T0329764

WHEN GOVERNMENTS FAIL

A PANDEMIC AND ITS AFTERMATH

WHEN GOVERNMENTS FAIL

A PANDEMIC AND ITS AFTERMATH

Edited by
VIKAS RAWAL
JAYATI GHOSH
C.P. CHANDRASEKHAR

 Tulika Books

in association with

Published by
Tulika Books
44 (first floor), Shahpur Jat, New Delhi 110 049, India
tulikabooks.in

in association with

International Development Economics Associates (IDEAs)
networkideas.org
and
Society for Social and Economic Research (SSER)
indianstatistics.org

First edition (hardback) 2021

ISBN: 978-81-947175-4-6

Printed at Chaman Enterprises, New Delhi

Contents

Tables and Figures

16 Impact on Indian Agriculture of the Covid-19 Pandemic

Covid-19 and the Economy

Initial Impacts across the World

Vikas Rawal, Jayati Ghosh and C.P. Chandrasekhar

The Covid-19 pandemic continues to rage across countries in different parts of the world, and it is clear that it has already wrought major changes that are likely to have prolonged impact on economies and societies. The development of vaccines that could contain the spread of the disease gives cause for hope for an eventual end to the pandemic, but the rate of inoculation suggests that will take several years over the entire world. Meanwhile, the economic damage could well persist even longer. The pandemic has highlighted and accentuated the extent of inequalities between and within countries. These have been reflected in the differential ability of different countries to deal with the disease and limit the contagion, as well as the impact on economies of both the disease and containment measures like lockdowns. Some countries have been remarkably successful in managing the disease, others have shown rapid spread despite severe lockdown strategies; economic policies in response to the health crisis have also varied greatly, and had very different outcomes in different parts of the world. On the whole, some regions like North America and Europe have been more affected in health terms, while much of the developing world has been more devastated by the impact on the economy.

How do we interpret these differing trajectories of the disease, policy responses and economic outcomes? What does this tell us about the current stage of global capitalism and the evolution of particular economies? This volume brings together a set of analyses that attempt to answer these questions at the global level as well as within particular countries. This allows for a comparative analysis of how the Covid-19 pandemic has affected the economy in the initial phases and assess what this can mean for the future. The contributions in this volume were originally delivered as online lectures in a series on 'Covid-19 and the Economy' organized by the Society for Social and Economic Research (SSER) and International Development Economics Associates (IDEAs) over 2020, and have been revised for publication. Together, they provide insights that allow us to understand the interplay between the ongoing health crisis, global and national power imbalances, and class structures. They also indicate the elements that will be crucial for envisioning a post-pandemic world that does not simply reinforce the existing inequalities and repeat the policy mistakes of the past, but lays the ground for more egalitarian, sustainable and resilient economies and societies.

Prabhat Patnaik opens the discussion by situating the pandemic in the context of globalized finance capitalism, which he argues had already reached a dead end and is in the throes of a protracted structural crisis. This results from the systemic downward pressure on wages across the world, while productivity increases allow the share of surplus to increase. The consequent deceleration of consumption and therefore of aggregate demand in turn depresses investment and generates stagnationist tendencies that have been sought to be alleviated through asset bubbles; but these strategies to generate expansion have also run out of steam. Two different trajectories have emerged for coping with this dead end reached by neo-liberalism. One approach seeks to revive a 'welfarist' approach that would restrict finance in some ways and seek to alleviate the suffering of people through enhanced public spending; the other is a fascist trajectory that remains under the hegemony of globalized finance but ruthlessly suppresses the people in the process. Because of the subservience to finance, the latter regimes (unlike classical twentieth-century fascism) would have little to show by way of economic achievements during or after the pandemic. Finance is opposed both to taxes on capitalists and to a fiscal deficit, which implies that governments worried about losing the 'confidence of the investors' are focused on reining in expenditures. While many governments dropped this fear and went ahead with debt-financed spending, some like the Government of India, where the effect of the pandemic and the lockdown on the poor and informal sector workers was devastating, chose to hold back on much needed fiscal transfers and stimulus spending. However, economic and social deprivation and the associated low level of wages in countries like India in the midst of globalization result, on the one hand, in underconsumption that perpetuates recessionary conditions and delegitimizes neo-liberalism, and, on the other, in a turn to authoritarianism to retain political power.

These arguments about the current nature of global capitalism are echoed by Erinç Yeldan, who notes the multiple crises that were already evident before the pandemic swept through the world. He notes that the

Covid-19 pandemic is being experienced as a multidimensional systemic crisis based on simultaneous manifestations of supply, demand and financial shocks, in a world economy already in a slowing trend exhibiting signs of deindustrialization. There has been a shift from 'jobless growth' to 'wageless growth' with growing concentration in global commodity and service markets. The effects of these processes were already being realized in the exacerbation of deep inequalities in income distribution, in functional, regional and gender terms; in access to public services that are commercialized; and therefore, in an environment where poverty is experienced along with social exclusion. Now, coping with the crisis is exposing further inequalities, as developing countries face distinct pressures and constraints that make it significantly harder for them to enact effective stimulus without facing binding foreign exchange constraints.

Despite regional and country variations, there are some tendencies common across countries, as the pandemic and associated economic crisis have been affected by and impacted upon existing inequalities of class, race, ethnic origin, caste and gender. Jayati Ghosh considers the specific ways in which the Covid-19 crisis has impacted women, and how gender constructions of society have affected both policy responses to the crisis and the ensuing macroeconomic processes. She shows how the pandemic, lockdowns and other policy measures have affected women as paid and unpaid workers and as national and international migrants, the survival needs of women in terms of access to food and to health care including reproductive health, and how they have reinforced relational inequalities and power structures that enable patriarchal oppression within households and communities. Official public policy responses have not only been inadequate to counter these trends but have even, in some cases, further accentuated them, relying on these gender inequalities as the shock absorber for the economy. She argues that effective global policy responses have to be designed along the lines of a 'multicoloured new deal' that would recognize the needs of the environment and climate alleviation as well as those of enhancing care activities and greater egalitarianism, through public spending for recovery, greater regulation and a focus on redistribution.

Several chapters dealing with some regional aspects follow. In a discussion on how the pandemic is playing out in Europe, Erik Reinert makes the interesting point that the fact that the pandemic had much worse spread and impact in the Southern countries can be traced to earlier and continuing differences within the European Union, and especially within the eurozone. The segregation between the 'responsible North' and the 'irresponsible South' that was actively promoted by Northern media resulted in no small part because of economic integration being forced through on the basis of unviable exchange rates, which supposedly gave an advantage to Southern consumers while destroying the competitiveness of Southern workers. The consequent deindustrialization of much of the South and the imposition of rigid fiscal rules had the further effects of reducing the resources available to states in the Southern periphery, resulting in much reduced per capita health expenditure. The consequences of that difference have played out in health outcomes during the pandemic.

The lack of international solidarity in dealing with the pandemic is also expressed clearly in Jose Antonio Ocampo's discussion of the experience of Latin America in this period. He shows how international cooperation, especially in terms of multilateral financing and moves to address sovereign debt problems of middle-income countries, was severely limited despite the scale and urgency of required measures. Indeed, multilateral actions have not even matched the relatively modest promises. Thus, even the urgent need to create international liquidity through an issuance of SDRs (special drawing rights) has not yet been forthcoming, while the International Monetary Fund's emergency credit lines have been relatively small and little used. An IMF swap facility has not yet been put in place. Debt restructuring moves, similarly, have been far too small and conditionality-driven to make much difference. All this has inevitably affected the ability of Latin American countries to deal with the disease and its economic fall-out. By contrast, regional arrangements like the FLAR (Latin American Reserve Fund) and regional development banks have responded better to the crisis, but they are limited by the size of their own available resources. Ocampo sees in this a lesson in terms of the need to revise the region's development strategy.

Given this external context and the associated constraints for Latin American countries, the chapter by Martín Abeles, Martín Cherkasky and Matías Torchinsky Landau describes how the twin crises have played out in the region and in specific countries. They note that the development pattern in the region was already showing symptoms of fatigue well before the emergence of Covid-19, including falling GDP growth rates, weaker investment spending, lower employment growth and slower poverty reduction. They argue that the same factors that account for the pre-pandemic sluggishness – widening productivity gaps, pervasive informality, stagnant exports, increasing foreign indebtedness – explain not only Covid-19's disproportionate impact in Latin America and the Caribbean, but also the projected post-pandemic slowness. This means that conventional counter-cyclical policies will not suffice to resume growth in Latin American and Caribbean economies in the short run. Since government spending has a low weight in aggregate demand, expansionary fiscal policies will have to be accompanied by a progressive redistribution of income in favour of wage-earners, especially of low wage-earners, to fuel private consumption and boost aggregate demand. In the medium term, both the prevailing institutional arrangements and the resulting set of economic policies, including unrestricted capital account openness, appeal for fiscal austerity and weak, or virtually inexistent, industrial policies need to be dramatically transformed. Like Ocampo, they too argue for a new development model for the region with redistribution at its core.

Sashi Kumar takes up the issue of how global media have reported the pandemic. As background to this, he traces some of the major shifts that have occurred in the Indian media landscape in recent years. Media consolidation under corporate auspices, the role of platforms in scavenging news for profit from traditional media sources without paying for it, and the decline in data prices leading to increased digital consumption and streaming with no clear revenue model in sight, have all contributed to a decline in 'news-based' journalism and a loss of objectivity. These changes have accelerated, during the pandemic, the tendency for a section of the mainstream media to aid, abet and promote the policies of the government. This makes it imperative in these times of Covid-19, he argues, to reinforce the adversarial and critical role of the media. There is a case for a supported media, even if by the state, because there is a limit to the media's growth as a business if it is to perform its public function.

The next set of chapters considers the experiences of specific countries. Jan Kregel's article questions mainstream analyses of the economic problems created by the coronavirus (focused on the impact on supply and demand) and the responses they recommended (most importantly, substantial state spending). They all missed the point that the only real response to the pandemic was a lockdown of appropriate severity for a required period of time to stop contagion and breakdown of the health system. A recession was the collateral fall-out of active policy decision. So, the economic problem was not to provide stimulus to offset the 'recession', but how to ensure that the economy could sustain the likely GDP and employment loss under lockdown. What was required was a guarantee not of income but of survival, of what we may call 'social provisioning', to make sure that everybody has enough to eat and survive without fear and the constraint of loss of income. What is needed is a reorganization of the food service sector into a food distribution sector. Moreover, everyone needed to be assured to survive the lockdown period in condition to recommence normal activity. This requires avoiding unnecessarily increased debt that will be carried over to the recovery.

Giovanni Andrea Cornia attempts to identify the factors that aggravate spread of Covid-19 infections in a country, and the factors that help protect a country's population from spread of the virus. In particular, he looks at the experience of Italy and India, not only comparing the trajectory of spread of Covid-19 infections in these two countries with other experiences, but also looking at the variations across different regions of these countries. In particular, Cornia points out that a greater proportion of elderly in the population and, in particular, a significant proportion of those living in nursing homes, have made countries of the North vulnerable. On the other hand, poverty and inequality in the low-income countries mean that a significantly higher proportion of population in these countries does not enjoy the possibility of working from home; homes and workplaces of people engaged in the informal economy tend to be congested. Along with this, he argues, high population density of urban areas, high mobility of the population and prior environmental contamination are factors that aggravate spread of Covid-19. Differences in the capacity of health systems, he finds, not only explain cross-country differences in the ability to respond to the pandemic, but also significant variations across different regions of countries like India and Italy.

Jomo Kwame Sundaram provides a cross-country analysis of diverse policy responses to contain the Covid-19 contagion. He points out that in East Asia and in the state of Kerala in India, early precautions and successful contact tracing helped contain the infection without resorting to full lockdowns. He argues that it is critical that lockdowns are complemented by targeted testing and contact tracing, are implemented through community cooperation and not mass repression, and are combined with relief measures to compensate for loss of livelihoods. The chapter then goes on to discuss the unevenness of recessions induced by Covid-19 across different countries. Jomo argues that relief and other policy measures taken by governments are critical for mitigating the effects of the shocks, and to 'guide, facilitate and accelerate' recovery. However, he points out that the main response of many governments and central banks has been in the form of massive injections of liquidity focusing mainly on monetary measures, as fiscal measures were eschewed because of widespread neo-liberal resistance to debt-financing. He argues that such injection of liquidity has enabled debt, inflation and financial speculation, keeping share markets buoyant while doing little to encourage the consumption and investment needed for recovery. He proposes some wide-ranging recommendations for a transformatory economic policy agenda in the post-Covid world, the key focus areas of which are progressive taxation, on the one hand, and public investment in productivity-enhancing investments and sustainable production systems, expansion of social protection, and universal health coverage, on the other.

Pasuk Phongpaichit and Chris Baker, in their study of the Thai experience, point to multiple factors varying from a developed and effective public health system that facilitated isolation and contact tracing, through social and cultural norms to climatic conditions (heat and dryness), to explain the low rates of infection and mortality. When some super-spreader events raised the threat of rapid spread, the government reacted with lockdowns which helped keep the case load down. However, though the pandemic in Thailand has been relatively mild compared to many other countries, the economic and social impact is likely to be heavy and long-lasting, they argue, given the Thai economy's large exposure to the outside world with exports amounting to two-thirds of GDP, and tourism being crucial to the economy with as many as 40 million tourists visiting the country in 2019.

In an analysis of the Indian experience, C.P. Chandrasekhar argues that the Covid-19 shock was particularly severe for two reasons. First, it intensified a recession that had engulfed the economy even before the pandemic. Second, the government's response, besides aggravating the crisis, did too little to mitigate its effects. Moreover, the recession itself and the crisis precipitated by the effects of the pandemic and the government's response to it have hugely aggravated the extreme inequalities that characterize a class- and caste-ridden patriarchal society. The poor, especially those dependent on precarious informal employment, were the ones devastated by the crisis.

Surajit Mazumdar argues that the series of lockdown announcements in response to the pandemic in India and the manner in which the measures were relaxed seem to lack any consistent underlying framework. Its severity was also not matched by its effectiveness in controlling the spread of the virus. The Indian story of the coronavirus pandemic was broadly what geography, its economic status and perhaps demographic characteristics like age structure of the population would indicate it should have been when restrictions started getting eased. On the other hand, the call to convert 'a crisis into an economic opportunity' was not backed by the required stimulus, despite a series of packages being announced. In the event, the mutually reinforcing combination of a sinking economy, a damaging epidemic and a larger public health crisis were the outcomes.

Mexico has emerged as one of the countries most affected by the virus, especially in terms of Covid-19-related deaths relative to population, but this was not so evident at the time when Alicia Puyana Mutis and Lilia Caballero wrote their chapter. Even so, their analysis remains completely relevant, because they show how the pandemic revealed the lethal effects of embedded inequality in Mexico, where a high share of labour informality reduces the feasibility and effectiveness of quarantines and other measures similar to those adopted in the developed world. Even when the government wishes to respond in a timely manner, a chronically underfunded and market-oriented health system reduces official room for manoeuvre and the effectiveness of policy.

Many discussions of the impact of the pandemic have tended to ignore or downplay the impact on agriculture; by contrast, this is an area considered in some detail in this volume. In the wake of widespread food insecurity and unemployment caused by an unplanned nation-wide lockdown imposed in India at a notice of barely a few hours, Utsa Patnaik reflects on her earlier work on causes of the Bengal famine to draw parallels between imperial policy-making in the early 1940s and the present government in independent India. She likens the blindness towards the impact on masses that led the British government in the early 1940s to use profit inflation to cause contraction of demand in India and use it to finance the war spending, to the one that led the present government in India to impose a nation-wide lockdown at short notice. She discusses the structural problems created by neo-liberal policies of the last three decades, and highlights the blows dealt by recent policy measures like demonetization on the Indian economy even before the Covid-19 lockdown was imposed. In that context, it is not surprising that the Covid-19 lockdown resulted in a massive crisis of employment and livelihoods. She argues that the only way to pull out of economic recession is by giving up the deflationary neo-liberal policies. In particular, she points to the need to provide cash assistance to those who have lost employment, expand public employment programmes and public distribution of food, expand public spending on employment-generating areas such as agriculture, and expand public spending on public health.

The chapter by Abhijit Sen and Vikas Rawal presents an analysis of the impact of Covid-19 crisis on Indian agriculture. They question the wisdom behind imposing a nation-wide lockdown at a few hours' notice when cases of infections were few and limited to only a few major cities. They argue that the policies to contain Covid-19 impacted Indian agriculture in many ways. These include disruption of agricultural market operations and supply chains due to sudden imposition of the lockdown, a massive contraction of demand, an adverse impact on the ability of rural households to invest in agriculture, and a disruption in the labour market. Although India had large public stocks of foodgrain when the Covid-19 pandemic struck, the government had been miserly in releasing it through the public distribution system, and did not use it to finance large-scale public works programmes. The chapter presents evidence to argue that the Covid-19 pandemic greatly accentuated the problem of rural unemployment, and that government initiatives in the direction of creating rural employment were grossly inadequate. The chapter ends by discussing the new farm laws that were enacted by the Indian government making use of the pandemic, and argues that these laws are unlikely to deal with the major problems that Indian agriculture is facing and are only going to deepen the agrarian crisis in India.

The chapter by Walden Bello provides a fitting end to this set of analyses, as he points to the major imperative revealed by the pandemic, of transforming food systems. He deals with fragility of global supply chains for food. He argues that globalization of agriculture over the last few decades and greater control of agribusiness corporations over food supply chains have contributed to many problems that the world is facing in the wake of the Covid-19 pandemic. These include vulnerability to disruptions in food supply, the possibility of food price spikes, adverse impact on incomes and livelihood of rural households, and an increase in food insecurity. He argues that, while it is important to keep global supply chains functional in the short run, it is important to strengthen agricultural production systems of less developed countries and move towards greater food self-sufficiency at the national level. In the long run, the world must respond to the crisis by moving away from corporate-controlled global food supply chains, bring greater focus on ecological issues in agriculture, and free food production and consumption from the dominance of world trade.

These lectures were delivered while the pandemic was largely in its first rising wave; yet the subsequent trajectory of the disease and the continued persistence of infection and vulnerability make them still very relevant. All the chapters in this volume go well beyond analysing the observed patterns and assessing the official responses, to proposing necessary and viable policy alternatives. If the world is truly to transcend this pandemic and its economic fall-out, and be in a position to confront other current and future challenges, the arguments made in this volume are likely to become even more important.

We would like to thank all the contributors to this volume for delivering the lectures in the SSER–IDEAs Lecture Series, for writing the papers, and for bearing with our repeated queries as the volume was being copy-edited. Alpana Khare designed the cover. The team at Tulika Books took meticulous care of the entire editorial and production process. Ankur Verma and Ambika Subash recreated all the figures in the book in a uniform style. Jesim Pais and Vivek Rawal helped in many ways, in conducting the lecture series and in the production of the book. We are grateful to all of them.

PART ONE

Global and Regional Trajectories

1
Globalization and the Pandemic

Prabhat Patnaik

I

The *differentia specifica* of the current globalization, I believe, is the globalization of *finance*. In earlier episodes of globalization – for instance, in the period before the First World War that Lenin had written about – each metropolitan power had a finance capital based within it, which was linked to its industry and had been mobile to a large extent within the 'economic territory' of that particular power. Now we have globalized finance whose country origin is of no great significance, and which goes all over the world looking for opportunities for gain unrelated either to the industrial capital or the strategic objectives of any metropolitan power. The fact that less than 2 per cent of cross-border financial flows is trade-related, is indicative of this dizzying movement across the globe of finance *per se*.

This globalization of finance in a world of nation-states, such as what we have, has profound implications. If the government of any nation-state pursues policies which are not to the liking of globalized finance, then the latter simply leaves the shores of that nation-state *en masse*, causing a financial crisis for it and acute hardship to its people. Every government therefore – as long as it lacks the gumption to take the country out of the web of global financial flows when necessary – feels the need to retain the so-called 'confidence of the investors' by pursuing policies to the liking of globalized finance.

This means, in a fundamental sense, an abridgement of democracy: *all* political formations when voted to power pursue more or less the same economic policies; and if perchance some formation with a different

---

Lecture delivered on 28 April 2020.

agenda happens to get elected (which itself is difficult because capital flight begins even before it comes to power, at the very prospect of its coming to power), it too soon falls in line and betrays its own earlier agenda (unless it has the gumption to delink from global financial flows). The people, in short, are denied any choice between different alternatives in the matter of economic policy. Or, put differently, the sovereignty of the people which democracy is founded on is replaced *de facto* by the sovereignty of global finance. And this is inevitable when the domain over which there is free movement of finance is not exactly co-terminus with, but rather goes well beyond, the domain over which the jurisdiction of the nation-state runs.

This *per se* would not matter much if the interests of the people coincided with the dictates of finance. Such, however, is not the case. Let me give an example to clarify the point. To overcome unemployment which has been growing in the capitalist world for some time now, what is required is state expenditure to stimulate demand, since monetary policy remains a blunt instrument. But such expenditure, to be effective, must be financed either by taxes on capitalists or by a fiscal deficit: financing state expenditure through taxes on the working people who spend much of their incomes anyway, simply substitutes state demand for that of the working people, without generating any net addition to aggregate demand. But finance is opposed both to taxes on capitalists and to a fiscal deficit; hence the dictates of finance prevent any amelioration of unemployment. Likewise, all transfers to the working people and all welfare expenditure of benefit to them, unless they are to be financed at the expense of the beneficiaries themselves (which therefore bring them no net benefits), get ruled out because of the dictates of finance.

Keynes, who had advocated state intervention for reducing unemployment, for otherwise he feared that capitalism would not be able to meet the challenge of socialism, was aware of this problem, i.e. the problem of the state being rendered incapable for fulfilling this task if finance was globalized. In 1933, in an article in *The Yale Review*, he had written: '. . . above all, finance must be national' (Keynes 1933). And the Bretton Woods system he helped to co-found after the Second World War had allowed member-countries to impose capital controls to ensure that finance remained 'national'. In the 1970s, however, with the collapse of the Bretton Woods system, the world got opened up for freer financial flows, ushering in the current era of globalization. Within this regime of globalization, we are confronted with the problem of nation-states having perforce to kowtow to the dictates of finance, and hence of giving short shrift to the interests of the people.

This conflict between the interests of the people and the dictates of finance, which underlies the entire phenomenon of globalization and characterizes the entire era of globalization, has come to a head with the current pandemic. The need to reach help to the working people during the pandemic, when they are without employment and without income owing to the lockdown, is urgent; but the dictates of finance, which frowns on taxing the capitalists or resorting to an enlarged fiscal deficit, stand in the way of doing so. The contradiction between the dictates of finance and the interests of the people has thus become absolutely acute during the pandemic.

In this situation, many countries have ignored the dictates of finance and have provided succour to the people by going back on the neo-liberal policies favoured by globalized finance. Spain has commandeered private hospitals to treat Covid-19 patients free of charge, exactly as they would be treated in government hospitals. In most advanced countries, there have been substantial relief packages for the people which have entailed enlarged fiscal deficits, far in excess of the limits imposed by finance capital. Thus, Germany has a fiscal package of 5 per cent of GDP (gross domestic product), Japan has a fiscal package of 20 per cent, and the US has a fiscal package, consisting of rescue and relief assistance, amounting to 10 per cent of GDP. Since in most countries, the fiscal deficit is limited by legislation at the behest of global finance to around 3 per cent of GDP (barring the US which has no such legislation), these fiscal packages clearly entail a substantial violation of the dictates of globalized finance.

Some other countries on the other hand, India included, have been extremely niggardly in providing assistance to the working people. The plight of the migrant workers in India – whose number is 8 crores even by the government's own admission but is actually much higher, closer perhaps to around 14 crores – is utterly heart-rending. Made jobless, income-less and homeless because of the lockdown announced with just four hours' notice, they poured into the streets to start moving towards the only refuge they knew, namely their village homes. Millions of them were on foot since no transport was available during the lockdown; and they were hungry. Many economists asked the government to provide free food to every individual and an income transfer to every family amounting to Rs 7,000 per month – covering the migrant workers' families as well but not confined to them – for a few months in order to tide over the crisis of the pandemic; the government however, having reduced the migrant workers to their miserable plight, offered them scarcely any assistance. Its total relief expenditure for all, not just the migrant workers but the entire population, comes to a mere 1 per cent of GDP.

This niggardliness no doubt is an expression of the complete lack of humanity on the part of the government; but its roots also lie in the pusillanimity of the government vis-à-vis globalized finance, its unwillingness to place the interests of the people over the dictates of finance.

The pandemic, in short, has brought out two contrasting responses from governments around the globe: with the contradiction between the dictates of finance and the interests of the people coming to a head, some governments have prioritized the interests of the people while others, including India, have prioritized the dictates of finance.

II

This contrast provides a clue to what lies ahead. Globalization under the hegemony of finance, or what is generally called neo-liberal globalization, has now reached a dead end. The crisis that capitalist economies were caught up in even before the pandemic struck was not just a cyclical downturn or a passing phenomenon from which there would be an automatic recovery. It was a prolonged, protracted structural crisis whose origins lie in the immense increase in income inequality in the world, or, as I would prefer to put it, in the increase in the share of the economic surplus in output in the world economy as a whole, as well as in individual economies.

The reason for this has to do with the very logic of globalization. The globalization of capital has meant the outsourcing of a whole range of activities from the advanced countries to the third world, especially to Asia, for meeting global demand. This has made the workers in the advanced countries compete against the low-wage third world workers; put another way, it has exposed advanced country workers to the baneful effects of the massive third world labour reserves. This not only has weakened the trade union movements in the former, but has also meant a virtual stagnation in the real wages of the workers there. Joseph Stiglitz, for instance, finds that the average real wage of a male American worker in 2011 was no higher than in 1968; in fact, it was marginally lower.

While the real wages of advanced country workers have not gone up, the real wages of third world workers have not done so either. This is because such relocation of activities to the third world has not dented the extent of labour reserves that exist there. There are two basic reasons for this. One is the fact that the rate of growth in labour productivity in the third world has been much higher than before, so that even in countries where higher rates of GDP growth have occurred, the growth rate of employment, which is the difference between the rate of growth of GDP and the rate of growth of labour productivity, has been even lower than under the earlier *dirigiste* regimes, and even lower than the rate of population growth.

The second reason for the non-exhaustion of third world labour reserves is the slowing down of the growth of peasant agriculture which makes it even lower than the rate of population growth. This slowing down itself is because of the withdrawal of support by the state from the peasant agriculture sector, a phenomenon associated with the neo-liberal regime of globalization. It forces a migration to cities from the rural areas, which, in the context of the sluggish rate of growth of jobs in the urban economy that we just discussed, simply swells the labour reserves in the cities. Of course, these reserves do not appear only in the form of open unemployment; rather, employment rationing takes all sorts of complex forms, which, besides open unemployment, include underemployment, disguised unemployment and casual employment. Such swelling of the labour reserves (relative to the workforce), exerts a drag on the real wages of all workers including of that small minority which constitutes the organized workforce.

Globalization therefore keeps down wages *everywhere* – in the advanced countries as well as in the third world. At the same time, it unleashes an increase in labour productivity *everywhere*, which results in a rise in the share of economic surplus in output. The observed increase in income inequality is an expression of this rise in the share of economic surplus.

This rise in the share of economic surplus, within countries and hence in the world as a whole, however, has a demand-depressing effect. Since it entails a shift from wages to surplus, and since consumption by the working people out of a rupee of income is greater than that of the surplus-earners, this shift slows down the growth of consumption. For any given time-profile of investment, therefore, aggregate demand tends to slow down with the rise in the share of surplus, which in turn has the effect of reducing the time-profile of investment itself, since investment responds to the growth of demand.

There is thus a tendency for a slowing down of aggregate demand and hence of output in the world economy as a whole and in individual countries. This tendency was countered for some time by the formation of major asset-price 'bubbles' in the US economy – first the 'dot-com' bubble of the 1990s and then the housing 'bubble' early this century. But after the collapse of the housing bubble, no similar bubble has appeared on the scene, since bubbles cannot be made to order; and the world economy has entered a protracted period of stagnation.

The tendency towards stagnation arising from the rise in the share of surplus could be countered in a more enduring manner by state expenditure, as Keynes had suggested, provided such expenditure was financed either by taxes on capitalists or by a fiscal deficit. But both these modes of financing state expenditure being anathema for globalized finance, no state can pursue such demand-increasing policies, *not even the US*. In the case of the US of course there is the additional fear that in normal circumstances, i.e. in the absence of protectionism of the sort that Trump introduced, such state-induced increase in demand would largely leak out abroad, generating little employment at home but increasing the external indebtedness of the US economy.

Neo-liberal globalization therefore has run into a dead end. It has entered a period of prolonged stagnation, with little possibility of any counteracting measures within the constraints imposed by this arrangement. The pandemic of course has added immensely to this crisis, but the crisis is not just a result of the pandemic that would disappear when the pandemic finally abates; it reflects deeper tendencies of the economic order with nothing to counteract them within the hegemony of globalized finance.

Even the more perceptive segment of the financial press is aware of this. It would want finance to be less exacting in its dictates, more accommodative of changes in the neo-liberal paradigm, in order to preserve the capitalist system itself which it recognizes as being subject to immense strains. Just as during the Great Depression of the 1930s Keynes had suggested repairing the capitalist system through state intervention, which had been unprecedented till then, in order to preserve the system itself, and Roosevelt had introduced the New Deal for this very purpose, a similar moment, it is believed, has once again arrived. Capitalism, according to *The Financial Times* of London, is once again facing a Keynes–Roosevelt moment. In an editorial on 3 April 2020, it wrote:

> Radical reforms in reversing the prevailing policy direction of the last four decades will need to be put on the table. Governments will have to accept a more active role in the economy. They must see public services as investment rather than as liabilities and look for ways to make the labour market less insecure. Redistribution will again be on the agenda. . . . Policies until recently considered eccentric such as basic income and wealth taxes will have to be in the mix.

One generally associates such views with Left economists from the Jawaharlal Nehru University (Delhi); but here is the most 'prestigious' financial newspaper of the world articulating a similar position, which is a matter of great significance. The reason is that the policies of the 'last four decades', i.e. the 'neo-liberal' policies associated with the phenomenon of globalization under the hegemony of finance, have become palpably unsustainable, in the sense that *their continuation henceforth is scarcely possible within a broadly democratic polity*.

The breakaway from the dictates of finance in implementing relief packages in several countries by enlarging the fiscal deficit acquires a deeper significance in this context. Though devised to meet the exigencies of the Covid-19 crisis, it could mark a more enduring change of course. But finance will not give up its hegemony so easily. Effective class intervention by the working people would be required if the new course, of prioritizing the interests of the people over the dictates of finance, is to be pursued in a more enduring manner. One must not forget in this context that Keynes's ideas were unacceptable to the capitalist establishment in the 1930s; they could be implemented only after the war under a Labour government enjoying the overwhelming support of the working class, and that too at a time when the victory of the Red Army in the course of the war had brought the so-called socialist 'threat' to the very doorsteps of Western Europe.

Likewise, Roosevelt's New Deal, once it had succeeded in reducing unemployment to a certain extent, was slackened under the pressure of finance which plunged the US economy once again into a recession in 1937. The US emerged from the Great Depression only when it started arming for the war; and state intervention in boosting demand, and that too through arms spending or what some have called 'military Keynesianism', became an accepted phenomenon only after the war, again under the socialist threat.

Once working class intervention is perceived to be necessary for changing the direction of development even in the manner suggested by *The Financial Times*, one must accept that new possibilities get opened up with regard to where these countries would be heading: whether towards an altered capitalism or further, through a sequence of developments, towards a socialist order. That becomes a matter to be decided by the course of class struggle in the coming days. Let us however turn now to the case of the other countries, including India, where there has been no effort to shake off the hegemony of finance.

III

The fact that the Indian government in the midst of one of the worst humanitarian crises in our post-independence history has been utterly miserly in its assistance to the distressed, has been already highlighted. This, as suggested earlier, is partly no doubt a result of its own inhumanity; in addition, it has also been affected by its timidity vis-à-vis globalized finance. In fact, finance capital prefers such regimes which faithfully obey its dictates even by sacrificing the interests of the very people they are supposed to represent. It is not surprising that the domestic corporate–financial oligarchy that is closely integrated with global finance capital funds the Bharatiya Janata Party (BJP) generously, to a far greater extent than it funds any other political formation.

Naturally, the Modi government's obeying the dictates of globalized finance to the exclusion of the people's interest is made possible by its suppressing democratic rights and civil liberties; using draconian laws to put political opponents and spokespersons for the poor in jail; subverting the independence of the judiciary and the media; and creating an atmosphere of dread which makes the practice of normal democratic politics impossible. We have been seeing such a tendency in the country of late.

In addition, since mere suppression of democratic rights cannot garner a political mandate for the ruling dispensation in any country, it tries to do so by other means, by shifting the discourse from economic issues to the threat from the 'other', typically a hapless minority group, which is blamed for all the ills of the nation. It divides the people along religious or ethnic lines, generates hatred for the minority among the majority, and thereby tries to obtain a political mandate by whipping up a phoney majoritarian sentiment that cares little for the genuine interests of the population belonging to the majority group itself.

We have seen in front of our eyes the Muslims being explicitly treated as the 'other', and a hatred being generated against them within the Hindu majority in our own country. Even in these distressing times, the pandemic itself was portrayed as a Muslim conspiracy by various votaries of *Hindutva* with no discouragement from Prime Minister Narendra Modi himself. All this represents the strategy of the ruling dispensation here to obtain majority electoral support, so that it can continue in power and yet pursue its policy of kowtowing to globalized finance.

This second trajectory that is followed by some countries in the context of the dead end at which contemporary globalization has arrived, is what I would call a fascist trajectory. It has all the essential features of classical fascism, namely the support it enjoys from finance capital, the creation of hatred against a hapless minority, and the suppression of civil liberties and democratic rights. At the same time, of course, the vastly changed historical context makes this fascism different in important ways from classical fascism, just as it makes contemporary globalization different from the earlier one and contemporary finance capital different from its earlier incarnation; but this difference must not make us lose sight of the basic fascist nature of several third world regimes, including the regime in India, which are currently busy kowtowing to globalized finance even in the midst of the pandemic.

IV

Let me sum up in conclusion. What I am suggesting is that, from the response of a regime to the pandemic we can surmise its response to the general phenomenon of the dead end of neo-liberalism itself. The former prefigures the latter. From what we observe during the pandemic we can therefore discern two different approaches or trajectories, which are currently being considered for coping with the dead end of neo-liberalism. One is a welfarist trajectory, or rather a revival of the welfarist trajectory, that had been pushed to the background 'four decades' ago by neo-liberal globalization; it visualizes, implicitly if not explicitly, restricting the hegemony of globalized finance in some ways. The second is a fascist trajectory which keeps the country trapped within the hegemony of globalized finance but which ruthlessly suppresses the people in the process.

There is however one important difference between the 1930s and now which must be remembered. In the 1930s, before large-scale military expansion by fascist powers had started, there had been substantial military expenditure undertaken by governments in those countries, which was financed largely by borrowing and which had quickly got those countries out of the Great Depression. Japan incidentally had been the very first country to come out of the Great Depression, entirely because of its military spending. That recovery had been made possible by overcoming whatever objections the largely home-based finance capital had put forward against fiscal deficits.

The current context being vastly different, kowtowing to the dictates of finance also means being fiscally conservative; hence the fascist regimes of today are utterly incapable of overcoming the crisis within their economies which the system has generated. Even after the pandemic is over, therefore, the crisis of the system that had existed prior to the pandemic and that would have got aggravated because of the irreversible effects of the pandemic itself, cannot be countered by the existing fascist regimes.

This only means that such regimes will have little to show, unlike classical fascism, by way of economic achievements – not just during the pandemic but even after the pandemic abates. This in turn will necessitate their becoming even more authoritarian, even more anti-worker, even more anti-minority, even more anti-women and even more ruthless in the days to come, in order to continue and camouflage their subservience to globalized finance.

The fact that the very period of the pandemic, and the lockdown generated in response to it when no normal political activity is possible, has been used in India as an occasion to put anti-CAA (Citizenship Amendment Act) activists in jail under the draconian Unlawful Activities Prevention Act (UAPA), the fact that labour laws which represent the achievement of the trade union movement after centuries of struggle are being abrogated in BJP-ruled states, are all indicative of the shape of things to come.

But precisely because this regime can achieve little by way of overcoming crisis and unemployment, it cannot also be a long-lasting one. Its historical potential is absolutely nil. Resistance to this regime and this trajectory will build up over time to bring about a very different *denouement* in our country to the crisis of contemporary globalization.

Reference
Keynes, John Maynard (1933), 'National Self-sufficiency', *The Yale Review*, vol. 22, no. 4, June: 755–69.

2

Capitalism in the Twenty-first Century

Lopsided Growth and Intensified Social Exclusion

A. Erinç Yeldan

Observations on Twenty-first Century Capitalism

For the global economy, the twenty-first century opened with prolonged recession, lopsided growth and widening income inequalities, along with consequent social exclusion, segmentation and escalating regional social conflicts. With the eruption of the financial crisis in the United States of America in September 2008, the global economy suffered negative growth rates with a total collapse of global products in 2009, for the first time since the 1930s' Great Depression.[1] The ensuing pathways of adjustment did not bring the expected recovery as both the centres of the global economy as well as its peripheries drifted into stagnation, rising inequalities in incomes and wealth, mounting indebtedness, and deepening segmentation of precarious working environments, along with increased duality along the lines of formal and informal jobs.

This study is about the dynamics of global capitalism in the twenty-first century. The century opened with a major crisis towards the end of the first decade – the so-called global financial crisis of 2008–09 – from which it has not recovered fully. Then, a decade later, we are facing another unprecedented crisis due to the eruption of the Covid-19 pandemic. The Covid-19 infections were first observed in the Wuhan region of People's Republic of China in November 2019, and announced as a *pandemic* by the World Health Organization (WHO) on 11 March 2020. In the course of the following six months, the pandemic had turned into a real threat to the global economy, affecting both the supply side by disrupting the value chains in trade and production, and the demand side by adversely affecting expenditures on consumption and fixed investments.

Lecture delivered on 12 May 2020.

In its most recent report, *World Economic Outlook*, the International Monetary Fund (IMF) projects that the world economy will shrink by as much as 3 per cent over the year 2020 (IMF 2020). Compared to earlier projections before the spread of the pandemic in January 2020, the new forecast announces a collapse of 6.3 per cent. Likewise, the United Nations Conference on Trade and Development reports that by the end of April 2020, losses in global exports would have already reached US$ 50 billion, and that by the end of the year, this figure is likely to reach US$ 800 billion in only the developing world (UNCTAD 2019).

Both the UNCTAD and IMF reports expect a severe contraction of global financial markets. Since the beginning of the pandemic in March 2020, outflows of capital from the developing and emerging economies (DEEs) have already exceeded US$ 70 billion. This has been accompanied by a severe rise of global debt to US$ 260 trillion (322 per cent of the global value added), clearly confirming the view that the adverse economic effects of the crisis will not be mitigated by monetary policies or by credit expansion alone.

Thus, the Covid-19 pandemic is being experienced as a *multidimensional systemic* crisis based on simultaneous manifestations of *supply, demand* and *financial* shocks. These effects have already been realized in the exacerbation of deep inequalities in income distribution, in functional, regional and gender terms, in access to public services that are commercialized and therefore in an environment where poverty is experienced with social exclusion due to severe inequalities of income. Saad-Filho (2020) describes the Covid-19 outbreak as 'a crisis that cannot be resolved without solidarity, industrial policy and public policy of the state'.

Given the experiences of the previous two decades, we are now in a position to summarize our main observations on the global economy:

1. The world economy is on a slowing down trend.
2. The nature of growth tends to switch from *jobless growth* to *wageless growth*.
3. There are tendencies of *concentration and monopolization* in the global commodity and services markets.
4. Industry's share in production and employment tend to decline (*deindustrialization*).

According to OECD's (Organization for Economic Cooperation and Development) projections (OECD 2014), the global economy is likely to slow down from its annual average of 3.6 per cent over 2014–30 to 2.7 per cent over 2030–60; and the growth rate of today's developed world will slow down to as much as 0.5 per cent by 2060. The OECD rests its projections on the ongoing decline in productivity, which is based on three factors: first, stagnation of fixed investment performance; second, the threat of a climate crisis; and third, intensified social exclusion and unrest given the worsening of income distribution worldwide. Tendencies towards intensified monopolization in the global commodity markets and deteriorating work conditions in the global labour markets are definitely parts of these processes.

It is these issues that we turn to in the sections below.

Financialization: Failed Hopes, Unavoidable Consequences

For the global economy, the late 1970s and 1980s are interpreted as a turning point. As pointed out by David Harvey (1989: 192), something has significantly changed since 1980 in the way capitalism is working. Acar, Voyvoda and Yeldan (2018) observe that

> the link between labour productivity and real wage remunerations is broken after 1980. This is known as the 'age of neoliberal reform' with increased flexibilization of the labour markets, reduction of the role of social welfare state, and an overall intensification of commercialization of the public services. But beyond all these, what lay at the heart of this restructuring was *the ascendancy of finance over industry*, a global process of *financialization* subjecting its logic of short-termism, liquidity, flexibility, and immense mobility over objectives of long term industrialization, sustainable development and poverty alleviation with social welfare driven states.

This dichotomy is most vividly shown for the US economy in Figure 2.1. Here, the hourly real-wage rates in US private manufacturing are contrasted with real productivity of labour over the post Second World War period. The period 1950–80 reflects the rise of the real-wage rate in tandem with the productivity cycle.

The main argument in favour of financialization was put forward by Mckinnon (1973) and Shaw (1973), who argued that *financial markets were under repression both nationally and globally, and that release from financial restrictions will result in higher savings performance, and both fixed capital investments and productivity rates will flourish in response.* Thus, starting with the US and the UK, all the major economies started to deregulate their financial markets, fully eliminating capital account restrictions on the mobility of finance. Financial deregulation has become a standard item in the conditionalities imposed by the International Monetary Fund (IMF) and the World Bank on indigenous economies of the developing world.

Figure 2.1 *Real hourly wage rates and productivity in private manufacturing in the US* (1982 = 100)

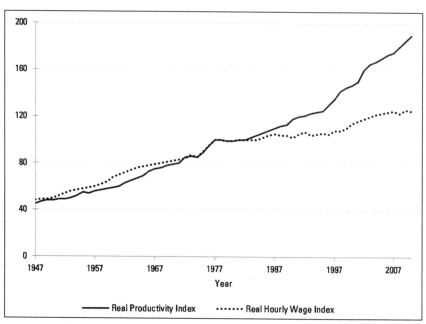

Source: Based on Shaikh (2011).

Financial deepening had indeed been realized after the 1980s as reflected in the rising ratios of financial assets to GDP (gross domestic product), and the introduction of many diverse forms of financial instruments. Contrary to expectations, however, neither savings nor investment performance have been elevated. As the world's financial centres turned the global markets into a financial soup, almost obeying no laws of gravity, funds devoted to fixed capital investments stagnated. This is best illustrated in Figure 2.2.

Here, on the left axis, the total financial assets and liabilities stock is portrayed against the path of investment expenditures as a share of GDP, which is displayed on the right axis. The escalation of the stock of financial assets is clearly visible and is mainly the end result of financial deregulation. This development, however, was not accompanied by any structural break with the investment performance, as had been hoped for under the prognostications of Mckinnon (1973) and Shaw (1973).

Many explanations underlie these observations. One is common to the inner tendencies of capitalist accumulation, the intensified consolidation and monopolization of capital. Evidence comes from an unexpected quarter, the IMF blog. Diez and Leigh (2019) made the following assessment:

Figure 2.2 *Financialization and investment expenditure in the developed economies*

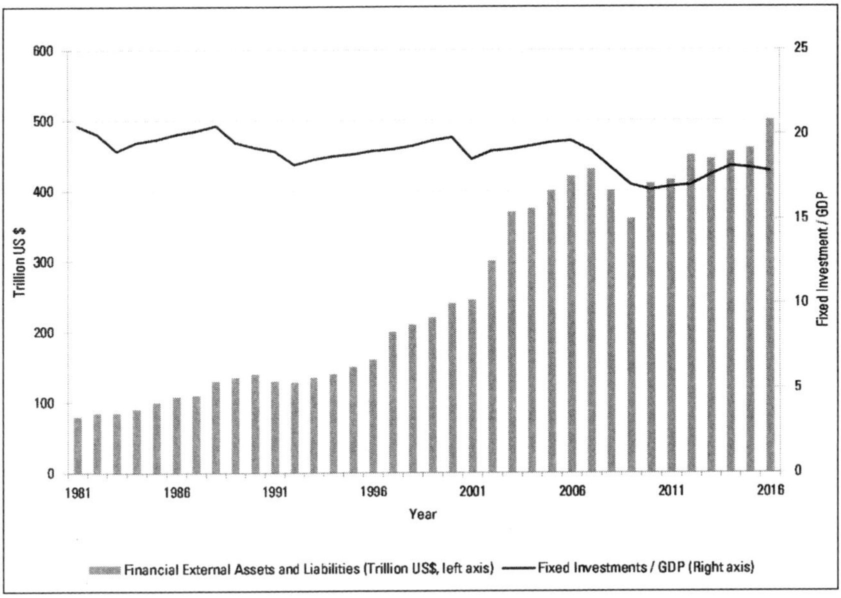

Source: UNCTAD (2018).

The growing economic wealth and power of big companies – from airlines to pharmaceuticals to high-tech companies – has raised concerns about too much concentration and market power in the hands of too few. In particular, in advanced economies, rising corporate market power has been blamed for low investment despite rising corporate profits, declining business dynamism, weak productivity, and a falling share of income paid to workers.

But more than that, the IMF researchers pointed to the fact that the ongoing concentration is asymmetric across the developed versus developing economies, and that the whole episode is actually driven by the new international division of labour.

The profit margins (mark-ups over costs) did indeed follow divergent paths, especially after the turn of the millennium. Profit margins continued their upward trend with further acceleration, while they are observed to have almost stagnated for the developing economies. The message of Figure 2.3 is clear: the diversion of the returns to capital across the globe has been unevenly distributed. 'As the top 2,000 oligopolies have increased their influence in the global commodity markets, they also led to declining business dynamism', as Diez and Leigh put it.

Figure 2.3 *Evolution of profit margins* (mark-up rates) (1990 = 1.0)

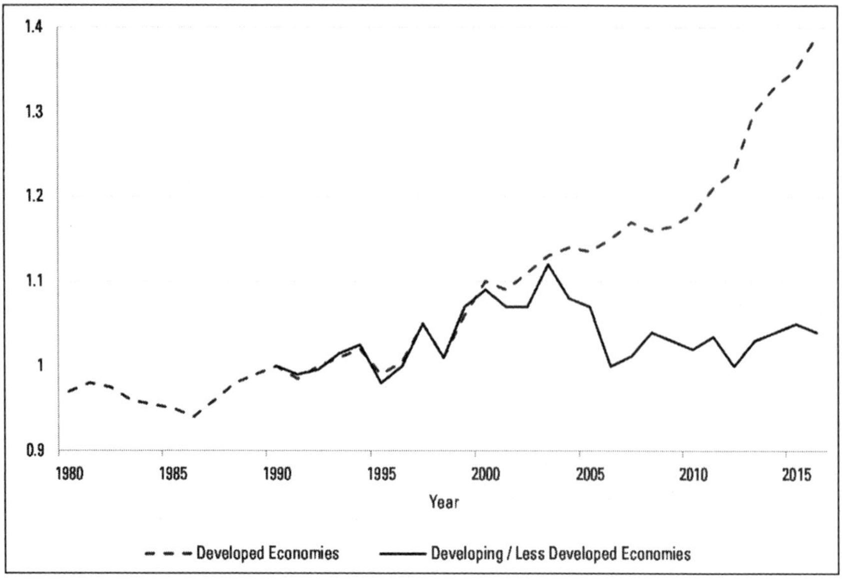

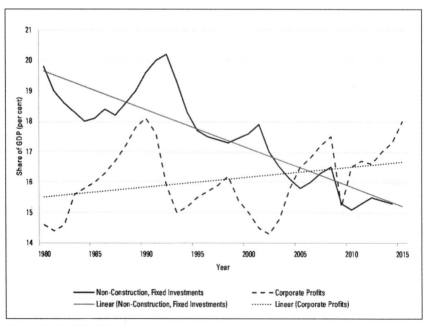

Source: Diez and Leigh (2019).

Figure 2.4 *Corporate profits and fixed investments in developed economies* (as percentage share of GDP)

Source: UNCTAD (2016).

Yet, what is enigmatic in this assessment is the fact that despite the rise in profitability, capital investment has not been forthcoming, as I have highlighted above. Increased profitability at the enterprise level did not accompany increased fixed investments, and this has taken a leading role in the explanation of poor productivity that ensued (see Figure 2.4). The overall result was declining productivity and a slowing down of the rate of growth.

Ecological Crisis

Earth scientists report that the surface temperature of our planet has warmed up by 0.9°C since the onset of the Industrial Revolution. They warn that life on our planet will be threatened very seriously with unforeseeable adverse consequences if the warming of earth's surface temperature exceeds 2°C. Hence, the scientific community has set an ultimate target for limiting the rise in global temperature to 2°C. It is estimated that in order to maintain this target, a maximum total of 450 ppm (parts per million molecules) of CO_2 (carbon dioxide) ought to be allowed in our atmosphere. According to United Nations Environment Programme (UNEP), our planet's atmosphere is estimated to have had 220 ppm of CO_2 around the time of the Industrial Revolution (UNEP 2011).

The total permissible emission of CO_2 to contain the temperature rise at 2°C is calculated to be of the order of 2,900 gigatons (1 gigaton = 1 billion tons). This figure is referred to as the global carbon budget, and it is estimated that 1,900 gigatons of this budget (65 per cent) has already been spent since then. This makes available roughly 1,000 gigatons of allowable CO_2 emissions to limit global warming at 2°C.

According to recent studies, our Earth has exceeded its ecological boundaries especially in the aftermath of the Industrial Revolution (Hahnel 2010). This is easily demonstrated by the ecological footprint indicator, which shows the amount of geographical area required by human beings in order to meet the natural resource needs of various economic activities, which serve consumption at the end. Based on the Global Footprint Network's recent data for the year 2010, it is stated that the only Earth we have cannot supply in a year the amount of natural resources warranted by our current annual consumption level, and consequently the natural resource stock has been rapidly declining. It was observed that, by 2010, 102 out of 139 countries had produced greater footprints of consumption than their own bio-capacities. It is possible for countries to consume more than the regeneration capacity of their own resources allows for only if they import resources from other countries, or otherwise their natural resource stocks will be depleted. It is clear that none of these paths are sustainable in the long run. Moreover, we cannot ignore the fact that those countries that meet the deficit between their consumption levels and their bio-capacities through imports exacerbate global inequalities in natural resource use, which will, in turn, have adverse social implications at a global level. (Acar, Voyvoda and Yeldan 2018: 58–59)

In Figures 2.5 and 2.6, I provide evidence of the extent of the deepening threat of climate crisis. Clearly, current trends of resource extraction and consumption patterns are simply not sustainable. The world economy has already surpassed the boundaries of our planet in replenishing itself. And yet it ought to be noted that most of the current industrialization and environmental problems originate from the excessive volatility of speculative finance flows characterizing the current realm of markets. This leads to excessive volatility of commodity prices and resource misallocation problems.

In fact, the quest for sustainable development, made more urgent because of the uncertainties about the future climate and technology, has recently led to the realization that while economic growth has been

Figure 2.5 *Atmospheric CO_2 concentration*

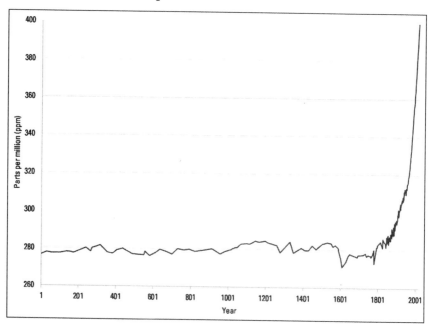

Source: Scripss CO_2 Program, 2018.

Figure 2.6 *Global annual and cumulative greenhouse gas emissions at various dates*

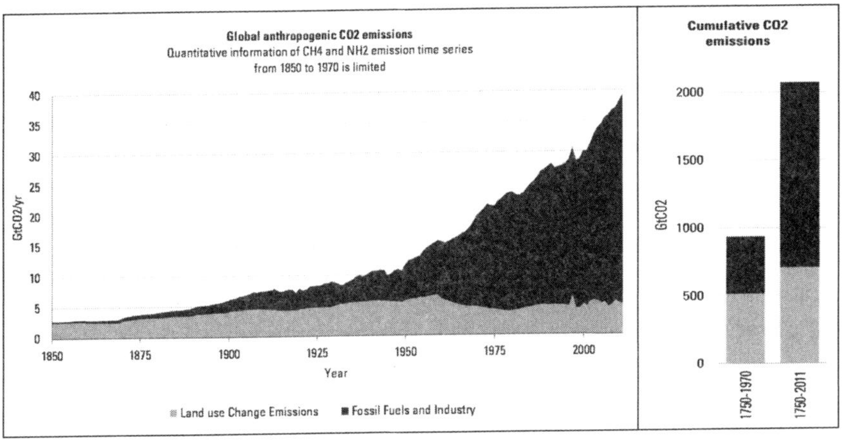

Global anthropogenic CO2 emissions
Quantitative information of CH4 and NH2 emission time series
from 1850 to 1970 is limited

Cumulative CO2 emissions

Land use Change Emissions ■ Fossil Fuels and Industry

Source: Based on Global Carbon Project (2019).

critical in improving the standard of living of millions of people in many parts of the world, its current patterns are not only unsustainable, causing significant environmental degradation, but are also characterized by deeply inefficient production and consumption processes and management of natural resources. At the root of these problems are market and governance failures for which basic economic and regulatory instruments are available, but their systematic use as part of broader policy packages has been lacking.

All this is happening at a time when new challenges and opportunities have emerged, including the recent and still ongoing food, fuel and financial crises, and the growing global concern about the impact of climate change and the destruction of ecosystems and biodiversity. A United Nations report (UN 2013) reveals that global greenhouse gas emissions maintain their upward trend, and calls for bold and decisive action. The rise in emissions has been mostly due to fast growth in the developing economies.

The report further notes that 'the present dominant model of development is facing simultaneous multiple crises such as, depletion of natural resources and the market failures that have already marked the first decades of the current millennium' (ibid.: 131). Accordingly, this model has been ineffective in enabling a productive and decent employment market, and has exacerbated the phenomenon of climate change with its various effects such as depletion of natural resources, degradation of biodiversity, energy and food security crises. In contrast, the report underlines that the 'green economy concept proposes to break away from the not very effective current model of development and move towards a more sustainable development paradigm that is merely characterized by low carbon emissions, rational use of resources and social inclusiveness' (Acar, Voyvoda and Yeldan 2018: 31).

Global Labour Markets and Deteriorating Income Distribution

The collapse of the Soviet system and the subsequent opening up of China and India to global markets has added 1.5 billion new workers to the world's economically active supply of wage-labour. This has meant almost a doubling of the global labour force and a reduction of the global capital–labour ratio by half. With intensified pressures of unemployment looming everywhere, wage-earners had witnessed a *race to the bottom* not only of their wage remunerations, but also of their social rights and work conditions. Complemented by neo-liberal policies invoking flexibility and privatization, global wage-labour had suffered serious informalization and vulnerability, consequent deterioration of income distribution, and increased poverty.

In Table 2.1, I provide information on the state of global labour markets. The fragility of global labour markets is evident from the fact that of the roughly 3 billion workers employed, 43 per cent (1.4 billion, or 1,369 million) are employed under *vulnerable* conditions.[2] The vulnerability ratio increases to 52 per cent for the developing economies.

Table 2.1 *Global labour markets: unemployment and vulnerability*

	Unemployed (million persons)			Unemployment rate (%)		
	2017	2018	2019	2017	2018	2019
World average	192.7	192.3	193.6	5.6	5.5	5.5
Developed economies	34.1	32.8	32.4	5.7	5.5	5.4
Less developed economies	158.6	159.5	161.2	5.6	5.5	5.5
	Vulnerable employment (million persons)			Share of vulnerable employment (%)		
	2017	2018	2019	2017	2018	2019
World average	1,391.3	1,409.0	1,426.4	42.5	42.6	42.7
Developed economies	56.7	56.5	56.3	10.0	9.9	9.9
Less developed economies	1,334.6	1,352.5	1,369.0	52.2	52.2	52.3

Source: Table 1.1 in ILO (2018b).

Global unemployment hit the young, first and foremost. The International Labour Organization (ILO) reports that open unemployment among the youth (15–24 years of age) has reached 71 million (ILO 2018b). Of these 71 million young unemployed persons, 53.5 million reside in the *newly emerging market economies* – the so-called dynamic manufacturers of the global factory. In these economies, the rate of youth unemployment is estimated to be 13.6 per cent, while the world average stands at 13.1 per cent. The problems of the young are not limited to the threat of being unemployed. According to the ILO, poverty stands out as a further serious threat among young persons who could have found a job; currently, 156

Table 2.2 *Women/men wage inequality* (per cent)

	Monthly wages	Highest 10% wage income group	Wages of women who have children/ who don't
USA	–23.50	–9.40	–4.30
Argentina	–25.00	–1.90	–10.50
Australia	–31.50	–5.20	–5.00
Brazil	–20.10	–1.20	–7.70
China	–19.00	–26.20	–10.40
Philippines	6.60	–48.10	–4.80
South Africa	–20.00	–12.40	–1.10
Switzerland	–36.00	–20.90	–7.30
Canada	–25.60	–8.70	–1.20
Korea	–36.70	–22.30	–12.60
Mexico	–20.20	–5.00	–5.80
Egypt	–13.50	–20.30	13.10
Peru	–21.20	–23.90	–12.90
Russia	–27.90	–22.90	–14.70
Chile	–21.60	–11.30	–2.40
Tanzania	–12.20	–17.90	–3.05
Turkey	–9.30	–19.10	–29.60
Ukrain	–25.40	–1.60	2.80
Uruguay	–23.00	–10.30	–6.10
Vietnam	–10.50	–6.90	0.96
World average	–20.5	–21.1	–

Source: ILO (2018a).

million young workers live under conditions of *absolute poverty*, according to ILO (2018b). ILO's researchers have fixed the limit of absolute poverty at 'US$ 3.10 per day', and disclose that this figure covers 37.7 per cent of those who are employed, i.e. one-third of all young employed persons are currently working under conditions of absolute poverty.

Another attribute of discrimination in global labour markets pertains to gender differences. The wage-gap across gender is an ongoing and intensified global problem, and is a common feature of both the developed and the developing world. In Table 2.2, data are given on several aspects of gender-based wage discrimination. The table shows that the gender wage-gap is particularly pronounced in Korea, the US and Switzerland. Furthermore, this is not necessarily only a problem of 'low'-wage occupations, but is seen among higher segments of wage income as well (column 2). Finally, in the last column we see that among women, those who have children are discriminated against as compared to women who had no children. Here, the gap is as high as 29 per cent for Turkey.

The Covid-19 Crisis and Beyond

The coronavirus pandemic hit the global economy under such adverse conditions. UNCTAD (2020) notes that 'projections of the potential impact of the Covid-19 shock on economies around the world for the year 2020 vary widely'. Further:

> For advanced country governments, now scrambling to contain the economic impact of the Covid-19 pandemic, the challenge . . . is compounded by persistent fragilities surrounding highly speculative financial positions, in particular, the already unsustainable debt burdens associated with highly leveraged corporate loans. These have been built up over the last decade of easy money and against a backdrop of heavily underregulated 'high-tech-cum-gig economies' and deeply ingrained income inequalities. . . . Developing countries, however, face distinct pressures and constraints which make it significantly harder for them to enact effective stimulus without facing binding foreign-exchange constraints. And as these countries do not issue international reserve currencies, they can only obtain them through exports or sales of their reserves. What is more, exports themselves require significant imports of equipment, intermediate goods, know-how and financial business services. Finally, the financial turmoil from this crisis has already triggered sharp currency devaluations in developing countries, which makes servicing their debts and paying for necessary imports for their industrial activity far more onerous. (Ibid.: 2)

In the words of Saad-Filho (2020),

. . . the crises of public health and the economy were not caused by failures of planning; instead, they reflected political choices, the dismantling of state capacities, staggering failures of implementation, and a shocking underestimation of the threat – for which, surely, reputations must be destroyed and heads must roll, as part of a systemic reckoning.

Notes

[1] See, for example, Akyüz (2012) for an evaluation of the first decade of the twenty-first century from a *Southern* perspective.

[2] In ILO's terminology, *vulnerable labour* refers to *unregistered workers* without any social security coverage, *self-employed* and *unpaid family labourers*.

References

Acar, Sevil, Ebru Voyvoda and A. Erinç Yeldan (2018), *Macroeconomics of Climate Change in a Dualistic Economy: A Regional Computable General Equilibrium Analysis*, London: Academic Press, Elsevier.

Akyüz, Y. (2012), *The Financial Crisis and the Global South: A Development Perspective*, London: Pluto Press.

Diez, F. and D. Leigh (2019), 'The Rise of Corporate Giants', available at https://blogs.imf.org, accessed 21 October 2019.

Global Carbon Project (2019), 'Supplemental Data of Global Carbon Budget 2019, Version 1.0 (data set)', Global Carbon Project, https://doi.org/10.18160/gcp-2019, accessed 3 September 2020.

Hahnel, R. (2010), *Green Economics: Confronting the Ecological Crisis*, London and New York: M.E. Sharpe.

Harvey, David (1989), *The Condition of Postmodernity: An Enquiry into the Origins of Cultural Change*, Oxford: John Wiley & Sons.

International Labour Organization (ILO) (2018a), *Global Wage Report, 2018/19*, Geneva.

———— (2018b), *World Employment and Social Outlook: Trends 2018*, Geneva.

International Monetary Fund (IMF) (2020), *World Economic Outlook*, Washington DC.

McKinnon, R. (1973), *Money and Capital in Economic Development*, Washington DC: Brookings Institution.

Organization for Economic Cooperation and Development (OECD) (2014), *Policy Challenges for the Next 50 Years*, Paris: OECD Publications.

Saad-Filho, Alfredo (2020), 'Coronavirus, Crisis, and the End of Neoliberalism', *The Bullet*, 15 April.

Shaikh, Anwar (2011), 'The First Great Depression of the 21st Century', in Leo Panitch, Gregory Albo and Vivek Chibber, eds, *Socialist Register 2011: The Crisis This Time*, vol. 47.

Shaw, Edward (1973), *Financial Deepening in Economic Development*, New York: Oxford University Press.

United Nations (UN) (2013), *Millennium Development Goals Report*, New York.

United Nations Conference on Trade and Development (UNCTAD) (2016), *Structural Transformation for Inclusive and Sustained Growth, Trade and Development Report*, Geneva.

———— (2018), *Power, Platforms and the Free Trade Delusion, Trade and Development Report*, Geneva.

———— (2019), *Financing a Global Green New Deal, Trade and Development Report*, Geneva.

_____ (2020), *The Covid-19 Shock to Developing Countries: Towards a 'Whatever It Takes' Programme for the Two-Thirds of the World's Population Being Left Behind, Trade And Development Report Update*, https://unctad.org/en/pages/PublicationWebflyer.aspx?publicationid=2698, accessed 6 March 2020.

United Nations Environment Programme (UNEP) (2011), 'Towards a Green Economy: Pathways to Sustainable Development and Poverty Eradication – A Synthesis for Policy Makers', www.unep.org/greeneconomy

3

The Gendered Macroeconomics of Covid-19

Jayati Ghosh

Introduction

The Covid-19 pandemic has served as an X-ray, revealing sharply the extent of inequalities between and within countries. We are clearly *not* 'all in this together', even though, in principle, a virus is no respecter of class or other socio-economic distinctions: it enters human hosts without checking for such attributes. And the rapid global spread of this particular virus has shown that it is no respecter of national borders either, which points to the more fundamental truth that as long as anyone anywhere has a contagious disease, everyone everywhere is under threat. This should have made it obvious that ensuring universal access to health care and prevention is not about compassion, but about the survival of all. Unfortunately, that obvious truth is still not adequately recognized, mainly because existing structures of authority and power imbalances ensure that the rich and the powerful continue to be more protected from both health risks and material privation.

Diseases tend to affect people differently depending not just on the strength of public health systems, but on existing fissures in society: of class, race and ethnicity, gender, caste, and other divisions. There are negative feedback loops between the squalor associated with income poverty and infectious diseases. In unequal societies, poor and socially disadvantaged groups are both more likely to be exposed to Covid-19 and more likely to die from it, because the ability to take preventive measures, susceptibility to disease and access to treatment, all vary greatly according to income, assets, occupation, location and the like. In developing countries, such divisions are often even sharper, because the extent and quality of public

---

Lecture delivered on 14 May 2020.

provision tend to be lower, and therefore ability to pay determines both the ability to protect oneself from the disease and subsequent treatment. Even governments' containment policies for Covid-19 within countries have generally shown class bias, with possibly the most extreme example coming from India, where migrant and informal workers have been at the receiving end of a particularly brutal yet ineffective lockdown that failed to control the virus yet devastated livelihoods.

Globally, developing countries have been particularly hard hit by the economic forces that have been unleashed by economic lockdowns, the collapse of international trade and the volatility of cross-border capital flows (Ghosh 2020a). The impact of the pandemic on global macro-economy is already sharply evident in the collapse of international trade, both in terms of volumes and prices; the decline in travel and tourism; the significantly increased volatility of capital flows, with net outflows from many developing countries and associated changes in currency markets; the concerns about global and local food supply chains; the reduced viability of external debt and other finance like insurance, at a time when debt levels were already seen to be problematic impact on actual and perceived 'fiscal space'. These forced many developing and emerging market econo-mies into severe crisis even *before* the health crisis really hit them, and since then, have also reduced their capacity to deal with the likely health impact. There are three features of the nature of the global economy that are driving the dramatic increase in spatial inequalities in the period of the pandemic. These are: the differences in degrees of formalization of labour market and legal/social protections available to workers; the nature of the external constraints, including volatile trade and capital flows; and the varying willingness and/or ability of governments to respond with fiscal stimuli (Ghosh 2020b).

But the economic responses and consequent outcomes have also varied quite widely across countries. The subsequent fiscal responses in most developing countries have also been much more subdued than after 2008 (IMF 2021), which in turn has affected the ability of governments to undertake spending that could affect people and reduce some of the negative impact. It is well known that such fiscal constraints have a par-ticularly bad impact on women, who are much more directly and indirectly reliant on public services because of the gendered division of labour within societies and families.

Within countries, the pandemic and associated economic crisis have been affected by and impacted upon existing inequalities of class, race, eth-nic origin, caste and gender in multiple ways. Here, I consider the specific ways in which the Covid-19 crisis has impacted women and affected their human rights, and also how gender constructions of society have in turn affected both policy responses to the crisis and the ensuing macroeconomic processes. The pandemic and the lockdowns and other policy measures have affected women as workers: both as paid workers, whether in formal or informal work, or self-employed; and as unpaid workers, in social reproduction and other productive work within homes and communities. They have affected women who are national and international migrants. They have affected the survival needs of women especially in developing countries, in terms of access to food and to health care, including reproductive health. And they have reinforced relational inequalities and the power structures that enable patriarchal oppression within households and communities. In what follows, I consider each of these in turn.

Women as Recognized and Remunerated Workers
One major problem with looking at the impact of anything on women workers is that this automatically excludes the far greater proportion of women who are engaged in only unpaid labour within households and communities. In this section, I consider only the impact on those who are in recognized and paid employment, thereby excluding not only unpaid care work but also unpaid workers in family enterprises. It turns out that, more or less across the board, such women workers have been disproportionately affected by the ongoing crisis, and the pandemic and related containment measures like lockdowns have impacted on women's livelihoods even more severely than for men.

To begin with, unlike in previous crises or recessions, women are disproportionately employed in what have been identified as the sectors more likely to be affected by the pandemic and the lockdown measures, and they are particularly over-represented in 'high-risk' sectors. Women are also much less likely to be involved in occupations that allow for remote work or telecommuting. The International Labour Organization (ILO) has categorized sectors by potential employment loss during and in the wake of the pandemic as follows, with the share of even more vulnerable own-account workers in that sector's employment given in brackets:

- High risk: wholesale and retail trade and repair of motor vehicles (45 per cent), manufacturing (19 per cent), accommodation and food services (29 per cent), real estate, business and administrative activities (21 per cent)
- Medium–high risk: arts, recreation, entertainment and other services (30 per cent), transport, storage and communication (31 per cent)

- Medium risk: construction (38 per cent), finance and insurance services (6 per cent), mining and quarrying (28 per cent)
- Low–medium risk: agriculture, forestry and fishing (55 per cent)
- Low risk: human health and social work activities (7 per cent), education (5 per cent), utilities (10 per cent), public administration and defence (2 per cent).

Obviously, these are broad-brush global categorizations, and the actual impact across sectors will vary across countries. But even so, it is evident that women workers are dominantly employed in the sectors with high or medium–high risk of greater job losses. According to the ILO (2020a), 40 per cent of all employed women (more than 500 million) are employed in sectors that are hard-hit by the pandemic, including accommodation and food services; wholesale and retail trade; real estate, business and administrative activities; and manufacturing. Some sectors considered to be 'moderately' at risk disproportionately employ women, who account for 61 per cent of employment in arts and entertainment, and other service workers. In any case, even in these affected sectors, women are more likely to be informally employed: 42 per cent of women workers in these sectors are informal compared to 32 per cent of men workers.

In developed countries, available data suggest that the impact on employment has already been much more severe: from the United States (Alon *et al.* 2020) to India (Deshpande 2020), women have faced disproportionately greater job losses. Meanwhile, open unemployment rates for women have also increased rapidly, even as other women choose to drop out of the labour force because of increases in unpaid labour due to the pandemic and lockdown.

There is the further negative impact on women's employment, of worsening labour market conditions in the aggregate. This means that even women working in sectors where they are less represented are likely to face further disadvantage. As Seguino and Braunstein (2018) have argued, across the world, women are more likely to be rationed out of better jobs in general; the crowding of women into lower quality jobs then has a negative effect on workers as a whole by dampening the labour share of income. And in crisis conditions these tendencies get greatly aggravated, so that when job losses occur, women are disproportionately more likely to lose their jobs or face reductions in incomes than men. This has been evident during the recent period of lockdowns and partial closures.

Evidence from some advanced economies confirms this. Women – especially women of colour – are more likely to have been laid off or furloughed during the Covid-19 crisis. In the US, around a quarter of the

Figure 3.1 *Employment of men and women by degree of risk of sector*

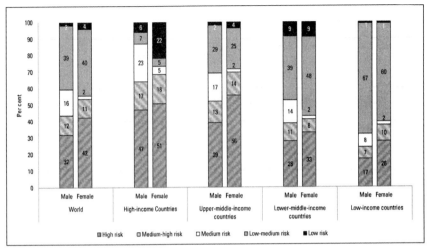

Source: Based on data from ILO (2020b).

women surveyed for annual Women in the Workplace study from LeanIn. org and consulting firm McKinsey & Company said they were planning to leave their jobs because of high levels of burn-out and tensions, since women with children were three times as likely as fathers to be responsible for a majority of the house work and child care amid the pandemic (Coury *et al.* 2020). Alon *et al.* (2020) note that during the Covid-19 recession in the US, women's unemployment rate rose by 12.8 percentage points between February and April 2020, i.e. 2.9 percentage points larger than men's increase of 9.9 percentage points. From February to August 2020 women's average hours worked for pay fell by 19 per cent versus a drop of only 12 per cent for men.[1]

Of course, this relates mainly to formal employment, and aggregate employment changes have varied across countries even in the developing world, because of the differing significance of informal work. For example, more than 90 per cent of all recognized workers in India are informal, and for women the proportion is even higher, at around 95 per cent, while many more women are involved in unpaid work that can be arduous and demanding but provides no income or protection at all. This means that formal employment-based compensation measures have little to no benefit for the vast bulk of women workers. And the job losses in informal employment are in any case much more extensive precisely because of the complete absence of legal protections. This situation in India may be extreme, but broadly similar patterns are found in many other developing countries. The ILO estimated that 67 per cent of informal workers and an even greater proportion of women workers live in countries with mandatory workplace closures, or full or partial lockdowns, which would inevitably affect their employment and earning capacity. Some of the most stringent lockdowns have occurred in countries like India with the most informality in labour markets. Among domestic workers (80 per cent of whom globally are women), 72 per cent lost their jobs during the pandemic and lockdowns (UN Women 2020). Apart from the problems of women farmers (many of whom are not even recognized as such), self-employed women and those running micro-enterprises – often in activities like trade, hospitality and personal services requiring physical contact – have also been heavily affected. Problems in micro-finance institutions resulting from the credit stringency apparent in most markets are also likely to affect such women.

The Unpaid Work of Women

Even when women are not in recognized employment, their often unacknowledged and unpaid contribution to social reproduction as well as to many economic activities has always been absolutely essential for the functioning of the system (Kalpagam 1994). All women are usually workers, whether or not they are defined or recognized as such. In all societies, and particularly in developing countries, there remain essential but usually unpaid activities (such as cooking, cleaning and other house-work, provisioning of basic household needs, child care, care of the sick and the elderly, as well as community-based activities), which are largely seen as the responsibility of the women. This pattern of unpaid work tends to exist even when women are engaged in outside work for an income, whether as wage workers or self-employed workers. This in turn means that it is impossible to understand women's work without situating it in the specific trajectory of capitalism in that society, and that issues relating to women's work and employment are qualitatively different from those of men workers (Folbre 2021). Just increasing paid employment does not always mean an improvement in the conditions of women workers. Women from poor families who are also engaged in outside work usually cannot afford to hire others to perform these tasks, so most often these are passed on to young girls and elderly women within the household or become a 'double burden' of work for such women (Elson 1995). These outcomes are critically affected by social relationships as well as economic policies and processes, which determine whether or not increased labour market activity by women is associated with genuine improvements in their economic circumstances. The recognized work participation rates of women as described by official statistics may not really be reliable indica-tors of the productive contributions of women, which are not just unpaid but also socially unrecognized. This is true of not just social reproduction, but other economic activity where women's work is rendered invisible by social perceptions.

As a result, it could be argued that women's work participation rate can be taken as one of the proxy indicators of women's overall status in society and of gender empowerment; in addition to the income that derives from paid employment, the engagement of women in such work adds to their social status. The productive contribution of women is typically less recognized in societies where women are engaged mostly in unpaid work and thereby undervalued in general. The significance of the unpaid–paid continuum in women's work is also evident in segmented labour markets and working conditions. Simply put, where there is a large amount of unpaid work that is performed in a society, and where the bulk of that is performed by women, the participation of women even in paid activities tends to be much more disadvantaged. Since the unpaid labour performed by women is not remunerated, and often not even socially recognized, it is easier for society to undervalue such work in general – particularly the types of care work and related activities that are typically performed within families. And this in turn leads to lower wages and worse working conditions, especially when many of the paid workers involved in such activities are also women. The very existence of the continuum therefore affects not only the bargaining power of women workers, but also social attitudes to them and to their work, and indeed their own reservation wages and self-perception.

The gender division of work, while determined in certain structural ways, is not completely fixed over time in any particular society. Rather, it tends to change according to the need to preserve not just male power over women, but also to ensure the greater economic exploitation of women to suit the needs of capital as required by particular accumulation trajectories. But also, the very possibility of extracting significant amounts of unpaid work from women enables the subsidization of 'formal' economic activities.

This has been sharply evident during the pandemic, when the gender construction of societies has enabled governments and employers to pass on many, if not most, of the burdens of adjustment to families, and therefore to unpaid labour of women and girls within them. There is much evidence that lockdowns and disruption of other services, including care and education services, have had differential impacts on adults within households, as the adults are forced to shoulder more of the care of children and the elderly who would otherwise have received socially provided services (whether public or private). As noted earlier, there is evidence across countries that more women also dropped out of the labour force because of child-care and other domestic responsibilities, as schools and day-care centres were shut. In general, care responsibilities within families have greatly increased during this period, first of all because this is primarily a health crisis which necessitates greater care activity, and secondly because of the temporary closure, postponement or lack of availability of many care services and associated facilities (for the care of the young, the elderly, the sick and the differently abled) that were earlier delivered through public or private providers.

This has had implications for time poverty, a feature that is typically ignored but is much more marked among women, and especially poorer women (Ghosh 2016). The loss of employment may appear to be associated with greater availability of time, both because of less paid work time and because commuting times have been greatly reduced if not eliminated altogether. But there is likely to have been a significant increase in unpaid labour time because of the increase in care requirements noted earlier. These increases in time use – and therefore in time poverty – are much more likely among poorer women.

Migrant Workers and the Globalized Care Industry

Migrant workers – both within countries and cross-border – have also been badly affected by the pandemic. Migrant care workers are typically less paid and protected than local care workers. Eighty per cent of all female cross-border migrant workers are domestic workers, who are part of a global supply chain of care services that has propped up economic activity and social reproduction in advanced economies. Yet now they are likely to be the most exposed and vulnerable.

Migration patterns are highly gendered, in terms of the causes and consequences of movement. International migration for work shows clear demarcations and separate niches for men and women workers. Male migrant workers tend to be concentrated in the production and construction sectors, and to a much lesser extent in service activities. Female migrant workers, by contrast, are dominantly found to be working in specific service activities – in the domestic work and care sectors, as well as in entertainment work. Demand for such workers is less dependent upon the economic cycle and more dependent upon longer-run demographic and social tendencies in the receiving countries. Ageing societies require more care providers. Societies in which women are more active in paid work participation, especially in higher-income activities, need more paid domestic workers.

A dominant part of the cross-border economic migration of women has been for employment in care activities. The globalization of care work has many aspects, and its gendered nature has generated much analysis, including in terms of how it has corresponded to the dynamics of capitalist accumulation in both sending and receiving countries. Yeates (2009) has shown how the cross-border migration of nurses maps on to institutional formations so closely that it is possible to speak of a global 'nursing labour migration–industrial complex', forming a global nursing care chain similar to the value chains that operate in manufacturing. For the sending countries, the benefits in terms of remittances received may be outweighed by the loss of such skilled workers within their own economies, as the (mostly developed) recipient countries effectively export their nursing care crises to the poorer countries of origin of migrant nurses.

The gender distribution of migrant workers has a macroeconomic impact on sending countries through the level and the volatility of remittance inflows, because both the ability and the willingness to send remittances is affected by economic cycles in the host economies. This is not only because women migrating for work have been known to send a greater proportion of their earnings back as remittances, and to send more regularly than men. It is also because typically, the nature of the work differs. Male migrant workers are much more immediately affected by business cycles in the host economies, tending to lose jobs or experience reduced incomes, which thereby affects the remittances they can send. Women working in services activities, by contrast, especially those in care services such as nurses or domestic workers, are less likely to be immediately affected by the business cycle as these activities are not the first to be curtailed. Therefore, their incomes and ability to send remittances are less affected. This means that countries that send more women migrant workers out are likely to show a more stable pattern of remittance inflow than countries with dominantly male out-migrants.

Similarly, the migration of women workers can lead to an international transfer of the job of providing care even in domestic contexts, as is illustrated by the example of migrant women workers from the Philippines. Many such women perform domestic tasks – the labour involved in social reproduction – that are still seen as the dominant responsibility of women in the more developed industrial societies in Europe or North America, or the more dynamic and rapidly growing developing parts of Asia such as Hong Kong, Singapore and South Korea, or the oil-exporting countries of West Asia and the Gulf. Migrant women domestic workers free locally resident women's labour for more active participation in the paid labour market and thereby contribute to the economic growth of the receiving country. At the same time, the migrant women's own household responsibilities back home must be fulfilled by other women, since the gender division of labour at both ends of the migratory spectrum still leaves women primarily responsible for doing the domestic work. This house work back home is often performed by women relatives such as mothers, sisters and daughters. But the very large wage differentials across sending and receiving countries can allow such migrant workers in turn to outsource their own domestic work through paid employment, by hiring poorer local women to care for their own children and perform necessary household tasks. In turn, such women may be migrants from rural areas of the sending country who have come into cities and towns in search of income.

All these have very specific implications during a time of pandemic, as restrictions on travel and mobility affect the possibility of outsourcing care work both within and across national boundaries, affecting both the possibility of more paid employment for women in such activities and the need to provide such care in whatever manner, possibly through unpaid time allocation within families and communities. The issue has been rendered more complex by the differing state responses across countries, with many countries not increasing public spending on health care to any substantial extent despite the health crisis. This leads to the critical question of women workers in health, sanitation and care activities, who have been critical in societal responses to the pandemic.

Women as Frontline Workers in Dealing with the Pandemic

Women dominate in health services: more than two-thirds of all health workers in 104 countries are women (Boniol *et al.* 2019). But they earn 28 per cent less than men on average, also because they are concentrated in lower-paid occupations like nurses and midwives. They are also less protected in all ways and more likely to be exposed to infection: it has been found that in the current pandemic, more women health workers (both paid and unpaid) are likely to be exposed to infection without adequate protection like PPE (personal protective equipment). Not only are women health workers more poorly paid in general, but there are additional occupational hierarchies to be navigated, from highly paid 'professionals' like specialist physicians down to nurses, ward attendants and cleaners. Unsurprisingly, the gender balance within each occupation changes as one goes down the pecking order, with women concentrated in the lower-status, worst-paid positions.

Globally, women hold 70 per cent of all health-care jobs.[2] But they are more likely to be nurses, midwives and community health workers, while men comprise a disproportionate share of better-paid occupations like surgeons, physicians, dentists and pharmacists. The gender gaps in wages are therefore marked, with women earning on average 28 per cent less than men in the health sector. Community health workers are perhaps the most exploited of all health workers, especially in developing countries. Often, they are not recognized as workers at all, but rather as 'volunteers' (as is true in India). As such, they rarely benefit from formal contracts that provide job security and a fair wage, let alone protections like health care.

Those who thought that a pandemic would make everyone realize the crucial role of care workers unfortunately have been proved wrong. With the coronavirus still spreading rapidly, frontline workers are more essential than ever, but at greater risk and often with even worse wages and working conditions than before.[3] Worse, as economies collapse and labour market conditions deteriorate, employers in the private and public sector alike have grown more cynical in their treatment of essential workers. Far from instilling a deeper appreciation for their employees, the pandemic-induced surge in unemployment has enabled employers to exploit workers even more.

Women health care workers are also more at risk in the current pandemic because they are more likely to be involved in activities that require close physical contact with patients. Among health care workers, women are three times more likely to contract Covid-19 infection than men (UN Women 2020). For a brief period after the pandemic first erupted, these workers were widely recognized for their critical contributions to society. Around the world, political leaders and members of the public applauded essential workers, singing their praises from balconies and leaving flower bouquets outside hospitals. But while health care workers at all levels were rightly described as 'heroes', that seems to have represented the extent of their reward. The public acclaim has not translated into better working conditions or higher wages, and certainly not systematic efforts to ensure their physical safety during the pandemic.

For example, in the United States, a brief period during which some companies offered their frontline workers slightly higher wages was soon followed by reversion to the norm: wages returned to their previous lows, and sometimes went lower.[4] Similarly, in the United Kingdom, Prime Minister Boris Johnson thanked the immigrant nurses[5] – 'Jenny from New Zealand', 'Luis from Portugal' – who saved his life when he was hospitalized with Covid-19. But then, he lost no time in trying to slap a surcharge on immigration fees on such workers and their cohort (ironically, for the purpose of funding the National Health Service).[6]

The situation in developing countries is even worse. Governments faced with falling tax revenues are practising austerity in the midst of a health emergency and recession, slashing non-Covid-19 health spending, forcing pay-cuts and longer hours on health workers, and avoiding the expense of procuring personal protective equipment. So blatant is the official disregard for essential workers that doctors and nurses in India have threatened to resign,[7] while health workers in the Democratic Republic of Congo have gone on strike[8] after months of working without pay. Likewise, the needs of underpaid and vulnerable sanitation workers have been systematically ignored.

Decades of public neglect and underspending[9] have meant that even an unprecedented global health emergency and economic collapse have not been enough to make mistreatment of low-paid essential workers socially and politically unacceptable. However, this is clearly a moment to recognize that greater social investment in care activities is not just an urgent necessity, but also an important opportunity. Obviously, the pandemic has exposed the critical need for massive investment in care economy across all societies, because one of the reasons Covid-19 has been able to do so much damage globally is the lack of development and/or hollowing-out of universally accessible health care facilities. But investing in care can also address future concerns about new technologies taking away jobs, especially in routine manufacturing and services tasks. Care work is relational and requires flexible responses, so it cannot be entirely replaced by machines. With changing demography, social changes and public health concerns, more skilled care services will be required. However, these *must* be provided through public intervention, as private markets will underprovide them. This means that public policy in all countries must recognize the crucial importance of care work and investment in good quality care services; invest adequately in skills and training for all types of care; make sure health care workers are trained, and have good wages and working conditions, workplace protection and social protection. In all of this, new technologies have to be enablers, not controllers of workers. This would serve public purpose at multiple levels: more and better quality employment, improved conditions of life, genuine (rather than false) productivity growth.

Other Specific Concerns of Women
There are several other gender-specific concerns that have emerged during the pandemic. It is now clear that the pandemic and the economic fall-out are pushing hundreds of millions of people into poverty, even extreme poverty. This is true not only of income poverty, but even more so of multidimensional poverty. Because of the intersectionality of gender concerns, this means that women from poor, marginalized and other disadvantaged social groups are directly at great risk. The emerging food crisis is

a critical area of concern, because when families have less access to food, it is known that women and girls suffer and are deprived of food even more than men and boys. And the environmental and climate crisis, which is already upon us, is likely to make all of these problems even more acute.

The pandemic and associated lockdowns have also involved greater threats to health and physical security for women. The substantial increase in domestic violence during lockdowns has been noted in many countries (UN Women 2020), and even these reports probably underestimate the extent of the problem. Pandemics in general are known to intensify other forms of violence and discrimination, and this has been particularly evident during the current pandemic. Meanwhile, official and societal support systems for victims of violence that were already weak have shrunk further. Health concerns have gone well beyond the impact of this particular virus. The single-minded focus on containing Covid-19 infections has led many governments to ignore or underplay the risk of other infections and diseases, and especially to underprovide reproductive health services. In India, for example, it has been estimated that institutional deliveries of babies came down by 40 per cent during the lockdown, exposing both mothers and infants to significantly greater risks and increasing the possibilities of maternal and infant mortality. Similarly, sanitary towels were not classified as essential goods in several countries during early phases of the lockdown, and anyway became less accessible for many when existing sources of distribution such as schools and health centres were closed. In some countries, such as the ones in South Asia, gender differences in access to health treatment have meant that women are more likely to die of Covid-19 than men, counter to the global trend.

The Way Forward: The Colours of the Future

The pandemic has sharply exposed existing forms of gender discrimination and relational inequality, and it clearly has the potential to increase and intensify all of them. Official public policy responses have not only been inadequate to counter these trends, but have even in some cases further accentuated them. Official gender blindness or apathy has meant that many government responses have further added to women's socio-economic disadvantages, and in some cases also reduced their voice and public participation. The contrasts across countries in this regard are striking and telling. It is now well known that countries run by macho leaders with authoritarian personalities have thus far performed very badly with respect to dealing with the pandemic. By contrast, several countries (especially some with woman leaders) have shown that the only way to defeat Covid-19 is through community involvement, cooperation and social solidarity – all of which require an explicit focus on improving gender relations and empowering women.

The challenges posed by the pandemic are enormous, but they may eventually pale into insignificance in comparison with the even greater existential threat posed by climate change, and the massive socio-political instabilities being generated by massively increased inequality. Clearly, the currently dominant policy paradigms and institutional arrangements are inadequate to deal with this, which is why there are growing calls for a Global Green New Deal (see, for example, Gallagher and Kozul-Wright 2019). It is clear that we need a Global New Deal – but it must be multicoloured. It requires a reliance on three planks: a focus on economic recovery based on significantly increased public expenditure, regulation and redistribution.

This New Deal must obviously be green, to address climate and environmental threats. Increased public spending has to be oriented towards recognizing, respecting and preserving the environment; reducing carbon emissions, addressing climate challenges and enabling adaptation; and changing patterns of production and consumption accordingly. It must also be blue, to deal with the growing shortages of clean water and the inequalities of access to water that are evident geographically and across classes, and have very strong gender-differentiated results. It must be purple, with an emphasis on care economy. The pandemic has exposed critical need for massive investment in care economy across all societies. With changing demography, social changes and public health concerns, more skilled care services will be required. This requires rewarding paid care work through increased public spending; recognizing, reducing and redistributing unpaid care work; and representing care workers and giving them greater voice. It must be red, with a critical focus on addressing and reducing inequalities: in assets, income, access to food, essential public services and employment opportunities. These have to be reduced across different dimensions: gender, race, ethnicity, caste, location, age. This requires more careful regulation of markets, including of financial markets, labour and land markets, and of interaction with the natural environment. It also requires more active redistribution, such that new public spending is financed by taxing the rich and the multinational companies that have managed to evade taxes by exploiting legal loopholes. All of this requires international cooperation, which is why this multicoloured new deal must be global in scope, with appropriate international architecture, with controlled finance and capital flows, revised rules for trade, investment flows and intellectual property rights that simultaneously prevent concentration and monopoly rent-seeking and encourage good quality employment generation.

This may seem like an impossible agenda, but the constraints are mainly political. The nations of the world have come together in the past to confront seemingly impossible challenges; now is the moment to find similar if not greater levels of ambition for humanity.

Notes

1. https://sites.google.com/view/covid-rps/home, accessed 22 October 2020.
2. https://www.who.int/hrh/resources/health-observer24/en/, accessed 23 October 2020.
3. https://www.project-syndicate.org/commentary/us-workers-need-higher-minimum-wage-new-tech-policy-by-daron-acemoglu-2020-07?barrier=accesspaylog, accessed 23 October 2020.
4. https://www.ft.com/content/6c7b59ad-be4f-46b3-8386-072f106a1960, accessed 23 October 2020.
5. https://www.washingtonpost.com/world/europe/boris-johnson-nurses-nhs/2020/04/13/51498d34-7bfa-11ea-a311-adb1344719a9_story.html, accessed 23 October 2020.
6. https://www.personneltoday.com/hr/extend-immigration-health-surcharge-exemption-to-care-workers-government-told/, accessed 23 October 2020.
7. https://www.newsclick.in/Delhi-Healthcare-Workers-Doctors-Threaten-Resignation-Unpaid-Salaries-Disbursed, accessed 23 October 2020.
8. https://www.barrons.com/news/dr-congo-virus-health-workers-strike-over-unpaid-wages-01594054805?tesla=y, accessed 23 October 2020.
9. https://www.project-syndicate.org/commentary/small-governments-big-failure-covid19-by-mariana-mazzucato-and-giulio-quaggiotto-2020-05?barrier=accesspaylog, accessed 23 October 2020.

References

Alon, Titan, Matthias Doepke, Jane Olmstead-Rumsey and Michèle Tertilt (2020), 'The Impact of Covid-19 on Gender Equality', National Bureau of Economic Research, Working Paper 26947, April.

Boniol, Mathieu, Michelle McIsaac, Lihui Xu, Tana Wuliji, Khassoum Diallo and Jim Campbell (2019), 'Gender Equity in the Health Workforce: Analysis of 104 Countries', Health Workforce Working Paper 1, March, Geneva: World Health Organization.

Coury, Sarah, Jess Huang, Ankur Kumar, Sara Prince, Alexis Krivkovich and Lareina Yee, (2020), 'Women in the Workplace Report', https://www.mckinsey.com/featured-insights/diversity-and-inclusion/women-in-the-workplace#

Deshpande, Ashwini (2020), 'The Covid-19 Pandemic and Lockdown: First Effects on Gender Gaps in Employment and Domestic Work in India', Working Papers 30, Department of Economics, Ashoka University, Haryana (revised June 2020), https://dp.ashoka.edu.in/ash/wpaper/paper30.pdf, accessed 6 March 2020.

Elson, Diane (1995), *Male Bias in the Development Process*, Manchester and New York: Manchester University Press.

Folbre, Nancy (2021, forthcoming), *The Rise and Decline of Patriarchal Systems*, London: Verso Books.

Gallagher, Kevin and Richard Kozul-Wright (2019), *A New Multilateralism for Shared*

Prosperity: Geneva Principles for a Global Green New Deal, Boston: Global Development Policy Centre and Geneva: UNCTAD.

Ghosh, Jayati (2016), 'Time Poverty and the Poverty of Economics', *METU Studies in Development*, vol. 43, no. 1, Special Issue in Honour of Fikret Senses.

Ghosh, Jayati (2020a) 'Global Inequality in a Time of Pandemic', *Real World Economics Review.*

———— (2020b), 'Covid-19, the Global Economy and Developing Countries', *Dissent Magazine.*

International Labour Organization (ILO) (2020a), *ILO Monitor: COVID-19 and the World of Work*, fifth edition, 30 June, Geneva: ILO.

———— (2020b), 'Impact of Lockdown Measures on the Informal Economy', ILO Brief, April, Geneva: ILO, https://www.ilo.org/wcmsp5/groups/public/---ed_protect/---protrav/---travail/documents/briefingnote/wcms_743523.pdf.

International Monetary Fund (IMF) (2021), *IMF Fiscal Monitor*, January, Washington, D.C.: IMF.

Kalpagam, U. (1994), *Labour and Gender: Survival in Urban India*, New Delhi: Sage Publications.

Seguino, Stephanie and Elissa Braunstein (2018), 'The Costs of Exclusion: Gender Job Segregation, Structural Change and the Labour Share of Income', *Development and Change*: 1–33, doi: 10.1111/dech.12462.

UN Women (2020), *From Insights to Action: Gender Equality in the Wake of Covid-19*, New York: UN Women.

Yeates, Nicola (2009), *Globalizing Care Economies and Migrant Workers: Explorations in Global Care Chains*, UK: Palgrave Macmillan.

4

Covid-19 in Europe

Aggravating North–South Tensions in the European Union

Erik S. Reinert

In Europe, the last serious pandemic was the Spanish flu, about a hundred years ago. My grandfather actually died from a complication of that Spanish flu – encephalitis lethargica – a sleeping disease that he contracted while on a business trip to Germany, and he died twenty years before I was born. But that was a late version of the disease which killed so many people. I recently found the name encephalitis lethargica in the statistics of pandemics that killed more than 1,00,000 people, so there is some memory of the last time. Recently, a 90-year-old economic historian who was born in 1930 said that he looked up the journals from an economic weekly in Norway of 1920–21 and noted that the relationship to such deaths was so much more matter-of-fact then, with the journal simply stating the number of people who died each day. He contrasted the inevitability of how things looked in 1920 with what is happening now. Then, it is an aggravating separation that has been there for a long time, so I go into the background of that partition of the 'responsible North' and the 'irresponsible South'. The fact that the 'irresponsible South' was so much worse hit with Covid-19 than the 'responsible North' came to highlight the fact that Europe has become more disintegrated: as a result of the economic policies of the European Union (EU) after the introduction of the euro, the South has grown poorer compared to the North.

We have in Scandinavia an interesting natural experiment. Table 4.1 below, from the newspaper *Verdens Gang* of 8 May 2020, shows the key numbers of Covid-19-related casualties for the Nordic countries. The number of deaths due to Covid-19 infection was 3,040 in Sweden, 514 in Denmark, 255 in Finland and 217 in Norway. Sweden has about twice

---

Lecture delivered on 8 May 2020.

the number of inhabitants as Norway, and the number of deaths is about fifteen times higher. While Sweden's approach is not to close schools and to let everything go on as normal, the Norwegian approach is to 'flatten the curve'. Anders Tegnell, a Swedish doctor, and other spokesmen for the Swedish strategy have said that, in the end, Norway is probably going to have just as many deaths per capita as Sweden. So it is an interesting experiment. But it looks pretty ugly at the moment.[1]

There are cultural differences as well. Norway is one of three countries in Europe that were never feudal. It was one of three countries – Iceland and Switzerland being the other two – that were asked to join the EU but refused. People do not like it when I point to the common element, i.e. no feudalism and the refusal to join the EU in Brussels. Norway has handled the crisis very democratically; it is the government – based on recommendations from the health authorities – that decides what policies are adopted. In Sweden, on the other hand, there is a single bureaucrat who has all the decision-making powers. So, while the expert(s) in Sweden run the show alone, in Norway the decisions are made by the government. Clearly, not all the differences come from this; there are other differences as well – one of them probably being that Norway is extremely sparsely populated. On the other hand, Denmark is much more densely populated than Sweden. Finland is the only country that still stores all the medical supplies from the Cold War. Most countries threw away their reserves of medical supplies for emergencies ten to fifteen years ago, but the Finns still kept them. As a result, Finland was better prepared.

As Table 4.1 shows, the number of hospitalized people (column II), those in intensive care (column III) and the number of confirmed cases (column IV) in May 2020 were also much higher in Sweden than in the other Nordic countries. The number of deaths per 100,000 inhabitants is

Table 4.1 *Number of persons infected, hospitalized and dead due to Covid-19 infections in Scandinavian countries, May 2020* (per 100,000 persons)

Country	Number of deaths	Persons hospitalized	Persons in intensive care	Persons infected
	(I)	(II)	(III)	(IV)
Sweden	30.1	21.1	4.7	243.8
Denmark	8.9	3.4	0.8	174.1
Finland	4.6	3.1	0.7	148.2
Norway	4.0	1.2	0.5	102.4

Source: *Verdens Gang*, 8 May 2020.

4 in Norway and 30 in Sweden. This makes the comparison even more interesting. A similar process is under way in the United States; but it is less of a clear picture there because of the conflict between the federal government and the different states, and the fact that the spread of cases is over a much larger terrain in the US.

The initial Covid-19 cases in Europe were heavily concentrated in Italy and Spain. In the beginning, the Scandinavian Covid-19 cases were thought to have come from Italy, which was logical to presume, because of the outbreak there. In fact, the story proved to be slightly more complicated, because most people had contracted the virus skiing in the Austrian part of the Alps but close to the Italian border.

Norway is not a part of the European Union, but Denmark, Finland and Sweden are. As the division within the EU between the 'responsible North' and the 'irresponsible South' gradually became clearer, the three Nordic countries became a natural part of the 'responsible North'. Seen from the North, the inflationary pressures and – after the introduction of the euro – the trade and budget deficits were signs of 'irresponsibility'.

In order to understand this division in Europe, we have to look back at what happened during the Cold War. We had a Marshall Plan, starting in 1947, in order to reindustrialize Europe after the Second World War. When its inventor – US Secretary of State George Marshall – received the Nobel Peace Prize in 1953, he emphasized that they had understood that the exchange between farmers and manufacturing was the basis of modern civilization. Therefore, reindustrialization was very important. But the Marshall Plan went beyond Europe, creating a sanitary belt of rich industrialized countries around the communist bloc. This was a very successful move, and very consciously based on the importance of manufacturing.

At the same time, in the late 1940s, Paul Samuelson restored David Ricardo's 1817 Theory of Comparative Advantage, which at the time was a marginal theory. In Samuelson's version of the Theory of Comparative Advantage, free trade created factor price equalization: wages and capital cost would tend to even out between rich and poor countries. The post-war history of Europe is that of a practice based on the logic of the Marshall Plan which slowly died out from 1947 till 1990. On the other hand, Samuelson's theory grew and replaced economic policies based on the ideas of the Marshall Plan over the same years. One reason why Samuelson's theory was so popular was that he created a kind of capitalist counter-utopia against the communist slogan, from each according to ability and to each according to need. Samuelson 'proved' that free trade would be even better. If you look at the theoretical background of the

Marshall Plan, there was an important link between economic structure and population density, and that link was lost.

US President Herbert Hoover was a mining engineer by profession. He was sent to Germany after the peace in 1945. Already in 1943, the Allies had decided to punish Germany for their warmongering, and the punishment was to prohibit manufacturing industry in the three Allied zones in Germany. Called the Morgenthau Plan, this was the worst punishment they could think of. This of course resulted in a big loss of industrial jobs, and people moved from West Germany to East Germany, to the Russian sector, which still had industry. This made the communist Eastern sector look more prosperous than the capitalist Western sector, and Hoover understood that the migration into East Germany had to be stopped. In a letter sent to Washington in early 1947, Herbert Hoover argued: 'There is the illusion that the new Germany left after the annexation can be reduced to a pastoral state [meaning, without industry], but it cannot be done unless we exterminate or move 25 million people out of it' (Hoover 1947). The word 'exterminate' was of course a very strong word in 1947, so from the Morgenthau Plan bringing deindustrialization, the logic of the Allies turned towards reindustrialization in a matter of months. This was the understanding that lasted until the fall of the Berlin Wall.

N-grams are useful things. If you look at the frequency of the names of three English economists, starting in 1817 when David Ricardo wrote his *Principles of Economics*, you will find that Ricardo was a minor

Figure 4.1 *N-gram showing relative frequency of reference to the English economists John Stuart Mill, James Mill and David Ricardo during the nineteenth century, showing how Ricardo was a marginal economist*

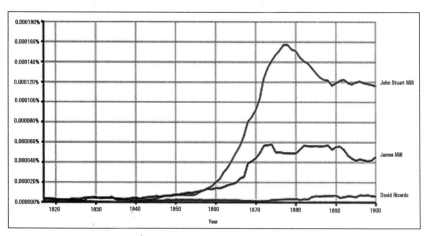

Source: Google Books Ngram Viewer.

figure for a long time (see Figure 4.1); around the 1840s his popularity grew a bit, but not very much. Those who were quoted were James Mill and his son John Stuart Mill, who had exactly the opposite theory to that of Ricardo when it came to third world countries: the idea that all countries need infant industry protection. In a sense, the Marshall Plan was starting from scratch again with infant industry protection, which was the strategy of the European Union until the Treaty of Maastricht in 1992, which brought in a more neo-liberal approach.

It is interesting to track the frequency of usage of the term 'comparative advantage': it was not used often after 1817; it began to be used in the 1920s and it really exploded during the Cold War; and then, interestingly enough, once the Cold War was won, the use of the term declined. This suggests that economics is very responsive to demand (see Figure 4.2). When there was a demand to prove that the market created economic harmony, the economists delivered. When communism had lost out and there was only one game in town – Thatcher's 'there is no alternative' – then 'comparative advantage' disappeared. As a result of this emphasis on static comparative advantage, what has been happening in Europe since the 1990s is that the southern periphery has been going through deindustrialization and the northern countries, especially Germany and Holland, have been doing well.

So we can say the EU has had different stages of ideology (Reinert and Kattel 2007). In the beginning, stage one, when everyone understood

Figure 4.2 *N-gram of David Ricardo's term 'comparative advantage' from its publication (1817) till today, showing how it became fashionable only during the Cold War*

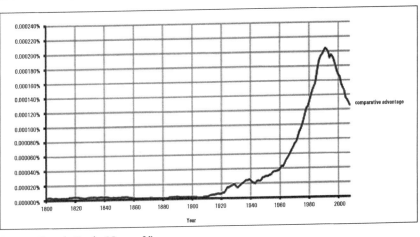

Source: Google Books Ngram Viewer.

that manufacturing matters, there were very strong industrial policies. This lasted through the 1980s with the integration of Spain. Economic integration was done very gradually, with the lowering of tariffs slowly over ten years and the addition of a lot of heavy-handed industrial policy. Then came stage two, when David Ricardo slowly took over from the Marshall Plan in determining the economic approach, policy practice yielded to new classical visions of economics as the science of harmony, and old goals became merely wishful thinking. Then, with the big Eastern integration on 1 May 2004, there was no longer any steering of the economic structure; and that is when the EU, in a sense, started coming apart. Eastern Europe was first deindustrialized and then integrated, which some of us described at that time as 'Europe's attempted economic suicide' (ibid.).

It is important to keep in mind that in the first phase, both the communist and capitalist strategies of the time were based on the ideas of German economist Friedrich List (1789–1846), the great industrializer. It is interesting that on an anniversary of Friedrich List, both Germanies issued stamps in his honour – and they even chose the same portrait of the man. He was probably the only hero the two countries had in common. The fact that both capitalism and communism were based on building manufacturing industry is something very important that was lost after the end of the Cold War. The space race was a part of this competition. Today, we have former World Bank chief economist Justin Yifu Lin confirming that Friedrich List was right: 'Except for a few oil-exporting countries, no countries have ever gotten rich without industrialization first.'[2] Now Southern Europe is becoming deindustrialized.

The theoretical argument for the single market was made by the Italian economist Paolo Cecchini (Cecchini 1988). He argued strongly for the common market, but around 85 per cent of the benefits from the single market appears to originate in economies of scale in manufacturing industry. This was still the Marshall Plan ideology in 1988, four years before Maastricht. If somebody had asked Cecchini the question, if some countries were to lose their manufacturing sector in the European Union, would it still be to their benefit to be in the European Union, the answer clearly would have been no. The gap between this official understanding and what actually happened is remarkable.

Even if we look outside the European Union, we can see something similar. Figure 4.3 shows a comparison of income distribution before the fall of the Berlin Wall and 2016. The countries to the left – Ukraine, Georgia, Serbia – were richer under communism than they are now under capitalism, which is remarkable. These countries have all tried to be democratic and have had to follow the rules of the World Bank and

Figure 4.3 *Percentiles of the population with income growth above/below the G7 average, 1989–2016*

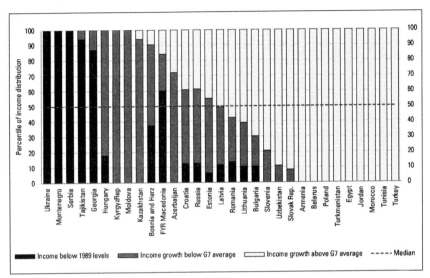

Source: Based on European Bank for Reconstruction and Development, Transition Report 2016–17: *Transition for All – Equal Opportunities in an Unequal World*, Chart 1.13, p. 17.

the International Monetary Fund (IMF). On the other hand, to the right in the figure are some countries which did this differently. Uzbekistan did exceptionally well and Belarus, the last communist country where Lenin still stands in the square with his hand raised, too did rather well. This is because they managed to save their industry. So it is a big problem in today's world system that the Washington Consensus – with the World Bank and the IMF – has created important disincentives to democracies: democracies have to follow their advice, which, in the present context of these countries, leads to deindustrialization and increasing poverty.

Once the euro enters the picture, the separation of North and South becomes serious. My explanation of this rift, which is really making the EU come apart during the coronavirus pandemic, is the industrial policy as it relates to exchange rates. When Germany was unified in 1990, the black market rate was 5 East German marks to 1 West German mark. The savings in East Germany were converted at 2 East German marks to 1 West German mark. But on 1 July 1990, wages were converted at the rate 1 to 1. Initially, the East Germans were very happy with their increased purchasing power. But their happiness was brief, because much of East German industry could not absorb the high wage costs, and factories closed down. There was a short-term benefit in terms of purchasing power, but since human beings play two roles in the economy – as producers and as consumers – it turned out that while East German consumers got a bonanza, the same persons as workers suffered. Thus, most East Germans came to see unification as an unfriendly takeover.

There are some interesting similarities of this process with what happened inside the EU, especially the euro zone. The euro was agreed upon in Maastricht in 1992, adopted in 1995 and bank notes were issued in 2002: all within a relatively short time-span. For political reasons, Southern Europe has had a history of inflation: communism and trade union pressure produced high wage increases and high inflation. I ran an industrial company in Italy for twenty years, so I witnessed this inflation machine that had a strange effect. If you were running an industry, wages were going up but the cost of capital was at times something like –8 per cent. So businesses invested heavily in new machinery, productivity increased considerably, and what had initially looked very irresponsible came out pretty well in the end, in terms of increasing real wages. Italy grew faster than Germany at the time. Just as with the unification of Germany, the euro appeared to have important advantages in Southern Europe. The low interest rates proved to be a big attraction to countries with high inflation. Instead of a 10 per cent interest rate or 12 per cent inflation rate, countries could now have an interest rate of 4 per cent or inflation rate of 5 per cent. But on the other hand, on the productive side of the economy, continued inflation combined with frozen exchange rates created cost problems for manufacturing in Southern Europe.

The euro created a similar death of industry, albeit much slower, in Southern Europe as unification did in former East Germany. Just as in East Germany, the unified exchange rate killed many manufacturing industries. Before the euro, imbalances were dealt with by adjusting exchange rates. If one country was a bit irresponsible – say, if Portugal was not doing well – it could be dealt with by devaluation that made the country competitive again. At the time most of the debt was in the national currency – and this was akin to the right-hand pocket owing money to the left-hand pocket – in effect there was no problem. But after the euro, the only adjustment mechanism was to move people, like in the United States. Michigan cannot devalue; if Detroit goes down the drain, people have to move out of Detroit. In the same way, the Greeks had to go to Germany even if they did not want to and the Germans did not want them.

This tension was there well before the coronavirus pandemic hit. It had worsened when Mario Draghi was the head of the European Central Bank (2011–19). During the inflationary years in Italy, Draghi and his family had been stuck with a huge amount of Italian treasury bonds, and they lost a lot of money because of inflation. In Draghi, the

Germans found somebody who hated inflation more than they did; so, in spite of being Italian, Draghi became the representative of the 'responsible North'. Most central banks have multiple goals to drive their strategies, but Mario Draghi managed to have inflation control as the only target of the European Central Bank. This reinforced the new culture clash: the responsible North versus the irresponsible South. Europeans have a lot of cultural differences, and the attitude towards inflation is an important one. The hyperinflation in Germany after the First World War created a lasting national aversion towards inflation. For the Germans, 'the black zero' is the goal for all budgets. Budget deficits are a sin (even forcing the German government to engage in off-budget spending to maintain this myth). This is a very different culture than, let's say, the one in Italy.

With the debt crisis this situation turned nasty. This was exemplified by the nationalist party in Finland (the 'True Finns') saying that we do not want to pay the nightclub bills of the Italians and the Greeks, not recognizing that Southern Europeans often work longer hours than people in Northern Europe. The cultural differences in attitudes towards inflation were not understood. Germany's huge trade surplus, more than what is allowed by the EU, is – virtually by necessity – mirrored by deficits in the 'irresponsible' southern periphery. In the end, imports have to equal exports, and the surpluses in Germany show up as deficits in the periphery, and the periphery gets deeper and deeper into debt. To me, it is not clear how Germany gets away with playing innocent: their surplus is also a big problem.

Expenditure on health in Italy was cut by €25 billion from 2010 to 2015, under the governments of Berlusconi and Monti, and a further €10 billion from 2015 to 2019. So, per capita health expenses in Italy now stand at €2,326, €2,000 less than in Germany. That is one of the reasons why things were so much worse in Italy than in Germany.

My family had economic bases in a couple of places in Italy. One of them was in Bergamo in Northern Italy, which happens to be where the crisis was at its worst. We wrote to friends who live 10 kilometres outside Bergamo to ask how they were doing. Their answer was that they were doing fine, but in Bergamo, people were dying like flies. It was very dramatic and we started wondering what, other than cuts in health spending, could be the cause of this. The increasing poverty in Italy makes it difficult for young couples to get their own housing. So it is becoming more and more normal that three generations live together. This would clearly be one reason for more infection. Northern Italy is also a haven for industrial pollution.

The European Union reacted very late to the situation in Italy.

Russia – before the crisis hit it – sent medical equipment to Italy with a message in Italian, 'From Russia with Love'. This was an important contrast to the complete lack of action from the EU. It was almost as if the EU had said, 'Well, of course, you in the irresponsible South get diseases. We in the responsible North do not.' Then, on 12 March 2020, Christine Lagarde of the European Central Bank made things much worse by saying, 'We are not here to close [bond] spreads, there are other tools and other actors to deal with these issues.' This statement was the exact opposite of what Mario Draghi had been saying for nine years, that we will do everything it takes to save the euro. Immediately after Lagarde said this in the middle of a serious crisis, interest rates in Italy skyrocketed and the stock market dropped by 17 per cent. It was really bad timing. In Italy, the president is not a political figure and is not supposed to make political statements. But at this point, President Sergio Matarrella reacted by saying that when Italy was grappling with the coronavirus crisis, the country had a right to expect solidarity rather than obstacles from beyond its borders. He did not mention institutions, he did not mention names, but it was clearly addressed to the European Central Bank.

Later, in March 2020, with the EU still hesitating, several Italian politicians made strong negative statements about the EU. Matteo Salvini is on the political right, but I quote him here because his statement on 27 March was the sharpest, even as similar opinions were expressed along the entire political axis: 'The EU which now takes fourteen days to decide what to do and whether to help, leaves us high and dry. First we win over the virus and then we have a rethink about Europe. And if that is our decision, we shall leave, without even saying thank you.'[3] He was really swearing at the EU, and it did not get better. A big problem is that Germany does not want to see the ills they are creating. Former Vice Minister of Finance Heiner Flassbeck tried to explain to Germany through his writings that what they are doing was wrong and why this was so damaging, but it did not get through.

Nations once again face what used to be called '*Zinsknechtschaft*' – 'debt serfdom'. This was a term used in Germany to describe their economic situation in the 1920s and 1930s. Now, the European periphery is in the same situation. A number of German words used in the 1920s and 1930s later became prohibited words: *Zinsknechtschaft* is one of those terms that one is afraid to use because it was used by the wrong kind of economists in the 1930s. But it actually describes a real phenomenon: a nation may fall into so much debt that a lot of its resources would have to go towards paying the interest. Something similar is happening in Ukraine and in Georgia, and also in Italy and especially in Greece. These countries should be allowed to go bankrupt. Here, the present imbalance of power between the real economy and the financial sector actually makes the economic situation much worse. Keynes had an expression, 'the paradox of savings' – that if you are in a deficit situation and you save too much, you actually shrink the whole economy. There is no doubt that this is happening, for instance, in Italy. The country is forced to save. But that saving will only be in the interest of foreign debt holders. It shrinks the domestic economy. The shrinking health budget is just one aspect of this. This represents fairly mainstream Keynesian thinking, but it is seemingly not able to penetrate the EU powerhouse.

I wrote an article in a Norwegian newspaper on the problems of Italy, and the newspaper carried a drawing alongside which showed Italy being grilled over the euro with viruses around. I think that is exactly apt.

Germany has strength in its long history of sophisticated medicine. It has traditionally produced vaccines and has a good health system as well. It is quite clear that the savings that were forced from Southern Europe reduced spending on the health system. Therefore it fell in Italy and other places, but not in Germany. There were also some strange regional differences: for example, north-eastern Italy – Veneto – seemingly had more money for health. The pressure that many are under may not immediately be seen, but over the long term there have been huge cuts in health services.

Due to the poverty in Italy, traditionally, generations have lived together. We now know that children can be infected by the virus and show no symptom at all, and that can be serious if they live with their grandparents. Traditionally, and also because it helps savings, in Italy, couples have to wait much longer before they can buy their own house; and that squeezes three generations into a house, which again helps spread disease. Clearly, savings were made in the wrong place. Finland kept its medical stockpile a secret – it had stocks of medical supplies of all kinds that it had been renewing since the Cold War ended – so the Finns are in one sense in an opposite situation, in that they were prudent and did all the right things, whereas Italy was forced to build on an already depleted health system.

Further to these differences between countries, it is now reasonably clear that Sweden indeed permanently paid a high price in terms of lives lost. There is no evidence that the countries that did better – Finland and Norway – only delayed the deaths. Their 'flattening of the curve' actually had the permanent effect of radically reducing the number of deaths as a percentage of the population.

Sweden experienced a very small decline in GDP, whereas Norway had a bigger one. So, in the short term, the extreme responses have had different costs: Norway's is costly and Sweden has saved money. The question is, how will this look in the long run. There are some important implications and a terrifying thought is that in the third world, where ever the governments do not have money, there might be very little you can do

One important difference has been in the case of old people's homes. In Italy, you tend to care for your parents if possible; you do not automatically send them off to old people's homes. In Scandinavia, parents are kept at home in some cases, but it is not the normal thing to do. In Canada and the US, as we have seen, old people's homes have seen terrible tragedies, and in Sweden too, apparently, they have seen a lot of deaths. The experts in Sweden shocked me when they said, 'Well, we have had a health problem in old age homes already so this just made it worse.' It is an already existing problem in many countries in Europe: not enough money being given to old people's homes. These are some of the existing weaknesses that are being magnified, and I think it is driving Europe more apart.

A key element in western and other cultures has been the prevention of hoarding. In other words, making sure money was circulating and not kept idle. The biblical term for idle money is *mammon*. We find a clear expression of this principle in the Bible, where servants are given money (*talents*) and later, the servant who has simply buried the money – instead of putting it in circulation – is severely punished (Mathew 25; 14–30). Below, we shall see how the fourteenth-century monetary theorist Nicolas Oresme testified to the importance of keeping money in circulation in order for the real economy – and the very process of life – to keep going. We find this issue also raised by Martin Luther (1483–1546), whose measure of good and bad was, 'does it serve life?'. This separation was culturally even more important in many other parts of the world.

This cultural tradition is important to keep in mind today when financial capitalism takes over from production capitalism. Continental European economics has always continued this 'biblical' separation of the *financial economy* from the *real economy*. We find this in Marx (in volume 3 of *Das Kapital*) on the left of the political axis, and in the conservative Schumpeter on the right. Schumpeter had the idea of separating the *money* (*Rechenpfennige*/accounting units) from what you can buy for money in the *real economy* (*Güterwelt*, the world of goods and services). Of course, this also has to do with the balance between the worlds of goods and services, the real economy and the financial economy. In good times, they support each other – money helps build the real economy.

A few years ago, when I was working for the European Union, in their think-tank in Seville in Spain, a taxi driver tried to explain to me what the hidden laws of the economy were: 'Well, you see, Mario Draghi and the European Central Bank are printing a lot of money. That money makes all the apartments in Spain more expensive. At the same time, the wages of taxi drivers and other people are shrinking.' The taxi driver's account was a good summary of what is happening in Europe. Real wages are going down in the South and a lot of people are moving from Southern Europe. Portugal has deindustrialized almost totally; Spain is suffering, Italy is suffering and Greece is suffering the most.

In 1848, there was a big crisis. Before that, in 1846, the repeal of the Corn Laws was the first triumph of free trade. England stopped protecting agriculture and tried to convince the rest of the world that they should not protect industry. Friedrich List was so upset by this that he committed suicide, thinking he had lost his cause of industrializing the European continent. So 1846 was the triumph of liberalism, but then in 1847 there was a huge financial crisis, especially in England. In 1848, harvests in many parts of Europe, from Finland to Spain, were very bad – and that year saw revolutions in all the large European countries except England and Russia. So 1848, in my view, was the moment when the previous ideology collapsed. The background for what happened in 1848 was the period called 'the hungry forties'. Charles Dickens's novels give a vivid picture of the poverty in England at that time. This was also a period of intense poverty in France, and even in Denmark. Hans Christian Andersen's story 'The Little Match Girl' was set in 1843. The same symptoms of poverty you had in the 1840s, you find now in the European periphery. So the optimistic interpretation could be that if things go really bad, then it might actually lead to a change of the economic system.

The initial North–South dimension of the pandemic and the lack of assistance from the European Union almost created a crisis within the EU. However, on 20 July 2020, at the initiative of the French president Macron, the EU changed its policies drastically and reached a historic agreement on a €750 billion coronavirus pandemic recovery fund.

Going back to Nicolas Oresme (*c*. 1320–1382), with the pandemic recovery fund the European Union can be said finally to have followed the logic of Theodoric, king of Italy from 493 to 526:

> And therefore so much of them [gold and silver] ought not to be allowed to be applied to other uses that there should not be enough left for money. It was this consideration that led Theodoric, king of Italy [493–526], to order the gold and silver deposited according to pagan custom in the tombs, to be removed and used for coining for the public profit, saying: 'It was a crime to leave hidden among the dead and useless, what would keep the living alive.' (Oresme 1956)

Notes

[1] *Editors' note*: The difference in death rates per million people was even greater by December 2020 – 504 in Sweden compared to 71 in Norway, available at https://ourworldindata.org/coronavirus, accessed 5 December 2020.

[2] https://www.project-syndicate.org/commentary/industrialization-s-second-golden-age?barrier=accesspaylog, accessed 8 May 2020.

[3] https://www.ilfoglio.it/politica/2020/03/27/video/salvini-dimostra-che-l-irre-sponsabilita-non-e-reversibile-307300/, accessed 8 May 2020.

References

Cecchini, Paolo (1988), *The European Challenge, 1992: The Benefits of a Single Market*, Aldershot: Gower Publishing Ltd.

Hoover, Herbert (1947), 'The President's Economic Mission to Germany and Austria', Report Number 3, https://cdn.mises.org/The%20De%20Moneta%20of%20 Nicholas%20Oresme%20and%20English%20Mint%20Documents_2.pdf, accessed 8 May 2020.

Oresme, Nicholas (1956), *The De Moneta of Nicholas Oresme and English Mint Documents*, trans., Charles Johnson, London: Thomas Nelson and Sons Ltd., https://cdn. mises.org/The%20De%20Moneta%20of%20Nicholas%20Oresme%20and%20 English%20Mint%20Documents_2.pdf, accessed 8 May 2020.

Reinert, Erik S. and Rainer Kattel (2007), 'European Eastern Enlargement as Europe's Attempted Economic Suicide?', The Other Canon Foundation and Tallinn University of Technology Working Papers in Technology Governance and Economic Dynamics, No. 14, http://technologygovernance.eu/files/main//2007070309122525.pdf, accessed 8 May 2020.

5

International Financial Cooperation to Address the Latin American Economic Crisis

José Antonio Ocampo

Introduction

The Covid-19 pandemic, the worst in a century, has engendered a global economic crisis that has been described by the managing director of the International Monetary Fund (IMF) as the worst recession since the Great Depression of the 1930s (Georgieva 2020). The containment measures adopted to manage the public health problems have had a profound effect on the economy, as they have paralysed 'non-essential' activities which may account for 50 per cent or more of economic activity in many countries. The turmoil in the financial markets has also been profound, and has prompted the worst flight in history of portfolio capital from emerging economies, although the bond markets in hard currencies for these economies have recovered since mid-April 2020. At the same time, international trade has contracted sharply, deepening the process that had already started in late 2019 as a result of the global economic slowdown and the 'trade wars', especially between the United States and China. In addition to this, the prices of an important group of commodities have dropped, reinforcing the negative trend seen over the last five years. Exports of services have also fallen, due in particular to the paralysis of tourism and air passenger traffic. In addition, remittances from migrant workers to their countries of origin will plummet, and new controls are being imposed on international migration.

The pandemic arrived relatively late in Latin America, but began to have significant effects in terms of infected people and the mortality rate in several countries, especially Brazil.[1] In economic terms, the pandemic hit the region after five years of slow economic growth, which can be described

---

Lecture delivered on 16 May 2020.

as a 'lost half-decade' (Ocampo 2020). Apart from the direct impact of the containment measures decreed in several countries, or those that people have adopted voluntarily to protect themselves, the economies of the region are also feeling the effects of the global crisis. Latin America will suffer the steepest drop in economic activity in the developing world, echoing the pattern it has experienced in recent decades, although with varying effects among the different countries. The 2020 recession will, moreover, be the worst since the Second World War, and there is thus the danger (and almost certainty) that the lost half-decade will turn into another lost decade.

Against this adverse backdrop, international economic cooperation has been very weak so far, in contrast to the strong multilateral collaboration led by the Group of 20 (G20) during the North Atlantic financial crisis of 2008–09.[2] This article analyses the discussions surrounding and the decisions taken on international financial cooperation, and the extent to which it benefits Latin America.[3] The article is divided into six sections, the first of which is this introduction. As a background, the second section offers some considerations on the global context as well as that of Latin America. A general analysis of international financial cooperation is presented in the third section. Analyses of monetary cooperation and the support from multilateral development banks and their impact on Latin America are discussed in detail in the fourth and fifth sections. Some brief conclusions are set out in the last section.

Academics have made enormous contributions to the ongoing discussions.[4] I am unable to do all of them justice here, although I will refer to proposals made by some authors. My analysis is rooted in international discussions and decisions taken by the major multilateral agencies to address the financial problems faced by emerging economies.

The Global and Latin American Context

The IMF's most recent *World Economic Outlook* projects a decline in global GDP (gross domestic product) based on market exchange rates of 6.1 per cent in 2020 (IMF 2020g).[5] This is the result of falls of 8 per cent in the major developed economies and 3 per cent in the emerging and developing economies, with Latin America as the worst performing region among the latter group of countries. The sharp downturn reflects the devastating effects of the pandemic containment measures on economic activity: quarterly contractions that were already severe in the first quarter,[6] and that will reach double digits in many economies in the second quarter. The basic IMF forecast assumes that these effects will gradually dissipate, but clearly, there is uncertainty as to whether there will be the medical means to prevent further outbreaks.

This crisis, which is truly global in scope, will certainly be more severe than that suffered by the global economy during the North Atlantic crisis (–2 per cent at market exchange rates in 2009, according to IMF figures), which did not occur in a large group of emerging and developing economies. Compared to the Great Depression, the current economic contraction has happened more quickly, but may be less deep and, above all, less protracted.[7] The basic IMF projection is that growth will be 5.3 per cent in 2021, which would not fully offset the 2020 recession. The outlook would be worse if it takes longer than expected to contain the pandemic in the current year, and/or if there is a second outbreak in 2021.[8]

In the light of the above, developed countries have been adopting aggressive measures in terms of increasing public spending, reducing or delaying tax payments, and providing liquidity, credit lines and guarantees for the business sector. In both fiscal and monetary terms, the IMF concludes that the packages are stronger than those adopted to deal with the North Atlantic crisis, although with differences between countries (IMF 2020b, 2020c). By contrast, China's recovery measures have been less pronounced than those adopted in 2009 because it has a smaller fiscal margin today, an issue that affects many emerging and developing economies more generally.

Initially, the effects on the financial markets were devastating. However, thanks to forceful interventions by central banks, the market falls were less pronounced than in 2008–09, and even led to a partial recovery from late March 2020 (IMF 2020b). A notable effect was the worst portfolio outflows in history from emerging economies, exceeding US$ 100 billion (Brooks and Fortun 2020; IMF 2020b). However, as will be seen later in this article, although risk spreads for these economies have remained high, bond yields and the cost of new financing have fallen to relatively moderate levels, thanks to the decline in benchmark interest rates (those of the United States Treasury Bonds), and several countries began to issue bonds on the international markets in mid-April 2020, much sooner than in past crises.

Another effect of the crisis has been a sharp contraction in international trade. Trade volumes and value, which began to fall in late 2019, have plunged further.[9] The World Trade Organization (WTO) expects that trade volume will fall by between 13 per cent under the baseline scenario and 32 per cent under the most pessimistic one (WTO 2020). The crisis may lead to the destruction or shortening of many international value chains. For this reason, trade may recover much more slowly than it did in 2010, which more than offset the fall seen in 2009. With regard to commodities, the crisis has caused oil and other energy prices to plummet, a more modest fall in prices of basic metals and diverse trends for agricultural products.[10]

Figure 5.1 *Latin America: GDP growth, 1950–2020*[*] (percentages)

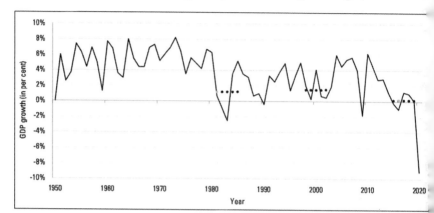

Note: * Figures for 2020 are the April ECLAC (Economic Commission for Latin America and the Caribbean) projections recorded in Table 5.1. The dotted lines indicate average annual growth during the aforementioned three five-year periods of low growth, specifically 1980–85, 1997–2002 and 2015–19.
Source: Prepared by the author on the basis of data from the Economic Commission for Latin America and the Caribbean (ECLAC).

Latin America is dealing with these serious external shocks after five years (2015–19) of anaemic growth, the worst since the Second World War, even worse than the five years of slowest growth during the Latin American debt crisis and the five years after the 1997 Asian financial crisis (see Figure 5.1). In the last five years, regional GDP growth barely reached 0.2 per cent (0.9 per cent if the Bolivarian Republic of Venezuela is excluded). This poor performance reflects not only economic problems, but also complex political crises and transitions in several countries.

However, Latin America's economic problems began long before the recent wave of economic and political instability. Economic growth in the region over the last three decades (1990–2019) was only 2.7 per cent per year, half of that seen in the thirty years preceding the lost decade (average annual growth was 5.5 per cent in the period 1950–80). Almost all the economies of the region have grown less than during those thirty years (with the exception of Chile, the Plurinational State of Bolivia and Uruguay); the downturn was particularly serious in the Bolivarian Republic of Venezuela, Brazil and Mexico. This indicates that, regardless of the current crisis, the region's development patterns need to be considered in depth.

All the multilateral organizations forecast a major recession in Latin America in 2020, with only a partial recovery in 2021 (World Bank 2020b; ECLAC 2020a and 2020b; IMF 2020b; Nuguer and Powell 2020). As shown in Table 5.1, these organizations expected a drop of around

Table 5.1 *Latin America and the Caribbean: economic growth in 2019 and projections for 2020–21* (percentage growth rates)

	ECLAC		IMF	World Bank
	2019	2020	2020	2020
Argentina	–2.2	–6.5	–5.7	–5.2
Brazil	1.1	–5.2	–5.3	–5.0
Colombia	3.3	–2.6	–2.4	–2.0
Chile	1.1	–4.0	–4.5	–3.0
Ecuador	0.1	–6.5	–6.3	–6.0
Mexico	–0.1	–6.5	–6.6	–6.0
Peru	2.2	–4.0	–4.5	–4.7
Venezuela (Bolivarian Republic of)	–25.5	–18.0	–15.0	n.d.
Latin America and the Caribbean				
2020		0.1	–5.3	–5.2	–4.6
2021			3.4	2.6

Source: Prepared by the author on the basis of ECLAC (2020a), IMF (2020a) and World Bank (2020b).

5 per cent in April for the region as a whole, with particularly severe downturns in Argentina, the Bolivarian Republic of Venezuela, Brazil, Ecuador and Mexico; Peru has been added to the list according to more recent projections. Among the larger countries, Chile and Colombia will perform comparatively. Later projections in June by ECLAC (2020c) and IMF (2020g) indicate that the contraction would be much worse, –9.1 per cent and –9.4 per cent respectively.[11] In general, the smaller countries, with the exception of Ecuador, will perform better. For the region as a whole, the 2020 recession will be the worst since the Second World War (much worse, in fact, than that of 1983, the worst year of the Latin American debt crisis) and one of the most painful in history.[12]

The multilateral organizations recognize the region's poor economic performance over the last five years, as well as the economic shocks they face as a result of the Covid-19 pandemic. In addition to the aforementioned financial shocks, the contraction in international trade and the decline in commodity prices, it is expected that intra-regional trade will fall sharply and tourism will collapse. On top of that, remittances – from both abroad (especially the United States and Spain) and within the region – will tumble by 19 per cent in 2020 according to World Bank forecasts (World Bank 2020c).

In terms of economic policy, the major constraint is the fiscal space available to the countries of the region, which is much more limited than it was during the North Atlantic crisis, a point that has been highlighted by several analysts from the Inter-American Development Bank (IDB). Izquierdo and Ardanaz (2020) note that the average deficit of the region's countries was 3 per cent of GDP in 2019 as compared to 0.4 per cent in 2008, while the average public debt was 62 per cent of GDP in 2019 as compared to 40 per cent in 2008.

The response of the countries of the region has been in line with international trends. Central banks have provided liquidity (with obvious restrictions for dollarized economies). Governments have adopted fiscal programmes, principally to support the health care sector and poor and vulnerable households, and measures to reduce or defer payment of some taxes, but the scale of the packages varies widely. According to IDB estimates, the largest packages as a percentage of GDP are those of Brazil, Chile, El Salvador and Peru (Pineda, Pessino and Rasteletti 2020). Some countries have introduced credit lines or loan guarantees on a large scale, most notably Chile, Colombia, Peru and Uruguay. Despite this, the magnitude of support provided by the majority of the region's countries is modest compared to that mobilized by developed countries.

The social repercussions will be evident, as ECLAC (2020b) has noted. Moreover, these will occur in a context of social conditions that have been deteriorating since 2014 as a result of poor economic performance. Underinvestment in health care is reflected in weak and fragmented health systems that do not guarantee universal access in many countries. The suspension of face-to-face classes has interrupted school feeding programmes, which several countries have sought to carry out in various ways including through cash subsidies. The large digital divide means that students from low-income backgrounds are unable to access virtual education. Furthermore, labour informality means that a high proportion of households are left without income, possibly without the support provided by conditional transfers, especially those that are not considered to be poor but are vulnerable. Many micro, small and medium-sized enterprises (MSMEs) may go bankrupt, which is a very worrying prospect as they are responsible for creating a high proportion of the jobs in the region. As a result ECLAC (2020b) estimates, under its worst scenario, which is the most likely, that poverty levels will increase from 30.3 per cent in 2019 to 35.8 per cent in 2020, equivalent to 36 million more people living in poverty.

An Overview of International Financial Cooperation During the Crisis

The international debate has highlighted that although the pandemic affected Western Europe and the United States earlier and to a serious degree, and reached the developing countries later, the latter are more vulnerable in economic and social terms. There are many reasons for this: containment measures are more costly for people with limited resources in developing countries who live in small, crowded spaces, sometimes without access to running water; support mechanisms for sectors living in poverty do not exist or do not reach the target population; health care systems are of a poor quality and do not cover the entire population; and labour informality rates are high which means that containment measures leave a wide range of workers without income. Added to this, the fiscal space is narrower and governments' access to credit is more limited. For this reason, there is agreement on the need to adopt ambitious policies to support the emerging and developing economies. The financial requirements of these countries are immense: US$ 2.5 trillion, according to estimates by both IMF (2020d) and the United Nations Conference on Trade and Development (UNCTAD 2020a).

In the light of these vulnerabilities and needs, the international cooperation agreed upon so far is very limited, in terms of both the measures adopted and the resources to which emerging and developing economies will have access. This is particularly true of the group of middle-income countries, to which almost all Latin American countries belong. As detailed below, the measures taken with respect to lower-income countries have been somewhat more relevant – although still insufficient – and are much more likely to be stepped up.

The shortcomings of multilateral cooperation were particularly evident at the meetings of G20 and the Bretton Woods institutions in April 2020. These meetings will be remembered, not only for being the first in history to be held virtually, but also for the limited international decisions taken in the face of the magnitude of the current crisis.

There have of course been expressions of international solidarity. At the end of March 2020, the G20 leaders committed to 'do whatever it takes and to use all available policy tools to minimize the economic and social damage from the pandemic, restore global growth, maintain market stability, and strengthen resilience' (G20 2020a). The G20 finance ministers and central bank governors expressed something similar in their statements at the meetings of the Bretton Woods institutions.

However, multilateral measures have not lived up to these promises. The actions being carried out diverge from those provided for in the

G20 Global Plan for Recovery and Reform adopted at the G20 Summit in London on 2 April 2009 to address the crisis at that time (G20 2009). This statement led to the most significant reform of IMF credit lines in the Fund's history: the largest issuance of IMF special drawing rights (SDRs), the capitalization of and massive increase in lending by multilateral development banks, and an ambitious reform of financial regulations. It also eventually led to work, beginning on efforts to strengthen international tax cooperation, overseen by the Organization for Economic Cooperation and Development (OECD); to the adoption in 2012 of the IMF institutional view on capital flows; and to the increase and redistribution of IMF quotas. Unfortunately, it took five years to implement the latter because of how long it took the United States Congress to approve the corresponding resources.[13]

Compared to these actions and to the needs of emerging and developing economies, the measures announced at the meetings of the Bretton Woods institutions and parallel actions adopted by the G20 countries have been meagre. This limited international cooperation contrasts with the ambitious domestic policies adopted by the developed countries. This is particularly true of the United States, whose domestic policies have been much more vigorous than those adopted to address the 2008–09 financial crisis, and whose support for international actions has been very limited during the current crisis, in contrast to the international leadership it exercised during the 2008–09 crisis. European countries have also adopted clearly counter-cyclical policies, but they have been more open to multilateral cooperation. The contrast between the decisive domestic economic policies of developed countries and the limited international cooperation seems to be a key feature of the current crisis.

International Monetary Cooperation and Its Effects on Latin America

The international agenda for monetary issues covers six areas: (i) the provision of international liquidity; (ii) the establishment and expansion of IMF credit lines; (iii) guarantees that IMF will have adequate resources; (iv) the possible coordination of the regulation of capital flows and of the decisions of credit rating agencies; (v) actions aimed at managing the over-indebtedness of several emerging and developing economies; and (vi) the active use and expansion of regional monetary arrangements (Gallagher *et al.* 2020).

With regard to liquidity provision, the proposal that has received the most support has been the issuance of SDRs in the amount of at least US$ 500 billion, doubling the value of the issuance in 2009.[14] To make better use of this issuance, a special fund could be created for countries to lend to IMF the SDRs that they do not use, in order to finance its programmes or to support other development projects (to capitalize multilateral banks or increase official development assistance). It would be preferable to distribute the SDRs based on criteria other than those used to determine national quotas,[15] but that would require a change in the IMF Articles of Agreement.

Given the share of Latin American countries in IMF quotas, this issuance of SDRs would imply an increase in their international reserves of US$ 37.740 billion, equivalent to slightly less than 5 per cent of those reserves as at the end of 2019 and a little more than 40 per cent of the net balance of the region's capital and financial account for that year.[16] The distribution by country would be as shown in Table 5.2: as a percentage of GDP, it would be 0.7 per cent on average, ranging from 0.6 per cent to 0.8 per cent for most of the countries, but higher for countries whose GDP in US dollars has decreased significantly in recent years.

More ambitious proposals have been put forward: for example, to issue SDRs worth US$ 1 trillion (see Cardoso *et al.* 2020). While this would be useful, it would require the explicit approval of the United States Congress because the US would receive more SDRs than its quota, so Congress cannot simply be informed. This would undoubtedly delay the issuance. Therefore, in order to avoid having to seek Congress's approval, the maximum issuance value must be equal to the total IMF quotas, some US$ 650 billion.

Although the proposal for a large issuance of SDRs had broad support among IMF member-countries and the public, it was vetoed by the United States at the 2020 Spring Meetings of the Bretton Woods institutions, on the grounds that about 70 per cent of the resources would go to G20 countries, most of whom do not need them (Mnuchin 2020). Surprisingly, India supported this position. While it is true that just under two-fifths of the SDRs issued benefit emerging and developing economies, it is also true that this is the only opportunity these countries have to share in the creation of international money (so-called 'seigniorage' benefits). Many low-income countries would benefit significantly from the SDR issuance (Collins and Truman 2020).

To help create international liquidity, the United States Federal Reserve re-established its currency swap lines with other central banks, following a practice it had already implemented during the North Atlantic crisis. However, only four emerging economies have access to this mechanism: Brazil, Mexico, the Republic of Korea and Singapore. It also set up a new mechanism: a repurchase agreement (repo) instrument, which allows

Table 5.2 *Latin America: IMF member-country quotas*

	IMF quota			Effect of a US$ 500 billion issuance	
	Millions of SDRs	Millions of dollars	Percentage of total	Millions of dollars	Percentage of GDP
Brazil	11,042	15,120	2.31	11,574	0.62
Mexico	8,913	12,204	1.87	9,342	0.77
Venezuela (Bolivarian Republic of)	3,723	5,097	0.78	3,902	2.52
Argentina	3,187	4,364	0.67	3,341	0.65
Colombia	2,045	2,799	0.43	2,143	0.65
Chile	1,744	2,388	0.37	1,828	0.62
Peru	1,335	1,827	0.28	1,399	0.63
Ecuador	698	955	0.15	731	0.68
Dominican Republic	477	654	0.10	500	0.59
Uruguay	429	588	0.09	450	0.76
Guatemala	429	587	0.09	449	0.62
Panama	377	516	0.08	395	0.61
Costa Rica	369	506	0.08	387	0.65
El Salvador	287	393	0.06	301	1.16
Nicaragua	260	356	0.05	273	2.09
Honduras	250	342	0.05	262	1.10
Bolivia (Plurinational State of)	240	329	0.05	252	0.63
Paraguay	201	276	0.04	211	0.53
Latin America	36,006	49,302	7.55	37,740	0.72

Source: Prepared by the author on the basis of current quotas according to the International Monetary Fund (IMF), converted from SDRs to dollars at the exchange rate of 1 May 2020, and 2018 nominal GDPs according to the Economic Commission for Latin America and the Caribbean (ECLAC).

the Federal Reserve to buy back the treasury bonds that countries wish to sell; however, this mechanism only benefits countries with large amounts of foreign exchange reserves.

In terms of creating and extending credit lines, the most important reform has been the doubling of the IMF emergency credit lines, including the rapid financing instrument (RFI) available to middle-income countries.[17] In the context of simplifying and streamlining procedures, and the absence

Table 5.3 *Rapid financing instrument (RFI) loans granted to Latin American countries, 2020*

Country	Millions of SDRs	Date of approval	Millions of dollars
Bolivia (Plurinational State of)	240.1	17 April	328.8
Costa Rica	369.4	29 April	505.8
Dominican Republic	477.4	29 April	653.7
Ecuador	469.7	1 May	643.2
El Salvador	287.2	14 April	393.3
Panama	376.8	15 April	515.9
Paraguay	201.4	21 April	275.8
Total	2,422.0		3,316.4

Note: SDR values are converted to dollars at the exchange rate of 1 May 2020.
Source: Prepared by the author on the basis of data from the International Monetary Fund (IMF).

of *ex ante* conditionality, this reform has given rise to the rapid approval of a plethora of loans for a wide range of countries.[18] As on 1 May 2020, seven Latin American countries had made use of these credit lines, totalling slightly more than US$ 3.3 billion (see Table 5.3); no additional loans were requested by countries of the region in the remainder of the month of May.

In addition to this instrument, there are other credit facilities which some countries took advantage of before the current crisis: the pre-existing flexible credit lines to Mexico and Colombia (the latter was renewed on 1 May) and the new ones granted to Peru and Chile at the end of May;[19] standby arrangements for Argentina and Honduras, with the latter augmented on 1 June; and the extended arrangement under the extended fund facility for Ecuador, although this was suspended on 1 May (see Table 5.4).[20] Thus, thirteen countries of the region have already received some form of support from IMF. As flexible credit lines act as a kind of insurance for countries, they have not been disbursed yet; disbursements from the other credit lines total just over US$ 45.7 billion (most of it going to Argentina). The exception in terms of access is the Bolivarian Republic of Venezuela, whose request for a US$ 5 billion loan was rejected in March by IMF on the grounds that there is no clarity among the Fund's member-states as to who is the legitimate president of that country.

Another recommendation that has been discussed is the creation of an IMF swap line. This recommendation was made by IMF staff two years ago (IMF 2017b), but was rejected by the executive board. The G20

Table 5.4 *Regular IMF-approved loans to Latin American countries, as of May 2020*

	Date of approval	Maturity	Loan value		Amount disbursed
			(Millions of SDRs)	(Millions of dollars)	(Millions of dollars)
A. Flexible Credit Line (FCL)					
Mexico	22 Nov. 2019	21 Nov. 2019	44,563.5	61,019.9	0.0
Colombia	1 May 2020	30 April 2022	7,849.6	10,748.3	0.0
Peru	28 May 2020	27 May 2022	8,007.0	10,963.8	0.0
Chile	29 May 2020	28 May 2022	17,443.0	23,884.4	0.0
B. Standby Agreements (SBA)					
Argentina	20 June 2018	19 June 2021	40,714.0	55,748.9	43,698.8
Honduras*	15 July 2019	14 July 2021	387.2	530.2	376.3
C. Extended Fund Facility (EFF)					
Ecuador	11 March 2019	10 March 2022	3,035.0	4,155.8	1,653.9
Total			121,999.3	167,051.2	45,729.0

Notes: SDR values are converted to US dollars at the exchange rate of 1 May 2020.
*Includes the resources approved under the Standby Credit Facility (SCF) and the increase approved on 1 June 2020; the amount authorized on the latter date includes a disbursement.
Source: Prepared by the author on the basis of data from the International Monetary Fund (IMF).

Eminent Persons Group on Global Financial Governance subsequently made a similar recommendation (G20 Eminent Persons Group on Global Financial Governance 2018). The IMF created the short-term liquidity line in April 2020 in response to this, but it is a very limited response. It will act as a revolving credit line for up to 145 per cent of the country's quota and without *ex ante* conditionality, but only member-countries 'with very strong policies and fundamentals' will have access to it, as is the case with the flexible credit line. However, it is less attractive than the flexible credit line because fewer resources are available and it cannot be combined with other loans from the Fund. Therefore, it is highly likely that it will not be used.

In order to finance the increased demand for credit, IMF needs to expand its resources to an amount estimated by the managing director at US$ 1 trillion. In this regard, an unfortunate decision was taken in 2019 to defer the increase in quotas until 2023. It is regrettable that the G20 countries have not accelerated this process, given that it is widely recognized by these countries that this should be the Fund's core resource. The additional funds will come from a doubling of the New Arrangements to Borrow (NABs), approved in January 2020, to around US$ 500 billion, and from bilateral borrowing agreements with several countries. The main contribution of the United States will be its support for NABs.

A fourth line of action that has been proposed by several analysts is the possible coordinated regulation of capital flows in an effort to curb, in particular, capital flight from emerging economies. This action would be in line with the institutional view on capital flows approved by IMF in 2012 (IMF 2012). Similarly, it has been proposed that credit rating agencies should suspend their downgrades (or the outlook on a rating) during the crisis, as these fuel capital flight.[21] Mexico and Colombia have already been affected by such decisions, although they have maintained their investment-grade rating. Neither G20 nor IMF has taken a position on these issues.

The fifth issue, debt relief, has been the subject of a wide range of proposals by both institutions (United Nations 2020; UNCTAD 2020b) and analysts (see, in particular, Bolton *et al.* 2020; Brown and Summers 2020; Reinhart and Rogoff 2020). This is an area where limited measures have already been taken in relation to low-income countries, but not middle-income countries.

IMF decided that twenty-five of its most vulnerable members (to which four more could be added in the near future) will be exempt from repayment and interest on their IMF debt obligations for six months, using resources from the Catastrophe Containment and Relief Trust (CCRT). In turn, the G20 countries offered to introduce a debt repayment standstill for countries supported by the International Development Association (IDA) for the rest of 2020, a measure that, according to Brown and Summers (2020), should be extended to the end of 2021. The Paris Club has already taken the necessary decision. It is not clear, however, whether private creditors will adopt it, as the G20 countries have requested. This programme does not cancel the debt, which will remain outstanding and continue to accrue interest.

With regard to middle-income countries, there are critical cases that require debt restructuring. The most important in Latin America are Argentina and Ecuador. While there are proposals for relatively widespread debt repayment standstill for emerging and developing economies (see in particular UNCTAD 2020a and 2020b; and Reinhart and Rogoff 2020), other proposals favour voluntary mechanisms.

The most interesting proposal is that made by Bolton *et al.* (2020), who suggest that the World Bank or regional development banks create a central credit facility to which countries would go voluntarily, and which would facilitate a deferral of amortizations and the use of interests due to fund the response to the health emergency. Countries' obligation would remain in place and therefore the proposed facility would act as a rollover mechanism during the crisis. It would apply to all bilateral and commercial debts on an equal basis. Apart from its voluntary nature, the facility would be subject to intermediation and strict monitoring by the multilateral bank that manages it.

Beyond short-term measures, the United Nations and UNCTAD have suggested that an institutional mechanism should be created for restructuring sovereign debt, an issue that has been under discussion for the last two decades, with progress limited to the definition of principles and clauses that allow each country to renegotiate with its creditors, but without a specific institutional framework.[22]

It does not make sense for Latin America to adopt a uniform rule in this area. As Figure 5.2 shows, although risk spreads on bonds issued by emerging economies have increased, they have remained below those seen during the North Atlantic crisis and especially after the Russian default in August 1998 (which in turn followed the 1997 Asian crisis). More importantly, with the sharp fall in the yield used as a benchmark to calculate these spreads (10-year United States Treasury Bonds), the bond

Figure 5.2 *Risk spreads and yield on emerging economies bonds, 1998–2020* (emerging market bond index)

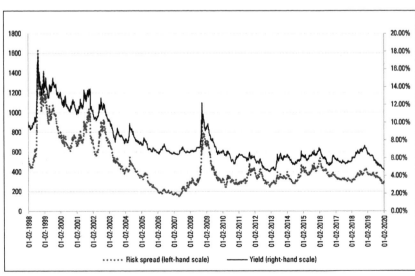

Source: Prepared by the author on the basis of data from Bloomberg.

yields of emerging economies have remained well below those reached during the two previous crises, and even those seen during the turmoil in emerging economies' bond markets in 2018.

Moreover, bond markets for emerging economies have opened up more quickly than they did after the North Atlantic crisis, when it took just over twelve months after the collapse of the United States' investment bank, Lehman Brothers. This indicates that several investment funds in the developed countries are again searching for yield. Two signs of this are the sharp reduction in risk spreads since the end of March (see Figure 5.2), and that capital outflows from emerging economies, which peaked at US\$ 66.1 billion in March, fell to US\$ 11.3 billion in April and US\$ 10 billion in May, when the flow of hard currency bonds became positive (JP Morgan 2020).

Eight Latin American countries have already issued bonds: Panama at the end of March, and since mid-April, Peru, Guatemala, Mexico, Paraguay, Chile and Colombia, two Colombian public sector companies (Ecopetrol and Grupo Energía de Bogotá, both with minority private shareholders), two Chilean public sector companies (Corporación Nacional del Cobre de Chile [CODELCO] and Metro de Santiago) and one Brazilian public sector company (Petrobras). In addition, the Development Bank of Latin America (CAF, according to its historical acronym for Corporación Andina de Fomento) and the Central American Bank for Economic Integration (CABEI) have also issued bonds. Through the hard currency bond markets, US\$ 24 billion have been raised between mid-April and 1 June 2020.

In this context, a uniform solution for the debt problems of the countries of the region – and for middle-income countries in general – does not make sense. There are three different situations that should be dealt with separately: (i) countries whose debts need to be thoroughly restructured; (ii) countries that can have recourse, at their discretion, to a debt standstill mechanism such as that proposed by Bolton *et al.* (2020); and (iii) countries with access to new private financing that will continue to service their debts, and combine that financing with loans from the IMF and multilateral development banks.

Lastly, it is worth highlighting the role of regional monetary mechanisms. These mechanisms have expanded significantly since the North Atlantic crisis and now have US\$ 585.4 billion at their disposal, equivalent to approximately 60 per cent of the resources available to IMF, although they are concentrated in European funds and the East Asian Chiang Mai Initiative (Gallagher *et al.* 2020). Active steps must be taken to deepen the relationship between the IMF and regional financing arrangements in order to strengthen the global financial safety net, as has been recognized by both IMF (2017a) and Gong Cheng *et al.* (2018).

This collaboration must be based not only on complementarity, but also the independence of the institutions and respect for their respective mandates and governance structures, and should not follow any hierarchical principles.[23] Moreover, it is not appropriate to have a formal relationship with IMF programmes which were the subject of much criticism during the eurozone crisis, and is one of the reasons why the resources of the Chiang Mai Initiative have not been used.

In Latin America, there is the Latin American Reserve Fund (Fondo Latinoamericano de Reservas [FLAR]) with eight member-countries. This Fund has a very successful record of supporting its members during the various crises they have faced, acting sometimes as a substitute for and sometimes as a complement to IMF resources. In any case, given the limited resources available to FLAR, IMF support is indispensable for large-scale programmes. As part of the measures to strengthen the global financial safety net, an important task is to expand the membership of this regional Fund until it comprises all the Latin American countries.

Table 5.5 shows the maximum amounts that member-countries can receive as loans from FLAR, both in terms of total financing and through its specific credit lines (balance of payments, liquidity and contingency). The total amount available to member-countries is just over US$ 6.5 billion. Nearly all of that amount is available because only one loan is currently active, to Ecuador (for balance of payments) of US$ 205 million, since the other credits, which had been granted to Costa Rica and the Bolivarian Republic of Venezuela, were settled at the beginning of 2020. As the capital contribution of the Bolivarian Republic of Venezuela to the Fund was used to pay off the loan, the Fund can give that country only limited support now.

The great advantage of FLAR is that its programmes do not have any *ex ante* conditionality, although countries requesting a loan must submit a macroeconomic programme to the Fund. Its main disadvantage is the amount of available resources, such that FLAR programmes will almost certainly have to be supplemented by IMF loans. In this case, countries can use FLAR programmes as a complement or as a bridge to an IMF loan, taking advantage of the more streamlined system of the regional Fund to approve financing. Another disadvantage in the current crisis is that FLAR facilities can only be used for balance of payments needs, and therefore cannot be used to finance governments at a time when demand for resources is very high. Thus, a temporary exception might be appropriate, allowing balance of payments credits to be used for fiscal purposes as well.

Table 5.5 *Capital contributions and maximum credit limits of the Latin American Reserve Fund* (FLAR) (millions of dollars)

Country	Subscribed capital	Paid-up capital	Maximum credit limit	Maximum credit limit by type of financial support		
				Balance of payments support	Liquidity facility	Contingency facility
Bolivia (Plurinational State of)	328.1	256.4	666.6	666.6	282.0	538.4
Colombia	656.3	512.9	1,282.3	1,282.3	512.9	1,025.9
Costa Rica	656.3	513.1	1,282.7	1,282.7	513.1	1,026.1
Ecuador	328.1	256.5	666.8	666.8	282.1	538.6
Paraguay	328.1	256.0	640.0	640.0	256.0	512.0
Peru	656.3	512.9	1,282.2	1,282.2	512.9	1,025.8
Uruguay	328.1	257.0	642.4	642.4	257.0	513.9
Venezuela (Bolivarian Republic of)	656.3	30.7	76.7	76.7	30.7	61.3
FLAR total	3,937.5	2,595.4	6,539.7	6,539.7	2,646.6	5,242.0

Source: Prepared by the author on the basis of data from Latin American Reserve Fund (FLAR).

Multilateral Development Banks' Cooperation

The development banks are one of the most important financial instruments available to the international community and a wide range of countries, both developed economies, and emerging and developing economies. The fundamental objective of these institutions is to support long-term development policies – to foster innovation, improve infrastructure, and promote social and regional equity and environmental sustainability – but their financing can also be used as a counter-cyclical instrument. Moreover, some projects associated with long-term strategies can be launched during crises to support economic recovery.

The network of development banks encompasses more than 400 institutions worldwide, with total assets of more than US$ 11 trillion, and they lend some US$ 2 trillion per year, according to estimates by the French Development Agency (Agence française de développement [AFD]). They include the World Bank Group, as well as a number of regional (such as IDB and CAF),[24] sub-regional (CABEI) and inter-regional banks (the

Islamic Development Bank), and a wide range of national banks of varying sizes. One of the major potential benefits is that the institutions act as
a network, with the multilateral banks supporting the actions of national
banks. If the development banks in this network were to increase their
activity by 20 per cent, they could mobilize an additional US$ 400 billion
a year; by leveraging private resources, this amount could be doubled
(Griffith-Jones, Marodon and Ocampo 2020).

During the North Atlantic crisis, the multilateral development
banks played an important counter-cyclical role that was recognized explicitly by the banks themselves and by the economic authorities (Ocampo *et
al.* 2011). The lessons of the past indicated that, in addition to the provision
of liquidity in times of crisis by international monetary institutions, it was
equally important that multilateral development banks provide long-term
financing to support public spending and public and private investment.

Overall, these institutions increased their lending commitments
to emerging and developing economies by 71 per cent between 2008 and
2009; their disbursements grew by 45 per cent in 2009 and continued to
trend upwards in 2010 (ibid.). This lag in disbursements occurred despite
the measures taken to accelerate them. Interestingly, the response to the
needs of middle-income countries was more vigorous than that for low-
income countries, with credit commitments to the latter falling from 32
per cent in 2007 to 22 per cent in 2009.

The banks' responses were determined in part by their limited
capital. For this reason, as noted earlier, the G20 countries agreed to
support capitalization of the multilateral development banks in the plan
adopted at their London meeting in April 2009. The capitalization of the
Asian Development Bank and the African Development Bank were rapid
and massive: a 200 per cent increase in 2009 in both instances. The capitalization of IDB, approved in March 2010, was less ambitious (about
70 per cent), happened gradually, and was for an amount less than the
Latin American and Caribbean countries had hoped. The World Bank
was capitalized in April 2010 and for an even more modest amount. It
was part of a set of reforms aimed at increasing the share of emerging and
developing economies in the capital of the World Bank.

This counter-cyclical response moderated, although it certainly did
not completely offset, the impact of the sharp drop in private capital flows
to these countries. Another area where multilateral development banks
played an important role was in the rapid provision of commercial credit
lines, which were used by a wide range of private banks.

Two important lessons to be learned from the response of the
multilateral banks during the North Atlantic crisis, therefore, are the need

...or good mechanisms for rapid disbursements during crises, and for their :apital to be replenished more automatically. An alternative to accelerate lisbursements that was used during the 2009 crisis and, as we will see, ıas been used by some institutions during the current crisis, is to allow ılready approved loans to be reallocated for other emergency purposes. Another might be to defer debt service payments to the institutions – a oractice that could, however, affect banks' credit ratings.

The relative importance of multilateral development bank support :o Latin American countries has increased dramatically in recent decades. The World Bank played a leading role until the 1980s. However, as Figure 5.3 shows, the amount it loaned to the region has remained fairly stable since the 1990s. Nevertheless, the World Bank has continued to play a critical role during crises, as indicated by the increase in its lending to the region in 1998–99 and especially in 2009–10.

The top lender to the region in the 1990s was IDB, before it was challenged by the rapid growth of CAF and CABEI. The uptick in the CAF lending trend has been particularly significant; it has provided as many loans as IDB in the last five years. Although CABEI is a much smaller institution, it has particular importance for the Central American

Figure 5.3 *Multilateral development bank lending to Latin America, 1990–2019* (millions of dollars)

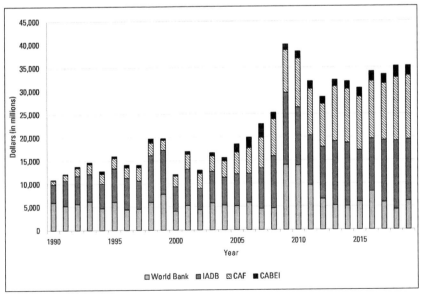

Source: Prepared by the author on the basis of data from World Bank, Inter-American Development Bank (IDB), Development Bank of Latin America (CAF) and Central American Bank for Economic Integration (CABEI).

countries and, in recent years, has been rivalling IDB as the main source of financing for the sub-region.

It should be noted, however, that the capacity of the World Bank and IDB to respond to the 2008–09 crisis was much larger than that of CAF and CABEI. This indicates that during times of crisis, the implicit support of the developed countries, in particular the United States, facilitates access to capital markets on advantageous terms. Conversely, CAF and CABEI may be affected, at least partially, by the fact that capital markets are closed to emerging economies during these periods. Nevertheless, both of these development banks joined the recent wave of Latin American bond issuances.

As Table 5.6 shows, CAF was the bank with the highest growth in terms of authorized capital and equity between 2007 (before the outbreak of the North Atlantic crisis) and 2019. Both CAF and CABEI were capitalized earlier than the World Bank and IDB during the 2009 crisis. A new World Bank capitalization was approved in 2018: an increase in the paid-up capital of the International Bank for Reconstruction and Development (IBRD) of US$ 7.5 billion and of the International Finance Corporation (IFC) of US$ 5.5 billion. Overall, IFC capital has grown much more than that of IBRD since the 2008–09 crisis (by 95 per cent), based primarily on the reinvestment of profits. In turn, an increase in the capital available to CABEI from US$ 5 billion to US$ 7 billion was approved in December 2019 and made official in April 2020, so it now exceeds CAF in terms of the growth of its capital since 2007.

All banks providing services to the region have adopted special support measures during the current crisis: granting special, fast-tracked credit lines to tackle the crisis, albeit with modest resources; increasing the scale of credit programmes, within their capital restrictions; streamlining credit approvals; and, in several cases, allowing already approved loans to be reallocated to meet urgent needs.

According to the remarks delivered by the president of the World Bank Group to the Development Committee (formally known as the Joint Ministerial Committee of the Boards of Governors of the Bank and the Fund on the Transfer of Real Resources to Developing Countries) on 17 April 2020, the programme to address the crisis is based on three pillars: (i) to protect the poorest and most vulnerable households; (ii) to support businesses and save jobs; and (iii) to help developing countries implement emergency health operations and strengthen economic resilience (World Bank 2020d). Two important elements of the packages announced are the significant weight of resources going to low-income countries – thus correcting one of the problems with the World Bank's actions during the

Table 5.6 *Authorized capital and equity of the multilateral development banks serving Latin America, 2007–19* (billions of dollars)

Year	Authorized capital				Equity			
	IBRD	IDB	CAF	CABEI	IBRD	IDB	CAF	CABEI
2007	189.801	100.953	5.000	2.000	39.926	20.353	4.127	1.636
2008	189.801	100.938	10.000	2.000	41.548	19.444	4.554	1.708
2009	189.918	104.980	10.000	5.000	40.037	20.674	5.287	1.813
2010	189.943	104.980	10.000	5.000	37.555	20.960	5.753	1.929
2011	193.732	104.980	10.000	5.000	39.683	19.794	6.351	2.028
2012	205.394	116.880	10.000	5.000	36.685	20.681	6.865	2.142
2013	223.181	128.781	10.000	5.000	39.523	23.550	7.817	2.268
2014	232.791	144.258	10.000	5.000	38.985	23.697	8.763	2.396
2015	252.821	156.939	15.000	5.000	38.637	25.253	9.524	2.573
2016	263.329	170.940	15.000	5.000	37.063	26.460	10.474	2.723
2017	268.937	170.940	15.000	5.000	39.798	32.247	11.122	2.831
2018	274.730	170.940	15.000	5.000	41.844	32.929	11.863	3.198
2019	279.953	170.940	15.000	5.000	42.115	33.871	12.797	3.300
Growth								
2007–19 (per cent)	47.5	69.3	200.0	150.0	5.5	66.4	210.1	101.8

Source: Prepared by the author on the basis of data from International Bank for Reconstruction and Development (IBRD), Inter-American Development Bank (IDB), Development Bank of Latin America (CAF) and Central American Bank for Economic Integration (CABEI).

crisis a decade ago – and the emphasis on measures aimed at the private sector carried out through IFC, offering international trade loans, working capital support and medium-term financing to private companies struggling with breaks in their supply chains.

The immediate support package approved by the World Bank in mid-March made US\$ 14 billion of new financing available to countries expeditiously. Fast-track facility resources have already been disbursed to six Latin American countries – Argentina, Ecuador, El Salvador, Honduras, Paraguay and Uruguay – in April and May, although the loans were for modest amounts, totalling US\$ 135 million (each country received US\$ 20 million each, except Argentina, which was loaned US\$ 35 million).

In addition to the emergency programme, in late March 2020, the World Bank approved a US\$ 160 billion package covering the next fifteen months. This is substantially more than the annual average of

World Bank loans approved in 2009–10, which was US$ 64.4 billion. This broader package includes emergency loans and the possible reallocation of funds from existing projects. Five Latin American countries have already benefited from this broader package in April and May 2020: Colombia, the Dominican Republic, Honduras, Panama and the Plurinational State of Bolivia. Together with emergency credits, the World Bank approved US$ 1.119 billion in lending to Latin America in April and May, which is higher than the monthly average for the last five years, but still less than the monthly average approved for the region in 2009–10.

The president of the World Bank Group told the G20 finance ministers in March that recovery policies must be linked to structural reforms: 'Countries will need to implement structural reforms to help shorten the time to recovery and create confidence that the recovery can be strong' (World Bank 2020e). It is regrettable that he made this link to structural reforms, given that an increasing number of emerging and developing economies have rejected this view as it bears very little relation to the economic emergency.

The programme announced by IDB to address the crisis is underpinned by the principle that the virus affects not only human health, but also the economy, the survival of many firms and families' finances, and that if not properly managed, it can create a social crisis. The bank has identified four priority areas for its support programmes: (i) the immediate public health response; (ii) safety nets for vulnerable populations, specifically measures to protect the income of the most affected populations through existing transfer programmes, as well as extraordinary transfers to workers in the informal sector and support for companies in sectors particularly affected by the crisis; (iii) assistance to small and medium-sized enterprises (SMEs) through financing programmes and liquidity guarantees, foreign trade financing, loan restructuring and support for strategic supply chains; and (iv) fiscal policies for the amelioration of economic impacts in the form of support to countries in designing and implementing fiscal measures to finance the response to the crisis, plans for the execution of expenditures and public procurement, and measures to support the economic recovery.

The programme includes an adjustment of IDB lending instruments and a streamlining of approving processes. In terms of resources, it includes the allocation of an additional US$ 3.2 billion to the loan programme initially stipulated for 2020. These funds, added to the available resources already programmed for this year, would make up to US$ 12 billion available to countries. This amount, however, is very similar to the annual lending average over the last five years, which is why, more than the amount loaned, the priority has been reallocating resources and accelerating loan approvals, which increased from US$ 2.6 billion to US$ 3.7 billion in the first five months of 2020 as compared to 2019. In immediate terms, it has also offered countries the possibility of reallocating resources from already approved loans to meet the new priorities created by the emergency, in an amount equivalent to 10 per cent of each loan or up to US$ 50 million (whichever is greater). IDB Invest, the private sector arm of the IDB Group, has contributed an additional US$ 5 billion to support the financing of production chains and trade, and banks, in a context of severe liquidity constraints.

In addition, both IDB and non-regional partners are providing technical cooperation resources that prioritize exchange and learning platforms. Analyses of the effects of the various dimensions of the crisis and of alternative methods to address them, which are published in the blog 'Ideas Matter', have also been very important.

Meanwhile CAF is helping to tackle the emergency through four specific actions. The first is a contingent credit line, approved in early March 2020, of up to US$ 300 million (up to US$ 50 million per country) to respond quickly to the needs of public health systems. The second is a rapid disbursement emergency credit line, approved in late March 2020, of up to US$ 2.5 billion, to streamline the approval of operations that support the emergency measures being adopted by countries. The third is the possibility of reprogramming existing loans, even allowing their objectives and destinations to be changed. The fourth is prioritizing collaboration with national development banks to support SMEs. It is not clear, however, whether CAF can substantially increase its credits over the high levels reached in 2018–19 without additional capital. In any case, it accelerated loan approvals in the first five months of 2020 to US$ 3.9 billion, compared to US$ 2.3 billion in 2019. In addition, non-reimbursable technical cooperation resources of up to US$ 400,000 per country are available, which several members have already received.

Lastly, CABEI launched the Emergency of Support and Preparedness Programme for Covid-19 and Economic Reactivation on 31 March 2020, worth US$ 1.96 billion. The programme includes three credit components: US$ 1 billion in loans to support the liquidity management of central banks of founding and non-founding regional members;[25] US$ 600 million in emergency budget support; and US$ 350 million in liquidity support for the financial sector in countries to support MSMEs. Unlike IDB and CAF, the recent capitalization of CABEI and the bond issuance at the end of April 2020 will allow it to significantly increase its lending, up to around US$ 3 billion, representing growth of 45 per cent in relation to the average for the last five years.

In the absence of additional capitalizations for IDB and CAF – the two most important multilateral banks for Latin America – the resources provided by these institutions to the countries of the region will increase modestly compared to the response to the North Atlantic crisis, even though the current crisis is more severe. CABEI is the notable exception. For this reason, actions in this area, as well as on the monetary front, must be strengthened substantially to tackle the severe economic and social problems caused by the Covid-19 pandemic.

Conclusions

The current economic crisis will be remembered not only as the worst since the Great Depression and one in which developed countries have adopted ambitious domestic policies, but also for the limited multi-lateral financial cooperation that has been agreed. This is particularly true of measures that aim to support middle-income economies. Actions to help lower-income countries have been more substantial, but also insufficient. Clearly, the multilateral actions have fallen far short of the commitment 'to do whatever it takes', made by the G20 leaders at the end of March 2020.

In the area of international monetary cooperation, the most frustrating aspects have been the refusal to issue IMF SDRs, the failure to take a decision on or even to suggest bringing forward the increase in IMF quotas, and the lack of collective measures to tackle capital flight from emerging economies and to stop credit-rating agencies from downgrading countries. Latin American countries have benefited from IMF emergency loans, albeit for modest amounts, and flexible credit lines (in the case of four countries), and can access other IMF facilities if they so wish. The eight member-countries of FLAR are also able to benefit from the support of this regional body, but it is recommended that they be allowed, at least temporarily, to use those resources for fiscal purposes. Efforts to expand the membership of FLAR should also be stepped up as a result of the crisis.

With regard to foreign debt, it is recommended that a diverse approach be adopted that supports ambitious foreign-debt restructuring for countries that need it (Argentina and Ecuador), and creates a volun-tary and multilaterally monitored debt standstill mechanism for those economies that may require such support. Meanwhile, the early recovery of the emerging economies' bond market that began in mid-April 2020 is good news, and has allowed several countries and public sector firms, as well as CAF and CABEI, to access private financing. In addition to short-term measures, the creation of an institutional mechanism to renegotiate sovereign debts must be put back on the table.

The multilateral development banks have created several emergency credit lines to address the crisis, streamlined their procedures, and several of them have allowed loans already approved to be re-channelled to tackle the health, social and economic emergencies caused by the Covid-19 pandemic. In Latin America, the work of CABEI, supported by the recent capitalization, has been the most noteworthy. The World Bank has increased its lending to the region, although these loans amount to less than those granted during the North Atlantic crisis. The two main multilateral banks for the region, IDB and CAF, have also adopted important measures, but they have reached the limit of their lending capacity and need to be recapitalized to provide more robust support to the countries of the region during the crisis. On the whole, in terms of resources, the multilateral banks' programmed support for Latin American countries is, so far, insufficient.

Lastly, the economic problems of a wide range of Latin American countries were already acute during the five years preceding the current crisis, and the sluggish growth during those years acted as a drag on and partly reversed the improvement in social indicators seen since the beginning of the century. Economic growth in the region has also been slow over the past three decades, and the region is still beset by multiple social problems, including having one of the worst income distributions in the world. Moreover, a contraction in global economic growth and trade, and fewer opportunities for Latin American migrants will be the grim legacy left behind by the crisis, among other adverse effects.

Therefore, beyond the crisis, the region's development strategy must be reformulated, to include a big push for scientific and technological development, reindustrialization, solid and depoliticized support for regional integration, and a firm commitment to reducing inequality and to making a major contribution to global efforts to combat climate change and protect biodiversity. On all these issues, which are beyond the scope of this article, the support of the development banking system will also be critical.

This chapter was prepared for the United Nations Development Programme (UNDP) and published as part of its *COVID-19 Policy Documents Series* (UNDP LAC C19 PDS N°7), May 2020. This updated and shorter version was originally published by the *CEPAL Review No. 131*, Economic Commission for Latin American and The Caribbean (ECLAC), August 2020, Copyright: ©Naciones Unidas 2020, all rights reserved. Given the speed with which the situation is evolving, it is analysed in the light of the information available and policy decisions taken up to 1 June 2020, and IMF reports available up to June 2020. The author wishes to thank Marcela Meléndez and Miguel Ángel Torres for their comments on previous versions, and María Luisa Montalvo and Víctor Alejandro Ortega for their collaboration on its drafting.

Notes

[1] See the updates by IDB (Inter-American Development Bank) on the spread of the pandemic in the region, in IDB (2020).

[2] I prefer this term to the more commonly used 'global financial crisis' because, although its effects were global, the crisis was concentrated in the United States and Western Europe.

[3] My analysis of Latin America does not include Cuba, which is not a recipient of the international financial cooperation under analysis, or Haiti, which is but through special mechanisms for very low-income countries, to which I make only marginal reference. The Bolivarian Republic of Venezuela also faces particular problems in its dealings with some of the international financial institutions mentioned throughout this article.

[4] See, among many others, Baldwin and Weder di Mauro (2020), Levy (2020), Stiglitz *et al.* (2020), and my contributions with other colleagues in Gallagher, Ocampo and Volz (2020), Gallagher *et al.* (2020), and Griffith-Jones, Marodon and Ocampo (2020).

[5] The IMF headline estimate is –3.0 per cent, calculated at purchasing power parity prices. This estimate is not comparable with those based on market exchange rates used by the United Nations, the World Bank and most private analysts.

[6] Down 6.8 per cent in the case of China, the country that was affected the earliest, 4.8 per cent in the United States and 3.8 per cent in the eurozone.

[7] This is particularly true of the United States, which saw three consecutive years of economic contraction during the Great Depression, with a cumulative downturn of 27 per cent according to the historical figures compiled by Maddison (2010), only returning to 1929 levels of growth a decade later.

[8] See an analysis of these risks in IMF (2020a).

[9] See the statistics published monthly by the Netherlands Bureau of Economic Policy Analysis (CPB). These figures indicate that growth in the twelve-month moving average of the volume of global exports was negative from October 2019, while that of global export values has been negative since August 2019 (CPB, n.d.).

[10] IMF (2020f) data on commodity prices indicate that the price of energy products has declined by 59.5 per cent compared to the average for 2019 (oil prices are down by 65 per cent), basic metals by 14.7 per cent and agricultural products used as industrial inputs by 9.4 per cent, but that food and beverage prices have fallen by just 5.5 per cent. World Bank (2020a) projections for the whole year follow this pattern.

[11] According to the most recent IMF projections, Argentina, Brazil, Mexico and Peru will shrink between 9 and 14 per cent, and Chile and Colombia between 7 and 8 per cent. Venezuela is expected to shrink by 26 per cent according to ECLAC.

[12] According to data from the ten economies for which information is available dating back to 1900 (see Table 1 of the Statistical Appendix of Bértola and Ocampo [2012]), the situation was only worse in 1914 and 1930. However, if the current crisis deepens, as it is very likely to do, it will be the worst in history.

[13] For a detailed analysis of these issues, see Ocampo (2017).

[14] For a preliminary version of this proposal, see Gallagher, Ocampo and Volz (2020). See also Collins and Truman (2020).

[15] As reflected in the long-standing discussions, alternative criteria could be different economies' level of development and demand for international reserves (Ocampo 2017, chapter 2).

[16] The reference data are taken from ECLAC (2019).

[17] See IMF (2020e) for more details on this and other IMF reforms.

[18] Countries may also make use of other IMF instruments, but the allotted value of emergency credit lines is generally less than the country's quota. This was the case for Ecuador, when an RFI was approved for 67.3 per cent of its quota on 1 May.

[19] The flexible credit lines approved for Chile and Peru were 10 and 6 times their quotas respectively, much higher than those extended to Mexico and Colombia, which are 5 and 3.8 times their quotas respectively.

[20] On the same date, Ecuador was given access to the emergency credit line. Ecuador will however seek another long-term IMF loan.

[21] See Gallagher *et al.* (2020) for more discussion of this issue.

[22] See Ocampo (2017), chapter V, for an overview of the discussion.

[23] Therefore, the 'lead agency' model proposed by IMF (2017a) should not be adopted.

[24] As reflected by its growing membership and new name, adopted in 2010, CAF is a regional development bank, although the acronym of its former name (the Andean Development Corporation, or *Corporación Andina de Fomento*) is still used.

[25] The founding regional members are Costa Rica, El Salvador, Guatemala, Honduras and Nicaragua, and the non-founding regional members are Belize, the Dominican Republic and Panama.

References

Baldwin, R. and B. Weder di Mauro (eds) (2020), *Mitigating the COVID Economic Crisis: Act Fast and Do Whatever it Takes*, London: Centre for Economic Policy Research (CEPR).

Bértola, L. and J.A. Ocampo (2012), *The Economic Development of Latin America since Independence*, Oxford: Oxford University Press.

Bolton, P., L. Buchheit, P.O. Gourinchas, M. Gulati, Ch.T. Hsieh, U. Panizza and B. Weder di Mauro (2020), 'Necessity is the Mother Of Invention: How to Implement a Comprehensive Debt Standstill for COVID-19 in Low- and Middle-Income Countries', London: Centre for Economic Policy Research (CEPR), 21 April, available at https://voxeu.org/article/debt-standstill-covid-19-low-and-middle-income-countries, accessed 1 June 2020.

Brooks, R. and J. Fortun (2020), 'COVID-19 Capital Flow Exodus from EM', *Global Macro Views* (GMV), no. 3830, Washington, D.C.: Institute of International Finance (IIF), 2 April.

Brown, G. and L.H. Summers (2020), 'Debt Relief is the Most Effective Pandemic Aid', Project Syndicate, 15 April, available at https://www.project-syndicate.org/commentary/debt-relief-most-effective-covid19-assistance-by-gordon-brown-and-lawrence-h-summers-2020-04, accessed 1 June 2020.

Cardoso, F.H. *et al.* (2020), 'A Roadmap for Confronting COVID-19 in Latin America', *Americas Quarterly*, 15 April, available at https://www.americasquarterly.org/article/a-roadmap-for-confronting-covid-19-in-latin-america/, accessed 1 June 2020.

Collins, C. and E. Truman (2020), 'IMF's Special Drawing Rights to the Rescue', 10 April, Peterson Institute for International Economics (PIIE), available at https://www.piie.com/blogs/realtime-economic-issues-watch/imfs-special-drawing-rights-rescue, accessed 1 June 2020.

CPB (Netherlands Bureau of Economic Policy Analysis) (n.d.), 'World Trade Monitor', available at https://www.cpb.nl/en/worldtrademonitor, accessed 1 June 2020.

Economic Commission for Latin America and the Caribbean (ECLAC) (2019), *Preliminary Overview of the Economies of Latin America and the Caribbean*, (LC/PUB.2019/25-P), Santiago.

———— (2020a), 'Measuring the Impact of COVID-19 with a View to Reactivation', *Special Report COVID-19*, no. 2, Santiago, 21 April.

———— (2020b), 'The Social Challenge in Times of COVID-19', *Special Report COVID-19*, no. 3, Santiago, 12 May.

———— (2020c), 'Addressing the Growing Impact of COVID-19 with a View to Reactivation with Equality: New Projections', *Special Report COVID-19*, no. 5, Santiago, 15 June.

Gallagher, K.P., J.A. Ocampo and U. Volz (2020), 'It's Time for a Major Issuance of the IMF's Special Drawing Rights', *Financial Times*, 20 March, available at https://ftalphaville.ft.com/2020/03/20/1584709367000/It-s-time-for-a-major-issuance-of-the-IMF-s-Special-Drawing-Rights/, accessed 1 June 2020

Gallagher, K.P., H. Gao, W.N. Kring, J.A. Ocampo and U. Volz (2020), 'Safety First: Expanding the Global Financial Safety Net in Response to COVID-19', GEGI Working Paper, no. 0037, Boston: Boston University, April.

Georgieva, K. (2020), 'Confronting the Crisis: Priorities for the Global Economy', Washington, D.C.: International Monetary Fund (IMF), 9 April, available at https://www.imf.org/en/News/Articles/2020/04/07/sp040920-SMs2020-Curtain-Raiser, accessed 1 June 2020.

Gong Cheng, D.M. *et al.* (2018), 'IMF-RFA Collaboration: Motives, State of Play, and Way Forward: A Joint RFA staff proposal', Discussion Paper Series, no. 4, Luxembourg, Publications Office of the European Union, October, available at https://www.esm.europa.eu/sites/default/files/esmdiscussionpaper4.pdf., accessed 1 June 2020

Griffith-Jones, S., R. Marodon and J.A. Ocampo (2020), 'Mobilizing $400 Billion: Using the Visible Hand of Development Banks', Washington, D.C.: Center for Global Development, 10 April, available at https://www.cgdev.org/blog/mobilizing-400-billion-using-visible-hand-development-banks, accessed 1 June 2020.

Group of 20 (G20) (2009), 'Global Plan for Recovery and Reform', paper presented at the G20 Leaders' Summit, London, 2 April, available at http://www.g20.utoronto.ca/2009/2009communique0402.html, accessed 1 June 2020.

———— (2020a), 'Extraordinary G20 Leaders' Summit: Statement on COVID-19', paper presented at the Extraordinary G20 Leaders' Summit, Riyadh, 26 March, available at http://www.g20.utoronto.ca/2020/2020-g20-statement-0326.html, accessed 1 June 2020.

———— (2020b), 'Communiqué', paper presented at the Virtual Meeting of the G20 Finance Ministers and Central Bank Governors, Riyadh, 15 April, available at http://www.g20.utoronto.ca/2020/2020-g20-finance-0415.html, accessed 1 June 2020.

G20 Eminent Persons Group on Global Financial Governance (2018), 'Making the Global Financial System Work for All', Report of the G20 Eminent Persons Group on Global Financial Governance, October, available at https://www.globalfinancial-governance.org/assets/pdf/G20EPG-Full%20Report.pdf, accessed 1 June 2020.

Inter-American Development Bank (IDB) (2020), 'COVID-19: Situation Update in Latin America and the Caribbean', available at https://www.iadb.org/en/coronavirus/current-situation-pandemic, accessed 1 June 2020.

International Monetary Fund (IMF) (2012), 'The Liberalization and Management of Capital Flows: An Institutional View', *Policy Papers*, Washington, D.C., 14 November.

———— (2017a), 'Collaboration Between Regional Financing Arrangements and the IMF', *Policy Papers*, Washington, D.C., 31 July.

———— (2017b), 'Adequacy of the Global Financial Safety Net – Considerations for Fund Toolkit Reform', *Policy Papers*, Washington, D.C., 19 December.

_____ (2020a), *World Economic Outlook: The Great Lockdown*, Washington, D.C., April.

_____ (2020b), *Global Financial Stability Report: Markets in the Time of COVID-19*, Washington, D.C., 14 April.

_____ (2020c), 'Policies to Support People During the COVID-19 Pandemic', *Fiscal Monitor*, chapter 1, Washington, D.C., 15 April.

_____ (2020d), 'Press Briefing by Kristalina Georgieva Following a Conference Call of the International Monetary and Financial Committee', Washington, D.C., 27 March, available at https://www.imf.org/en/News/Articles/2020/03/27/tr032720-transcript-press-briefing-kristalina-georgieva-following-imfc-conference-call, accessed 1 June 2020.

_____ (2020e), 'The Managing Director's Global Policy Agenda, Spring Meetings 2020: Exceptional Times, Exceptional Action', *Policy Papers*, no. 20/020, Washington, D.C., 14 April.

_____ (2020f), 'IMF Primary Commodity Prices', June, available at https://www.imf.org/en/Research/commodity-prices, accessed 1 June 2020.

_____ (2020g), *World Economic Outlook Update*, June.

Izquierdo, A. and M. Ardanaz (2020), 'Fiscal Policy in the Time of Coronavirus: Constraints and Policy Options for Latin American and Caribbean countries', Ideas Matter, Inter-American Development Bank (IDB), 31 March, available at https://blogs.iadb.org/ideas-matter/en/fiscal-policy-in-the-time-of-coronavirus-constraints-and-policy-options-for-latin-american-and-caribbean-countries/, accessed 1 June 2020.

JP Morgan (2020), 'EM Flows Weekly', 28 May.

Levy, S. (2020), 'Suggestions for the emergency', *COVID-19 Policy Documents Series*, no. 2 (UNDP LAC C19 PDS 2), New York: United Nations Development Programme (UNDP), March.

Maddison, A. (2010), 'Maddison Database 2010', Groningen Growth and Development Centre, University of Groningen, available at https://www.rug.nl/ggdc/historical-development/maddison/releases/maddison-database-2010, accessed 1 June 2020.

Mnuchin, S. (2020), 'U.S. Treasury Secretary Steven T. Mnuchin's Joint IMFC and Development Committee Statement', United States Department of the Treasury, 16 April, available at https://home.treasury.gov/news/press-releases/sm982, accessed 1 June 2020.

Nuguer, V. and A. Powell (eds) (2020), 'Policies to Fight the Pandemic', *Latin American and Caribbean Macroeconomic Report*, Washington, D.C.: Inter-American Development Bank (IDB), April.

Ocampo, J.A. (2017), *Resetting the International Monetary (Non)System*, Oxford: Oxford University Press.

_____ (2020), 'Can Latin America Avoid Another Lost Decade?', Project Syndicate, New York, 3 January, available at https://www.project-syndicate.org/commentary/latin-america-lost-decade-low-growth-by-jose-antonio-ocampo-2020-01?barrier=accesspaylog, accessed 1 June 2020.

Ocampo, J.A., S. Griffith-Jones, A. Noman, A. Ortiz, J. Vallejo and J. Tyson (2011), 'La gran recesión y el mundo en desarrollo', in J.A. Alonso and J.A. Ocampo (eds), *Cooperación para el desarrollo en tiempos de crisis*, Mexico City: Fondo de Cultura Económica.

Pineda, E., C. Pessino and A. Rasteletti (2020), 'Policy and Fiscal Management during the Pandemic and Post-Pandemic in Latin America and the Caribbean', 1 May, https://blogs.iadb.org/gestion-fiscal/en/policy-and-fiscal-management-during-pandemic-and-post-pandemic-latin-america-and-the-caribbean/, accessed 1 June 2020.

Reinhart, C. and K. Rogoff (2020), 'Suspend Emerging and Developing Economies' Debt Payments', Project Syndicate, New York, 13 April, https://www.project-syndicate.

org/commentary/suspend-emerging-and-developing-economies-debt-payments-by
carmen-reinhart-and-kenneth-rogoff-2020-04, accessed 1 June 2020.

Stiglitz, J.E. *et al.* (2020), 'How the Economy Will Look After the Coronavirus Pandemic',
Foreign Policy, Washington, D.C., 15 April, https://foreignpolicy.com/2020/04/15,
how-the-economy-will-look-after-the-coronavirus-pandemic/, accessed 1 June
2020.

Tooze, A. (2020), 'The Coronavirus is the Biggest Emerging Markets Crisis Ever', *Foreign
Policy*, Washington, D.C., 28 March, https://foreignpolicy.com/2020/03/28/
coronavirus-biggest-emerging-markets-crisis-ever/, accessed 1 June 2020.

United Nations (UN) (2020), *Debt and COVID-19: A Global Response in Solidarity*, New
York, 17 April, https://www.un.org/sites/un2.un.org/files/un_policy_brief_on_
debt_relief_and_covid_april_2020.pdf, accessed 1 June 2020.

United Nations Conference on Trade and Development (UNCTAD) (2020a), 'The COVID-
19 Shock to Developing Countries: Towards a "Whatever It Takes" Programme
for the Two-Thirds of The World Population Being Left Behind', *Trade and
Development Report Update* (UNCTAD/GDS/INF/2020/2), Geneva, March.

_____ (2020b), 'From the Great Lockdown to the Great Meltdown: Developing Country
Debt in the Time of COVID-19', *Trade and Development Report Update*
(UNCTAD/GDS/INF/2020/3), Geneva, April.

World Bank (2020a), *Commodity Markets Outlook: Implications of COVID-19 for
Commodities*, Washington, D.C., April.

_____ (2020b), *Semiannual Report of the Latin America and Caribbean Region: The
Economy in the Time of COVID-19*, Washington, D.C., April.

_____ (2020c), 'COVID-19 Crisis through a Migration Lens', *Migration and Development Brief*, no. 32, Washington, D.C., April.

_____ (2020d), 'World Bank Group President Malpass: Remarks to the Development
Committee', 17 April, https://www.worldbank.org/en/news/statement/2020/04/17/
world-bank-group-president-malpass-remarks-to-the-development-committee,
accessed 1 June 2020.

_____ (2020e), 'Remarks by World Bank Group President David Malpass on G20
Finance Ministers Conference Call on COVID-19', 23 March, available at https://
www.worldbank.org/en/news/speech/2020/03/23/remarks-by-world-bank-group-
president-david-malpass-on-g20-finance-ministers-conference-call-on-covid-19,
accessed 1 June 2020.

World Trade Organization (WTO) (2020), 'Trade Set to Plunge as COVID-19 Pandemic
Upends Global Economy', Press Release (Press/855), Geneva, 8 April, https://www.
wto.org/english/news_e/pres20_e/pr855_e.pdf, accessed 1 June 2020.

6

Economic Impact of Covid-19 in South America

Martín Abeles, Martín Cherkasky and Matías Torchinsky Landau

Introduction

The economic downturn of Latin America and the Caribbean in 2020 is expected to be the most severe among the world's developing regions (IMF 2020a). By the end of the year, per capita GDP (gross domestic product) figures in Latin American and Caribbean countries will retreat to their 2010 levels (ECLAC 2020b), and poverty rates to their 2005 levels (ECLAC-ILO 2020). Further, the region's post-pandemic recovery is projected to be among the slowest within the developing world (Table 6.1).

This chapter argues that such a disheartening outcome should not come as a surprise. The development pattern of Latin America and the Caribbean began to reveal symptoms of fatigue way before the emergence of Covid-19, including falling growth rates, weaker investment spending,

Table 6.1 *GDP growth per developing region, projections 2020–21* (percentage change)

	Projections	
	2020	2021
Emerging and Developing Asia*	−1.7	8.0
Emerging and Developing Europe*	−4.6	3.9
Middle East and Central Asia*	−4.1	3.0
Sub-Saharan Africa*	−3.0	3.1
Latin America and the Caribbean**	−9.1	3.6

Source: *IMF (2020a, 2020b); **ECLAC (2020d).

Lecture delivered on 20 May 2020.

lower employment growth and a slower pace of poverty reduction. Taking on a structuralist perspective, we claim that the same factors that accounted for pre-pandemic sluggishness – widening productivity gaps, pervasive informality, stagnant exports, increasing foreign indebtedness – explain not only Covid-19's disproportionate impact in Latin America and the Caribbean, but also the projected post-pandemic slowness.

Against this backdrop, we suggest that conventional counter-cyclical policies will not suffice to resume growth in Latin American and Caribbean economies in the short run. Given the relative low weight of government spending in aggregate demand, expansionary fiscal policies will have to be accompanied by a progressive redistribution of income in favour of wage-earners, especially of low-wage-earners, to fuel private consumption (the weightiest component of aggregate demand), boost aggregate demand and effectively restart growth.

From a longer-term perspective, we claim that, despite pandemic-related counter-cyclical efforts, which have been significant in many cases, if the prevailing institutional arrangements and the resulting set of economic policies, including unrestricted capital account openness, appeal for fiscal austerity and weak – or virtually non-existent – industrial policies are not appreciably transformed, Latin America and the Caribbean are likely to go back to their pre-pandemic malfunctioning, even if they are able to regain some movement in the short term.

This chapter focuses on South America's commodity-exporting economies, and is organized as follows. The first section describes South America's pre-pandemic economic situation and trends. The second section discusses the structural factors that account for these trends, including the resulting macroeconomic vulnerabilities as faced by most South American countries on the verge of the Covid-19 outbreak. The third section describes the impact of Covid-19 in South America, and discusses the effectiveness of conventional counter-cyclical policies under the said structural vulnerabilities. The fourth, and last, section concludes the chapter.

Pre-Pandemic Economic Stagnation

South American economies had been slowing down consistently since 2014, prior to the Covid-19 outbreak, after a major drop in international commodity prices. Excluding Venezuela – which was struggling with a full-blown depression at the same time – South America's growth rate averaged 1.9 per cent between 2014 and 2019, as compared to 5.7 per cent in the commodity boom period of 2004–08. Excluding Argentina and Brazil – which had also experienced several recessive episodes in that period – South America's growth rate averaged 2.6 per cent between 2014 and

Figure 6.1 GDP growth rate, South America (annual, simple average)

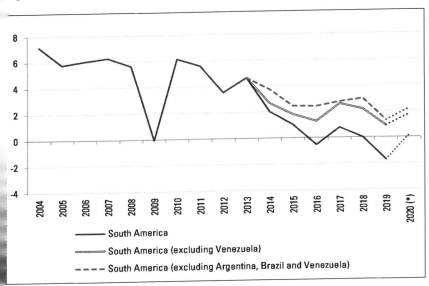

Note: * ECLAC's projection (December 2019).
Source: Based on ECLAC (2019).

2019, well below the 5.5 per cent average of the 2004–08 period (Figure 6.1). Furthermore, by the end of 2019, before the eruption of Covid-19, ECLAC (United Nations Economic Commission for Latin America and the Caribbean, or CEPAL) forecast another anaemic performance for South America in 2020, of barely 1.7 per cent growth (excluding Venezuela). Bolivia and Paraguay, with relatively lower per capita GDP levels, were the only two countries that managed to sustain moderate growth rates before the pandemic, of 4.2 per cent and 3.1 per cent on average between 2014 and 2019. Without Bolivia and Paraguay, South America's already low growth rates in 2014–19 would have been even lower.

Logically, the 2014–19 pre-pandemic economic slowdown brought about rising unemployment rates in most South American countries, especially Brazil (+4.7 percentage points), Uruguay (+2.4), Argentina (+2.8) and Paraguay (+1.6).[1] On average, the unemployment rate went up from 5.6 per cent in 2013 to 7.3 per cent in 2019, after a full decade of continuous improvement (Figure 6.2). Inequality, which had also fallen significantly in the preceding decade, stopped falling as of 2014. Stagnant (or, in some cases, growing) inequality, coupled with rising unemployment, also brought the downward trend of poverty rates to an end (Figure 6.2).

Higher unemployment and falling real incomes hit private consumption, which represents nearly two-thirds of aggregate demand in South

Figure 6.2 *Unemployment and poverty rates, South America* (simple average)

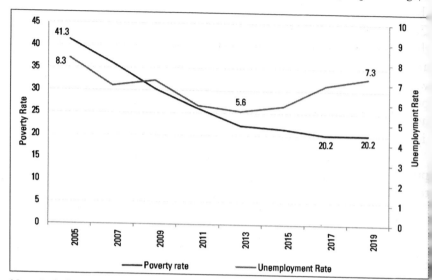

Note: Includes Argentina, Bolivia, Brazil, Chile, Colombia, Ecuador, Paraguay, Peru and Uruguay.
Source: Based on CEPALSTAT (https://estadisticas.cepal.org, accessed November 2020).

American economies. Negative feedback between higher unemployment, lower incomes and falling consumption reinforced the slowdown in economic activity, and activated new contractionary factors, such as falling investment. Indeed, the investment rate also exhibited a falling trend prior to the pandemic. Gross capital formation as a percentage of GDP fell from an already mediocre 22.8 per cent in 2013 to 20.8 per cent in 2019 (excluding Venezuela). Falling investment slowed down – or sometimes impeded – productivity growth, making the needed reversion of the structural faults that lay behind anaemic growth much more difficult (more on this below). Excluding, also, Argentina and Brazil – not only the two largest, but also the two worst performing South American countries at that time, after Venezuela – the average investment rate also fell by close to 2 percentage points, albeit from a slightly higher start point, from 23.7 per cent to 21.5 per cent in the same period.

This situation of low and weakening growth rates – which look meagre not only in historical terms but also when compared to other developing regions[2] – begs the question: What is it that explains, and how does one interpret, this downward and seemingly regressive trend? According to conventional (orthodox) wisdom, mediocre growth in Latin America is (and has been) due to long-lasting institutional deficiencies, including the lack of depth in financial markets, a plethora of distortive axes, the excess or inadequacy of labour market regulations, and/or the persistence of oversized social protection systems (see, for example, Cavallo and Powell 2018). Allegedly, those deficiencies reveal – still, after three decades of ubiquitous market reforms – the continuance of certain archaic rules of the game, which increase the legal uncertainty associated with investment decisions, generating a 'problem of appropriability' that prevents the efficient allocation of resources.[3] In short, even if veiled by a neo-institutionalist hypothesis, according to this view, the fault seems to lie in the unfinished agenda of market-oriented reforms.

In what follows, we put forth an alternative, structuralist interpretation, that South America's recent (pre-pandemic) stagnation is due to its structural (endemic) external constraint on growth.

Pre-Pandemic Macroeconomic Vulnerabilities

Indeed, South American exports slowed down significantly after the 2008–09 international financial crisis and their growth rate has remained at a historically low level since then, especially after 2013–14. This was not merely an effect of the contemporaneous drop in international commodity prices.[4] As shown in Figure 6.3, annual export growth rates fell significantly, from 7.7 per cent in 2004–08 to 1.6 per cent in 2014–19, even when computed in real terms. Even though decreasing exports do not fully account for the reduction in growth rates, given their limited participation

Figure 6.3 *Growth of exports, South America* (constant prices, three-year moving average)

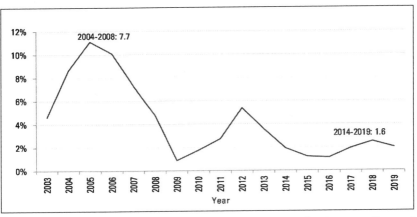

Note: Includes Argentina, Bolivia, Brazil, Chile, Colombia, Ecuador, Paraguay, Peru and Uruguay.
Source: Based on World Bank Open Data (https://data.worldbank.org/, accessed November 2020).

on aggregate demand, especially in the largest South American economies, such a deceleration was anything but inconsequential.

As pointed out originally by Raul Prebisch (1949) and formalized later by Anthony Thirlwall (1979), the growth potential of peripheral economies – defined as those that do not issue international reserve currencies – is restricted by their ability to obtain external income. In the short run, such income may be attained via exports or external finance in its various forms, from short-term portfolio flows to foreign direct investment. But in the long run, the availability of foreign exchange will inevitably depend on the peripheral country's ability to generate foreign proceeds via exports (Setterfield 2011).

Thirlwall's law states precisely this – that, assuming the real exchange rate stays relatively constant over time, the long-run sustainable growth rate of a peripheral country, consistent with balance of payments equilibrium, can be approximated by the ratio of the growth of its exports to the income elasticity of demand for its imports (Thirlwall 1979). The growth rate of a country's exports can in turn be expressed as the product of the income elasticity of exports to the growth rate of the rest of the world (or, typically, of the peripheral country's main trading partners). A country's elasticity of exports may be conceived of as a structural feature or parameter (which conditions the short term but cannot be willingly modified in the short term) that reflects the economy's technological capabilities and resulting pattern of specialization. The same can be said about a country's income elasticity of demand for imports (ECLAC 2020a).

From this angle, changes in the ratio of export to import elasticities, which we may call 'Thirlwall's coefficient', comprise a concise representation of an economy's structural change. As argued by Prebisch, South American economies are prone to face balance of payments difficulties due to their 'asymmetric' productive structures. In these structures, a few natural resource production and processing activities, some capital-intensive services (electricity, telecommunications, banking), and a small number of large enterprises exhibit high production standards, while the rest (a very large part of the production system) show very low productivity indicators.

The ensuing production structures – highly concentrated in low-technology activities – tend to generate a disproportionate demand for imports during upswings (high import elasticity), due to the virtual absence of several industries, particularly technology-intensive ones. On the contrary, exports do not respond as readily to the increase in external demand, given the prevalence of natural resource-based activities which display not only less elastic supply, but also lower responsiveness to global growth, resulting in low export elasticity.[5, 6]

Going back to the data, the fact that the sharp deceleration in South American exports between 2014 and 2019 was more severe than the slowing down of international trade – which hit historical lows at the time – points to the likely weakening in the region's income elasticity of exports. Figure 6.4 shows, precisely, the decline of the income elasticity of exports in the last two decades in most South American countries, as well as the fall in Thirlwall's coefficient.[7] From a structuralist perspective, key to increasing peripheral countries' growth rate in a (balance of payments) sustainable manner is the implementation of policies that bring about the increase of Thirlwall's coefficient. The trend portrayed in Figure 6.5 comprises, from that point of view, a significant structural regress – related, as verified in different analyses, to a 're-primarization' of South American economies (ECLAC 2012) – and suggests that the deceleration of exports in the 2014–19 period is not merely due to the exogenous slowdown in international trade – which, of course, did not help – but also to this structural backslide.

The fall of international commodity prices after 2014, and the pronounced deceleration of exports henceforth, did not bring about more acute and widespread symptoms of economic distress – apart from the economic slowdown – due to the ample liquidity obtainable in international

Figure 6.4 *Import and export elasticities, South America, 1998–2008 and 2010–16*

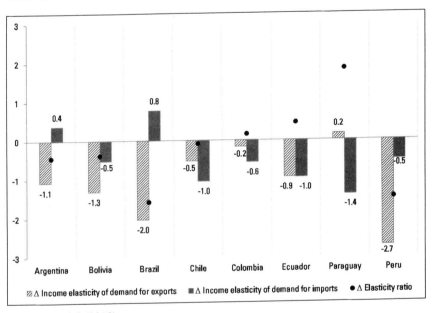

Source: ECLAC (2018).

financial markets at the time. Fluid access to external financing in most South American economies was, to be sure, a key factor that softened the impact of the fall in international commodity prices and external demand between 2014 and 2019, prior to the pandemic.

But the fall in exports and the consequent deterioration of current account balances led to a greater dependence on international financial markets (Figure 6.5). South America's average current account balance fell from +1.5 per cent of GDP in 2004–08 (the commodity boom period) to –2.1 per cent in 2014–19 – a substantial current account deficit considering the significant slowing of economic activity. In tandem, external debt as percentage of GDP rose sizeably, from an average of 31 per cent in 2013 to 48 per cent in 2019.[8] Consequently, the foreign interest net outflows increased on average from 1.1 per cent to 2 per cent of GDP between 2013 and 2019. Increasing debt intensified an already noticeable shift towards fiscal austerity in some countries – particularly in the largest economies in the region – dampening growth rates further, which often fell short of those allowed by the corresponding external constraints.[9]

These vulnerabilities can be assessed and portrayed straightfor-

Figure 6.5 *External debt and current account balance, South America* (as per cent of GDP, simple average)

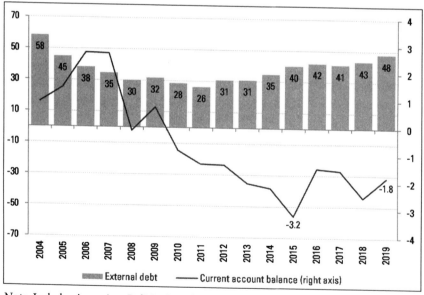

Note: Includes Argentina, Bolivia, Brazil, Chile, Colombia, Ecuador, Paraguay, Peru and Uruguay.

Source: Own calculations based on IMF BOP/IIP (http://data.imf.org/BOP, accessed November 2020), and CEPALSTAT (https://estadisticas.cepal.org, accessed November 2020).

vardly as the ratio of external debt (net of international reserves) to annual exports, as in Figure 6.6. The ensuing external vulnerability indicator goes down with lower foreign indebtedness, higher international reserves and higher exports, and vice versa, and is consistent with Thirlwall's long-term concern with external constraints to growth (Bhering, Serrano and Freitas 2019). As shown in Figure 6.6, external vulnerability as measured by this indicator increased significantly before the outbreak of the pandemic. According to this indicator, while prior to the 2008–09 international financial crisis South American economies would have required, after using up their international reserves (theoretically, of course), only 40 per cent of annual exports to settle their entire foreign debt (public and private), prior to the Covid-19 crisis this percentage rose three-fold, reaching almost 120 per cent. This worsening of external vulnerability resulted, in most cases, from the composite effect of growing foreign indebtedness, diminishing international reserves and declining exports.

Summing up thus far, the re-primarization of South American economies increased their exposure to fluctuations in international commodity prices and worsened their sustainable growth potential (vis-à-vis their balance of payments constraints), as reflected in the decline in Thirlwall's

Figure 6.6 *External vulnerability indicator, external debt (net of reserve assets) as percentage of exports, South America* (simple average)

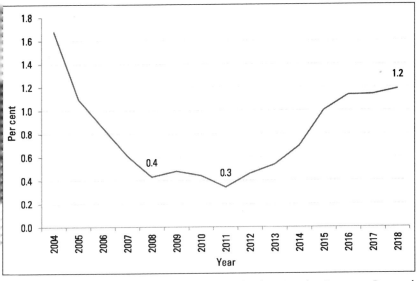

Note: Includes Argentina, Bolivia, Brazil, Chile, Colombia, Ecuador, Paraguay, Peru and Uruguay.
Source: Same as for Figure 6.5.

coefficient. The consequent deterioration of current account balances led to greater dependence on international financial markets – reflected in growing foreign indebtedness – and, consequently, greater exposure to international liquidity cycles. At the same time, the deceleration of economic activity deterred capital formation – a first order requirement for the much needed structural change. The concurrence of growing foreign indebtedness, falling investment and the regressive transformation of domestic production structures – a sign of lax capital account management and weak domestic industrial policies – is likely to reinforce foreign sector vulnerabilities in the medium to long term, if the prevailing policy arrangements, and the resulting development model, do not change substantially.

Impact of Covid-19 and Alternatives for Economic Recovery

Despite the global reach of Covid-19, the South American countries, from a strictly economic perspective, did not experience the pandemic as an 'external' shock. As stated by José Antonio Ocampo in this volume, international commodity prices – except for oil – did not plummet as significantly as during the 2008–09 'Great Recession'; international credit markets also recovered more quickly (after some early financial turmoil[10]) when compared to that crisis, and so did international trade.

The severe decline in South American economic activity after the spread of the pandemic was mainly due to a collapse in household consumption, which on average accounted for approximately two-thirds of the total GDP contraction in the second quarter of 2020 (Figure 6.7). Contrariwise, reduction of exports accounted for only one-third of GDP's fall at the same time and, net of imports, it explained only 1 per cent of the total decline. This was the case not only in the largest South American economies, with relatively sizeable domestic markets (Argentina, Brazil, Colombia, Peru), but also in the smaller and more open ones (Chile, Ecuador, Paraguay, Uruguay).

The contraction in household consumption began with the sudden and acute fall in mobility caused by social distancing measures. Fear of contagion also played a contractionary role. In that context, very few industries (for example, food, personal hygiene products, pharmaceuticals, telecommunication services) dedicated to the production of essential goods and services managed to sustain pre-pandemic production levels. The rest of the production apparatus faced an unprecedented pause, particularly the services industries, engendering additional negative feedback.

Indeed, the initial drop in private consumption, in tandem with total or partial lockdowns, led to significant second-round effects – also contractionary in nature – owing to the fall of households' disposable

Figure 6.7 *Contribution to GDP growth by final demand components, South America* (y/y change, constant prices, Q2-2020)

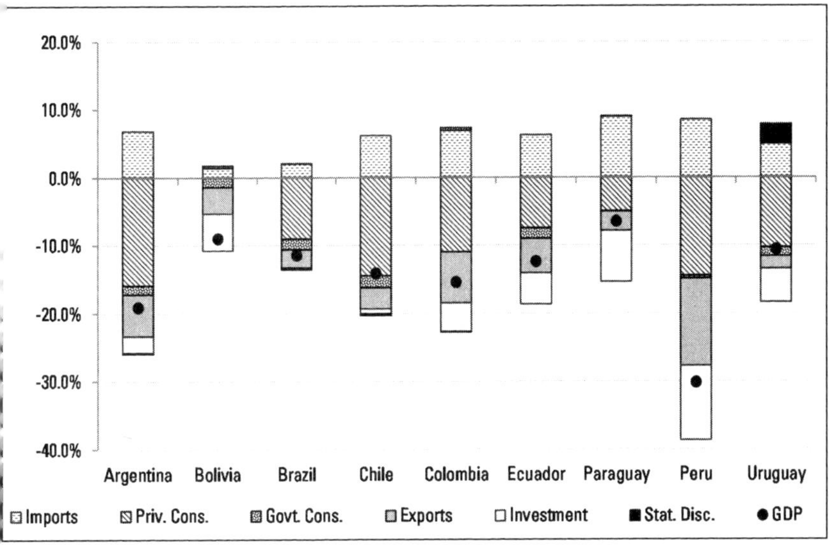

Source: ECLAC, based on national statistics offices.

income. As a result, employment went down further and, on average, fell by more than 10 per cent in South American countries, amid massive business closures (ECLAC 2020c). The prevalence of informality due to the predominance of low-productivity activities only contributed to make things worse, producing massive job losses and a generalized fall in real wages (of –2.8 per cent, on average, in the second quarter of 2020 alone) (Figure 6.8). While the fall in formal jobs was moderate, considering the impact on economic activity (except in Colombia), the impact on informal jobs was significantly higher, and some countries lost as much as one-third of their informal positions in the second quarter of 2020. The unparalleled collapse of private consumption can only be understood as the compound effect of falling employment and wages. Logically, the resultant low levels of capacity utilization – not to mention the prevailing economic uncertainty – brought investment spending to a halt, causing an additional cutback (–5.3 per cent) to GDP in the second quarter of 2020.[11]

Against this background, most South American governments put forth sizeable counter-cyclical policies. On the fiscal side, these included wide-ranging income transfer programmes to both households and firms (ECLAC 2020d), as reflected in the increase of primary expenditures (Figure 6.9). On the monetary side, central banks cut interest rates and helped fund – directly or indirectly – various subsidized credit programmes.

Figure 6.8 *Employment and real wages, South America* (y/y change, Q2-2020

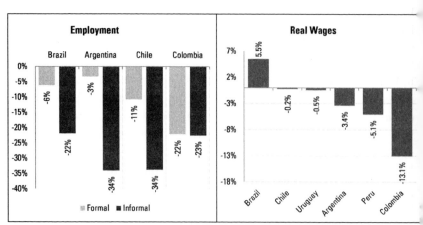

Note: The data for Peru and Paraguay comprises only formal employees, and for Argentina, Brazil, Chile and Uruguay, includes all employees (excluding self-employed). Colombia's employment data are for the period May–July and considers all employees (also excluding self-employed), but real wages data is only for the manufacturing sector.
Source: ECLAC, based on national statistics offices.

Figure 6.9 *Government expenditures, South America* (y/y change, constant prices, 2020)

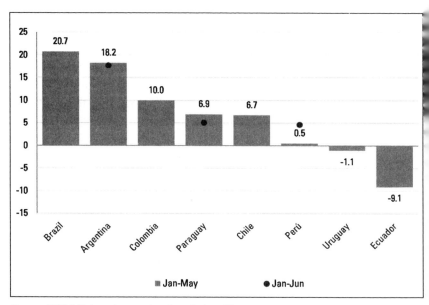

Source: ECLAC, based on national statistics offices.

Fiscal expansions were crucial to sustain economic activity levels: the IMF (2020b) estimates that GDP would have fallen, on average, 5 percentage points more than it actually did without the implemented fiscal support. But despite their magnitude, expansionary measures did not suffice to compensate the pandemic's blow to aggregate demand – not even in Brazil, which applied the largest fiscal expansion and is recognized for its relatively high fiscal multipliers. But the low effectiveness of counter-cyclical fiscal policies thus far was not only due weak fiscal multipliers.[12] It was also due to the relatively low contribution of government spending to aggregate demand vis-à-vis private consumption. Every percentage point lost in private consumption is, on average, equivalent to 2.5 percentage points lost in primary government spending. By way of illustration, for GDP to return to its 2019 levels by 2021, an extraordinarily large fiscal expansion would be required, ranging from 3.4 per cent to 6.1 per cent of GDP (depending on the case).[13] For that to occur, public expenditures would have to go up between 15 per cent and 26 per cent y/y in real terms, depending on the country. Such an expansion – it is higher than 2020's largest fiscal packages – is not only difficult to finance,[14] but also difficult to execute.

In short, typical counter-cyclical policies are likely to be insufficient to set South American economies back on a sustainable growth path. While required, the size of fiscal expansion will not be able to match the size of the needed boost to aggregate demand.[15] Investment spending, given low capacity utilization, is unlikely to lead the way either. The recovery of international trade and the consequent export rebound, if it ever materializes, would also be insufficient to push economic activity to the needed extent. As shown in Figure 6.10, a 5.2 per cent recovery of global demand in 2021 – as expected by the IMF (2020a) – would not contribute much to GDP growth, ranging between 0.8 per cent (Colombia) and 1.7 per cent (Chile). This reflects, essentially, the region's low income elasticity of exports, as pointed out earlier.

This leaves us with private consumption as the only potentially effective lever for recovery. Private consumption represents between 51 per cent and 60 per cent of GDP in South America, compared to government primary spending (between 13 per cent and 21 per cent), investment (between 15 per cent and 22 per cent) and exports (between 12 per cent and 30 per cent). Its movement is of course mainly defined by changes in the real wage bill, which is determined by changes in employment and real wages. Given their different relative weights in aggregate demand, comparatively small improvements in real wages can have a much larger impact on aggregate demand than similar increases in, say government

Figure 6.10 *Expected GDP fall, and impact of fall and recovery of trade partners, South America*

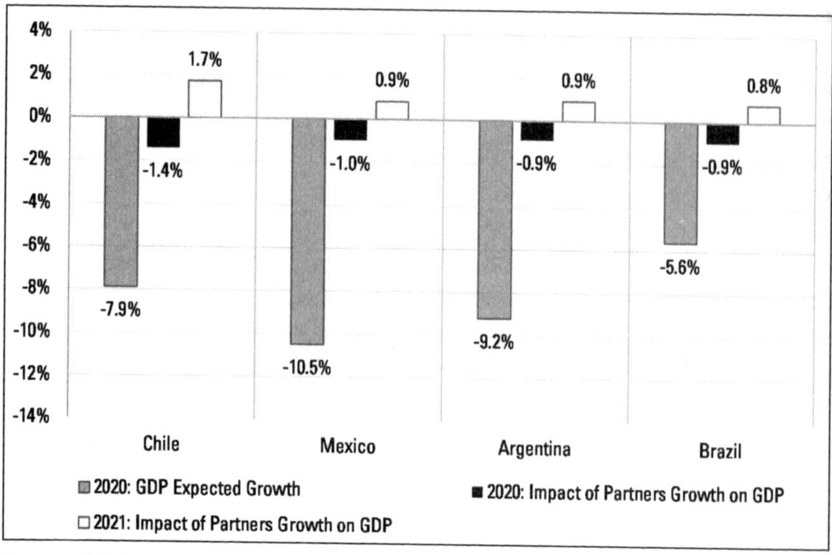

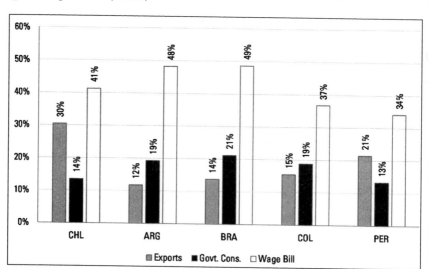

Source: ECLAC, based on ICIO-OECD (http://oe.cd/icio, accessed 19 November 2020) and IMF (2020a).

Figure 6.11 *Exports, public spending and wage income, South America* (percentage of GDP, 2015)

Source: ECLAC, based on IMF (2020a) and ICIO-OECD (http://oe.cd/icio, accessed 19 November 2020).

pending. To exemplify the expansionary potential of progressive redistribution of income (i.e. a rise in real wages), Figure 6.11 compares the relative weights of exports and public spending in GDP to the wage share.

The introduction or strengthening of minimum wage legislation, the promotion of inclusive labour market regulations, the support of progressive tax reforms cum redistribution policies (for example, via expanding cash transfer programmes, education grants, social security coverage and so on) are policies that would not only enable a much needed improvement in income distribution but more effectively fuel growth. Such an approach, in the midst of mounting unemployment and falling real wages, would have no bearing on typical concern with profitability and/or competitiveness of business,[16] and need not exert inflationary pressures either (Bresser-Pereira 2020).

Moreover, these policies would not necessarily lead to unsustainable external positions, at least in the short term. For most South American countries, the fall in imports caused by the recession exceeded that of exports. The balance of payments deficit, which reached 79 billion dollars in 2019 (2.3 per cent of regional GDP), is therefore expected to fall to only 16 billion in 2020 (0.6 per cent of GDP) (IMF 2020a). The only exceptions to this trend were Uruguay and Ecuador, as shown in Figure 6.12, whose exports declined more than imports. For most countries, these deficits should be relatively easy to finance, considering that their risk premia (measured by the EMBI+ in Figure 6.12) returned to relatively low levels

Figure 6.12 *Current account and *EMBI+, South America, 2019–20*

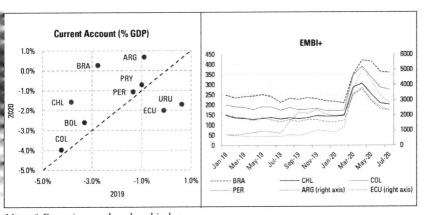

Note: * Emerging markets bond index.
Source: ECLAC, based on IMF (2020a) and World Bank Data (https://datacatalog.worldbank.org/jp-morgan-emerging-markets-bond-indexembi, accessed 19 November 2020).

Figure 6.13 *Potential policy mixes to reach 2019 GDP, South America*

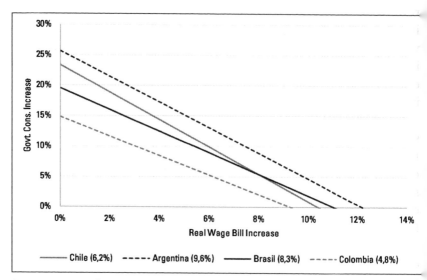

Source: ECLAC, based on IMF (2020a) and ICIO-OECD (http://oe.cd/icio, accessee November 2020).

after reaching a peak in February–March, although they remain highe than they were before the burst of the pandemic.

To expose the effectiveness of progressive redistribution as a mac-roeconomic policy lever for recovery, Figure 6.13 shows various combina-tions of fiscal and progressive redistribution policies that would allow South American economies to recover their 2019 GDP levels in 2021. Take, for instance, the case of Colombia. Assuming (as in all other cases) a positive impact from the expected growth in global demand, Colombia would require a 15.6 per cent increase in government spending (equivalent to 3.4 per cent of GDP) in order to recover its 2019 GDP level, if the real wage were to remain at the same level (i.e. at its depressed 'pandemic level'). If the real wage bill could be raised by 3 per cent (equivalent to 1.1 per cent of GDP), government spending would need to grow only by 10 per cent (2.3 per cent of GDP) to achieve the same result.

Conclusions

In sanitary terms, Latin America and the Caribbean, especially South America, has been among the hardest hit regions in the world (IMF 2020a; ECLAC 2020a, 2020b). These circumstances are typically associ-ated with structural factors, including urban agglomeration, inadequate state capacity and weak health systems, which have made it difficult for the region to contain the pandemic.

These structural factors not only explain the region's struggle to restrain the death toll, but also the severity of Covid-19's socio-economic impact. Insufficient hospital capacity forced stricter isolation measures when compared to developed countries. In combination with high labour informality – Latin America's Achilles' heel – these stricter measures heightened the pandemic's socio-economic impact, exacerbating the disruption in supply chains and related jobs, and income losses.

Covid-19 not only exposed South America's faulty public health systems, it also revealed the profound weaknesses of its development model. Persistent and ubiquitous informality is nothing but a direct symptom of South America's faulty production structures, and explain why what started as a sanitary crisis turned out to be 'the worst economic and social crisis in a century' (ECLAC 2020a), comparable to the 1980s' debt crisis (Palma 2020).

Warning indicators had surfaced early on from almost every conceivable angle – except for, perhaps, long-lasting low inflation rates in most South American economies. As pointed out in the first section of this chapter, Covid-19 hit the region against the backdrop of decelerating growth, growing unemployment, declining exports, falling investment, rising foreign indebtedness and intensifying external vulnerabilities. These growing external vulnerabilities did not embody an unfortunate, fortuitous outcome. They were the foreseeable result of a malfunctioning development model that combined (and still to a large extent does) weakening industrial policies with unrestricted international financial integration, which, as we know, comes with a taste for fiscal austerity. While for some countries, external conditions are less stringent and growth could be restored without immediately affecting the external sector, other countries, particularly Argentina, Ecuador and Venezuela, do face a binding external sector and are likely to need international assistance.

South America's high rate of labour informality, which proved so pernicious during the pandemic, is the flip-side of the production system's well-known structural heterogeneity. Primarization of production and informalization (precarization) of urban labour markets not only tend to come together, but also exacerbate the external constraints to growth described in the second section, and related foreign sector vulnerabilities. These vulnerabilities reduce macroeconomic policy space, hindering the possibility of applying expansionary fiscal policies when needed, and contribute to locking in the institutional setting and power structure – the 'rules of the game', as Joan Robinson (1956) would have put it – that get in the way of a more progressive distribution of income.

As we suggest in the second section, a progressive redistribution of income may be, precisely, the most effective way to restart South American economies, in tandem with bolder expansionary fiscal policies. But redistributive policies are seldom conceived of as part of the macroeconomic toolkit and are barely on the agenda. Challenging the pre-pandemic rules of the game will require, if South America is to overcome its endemic weaknesses, placing redistribution as a crucial component of the new development model.

Notes

[1] In Bolivia and Ecuador, unemployment rates remained unchanged during this period.

[2] Emerging Asia, for instance, grew by 4.5 per cent on average during the same period (2014–19), with twenty-six out of thirty economies growing faster than the South American economies.

[3] There is nothing wrong in seeking an efficient allocation of resources. But there are various conceptions of efficiency that inform different policy options and development models. The notion of efficiency implied in the orthodox view refers to static comparative advantages, which in South America are generally linked to natural resources. For a distinction between static (Ricardian) efficiency and dynamic (Schumpeterian or Keynesian) efficiencies, see ECLAC (2012).

[4] The IMF's primary commodity price index fell by 30 per cent between 2013 and 2019.

[5] Empirical evidence shows that industrial manufactures, especially those of high technological content, have a greater exports elasticity (respond to world demand), in contrast to commodities (see Dosi, Pavitt and Soete 1990; ECLAC 2007; Cimoli and Porcile 2013).

[6] Besides its impact on the balance of trade, the 'duality' of the productive structure leads to a more obvious consequence: the prevalence of low productivity industries and the resulting predominance of informal jobs, which, as discussed in the next section, led to a much more severe impact on the labour market and economic activity than in developed countries.

[7] The only country that experienced a slight improvement in the income elasticity of its exports was Paraguay. The low (and falling) income elasticity of South American exports contrasts with that of most Asian economies (Abeles and Cherkasky 2019).

[8] Especially in Argentina (+37 percentage points), Ecuador (+29 percentage points) and Chile (+21 percentage points).

[9] Note that the maximum growth rate allowed by the external constraint is not an 'attractor', but a long-run limit to growth. Reaching this threshold, or surpassing it (if external finance permits), requires growing aggregate demand (Amico 2013; Serrano and Summa 2015).

[10] In February–March of 2020, global financial markets were upset by massive sell-offs in equity markets and pervasive 'flight to quality', hitting emerging markets and developing economies harshly. Many South American economies, which as pointed out above had been running current account deficits for some time – and were thus highly dependent on short-term capital inflows – experienced a characteristic 'sudden stop' at that time. But the shortfall in foreign finance, which exerted worrying downward pressures on national currencies and rising sovereign risk premia across, was soon averted by massive monetary intervention by the Federal Reserve and the European Central Bank.

[11] Incidentally, as suggested by UNCTAD (2020), given the resulting low capacity utilization figures, it is very unlikely that investment works as a major driver of aggregate demand any time soon.

[12] Abeles, Caldentey and Porcile (2020) discuss the structural factors that lie behind low fiscal multipliers in Latin America and the Caribbean.

[13] This and subsequent estimations are based on the calculation of type II input–output multipliers using the 2015 Inter-Country Input–Output (ICIO) matrix developed by the OECD (Organization for Economic Co-operation and Development) (see Miller and Blair 2009). In these estimations, workers are assumed to save part of their income (the OECD average propensity to save) and spend the remaining income on both national and imported goods according to each country's consumption vector. This leaves four sources of autonomous demand for each country: autonomous private consumption, government consumption, investment and partners' autonomous expenditures (which determine exports).

[14] Covid-19 fiscal and monetary responses tended to be much smaller in developing countries than in developed countries, due precisely to their external constraints (Bonizzi, Kaltenbrunner and Mitchell 2019). As Tinti (2020) shows, developed countries not only announced larger Covid-19 fiscal packages than developing economies, but also displayed a higher variance in their size relative to GDP, suggesting that while fiscal policy is a matter of policy decisions for the latter, it is much more about the existing constraints for the former.

[15] For reasons discussed in Abeles, Pérez Caldentey and Porcile (2020), monetary policy is even less likely to do the job.

[16] It also would have a positive effect on investment due to the resulting increase in capacity utilization, even in those economies where profitability is the main factor driving investment (Foley and Nikiforos 2011).

References

Abeles, Martín and Martín Cherkasky (2020), 'Revisiting Balance-of-Payments Constrained Growth 70 Years after ECLAC'S Manifesto: The Case of South America', *Revista de Economia Contemporânea*, vol. 24, no. 1, pp. 1–24.

Abeles, Martín, Esteban Pérez Caldentey and Gabriel Porcile (forthcoming), 'La Crisis del Covid-19 y Los Problemas Estructurales de América Latina y El Caribe: Responder a La Urgencia Con Una Perspectiva de Largo Plazo', *Revista de la CEPAL*.

Amico, Fabián (2013), 'Crecimiento, Distribución y Restricción Externa en Argentina', *Circus: Revista Argentina de Economía*, vol. 5, pp. 31–80.

Bhering, Gustavo, Franklin Serrano and Fabio Freitas (2019), 'Thirlwall's Law, External Debt Sustainability, and the Balance-of-Payments-Constrained Level and Growth Rates of Output', *Review of Keynesian Economics*, vol. 7, no. 4, pp. 486–97.

Bonizzi, B., A. Kaltenbrunner and J. Michell (2019), 'Monetary Sovereignty is a Spectrum: Modern Monetary Theory and Developing Countries,' *Real-World Economics Review*, vol. 89, pp. 46–61.

Bresser-Pereira, Luiz C. (2020), 'Financiamento da Covid-19, Inflação e Restrição Fiscal', *Revista de Economia Política*, vol. 40, no. 4, pp. 604–21.

Cavallo, Eduardo and Andrew Powell (eds) (2018), 'La hora del crecimiento, Informe macroeconómico de América Latina y el Caribe de 2018', Washington, D.C.: Banco Interamericano de Desarrollo.

Cimoli, Mario and Gabriel Porcile (2013), 'Technology, Structural Change and BOP-Constrained Growth: A Structuralist Toolbox', *Cambridge Journal of Economics*, vol. 38, no. 1, pp. 215–37.

Dosi, Giovanni, Keith Pavitt and Luc Soete (1990), *The Economics of Technical Change and International Trade*, Brighton: Wheatsheaf.

ECLAC (2007), *Progreso Técnico y Cambio Estructural en América Latina*, Santiago de Chile.

ECLAC (2012), *Cambio Estructural Para la Igualdad: Una Visión Integrada del Desarrollo*, Santiago de Chile.

ECLAC (2019), *Balance preliminar de las Economías de América Latina y el Caribe 2019*, Santiago de Chile.

ECLAC-ILO (2020), 'La Dinámica Laboral en Una Crisis de Características Inéditas: Desafíos de Política", *Coyuntura Laboral en América Latina y El Caribe*, Santiago de Chile.

ECLAC (2020a), *Building a New Future: Transformative Recovery with Equality and Sustainability*, Santiago.

ECLAC (2020b), *Reconstruction and Transformation with Equality and Sustainability in Latin America and the Caribbean*, Santiago de Chile.

ECLAC (2020c), 'Sectors and businesses facing Covid-19: emergency and reactivation', Covid-19 Special Report, no. 4, Santiago.

ECLAC (2020d), 'Addressing the Growing Impact of Covid-19 with a View to Reactivation with Equality: New Projections', Covid-19 Special Report, no. 5, Santiago.

Foley, Duncan and Michalis Nikiforos (2011), 'Distribution and Capacity Utilization: Conceptual Issues and Empirical Evidence', *Metroeconomica*, no. 1, pp. 200–29.

IMF (2020a), *World Economic Outlook: A Long and Difficult Ascent*, Washington, D.C., October.

IMF (2020b), *Regional Economic Outlook for Western Hemisphere: Pandemic Persistence Clouds the Recovery*, Washington, D.C., October.

Miller, Ronald E. and Peter D. Blair (2009), *Input Output Analysis*, Cambridge: Cambridge University Press.

Palma, Gabriel (2020), 'Latin America in Its "Gramscian Moment": The Limitations of A "New European Social Democracy"-Style Exit to This Impasse', *El Trimestre Económico*, vol. 87, no. 348, October–December, pp. 985–1031.

Prebisch, Raúl (1949), *El Desarrollo Económico de La América Latina y Sus Principales Problemas*, Santiago de Chile: ECLAC.

Robinson, Joan (1956), *The Accumulation of Capital*, London: Macmillan.

Serrano, Franklin and Ricardo Summa (2015), 'Aggregate Demand and the Slowdown of Brazilian Economic Growth in 2011–2014', *Nova Economia*, 25, pp. 803–33.

Setterfield, Mark (2011), 'The Remarkable Durability of Thirlwall's Law', *PSL Quarterly Review*, vol. 64, no. 259, pp. 393–427.

Thirlwall, Anthony (1979), 'The Balance of Payments Constraint as an Explanation of the International Growth Rate Differences', *PSL Quarterly Review*, vol. 32, no. 128.

Tinti, Eduardo (2020), 'Pandemic: What About the "Third World"?', EPOG Policy Briefs, No. 14.

United Nations Conference on Trade and Development (UNCTAD) (2020), *Trade and Development Report*, Geneva.

7

The Coronavirus and the Emerging Media Ecology

Sashi Kumar

We need to look at what the coronavirus has done to the media as much as what the media is doing to the coronavirus, in terms of communicating effectively to the people that the media is supposed to represent. The coronavirus, of course, has compounded the problems that the media was facing over the last decade or so. There have been so many game changers that have affected our idea of the freedom of news media, of journalism itself, and the coronavirus has come as yet another twist, so to speak, in the narrative.

A good entry point to begin this narrative would be the early 2000s, when we had a spate of mergers and acquisitions in the media, something of the order of 300 billion dollars. Of course, there were a few even earlier, in the 1990s, when Google was already on the scene. When the dust settled on these mergers and acquisitions, nine media conglomerates were responsible for much (almost 90 per cent) of what we read, saw or heard on the media. These multinational companies were – all except one – American: Sony, the News Corporation, AT&T Broadband, General Electric, AOL Time Warner, Disney, Viacom, Vivendi, Bertelsmann.

The Game Changers

What is specifically a game changer at this time is what happens to the media vis-à-vis journalism. As part of these mergers and acquisitions, one distinct trend was that the bigger players were acquiring stand-alone news media entities of repute that were influential brand names, and making these a subset or small part of the corporate entity. So much so that the journalism or news portion really shrank to a relatively insignificant

---

Lecture delivered on 30 April 2020.

part of the corporate entity, in terms of the revenues or the profits that i
fetched. For example, when ABC News – quite a big name in the Unite
States – was acquired by Disney Group, it represented less than 2 per cen
of the total profits of this corporation. Times Incorporated represente
only single-digit profits as a percentage of AOL Time Warner's revenue
Similarly, NBC News contributed an equally minuscule part of the tota
profits of General Electric.

When journalism becomes a small subset of a larger media propo
sition, there are pulls and pressures between the media, on the one hand
and journalism, on the other. Therefore, when it is said that the media i
doing well, it does not – after this point – mean that journalism is doing
well. The media could be laughing its way to the bank and journalism
could be languishing, both in terms of quality and even survival. So thi
has been a major game changer.

As we move further into the twenty-first century, the advent o
social media becomes very important. Google has been there for some
time, Facebook made its appearance in 2004, and other social media platforms, like WhatsApp, Instagram and Twitter, have come in, in a very big
way. And very soon, they find huge constituencies, huge catchment areas
and consumer relationships. What is also important is that some of these
technological platforms, like Google and Facebook, are really media or
journalistic enterprises. They may be aggregators; they may be cannibal-
izing news that is sought and sourced, worked for and paid for by others.
In this situation of crisis, there is already a strident voice emerging, in
Australia and other parts of the world, and in India as well, that Google
and Facebook should share their revenues with the legacy and mainstream
news media players whose content they are using on their platforms, and
thereby calling their bluff that they are only technology platforms. They
are the super competitors of our time, just as AOL Time Warner, Sony or
Bertelsmann were, a decade or two ago.

In the favourable telecom regulatory world of early twenty-first-
century India, Reliance emerges in a major way. The next big game changer
is in September 2016, when Reliance Jio's entry into the media ecology
makes a huge difference as data prices collapsed as much as 93 per cent.
Streaming becomes much more accessible, smartphones become that much
more attractive and affordable, and 65 million viewers are estimated to
be added every year to this media environment. And therefore, there is a
huge spurt in consumption. The narrative is really one about consumption – more and more consumption, more and more page views, more
and more web impressions – but without an inkling of a revenue model.

The Elusive Online Revenue Model

There were so many consumers, but there was no revenue model that could monetize the consumption. By then, the advertising revenue model was already shrinking, the economy was on a downturn, and it was slipping very fast. There was talk of near-recessionary conditions on the horizon, particularly because the sectors that had been advertising were important ones – like the automotive sector, the services sector, the e-commerce sector, which were all in the doldrums. We had a situation when the mainstream media players found that advertisers were forsaking them, and the online revenue model had not yet kicked in.

One of the big international media players, *The Guardian*, has been trying with a digital-only presence, without any paywall, and asking viewers to voluntarily pay for the content. *Financial Times* and *New York Times* have gone into 'Premium' kind of models, where some content is free but the important part is put behind a paywall. These models were beginning to work, but in India, media players were still trying to make sense of them when the coronavirus hit us the way it has.

During the past few months, we have seen a huge spurt – 50–60 per cent increase – in digital usage in India, which looks great, of course. However, there is not a smattering of an idea as to how to monetize this usage. Those who were using the online media were used to free content, and it took some time for them to habituate themselves to pay for it. That hasn't really happened. Advertising has become even more scarce, and is not likely to be there in the near future. At the same time, the revenue model is not working for the digital content. This is one kind of crisis the news media is faced with.

In the midst of the coronavirus crisis, we have seen greater concentration of the powerful media. The most striking deal is that Facebook, which has enormous reach and influence, has bought Reliance Jio. The consequences of this deal will play out much, much later. This trend will only continue, even worsen, especially when revenue models are collapsing. The big media players are now resorting to retrenchment, deferred payments and other devices in order to sustain themselves. Start-ups are in an even more pathetic state, with very short runways. They have to think of ingenious ways to extend the runway, stretch it as much as they can, and hope against hope in the meantime that some subscription model, comprising a revenue model, advertising or a grant will work.

Grants are likely to play some role in the future in media revenue models. Already, we can see that newer forms of media practice are emerging. That's the vibrant part of the story, and particularly among the small and medium players, we find innovation, we find re-imagination, we find the idea of a dispersed newsroom where work from home has actually increased productivity, especially where stories have to be told. With the new smartphones, apps and devices, journalists are able to present multi media content from anywhere. Work from home hasn't meant shrinkage in terms of the content that is put out into the ecology.

However, the big questions remain. How do you monetize and sustain this – even in the short term, but certainly after the coronavirus has passed? How do we sustain autonomous, stand-alone media creation centres and devolution in media operations? How and why is there distrust of the media by those in power, on the one hand, and even by the consumers, on the other? Of course, fake news, misinformation and disinformation have played a role in this credibility crisis, largely due to the presence of social media. But the vast expanse of social media is variegated, with biases and prejudices, along with vibrancy, hope and innovation. It is quite a strange and fascinating mix.

Erosion of Media Credibility

This is the time to ponder over the credibility of the media, and whether the media belongs to the 'marketplace of ideas', as Justice Oliver Wendell Holmes Jr. mentioned a century ago, in 1919, in his dissent note in *Abrams v. United States*. The phrase refers to ideas in the media competing with one another for a better-informed citizenry. But we know, that has not really happened. We know that the market hijacking of the media has made it less a public interest proposition and more a profiteering proposition.

We do know that the reputation and identity of the news media are in question, because a good section of the media, particularly television media, has chosen to become the propaganda arm of the ruling party. It is doing it so unabashedly, without any sense of ethical restraint, that it is a blatant misuse of the concept of journalism. Is this journalism? – we keep asking ourselves, and we are convinced it is not. But then, it is ruling the roost. In a context where political liberalism is on the back foot everywhere in the world, a heady cocktail of authoritarianism and populism is in control. This kind of appeal to people's prejudices, to their biases, to their baser instincts, is made by a hectoring media, and a media that 'others' by resorting to minority-bashing.

We saw the context of the large Muslim gathering of the Tablighi Jamaat in mid-March 2020, and the role that a section of the media played in conflating the spread of the coronavirus with this single event in Nizamuddin, Delhi. One would think that this event alone was responsible for the wide spread of the coronavirus in India. Nobody is an apologist for what happened there. The Tablighi Jamaat gathering was a foolish enterprise – it should not have been held in mid-March, especially when the participants knew that the coronavirus situation was worsening. But the point is that the event has been used as an opportunity by the media for denigrating the Muslim community. Normally, we speak of a crisis being used positively by the media. But in this case, it was used so negatively, so adversely, by a section of the media.

For some time now – even during the anti-CAA (Citizenship Amendment Act) protests in 2019–20 – the idea has emerged that the media should aid and abet, and promote the policies of the government, and not play spoilsport or criticize its point of view. It is not the duty of the media – it would seem, according to this understanding – to be questioning what is happening, but to support, advance and disseminate the government's projects and priorities to the people. A false sense of political propriety has taken hold of the media, or is sought to be imposed on the media, where journalists should do their bit or else be called 'anti-national', or dubbed a dissident or a traitor, or 'othered' as much as certain minority communities are. Unfortunately, a good section of the media lays itself supine before the government. Even before these journalists are asked to do it, they have accepted it, internalized it and have become, shall we say, cats' paws of the ruling party.

One of the first things we need to reinforce in this Covid-19 situation, therefore, is that the adversarial and critical role of the media is a very important role, and we should not lose sight of it. In fact, investigative journalism should be at a premium at this point of time, because this is when we need transparency on the part of the government. But at least as far as the Indian government at the centre is concerned, there is no transparency about why it is doing what it is doing. Why was the lockdown announced the way it was, with four hours' notice, creating this 140-million destitute workforce, these migrant workers, who did not know whether they were coming or going? Just as we were trying to tackle the coronavirus, the government had created a parallel crisis.

This is the big criminal underbelly of the coronavirus situation, and the journalist's critical function is paramount in such a situation. In fact, there was a story in *The Times* ('Coronavirus: 38 days when Britain sleepwalked into disaster') of 19 April 2020, about how Prime Minister Boris Johnson had deep-dived into the problem by mindlessly talking about 'herd immunity', not heeding scientific advice, missing crucial parliamentary meetings, thereby losing valuable time and thousands of lives in the battle against the virus. This was a culpable crime. It was not a sin of omission but a sin of commission. Similarly, if one looks at the migrant labour situation in India, it is a culpable crime on the part of the government. There was no need for the sudden, dramatic announcement of the lockdown. Giving a few days' time would have made a tremendous difference in terms of making the lockdown itself that much more effective.

The Constitution and the Right to Know

It is important, therefore, to place the media in the larger context of the right to information, or the right to know. There is an interesting and quick study done by the Commonwealth Institute for Human Rights Initiative (headquartered in Delhi), where it is pointed out that the institutions that have come into being after the passing of the Right to Information Act, 2005, haven't worked as well as they should have. And many of the state information institutions are defunct; they are not working at all. This is the crucial interface between the media and the government, and this is the point of time when important information that is valuable to the people is sought by journalists more than ever. If these institutions are not functioning well, then it shows the scant respect with which the government is treating these institutions, particularly at such a compelling time.

In fact, there have been two Supreme Court verdicts that equate the right to information to the right to life, underlying Article 21 of the Indian Constitution. In the 1988 case, *Reliance Petrochemicals Ltd v. Proprietors of Indian Express*, Justice Sabyasachi Mukharji and Justice S. Ranganathan actually read the right to know as an integral part and parcel of the right to life and personal liberty. And sixteen years later, in 2004, in a judgement on the case *Essar Oil Ltd. v. Halar Utkarsh Samiti & Ors*, Justice B.N. Srikrishna and Justice Ruma Pal make this idea even more explicit. Here is a sentence from the judgement: 'There is a strong link between Article 21 and the right to know, particularly where secret government decisions may affect health, life, and livelihood.' It is almost as if the honourable judges were presciently speaking of the coronavirus situation and to the present government.

There is a need for openness, a need for transparency about the process by which governments are going to tackle this pandemic of an unprecedented nature, by taking the people into confidence. We have seen press conferences everywhere, famously by the governor of New York, Andrew Mark Cuomo, and on the flip-side, by the President of the United States, Donald Trump. Here, in India, we have the unique distinction of a Prime Minister who refuses to give a press conference, and the coronavirus has made no change to that situation.

So, we see how important the right to information is today and, by inference, the role of the media as fair-minded and critical is that much more crucial today. We should be looking at the role of the media in the constitutional scheme of things, and the Indian Constitution has been a buzzword for some time now. All the subterfuges by the government to destabilize the social order in this country has led to a situation where the people have started clinging to the Constitution – as a last resort, as an oasis of sanity, in the midst of all this madness. The spirit of the Constitution continues to be very important in the period of the coronavirus and earlier. Article 14 (equality before the law), Article 19 (freedom of expression) and Article 21 (right to life and personal liberty) of the Indian Constitution have been centre stage, particularly during the past several months, in the anti-CAA protests, because of the communal unrest artificially created in the country.

This is also the time to reinforce the role of the media as the fourth pillar of democracy, and as an intrinsic part of a constitutional mechanism of separation of powers between the executive, the legislature and the judiciary. The media plays a check-and-balance function by supervising and invigilating the other three powers. Media freedom is an inferred right from Article 19, and not a prescribed right as in the USA, where the First Amendment of the US Constitution says: 'Congress shall make no law . . . abridging the freedom of speech, or of the press.' In India, even though media freedom is an inferred right, successive rulings by the highest court of the land allow people to give the media the moral high ground, and it is by virtue of this that the media exercises its right to freedom. Thus media freedom is almost a basic feature of the Constitution, and this cannot be changed even by a legislative act.

Unfreedom in the Indian Media

It would seem, however, that if you exercise your right under Article 19 brilliantly, you could forfeit your right under Article 21 and have a couple of people with country-made pistols killing you. The question is there in every journalist's mind: how will you be able to exercise your right to freedom of expression without becoming a target of attack? There is no point in having a right to freedom of expression without having a right as a consequence of that expression. Without the latter, 'freedom of expression' literally becomes a dead-letter phrase.

Even before the coronavirus pandemic kicked in, the government authorities yanked off two television channels in Kerala because of their coverage of the Delhi riots in late February 2020. What is astounding is the notice that was given to these two Malayalam channels, which said that they had fallen foul of the broadcast guidelines. One of the reasons for 'falling foul' of the guidelines was that they criticized the Rashtriya Swayamsevak Sangh (RSS), the cultural wing of the ruling Bharatiya

Janata Party (BJP). It was as blatant as that – as black and white. The minister concerned then realized that it was a huge *faux pas*, and implied that it had happened due to some bureaucratic bungling and that they were investigating it. We haven't heard of the result of the investigation, because other events overtook us in the meantime.

There have been several such pin-pricks, but graver than that was the incident where *The Wire* editor, Siddharth Varadarajan, was prosecuted by the Uttar Pradesh state authorities for having criticized the behaviour of Chief Minister Yogi Adityanath during the lockdown. We find that such issues keep cropping up and they continue to act as a deterrent in the coverage of the coronavirus. During the coronavirus pandemic, we are asked to stay at home, but the crisis is handled by the Ministry of Home Affairs at the centre. It is not a crisis that is actually being handled by the Health Ministry. The health authorities do play a role, but the coordinating agency is the Home Ministry. There is this fear, when it comes to the Home Ministry, about how much you can say and what you can say. We can be sure that there is pre-emptive censorship by the media, which prevents journalists from doing their tasks fully and effectively.

The Way Forward

Going forward, is there another paradigm for the media, where it can become more relevant? There are examples of the media working in tandem with the government. When we say that, it sounds strange, for in a situation where the government is hunting the media down, the government subsidizing the media sounds like a scandalous proposition. And yet, the Nordic countries (Norway, Sweden, Denmark, Finland) have dealt with the media far better than we have, and they occupy the top five or six slots in the World Press Freedom Index. In 2020, India occupied the 142nd rank out of 180 countries, even though we are the biggest democracy with the largest media sector in the world. Taking a lesson from the Nordic countries, we find that the idea of media freedom in these countries has been imprinted in the constitutional scheme of things since the eighteenth century. Sweden was talking about media freedom, and even passed the Freedom of Press Act, as far back as 1766, much before the French Revolution in 1789 or the institution of the First Amendment in the US Constitution in 1791. Since the 1960s, there has been government subsidy of the press (reflecting various viewpoints) in a few Nordic countries. This has created pluralism in society and led to democratic empowerment of their citizens.

In the Indian context, we find that small and big players, just because they have been critical of the government's policies, have been refused government advertising. On 8 April 2020, the president of the Congress party, Sonia Gandhi, said that the government should stop its advertisements in the media. When she said that, it seemed as if she was throwing out the baby with the bathwater, because government advertising is a lifeline for several small media entities. That the government uses its advertising in an uneven, unfair manner is the unfortunate part of the story.

Nevertheless, the point is that the role of the state in terms of subsidizing the media is not an unseemly proposition, because the media is in the public interest. An enlightened state should be able to provide succour to the media to sustain itself, without being propelled into the arms of the market to become the kind of profiteering media that we see before us. If the media is provided with the constitutional high ground, it is because people expect the media to represent them, and play a democratic role and that of a watchdog in society. The media should build agendas, and sometimes even set good agendas. But if the media's primary concern is to maximize profits, why should people treat journalists with kid gloves or as sacred cows?

So, we have to rediscover the role of the media. In the 1840s, while writing for the *Rheinische Zeitung,* Karl Marx had said that what we need is not a bourgeois capitalist press, but a '*Volkspresse*' or a people's press. Marx also said that the purpose of the press is not to be in business. That may be too utopian an idea to hold at the present time. But the media has to have a limit to its growth as a business, in order to perform its public function. The role of the state in enabling such a media should come back into the discourse of how the media can go forward in the post-coronavirus age.

PART TWO

The Impact of Policy Responses

8

The Pandemic Requires a Different Macroeconomic Policy Response

Jan Kregel

Let me start by noting that I have been on 'shelter in place' in New York since the beginning of March 2020, so that my comments will be coloured by conditions here. I would like to start by setting out an alternative approach to the economic problems raised by the pandemic, different from both the mainstream approach and some Keynesian-inspired policy responses.

My knowledge of the mainstream analysis comes from the widely ventilated interviews of economists on the major news programmes. Not surprisingly, these were usually couched in terms of the impact of the pandemic on supply and demand. Since the outbreak was first announced in China, and met with a rigid local quarantine, the initial focus was on the reduction in production due to disruption of global supply chains that put pressure on supplies and prices. When the contagion started to be visible in Europe, and then in the United States, leading to suspension of non-essential production activities, the discussion quickly shifted to the collapse of demand problem as workers were furloughed or dismissed. So, the discussion shifted quickly from an inflationary spiral to a recession or depression problem, or both. The dominant policy discussion was around the most appropriate remedies for the supply bottlenecks and failing demand. With the recent financial crisis in mind, most recommended financial support measures similar to those that had been employed after 2008 – higher government deficit spending and low or zero interest rates to offset the declines in output and to support demand. The Federal Reserve moved quickly on interest rates and expansion of its balance sheet while Congress produced multiple 'stimulus' packages to offset the loss of income

Lecture delivered on 11 May 2020.

and employment due to the pandemic. Keynesian Democrats joined Cheney Republicans to argue that there was nothing to fear from deficit spending and expanding national debt. I think this was the wrong place to start and led to the wrong policy response, because it was a mischaracterization of the problems facing the economy.

Was there an alternative point of departure and method of analysis? I am not a virologist or epidemiologist and thus totally unqualified to say anything at all on the impact of the coronavirus pandemic – and have attempted to keep silent. On the other hand, there is an alternative approach that is possibly relevant and that I am presumed to know something about – uncertainty and expectations. Quite early on, developments in China made it clear that the analysis of the coronavirus was a case of absolute, complete and total uncertainty as to its nature and impact. Keynes had already pointed out that the natural response to a case like this would be to presume that tomorrow would be much like today. Thus, the first response was to back to something that you know. And this is what happened – the references were to the experience of SARS (severe acute respiratory syndrome) and MERS (Middle East respiratory syndrome), to the death rates, contagion rates, which were contained at what were thought to be manageable values. The official response was, 'do not panic' – we know that SARS and MERS were eventually controlled, so we really don't have to be too concerned. Further, as was initially thought with MERS, there was no confirmed person-to-person contagion. With no idea what the virus was or what the impact was going to be, the natural response was that it would be like the past, so the first order of business was to prevent panic; which outside of China was quite easy as there was no real evidence of the presence of the virus before February.

But as evidence in China accumulated, the transmission rate turned out to be much higher than it should have been, and mortality was much higher than expected, reinforced by the rapid spread and mortality in parts of northern Italy. As the physical evidence of overcapacity in hospitals and morgues emerged from Wuhan and then Lombardy, it became necessary to form new expectations. Forecasters started to model the prospective evolution of infection and mortality based on parameters to reflect this new reality; and the numerous model projections of the spread of the disease quickly produced estimates that exceeded the capacity of potential treatment facilities. The panic was as much due to the fear of insufficient hospital beds and ventilators as to the potential explosion in the death rate.

But the basic parameters of these models, such as the now famous R_0 (or R-nought, the rate at which the virus is passed through the population) and the mortality rates, were just best guesses and were initially hought to be much higher than historical norms. And more importantly, eporting from China raised the suspicion that unlike the earlier episodes, here was clear evidence of asymptomatic viral shedding and person-to-person contagion (paradoxically, both had been characteristic of the Spanish flu, but there was no historical memory), which called into question the estimates of R-nought. If you don't know how many people are infected and spreading the disease before showing symptoms, you cannot know the spread rate. The same was true for the death rate, since asymptotic spread means that the real death rate would be much lower than recorded because the denominator is much higher than reported when as many as 25–40 per cent of the infections are asymptomatic. And this miscalculation was aggravated by the initial response of 'don't panic', which allowed the spread to ramp up largely unseen. As we now know, the virus had been identified in November 2019, and was already global and extensive in December in China and Europe, and in January in the US.

This meant that the parameters that were required for the model projections were not only uncertain, they were unknowable until full-scale testing determined asymptomatic infection and transmission rates. This problem was further aggravated in the US by the fact that test kits were in short supply, were defective and were only offered to those demonstrating clear symptoms. So, two months after the official Wuhan announcements, uncertainty was complete and total, and it appeared that health services would be wholly insufficient to provide even minimal treatment.

In these conditions, the only available medical response was to take physical measures to stop transmission – full-scale lockdown appeared to be the only way to avoid pandemic. The policy problem was no longer how to manage the impact on the economy to avoid recession, it was to influence R_0 to stop contagion and the breakdown of the health system. The economic problem became the management of expectations in pursuit of one objective: move $R_0 < 1$. The recession was thus the collateral result of active policy decisions to achieve that objective. Non-essential employment had to be suspended. It was not the result of cyclical movement in demand – it was imposed on the economy. The problem was to ensure that the lockdown could be maintained until the objective was achieved. And this presented another unknown. In Wuhan, the lockdown started end January and the relaxation in April – which was around three months. This suggested that the cost of fighting the virus would be something less than a quarter of GDP (gross domestic product) in lost income and production, depending on how rapidly the subsequent resumption of activity could take place.

Many economists responded with traditional policies to fight recession, not realizing that the economic problem was not to provide stimulus to offset the 'recession', but how to ensure that the economy could sustain the likely GDP and employment loss under lockdown. There was no possible 'stimulation' response – stimulus doesn't kill the virus; money is useless if you are sheltering in place and can't go out to shop except or Amazon. Job guarantee programmes are not useful if the point is not to work, if the employment loss is imposed. Guaranteed basic income pro grammes do not work if you have to provision public spaces.

What had to be done was to make sure that everyone managed to survive the pandemic, which meant staying quarantined at home in order to avoid public contagion and overcrowded hospitals. And, in the aftermath of the mistakes made with stimulus packages used in response to the Great Recession, it was important that the government stimulus should be done in an equitable manner, to ensure it did not make income and wealth inequality worse.

The response, thus, called for a different page from the New Deal response to the Great Depression of the 1930s – building confidence that the threat could be overcome. It is now recognized that there was no formal blueprint for a New Deal when Roosevelt took office, and indeed many of the policies implemented were borrowed from the Hoover Administration. But Roosevelt recognized the need to provide a sense of confidence and security, to free decisions from the fear of fear itself. Thus, he moved to restore confidence in the banking system via rapid legislation; and he moved to restore confidence by providing income through the myriad employment programmes and finally a blueprint for recovery. Ira Katznelson notes that what 'observers and commentators' of the dilemma facing the incoming administration shared was

> an understanding that theirs was a time when uncommon uncertainty at a depth that generates fear had overtaken the degree of common risk that cannot be avoided. . . . When deep uncertainty looms, the ability to choose is transformed. . . . Measurable risk generates worry. Unmeasurable risk about the duration and magnitude of uncertainty spawns fear. . . . Under conditions of fear . . . people develop a heightened mindfulness and self-awareness about the constraints on free action, and take, as a central goal, the desire to restore a higher degree of coherence and certainty; that is, they try to reduce deep uncertainty to ordinary risk. (Katznelson 2013: 33)

And this is precisely what was required in order to generate support for the only rational response to the virus – loss of income and employment via a strict lockdown. But it was necessary for this policy to recreate a sense of safety and security, of a clear path to exit from the threat of disease and unemployment, rather than fear and uncertainty of employment loss.

How could it have been done? It should seem quite clear that neither guaranteeing income nor providing government employment would work. Lockdown means not working, not working means no demand for labour, and staying home means you don't have the possibility to spend much anyway. What was required was a guarantee not of income but of survival, of what we may call 'social provisioning'. So, the first thing is to make sure that if everybody stays home, and even if they lose their jobs, they will have enough to eat and survive without fear and the constraint of loss of income.

The US has a minimum system of state-provided unemployment benefit and of food support (known by the acronym SNAP, Supplemental Nutrition Assistance Program), which provides food security for low-income families. One possibility would have been to support everybody's income by expanding these programmes to everyone classified as non-essential and subject to lockdown. These are cash transfer programmes that require the ability to use income for provisioning in the public market. But the essence of the lockdown means suspension of the market mechanism, of the labour market, of the consumption market, of public activity. Providing income transfers requires provisioning through participation in the market; if there is no market, then it cannot work. Provisioning must be provided by central organization, by government.

Here is where the New Deal comes in again. A food distribution organization – some sort of Civilian Conservation Corps – would have been required to make sure that everyone was provided with enough to eat. In most large cities, restaurants donate their excess supplies to food banks and other non-profit private or religious welfare agencies. It is obvious that in the shutdown, restaurants cannot operate; the supplies that they would have bought would become redundant. Here was excess supply that could provide food security – if only it could be organized and distributed. In the event, it took press reports that the excess food production from the countryside's producers was being trashed before a system was set up to channel it to the unemployed through non-profit beneficial agencies and soup kitchens. The first order of business should have been the reorganization of the food service sector into a food distribution sector, social provisioning to ensure a minimum subsistence and survival to everyone in lockdown. Hebert Hoover did this for Belgium in the First World War, so it clearly could have been done instead of sending everyone US$ 1,200 to chase down non-existent goods on empty store shelves, and benefiting speculators who profited from creating shortages and creating incentive to break quarantine in search of supplies (Nash 1989).

The next measure would have been to look at other types of expenditure. If you are a good Keynesian economist or stock-flow modeller you know that every income is an expense, and if you know your national accounting, you know that production creates income and expenditure to take off that production. The 'stimulus' response was a focus on incomes only – costs and sales were forgotten. A more sensible approach would have looked at the need for a balance between costs and incomes in the lockdown. If the firm is not producing, it is not earning; variable costs go down; it does not need a government loan to support employment if workers have to stay home. If households receive government-distributed food subsistence, they don't need wages from employment to survive.

But in the shutdown, there are also fixed costs that have to be met, for both the family unit and the firms – rents, mortgages, leases, etc. – which create insecurity if they are not met. But it is not necessary to provide income transfers to ensure that these payments are met. Fair burden sharing of the costs of the crisis implies that the rational approach is to suspend all fixed cost payments. A successful lockdown requires every economic unit to have minimum costs and minimum income, but to be assured to survive the lockdown period in a condition to recommence normal activity. Thus, suspending financial operations to avoid unnecessary increases in debt levels that will be carried over to the recovery period and create repayment difficulty is the order of the day to support and maintain social provisioning. Government support and finance, and organization of the production and distribution of subsistence, are required – not the provision of incomes to maintain capital values.

There is no reason why rental income or capital income should have preference over labour income. If everyone qualifies for social provisioning, the landlord gets food security just like the furloughed production worker. Here is the key to the idea of an equitable distribution of the burden of fighting the pandemic. Capital incomes and capital values have to be treated the same way as human capital and labour incomes. Household non-essential workers are losing, say, three months of income; so should all other wage- or capital-income recipients. Everyone should shoulder the capital loss created by the reduced flow of income, both human and financial.

The basic principle is that to stop all flow costs, since everybody's cost is somebody else's income, we don't have to give anybody money to cover those costs or offset the lost incomes. Capital incomes have to share in the costs of fighting the virus. This means not only that we suspend trading in capital assets, but that the incomes of all corporate administrative and management personnel are eliminated. They also now go down to subsistence provisioning. That's the way we try and share equitably the cost of the shutdown. This would also mean that the government does not have to engage in massive deficit spending aside from the support of social provisioning. The government would have to engage in a certain amount of organization; and for those who argue that it is difficult to act sufficiently quickly, refer back to the Roosevelt Administration's first 100 days. It took about a month to set up the Civilian Conservation Corps which provided employment for 300,000 young men in support of environmental projects (see Bremer 1975). We are not really interested in the impact on jobs and income, however, but the decisive action to set up the organization and management in record time. What was needed in this case was not government money – government did not need to spend a great deal in order to solve this problem. What was needed was to get the government to provide an equitable means for sharing the costs of quarantine to fight the virus, and to make sure that particular sectors and categories did not pay a higher price than others.

In the 2007–08 crisis, the government bailed out the banks and the management of private corporations, but let households lose their homes. Instead of an equitable distribution of capital loss, there was a capital transfer. This time was supposed to be different. But it looks very much the same in the US. There was stimulus support for banks, for firms, and this was supposed to maintain jobs – for workers the companies did not need. Should one be surprised that the job maintenance of these programmes was extremely low? The major impact of the stimulus was to expand government debt and produce fee income for the financial institutions managing them. And what of the income transfers and unemployment benefits? It is telling that household savings hit record levels during the period of quarantine.

And as a result of the attempt to stimulate during the lockdown, there is an increase in government debt. Is this a problem? We all know that it really doesn't make that much of a difference. And there are any number of Keynesians who support the debt finance government stimulus because they argue that deficits don't matter. And they don't. But if they are unnecessary, then there is a very big political cost, because every time the government deficit increases the debt, Congress attempts to cut essential services; which are precisely the things that are needed in order to respond to the crisis at the federal level.

However, in this regard the real problem is on the state level, where governments have been responsible for most of the health care costs. Since state governments run on a legally imposed balance budget principle, the eventual response is going to be cuts in state government expenditures that are primarily the income and employment of those essential workers in the forefront of the fight against the virus. Medicare and education, the basics that we need, are going to be cut as a result of the mistaken emphasis on stimulus.

But there is a much simpler argument against the use of stimulus to offset a policy-induced recession. Consider Keynes in *The General Theory* on the appropriate role of government expenditure:

> . . . if our central controls succeed in establishing an aggregate volume of output corresponding to full employment as nearly as is practicable, the classical theory comes into its own again from this point onwards. If we suppose the volume of output to be given, i.e. to be determined by forces outside the classical scheme of thought, then there is no objection to be raised against the classical analysis of the manner in which private self-interest will determine what in particular is produced, in what proportions the factors of production will be combined to produce it, and how the value of the final product will be distributed between them. . . . Thus, apart from the necessity of central controls to bring about an adjustment between the propensity to consume and the inducement to invest, there is no more reason to socialize economic life than there was before. (Keynes 1936: 378–79)

Those who justify additional deficit-financed stimulus expenditures with arguments about the unimportance of government debt rely on the first part of the argument, but overlook the fact that the market system which is presumed to function to allocate these expenditures to produce output and employment no longer functions, since the very response to the pandemic has been to shut down the labour market and suspend private decision-making. The appropriate policy should be the 'necessity of central controls' over federal expenditure, in order to offset rising unemployment that has been created by central controls suspending the market mechanism. If we take Keynes at his word, the response to the pandemic should have been not only central controls on aggregate output, but central controls on the determination of production and distribution. Without the latter the former is likely to be ineffective as response to the pandemic, as the equivalent of Keynes's well-known references to burying bank notes in the ground: better than nothing, but not efficient in fighting the virus. Better food distribution and building hospitals and providing loans to business operating in a system outside the market mechanism.

If the objective is to eliminate the virus contagion and it requires shutting down the economy, there is no need to support full-employment income through government expenditure. The problem is rather to provide the appropriate redirection of production and an equitable burden-sharing in which social provisioning is assured. Debt, deficits, transfer payments are not part of this. Central control of the market should be the goal. Relying on the crippled market mechanism cannot do it. If you fight a war, this is what has been required in the past.

As a final coda, there is the problem of the essential workers and those who manage to remain employed while in quarantine. This is part of the problem of equity. Since it is difficult to suspend these incomes, the appropriate solution would be a progressive tax on the incomes of home workers who can telecommute without loss of income to be used as a supplement to incomes of essential workers in the sanitary support sector, to offset the increased contribution and risks incurred in fighting the spread of the virus. As a metaphor, the idea is for the economy (like Snow White) to fall asleep, while the trusty essential workers manage to the fight against the coronavirus, and once R_0 is sufficiently reduced, the economy can resume without unacceptable disparity in the distribution of costs of the lockdown.

Postscript

Now, we all know this response to the crisis was not taken, and the four government stimulus plans have expired (those in support of incomes and employment payments) or those providing loans/grants to businesses have not been fully utilized. The increase in government deficits and debt has led to the expected response of an unwillingness of the Republicans in Congress to authorize additional programmes to prevent a relapse of the economy as Covid infection rates increase, and sales and employment have again started to fall. The call is for debt reduction rather than support. Economists have started to predict a tsunami of unemployment for the end of 2020. Yet this misses the main obstacle to successful recovery in the event of elimination of the pandemic.

Remember, Minsky's theory of financial fragility is based on the relation between cash inflows and cash outflows. In these terms the stimulus packages provided for limited cash inflows to firms (the payroll protection programmes) to meet cash outflows to households (cash transfers and increased unemployment benefit). But this provided no inflows to meet cash outflows for debt service. Thus, for most economic units, even with the stimulus programmes cash inflows were below cash outflows, and firms and households were either delinquent in debt service or had to find alternative financing. As the current stimulus plans expire and in the absence of replacement, this financing gap will only increase. This gap has been financed on the one hand by Fed policies of buyer of last resort for government and private-sector liabilities, and on the other, by increased borrowing of the non-financial corporate sector financed by bank lending or by the issue of new debt in the bond and equity markets.

In Minsky's terms, the initial impact of the pandemic was to increase the number of Ponzi units in the economy – borrowing to meet shortfalls in financing costs. The stimulus response measures, based on increased lending to Ponzi units, meant even more Ponzi financing. Think of the transportation sector, in particular airlines, who are still out of bankruptcy court only because of government support and the issue of new debt. The stock market continues to boom, and interest rates remain near zero, and debt issuance continues to rise, without any near-term prospect of increased cash inflows to service the increasing debt service ratios. This is the Ponzi pandemic, and the other side of the unemployment tsunami will be the Ponzi tsunami and the write-down of the assets held by the banks and the investing public.

References

Bremer, W. (1975), 'Along the "American Way": The New Deal's Work Relief Programs for the Unemployed', *The Journal of American History*, vol. 62, no. 3.

Katznelson, I. (2013), *Fear Itself: The New Deal and the Origins of Our Time*, New York: Liveright Publishing.

Keynes, J.M. (1936), *The General Theory of Employment, Interest and Money*, London: Macmillan.

Nash, G.H. (1989), 'An American Epic, Herbert Hoover and Belgian Relief in World War I', *Prologue Magazine*, vol. 21, no. 1, Spring.

9

Explaining the Differences in Covid-19 Mortality between the North and the South

Giovanni Andrea Cornia

Introduction

This chapter looks at the North–South Covid-19 mortality differentials on the basis of a unified framework even if some causes of the pandemic differ somewhat because of structural differences between the two regions. Yet the same causes seem to operate – if with vastly different intensity – in both the South and in the North. In carrying out this analysis, it is important to separate out the direct mortality effect of the disease from the indirect mortality effects caused by measures implemented by domestic governments (as lockdowns and other restrictions) and by the countries' international partners. The analysis is conducted using a general causal framework developed first for the countries of the North (Europe in particular) and then extended to the countries of the South. In Europe, Covid-19 arrived in January 2020, and it spread to all the regions from February, basically following the same trajectory in the main countries that adopted similar lockdown policies. The United Kingdom and Sweden, which initially decided to 'let the pandemic run its course', in the end introduced measures similar to those adopted in the rest of Europe. The number of deaths increased dramatically. So far, the large Western European countries have recorded between 30,000 and 50,000 deaths, and broadly followed a common pattern of mortality.

The chapter examines also to what extent the explanatory variables that account for the surge in mortality in the countries of the North explain the evolution of contagion and Covid-19 deaths in the developing countries. Finally, the chapter analyses, in both the countries of the

Lecture delivered on 22 May 2020. The data and trends cited in the lecture are therefore somewhat dated, though the paper's conclusions remain valid.

South (taking two Indian states as an example) and the North (taking two Italian regions as an example), the causes of the huge regional variations in infection and death rates recorded in many countries.

The key conclusion is that, if in Italy and India the national authorities had been able to push nation-wide the policies followed in Veneto and Kerala, one would have saved tens of thousands of lives.

A General Causal Framework of the Determinants of Covid-19 Infection and Death Rates

By and large, it is clear by now that the overall infection and lethality rate depend on the individual characteristics of the population, and on national structural characteristics that influence the number of contacts each individual has with potential carriers of the virus. Among the first, we include the following.

Age Structure of the Population

A key variable affecting the overall Covid-19-related mortality is the age structure of the population. In the countries of the North, in 2015–20, 5.3 per cent of the population were, on average, over 80 years of age (7.5 per cent in Italy). In developing countries, such number fell to 0.4 per cent (1 per cent in India, 0.3 per cent in Sub-Saharan Africa). People over 80 years of age are much more fragile, especially if they are or have been affected by serious comorbidities (including a growing number of cases of obesity and diabetes). They are therefore exposed to much greater risks of Covid-related death, as suggested by the large differences in age- and Covid-specific death rates (see Table 9.1). They are also affected indirectly by the number of deaths caused by a 'health diversion', as in all countries the existing medical resources were concentrated on dealing with the Covid-19 cases, with the effect that the number of deaths from cancers, strokes and heart attacks rose. Likewise, in developing countries, the diversion of health resources to deal with Covid-19 reduced the moneys and staff time allocated to immunization and infectious diseases, causing some increases in death rates in both cases.

As a result, in the countries of the North, a large share of the total

Table 9.1 *Age- and Covid-specific death rates, Italy*

Age-groups	20–29	30–39	60–69	70–79	80–89	Total
Death rate (in per cent)	0.1	0.3	10.5	27.0	40.8	13.4

deaths occurs among the elderly. For instance, in Italy, 84 per cent of all deaths were recorded among people of over 60 years of age. Difference in age structure across countries is not a problem that can be solved through medium-term policy changes. Now, the interesting thing is that the lethality rate – i.e. the number of people who died due to Covid-19 divided by the number of people who tested positive – is the highest in Belgium, followed by France, Italy, United Kingdom and Spain that share basically the same lethality rate. This finding remains unexplained. The United States has recorded the highest absolute number of deaths but has a population of 350 million people and so its lethality rate is not the highest.

Living Arrangements

People living, for whatever reason, in close contact with others face a higher risk of contracting the virus. With the decline of the three-generation family household, due *inter alia* to increased labour mobility and rising female labour participation rates, in practically all countries of the North, people of over 70 or 80 years of age now have to choose to live alone in their homes with the assistance of a carer who, in Europe, is often from Eastern Europe or South Asia. The number of the elderly living with relatives in urban areas is generally modest. Alternatively, the elderly may choose to enter nursing homes, especially if they are no longer self-sufficient. In less industrialized regions, especially in the countryside, one may instead still find three-generation families, but their number is declining, together with a drop in the total fertility rates.

Nursing homes are far more common – *ceteris paribus* – in the richer and more modern regions where employment, wages and pensions are higher. The model of social policy behind this approach basically states that, 'Ok, you have completed a very active working life and now need to rest in a nice nursing home endowed with pool, gymnasium, various types of entertainments, private rooms and, perhaps even small private apartments.' Medical personnel are always on call in these institutions. The main limitation of these nursing homes is that their guests share a lot of common space and activities with other elderly people. The risk of contagion in these institutions is thus very high.

Nursing homes are paid for with private and, increasingly, public funds, though the services are provided in most cases by private firms or cooperatives. These are supervised by public institutions which are supposed to ensure that the standard of service is adequate and the health norms to protect their guests are strictly respected. In practice, this model has not worked well for two reasons. The first is the objective difficulties encountered by the 'principal' (the public institutions) in monitoring the quantity and quality of the services provided by the 'agent' (the private service provider). The second problem is a sort of 'age discrimination' against the elderly, as 'they have already lived a long life, and are in any case in the final stretch of their existence'. In developing countries, one may frequently observe a health discrimination against children and women, but in the North such discrimination affects the elderly – who are no longer part of the labour force and are perceived to be a burden to society. So the thinking goes: 'It is not important to give them a ventilator or to take good care of them because they're about to die due to something else. It is better to focus on younger, potentially more productive people.' However, this conclusion is not correct if proper life-saving therapies are adopted also for them. Public policy thus has to change to ensure the 'right to life' for all people, independent of age, keeping in mind, of course, the cost of the therapies to be followed to extend the life of various age-groups.

Other circumstances in which people live very close to each other are observed in schools, universities, cruise ships and the navy, barracks, convents, and crowded slums that are common in the urban areas of some developing countries. In all these cases, people are more likely to be infected because of the unavoidable contact with other positive people.

Poverty and Inequality

Countries or communities with a high proportion of poor people (because the average national income per capita is low or is poorly distributed) face a higher risk of contagion. This happens in other types of crises (economic, financial) too. But in the case of Covid-19, poverty and inequality generate specific perverse effects. Because of the high degree of labour informality and the prevalence of daily work contracts, many people have to report to congested informal labour markets on a daily basis to look for a daily job and wage. This exposes them to a high number of contacts. Second, better off – and therefore better educated – people generally do 'smart work' from home, reducing in this way the number of potentially dangerous contacts (as observed empirically, for instance, in Argentina). And third, most of the poor in the cities purchase their food and other essential items in congested local markets where social distancing is not practised, as in the case of Lima, Peru (a city that accounts for over half of Peru's population). This is because they depend on receiving a daily wage. In addition, they lack refrigerators to conserve perishable food, and this forces them to go shopping daily in a crowded market that can be a source of contact and infection.

Latitude and Seasonal Changes

There is initial (if now disputed) evidence that the increase in infection rate has been higher in areas located between the 20th and 40th degree of latitude, which means basically in subtropical and temperate climates, like in Wuhan, Lombardy, New York, Madrid and so on. The virus does not seem to thrive in very warm climates. This view is now criticized by many who mention the recent increase in contagion in Brazil (that is characterized in many regions by a hot climate) and Peru. But this critique should be tested – *ceteris paribus* – i.e. assuming that all other determinants of Covid-19 have similar values than in the comparator country. But this is not the case in Brazil, a country characterized by a passive national Covid-19 policy that led President Bolsonaro to firing three ministers of health who wanted to change such an approach to deal with the disease.

Another aspect of the 'climate hypothesis' is that many virologists predicted a decline of infection rates in Europe during the summer. This did, in fact, happen, but it is unclear whether it was due to the temperature or other factors.

Prior Environmental Contamination

There are many (often inconclusive) studies on this, but it is plausible to argue that – *ceteris paribus* – a high pre-Covid-19 contamination of the air tends to increase the incidence of respiratory diseases for all age-groups and so weakens the people's resilience to airborne diseases. For instance, if we look at the pre-Covid map of CO_2 (carbon dioxide) and SO_2 (sulphur dioxide) incidence in the Po Valley (which includes the highly industrialized Lombardy and Emilia Romagna), we find that the pre-Covid incidence of chronic pulmonary diseases is higher than that in other less industrialized regions. The University of Bologna has also produced research which shows that the fine particulates produced by the exhaust fumes of cars can act as a 'carrier' of the virus (that does not fly all alone).

High Rates of Urbanization, Territorial Mobility and Domestic Migration

If you live and work in Mumbai (inhabited by ten to fifteen million people, depending on the time of the day), you are bound to run into many people on average. Milan has about two million people, but is surrounded by a very dense hinterland to which it is well-connected by a highly developed system of suburban trains, roads and highways. In brief, high rates of urbanization basically tend to increase the likelihood of contact among people and increase the potential for transmitting the virus. Urban density and territorial mobility can be proxied, for instance, by the number of kilometres of road and rail per square kilometre. If the value of such variables increases, the contact among people of different towns rises. An indirect proof of this proposition is given by Sondrio, a city with about 100,000 inhabitants, located only 70 kilometres away from Bergamo, the most Covid-19-affected city in Lombardy and Italy. The mayor of Sondrio was asked why the infection rate in his town was so low. He replied saying that his city is very difficult to reach by road and rail.Overall, in peri-urban areas, a 'high road and rail density' per square kilometre raises the likelihood of contact among people of different towns and the overall risk of contagion.

While a high degree of road/rail connectivity increases the potential for higher contact between people of nearby cities, places with a large number of returning migrants and students may also experience a higher risk of contagion as their travel to the place of destination often occurs in uncontrolled, stressful and unhealthy conditions. For India, estimates of migrant workers who were displaced because of a sudden and unplanned lockdown vary between five and thirty million. Apart from taking the contagion from a few urban centres to small towns and villages across the country, at least 173 migrant workers died in transit as they used most desperate means to reach home, and several others died of hunger (Table 9.2). In Italy, the government strongly discouraged the return home of students from the South studying in North Italian universities (as some of them were

Table 9.2 *Number of distress deaths caused by the lockdown and other Covid-related policies*

Category	Number of deaths
Death due to hunger/economic distress	288
Deaths of migrants in transit	173
Death due to police atrocities/retaliation	16
Lack of access to medical facilities	176
Lack of access to mental health care	19
Suicide/homicide due to fear/stigma	111
Deaths of addicts due to absence of help	83
Suicide because of separation from partner/family	14
Sexual assaults, domestic violence and honour killings	8
Deaths of providers of critical services	7
Other reasons	47

Source: https://coronapolicyimpact.org database, accessed 19 August 2020.

potentially positive). To this effect, the government drastically reduced the number of long-distance trains travelling from North to South Italy.

Health Approach Followed to Fight the Pandemic: Policy Commitment by Governments

We look here at the following three aspects of the problem.

Health preparedness

A factor that may reduce the incidence of the virus is vaccination against recurring viral diseases in the North and the South. In the Northern countries, the vaccination of people above 60 years of age against the common flu (which kills several thousand people every year) already covers 50–60 per cent of the target population in Italy, and has been shown to reduce the risk of contracting Covid-19. It is now recommended also for children. In countries of the South, vaccination against childhood diseases – BCG vaccine in particular – seems to be important for reducing the risk of contracting the Covid-19 virus later in life. This is a topic much debated nowadays in India and also in other developing countries where the full coverage of BCG has not been achieved, while its coverage is basically universal in the countries of the North, where tuberculosis has been eradicated in the past by vaccination.

Health approaches to the treatment of Covid-19

This point is further dealt with later in the chapter, but it is important to emphasize here that 'decentralized' approaches seem to be superior to a highly 'centralized' approach.

Overall national commitment to fight Covid-19

A third important policy factor concerns a country's overall commitment to combat Covid-19. This commitment ought to come from the central government, even where the implementation of practical measures depends on the regional authorities. The very high infection and death rates recorded in some countries (such as Brazil and the United States) likely are due, in part, to the weak commitment of their top political authorities to eradicating the disease. A series of unsupportive declarations by the national government for a universal lockdown in Sweden and the UK did not help either. These governments argued initially that it was more efficient to let the disease run its course. But both countries later changed this position. Global government commitment varies, of course, with the political cycle of each country, and it is difficult to identify a single variable that summarizes the degree of government commitment. One such variable could be, for instance, the number of viral tests carried out pe 1,00,000 people. But other measures have to be tried out.

Can Such Explanatory Models Explain the Differences in Infection Rates across Countries?

Can the model discussed above, which was initially developed fo the North, be used also for countries in the South, once account is take of the 'protective' and 'aggravating' factors evident in the countries of th South that are briefly reviewed below?

Protective Factors

In developing countries, the age structure of the population is sub stantially different than that of the advanced economies. In particular, th share of the population of over 80 years of age (who face a much highe death risk for biological reasons) is very low (around 1–2 per cent).

Second, the number of elderly persons living in infection-pron nursing homes is also very low, as extended family and other communit arrangements are still common, especially in rural areas. These arrange ments tend to reduce the number of contacts of a large number of th elderly living in narrow spaces.

Third, hotter climates may reduce contagion, although this view is now less accepted than before. The very high temperatures in Brazil are often cited in this regard, but before coming to conclusions, one should also consider that such a country lacks a national anti-Covid-19 policy that penalizes the slum and Indian populations who are dying in great numbers.

Fourth, except for urban slums, the environmental contamina tion (especially of the air) is less pronounced due to lower rates of indus trialization and the emission of noxious substances. Finally, except for large urban slums, population density and congestion (and therefore the number of contacts) may be less, although the nature of daily work and lack of refrigerators force people to travel to crowded parts of the city on a daily basis for food and other items, as noted in the case of Peru. In addition, in urban slums (which may accommodate 30–40 per cent of a city's population), overcrowding (and the risk of contagion) is endemic. Such problems do not exist in the still important rural areas, which enjoy some degree of self-protection in this regard. In a way, one could argue that the Southern countries may have a lower rate of infection because of these structural differences. But it must also be noted that their death registration system is less complete and only a (costly) survey could help disentangling these two effects.

Aggravating Factors

First, developing countries tend to have weak health infrastructure 1at often does not cover all areas of a country. It is argued, for instance, 1at low rates of child vaccination, including for BCG, may weaken people's nmune system in the long term. Second, the South is more affected by fall in incomes due to lockdown measures (and subsequent collapse of ;DP growth) introduced in the Northern countries to stop the pandemic. Jobody knows exactly, but the European Union will likely experience a ecline in GDP per capita of 8–10 per cent in 2020, resulting in a contrac- ion of all international transactions with developing countries. Thus, in he case of the latter, the indirect effect on death rates due to loss of income aused by a contraction of international transactions may well outweigh he direct impact due to the spread of the pandemic itself. People may not lie of Covid-19, but of reduced access to food and health services. Third, nany developing countries lack comprehensive social assistance cover- ıge in order to be able to compensate, if in part, the loss of earnings and ıousehold incomes of their citizens. True, in the 2000s–2010s there has ›een an important spread of cash transfer systems to the poor that covered, n the late 2010s, an estimated 900 million people worldwide, even if with arge regional variations. Thus, as noted, people in low-income developing :ountries may suffer more due to loss of income, growing poverty, mal- ıutrition, and stressful, forced return migration. The advanced countries ;hould be well aware of the knock-on effects on developing countries of neasures like their strict lockdowns and other restrictions introduced to ight Covid-19 domestically. True, the developed countries have the right to defend themselves from the pandemic, but they also ought to think about :he effects of their measures on developing countries linked to them through :rade, finance, tourism, migration and so on. In some cases, compensation provided by Northern countries may lead to a win-win situation. In Italy, for instance, during the Covid-19 pandemic, the government issued legal immigration permits to 400,000 formerly illegal migrants who can now find better paid jobs and remit home greater amounts of money.

Variations in Infection Rates within Countries of the South and North

In both the developing and developed countries, health and social policies play an important role in moderating or aggravating the incidence of the pandemic. To get an idea of the impact of social policies introduced at the sub-national level, one could, for instance, compare the situation of Maharashtra with that of Kerala in India. Maharashtra (capital, Mumbai) is possibly the richest Indian state on a per capita basis. It is endowed with a comparatively modern health infrastructure but cannot count on a capillary network of primary health care centres, while the lack of accompanying social policies to shelter the groups at risk (such as returning migrants has led to an increase in infection rates in and around Mumbai because of the limited reliance on an incomplete network of primary health care facilities. With the spread of the disease, the modern specialized hospital were overwhelmed by a large increase in the number of Covid-positive patients. The recovery rate was not high and by mid-May 2020, 1,390 deaths had been recorded (and this is certainly an underestimate).

Infection and death trends in Kerala have been quite different For several decades, Kerala has counted on a capillary network of private and public health care centres. Excellent results were achieved also in the fields of nutrition, education and labour policies. As a result of a large accumulation of human capital, many well-educated Keralites migrated to the Gulf to work in well-paid skilled or semi-skilled jobs. At the same time, many Indians from poorer states like Bihar and Uttar Pradesh migrated to Kerala, where minimum wages are higher than in the rest of India. Thus, in Kerala, the impact of the pandemic was moderated by reliance on a widespread system of primary health care centres developed over prior decades, and by a high number of tests per capita. Kerala also adheres explicitly to the World Health Organization's Covid-19 protocol (test, trace, isolate and support), and was helped in its efforts by a large number of health volunteers including students. As a result, by mid-May 2020, Kerala had reported 561 cases of Covid-19 and only four deaths. Of course, not everything is rosy, as there is now the return of a large number of migrants from the Gulf states (which have high average infection rates). To handle this emergency, the government has already requisitioned many hotels normally used by tourists. The Kerala government is also helping migrants from other Indian states to return safely to their communities by feeding them (three meals a day), providing temporary accommodation and sending them home by means of chartered trains. This is quite different from the long lines of migrants returning homes in other parts of India, where the migrants walk on the streets or along rail-tracks. Kerala thus protects its own people as well as any other group in need, and relies on a solid social infrastructure and the help of volunteers, respecting in this way the time-old political tradition of this part of India.

In the North, governments have adopted very different approaches to the fight against Covid-19. In many countries, health care and public expenditure are in the hands of regional (not central) authorities, that may therefore follow different approaches despite being part of the same country. Though health care in the advanced countries is also organized on three levels, in many states, the choice has fallen between a highly entralized system based on big, high-tech hospitals (at the third level of care) and a more decentralized approach. The centralized approach makes use of large and costly (and often privatized) facilities generally located in big cities. It has relied little on smaller territorial hospitals, many of which were closed 'for efficiency reasons' during the last two decades by conservative governments to save money, and because the health care model was basically pivoting on highly specialized public and privatized structures. But this choice has turned out to be inappropriate as the simpler territorial hospitals would have been very useful to identify people with mild symptoms at the beginning of the infection. These cases could have been followed up at home by travelling teams of doctors and nurses. These people were instead placed in large-scale hospitals filled to the brim with cases of advanced Covid-19 infection. There was also little tracing of prior contacts' of the infected people and little quarantine. In many cases, the big hospitals ran out of space, staff and equipment (see the column for Lombardy in Table 9.3).

The alternative – a more decentralized approach – makes greater use of all territorial health facilities, including at the primary and secondary levels of care, greater use of 'home care' of patients with mild symptoms assisted by a team of doctors and nurses who visit them regularly, greater testing and tracing, and greater voluntary self-isolation. A study done by the Hospital Gemelli in Rome compares the results of the two approaches in Lombardy and Veneto (Table 9.3). In view of their inferior results, over the last month, Lombardy has adjusted its approach towards fighting Covid-19, but much of the damage has already been done, as the death rate among people over 80 years of age has been extremely high

Table 9.3 *Results of centralized vs. decentralized health approaches in Italy*

	Lombardy	Veneto
Inputs		
ICU beds per 100 people	12.63	16.8
Rate of saturation of ICU beds (%)	103.0	36.0
Number of tests per resident population (%)	1.58	3.13
Outcomes		
Total deaths / Covid-19 deaths (%)	17.30	5.76
Incidence of Covid-19 deaths among people above 80 years	very high	high
Contagion among care providers (%)	5.4	12.8

(Table 9.3). As a result, Lombardy has had to import coffins from nearby Piedmont and bury people outside of the region. Likewise, the death rate among care providers has been extremely high (Table 9.3). As noted, the region of Veneto (capital, Venice) followed a more decentralized approach that has now become a blueprint for other regions of Italy and possibly for countries in the South.

Conclusions

This analysis leaves out several other factors that will have to be looked at carefully before policy conclusions are formulated. Most of the determinants of Covid-19 infection discussed in this chapter apply – if with very different intensities – to both countries of the North and of the South. The groups affected also vary. Also, while in the North, the large number of deaths recorded was a direct effect of Covid-19, in the South, an important part of the observed mortality was due to the indirect effects of the disease, i.e. to the loss of income induced by the contractionary measures applied in the North and the South to fight the pandemic.

The health approaches to fight the disease also have to be adjusted in view of the better outcomes recorded in Veneto in the North and in Kerala in the South. Had Lombardy followed the same health approach of Veneto, and all Indian states followed the 'Kerala model' to fight Covid-19, several thousand deaths would have been avoided.

The last problem that has to be discussed in greater detail concerns the impact of health measures (e.g., lockdown) introduced in the North on the economies and the Covid-19 death rates of the South. The North has, of course, a sacrosanct right to protect itself and to introduce those measures that are most efficient until a curative drug or a vaccine is discovered that will improve the health of Covid-19 patients all over. But it would make sense if the United Nations, the World Bank and other global economic institutions considered special programmes of assistance to compensate for the decline in resources experienced by the developing countries as a result of measures introduced by the North to stop Covid-19 in their countries.

The author would like to thank Frances Stewart for comments on a prior version of this chapter.

10

Look East, Not West

Comparative Lessons for Containing Covid-19 Contagion

Jomo Kwame Sundaram

Reviewing various experiences in trying to prevent or contain the Covid-19 contagion allows us to draw some lessons from how the pandemic has affected many societies. How have different types of policy responses been formulated? Essentially, political economy – more politics than economics – has been crucial in determining whether national authorities have been able to prevent or, failing that, contain the contagion. An 'all of government' approach has not only been crucial to ensure effective prevention or containment measures, but also for comprehensive 'whole of society' social mobilization.

First, differences in responses, particularly in relation to the initial outbreak, were important. The virus was first identified late in 2019 in Wuhan, for long the industrial hub of China during the twentieth century. Initially, the infections were presumed to be those of just another flu outbreak. Although local authorities in Wuhan may not have reacted to the new virus outbreak appropriately, national authorities intervened more appropriately, notifying the World Health Organization (WHO) at the end of 2019 and sharing genome sequencing information with the world two weeks later. This has been especially important for the later development of mRNA 'vaccines' and Covid-19 therapeutics.

This is necessary to emphasize because there is a great deal of confusion due to contradictory claims by media sources, and politicization of the virus outbreak. The Chinese authorities followed up by providing the genome sequencing of the virus to the world less than two weeks later. This has enabled a number of efforts to develop both cures and vaccines.

As with any multilateral organization, there is a WHO protocol to

---

Lecture delivered on 7 May 2020.

be followed. Eventually, after an official investigation team returned from China, the WHO declared Covid-19 an 'epidemic of international signifi cance' at the end of January 2020, four weeks after the initial discovery. This was actually most consequential, as its subsequent declaration as a pandemic in March 2020 really had much less operational significance for the WHO, an intergovernmental organization. There are now claims that information was suppressed by the Beijing authorities with considerable adverse consequences. And if there is *prima facie* evidence, the charges should be thoroughly investigated later.

Before going further, it is important to highlight certain different features of this viral outbreak. It is much more infectious than many other viruses, while the mortality rate is lower than for, say, the severe acute respiratory syndrome (SARS) epidemic of 2002–03. One big problem is that the virus does not lend itself to immediate detection. Available tests, especially during the first two to three months of 2020, could only identify the virus after about five days. Another much cheaper test, used by many poorer developing countries, could only confirm infection after about twice as long, i.e. ten to fourteen days. There are now new developments, which have potentially major implications. For example, in August 2020, a low-cost, fast and accurate saliva-based laboratory diagnostic test for infection was granted emergency use authorization by the US Food and Drug Administration (FDA).

There are multiple strains and mutants of the SARS-CoV-2 virus, which continue to spread geographically in unexpected ways. Strain B is the one found in China, apparently mutated from strain A, said to be from the US. Strain C is largely to be found in Europe. There is much specula- tion over the reasons for these distributions as well as for the apparently very varied rates of infection and fatality. There is also a great deal of speculation about possible cures, including those offered by homeopathy, traditional and alternative medical and pharmaceutical systems influential in various parts of the world.

Although several 'vaccines' are being developed, and some have been approved for conditional use, most provide partial immunization and none offers full immunity. Big data analysis and artificial intelligence have accelerated some research and development processes, but these will still require considerable time before a vaccine is universally and affordably available. Although several vaccine development firms initially pledged not to profiteer from the vaccine, intellectual property rights (IPRs) and exces- sive costs of tests, equipment, therapies and vaccines are now recognized as the major obstacle to ending the pandemic. Before the outbreak, the US government had been seeking to extend IPRs to naturally occurring ubstances termed 'biologics', which previously could not be subject to property rights, e.g., via the Trans-Pacific Partnership (TPP) Agreement. This is a contentious area with a number of recent trade agreements allowing IP of biologics. Potentially, for instance, the cost of insulin, naturally occurring in some mammals, can be significantly raised if such rights are successfully asserted by pharmaceutical companies.

Different Recessions, Different Lessons

The Covid-19 challenge raises a host of important issues. The nature of this crisis implies that it cannot be addressed by simply using a fiscal stimulus. The crisis has been massively disruptive from the supply side, which of course has important implications. Precautionary requirements, such as using face masks or 'physical', 'safe' or 'social' distancing, involve introducing a range of restrictions, particularly on social interactions, work processes and services requiring close interpersonal interactions.

The effects of the lockdowns have been massively disruptive, particularly for casual or daily-rated workers relying on daily sources of income in informal employment or even in the formal sector. There are also the petty, family or micro businesses. Supply chains, including credit lines, influence flows of funds which affect all businesses, albeit differently, depending on the nature of the business, the credit supply line, etc. Even recommendations using unconventional monetary measures have important limitations, especially when Covid-19 recessions involve supply-side and structural issues that are quite different from the challenges posed by financial crises.

It is important to recognize that different countries have responded to the contagion threat very differently. In East Asia and the state of Kerala in southwestern India, adequate early precautionary measures enabled them to contain the threat without resorting to 'stay in shelter' lockdowns. Sadly, the response in much of the rest of the world has been quite different with some national authorities dismissing the threat as a 'local' virus outbreak that does not threaten the rest of the world. Another view was that the contagion should be allowed to run its course, enabling populations to develop 'herd immunity'. This was the UK policy stance until the mid-March 2020 publication of the first study by Imperial College of London (ICL).[2] The ICL study projected a much higher fatality rate than previously presumed, shocking the Johnson government into changing UK policy. Sweden continues to maintain a modified herd immunity approach, although the authorities there effectively quarantine particularly vulnerable segments of the population.

It is sometimes said that East Asian countries and Kerala responded differently because of their recent experiences with viral outbreaks, which is quite important. Early suppression of information of the viral outbreak in Wuhan City by local authorities may have been due to ignorance in dealing with a completely new phenomenon involving a novel virus. Wuhan, a major industrial city, relies on commuting workers from three surrounding provinces. Thus the viral outbreak was not only in the city, but also involved commuters from surrounding provinces. Hence, the lockdown in China affected not only Wuhan, but also surrounding provinces where the contagion had spread. Other Chinese provinces were not subjected to lockdowns. This did not mean that nothing was done – appropriate and early precautionary and preventive measures were undertaken speedily by the authorities.

A WHO fact-finding committee sent to China emphasized that Chinese success in containing the outbreak was because of prompt early action and containment measures. The rest of the country was also urged to urgently take precautionary preventive actions. Workers in China have two major breaks annually, once in October, the so-called 'golden month', and the other for a week around the Lunar New Year, which fell on 25 January in 2020. The Chinese authorities dealt with the new threat by extending the usual one-week break to two weeks, from the last week of January into early February.

In much of the world today, right-wing ethno-populists, not progressive forces, are in ascendance. The fact that progressive forces have generally responded to the crisis reasonably well does not mean that most authorities will necessarily adopt these measures with democratic sensibilities. Some well-meaning colleagues have called for extraordinary wartime-like measures to address the crisis, but such responses have also become the pretext for repressive authoritarian actions. Hence, this recommendation needs to be reconsidered as right-wing populist, and other repressive regimes have used this as a pretext for instituting heavy-handed, harsh, even brutal measures.

South Korea had the second highest rates of infection and death in the early weeks of the outbreak. A significant cluster emerged around a secretive religious cult operating in Daegu. Although the Korean response to the outbreak was strong, they never introduced lockdowns. Many of the developing countries might not be able to emulate South Korea because of the high costs of the measures adopted (testing and monitoring). Until April 2020, Korea had the highest level of testing in the world, later exceeded by Norway and some other countries. Mass testing in South Korea was accompanied by tracing and monitoring. When infections were confirmed, efforts were taken to trace 'primary contacts' who had had face-to-face contact with the infected persons when believed to be infectious. This was done very effectively while ensuring that privacy is respected.

This has also been the case in Vietnam, which has been very careful about identifying patients by numbers rather than by name, except in one case involving a high-level official whom the Vietnamese government apparently wanted to use to demonstrate its even-handedness. The official was not allowed to get away after breaching its strict measures.

Hence, besides the three provinces around the Wuhan epidemic epicentre, there were no stay in shelter lockdown measures in East Asia. Without lockdown measures, Korea successfully contained and stopped the outbreak to 'flatten the curve'. It is generally acknowledged that different societies in different countries are differently prepared to cope with major crises. Flattening the curve refers to reducing new infections to contain the contagion so that the national health system is better able to cope.

If left completely unchecked, contagion is likely to spread exponentially. For example, in the case of China, the Chinese authorities deemed this impossible without lockdown measures in place in the three provinces surrounding Wuhan. In Korea, this could be achieved through mass testing, tracing and treatment of patients as well as other measures such as requiring the use of face masks and physical distancing – the matter could be handled without a lockdown. The same thing happened in Vietnam, except for a few infected communes out of hundreds. This is a time when targeting is appropriate and works well. Having a lockdown in a localized area effectively means quarantining the area. Simple measures adopted in many places in the world, including Kerala, a relatively poor state in India, have apparently been effective in checking the spread of the virus. While most countries have relief measures, Kerala's have been more biased to the most vulnerable.

Jair Bolsonaro, the current president of Brazil, has been 'outtrumping' Trump himself. Bolsonaro dismissed Covid-19 as nothing more than a flu virus, insisting that all the fuss was created by the media. Meanwhile, Brazil is rising rapidly in the international league of Covid-19 infection and death rates. New cemeteries have been opened and excavators are working round the clock to dig graves, expecting continued increases in deaths. Importantly, Bolsonaro has been at odds with Brazil's state governors. He even called for an army coup against his own government to strengthen centralized authority and eliminate the governors, as he expects to continue to be in charge after the coup. He has made little attempt to develop and implement a common national strategy.

After elections in Argentina, Alberto Fernandez, who was finance minister in the previous Cristina Fernandez de Kirchner government, became president in December 2019. He inherited a huge economic mess – an economy in recession, inflation exceeding 50 per cent, a poverty rate exceeding 40 per cent, and the currency falling by more than 60 per cent over 2019. He announced two priorities: first, improving the fiscal balance by increasing taxation; second, negotiating down the foreign debt. In March 2020, Argentina became the first Latin American country to decree a public health emergency in response to the pandemic. The new Fernandez government appointed a health minister to the cabinet, after the previous Macri administration had 'demoted' the post to that of secretary in the social development ministry. In Argentina, the policy measures reflect greater sensitivity to the plight of the most vulnerable, as in Kerala.

Unusually, Fernandez has engaged with all political parties; he declared the emergency in the presence of all political parties in the spectrum, in a show of national unity and to portray the effort as truly national. All the governors have been closely consulted on measures to be taken, including relief measures to be introduced. In a second display of national unity, Fernandez and other political leaders came out together to insist on new terms for sovereign debt resolution. Martin Guzman, the economy minister (there is no finance minister in Argentina), seeks new terms far less onerous than the previous Macri government had agreed to, in its ill-advised efforts to be more acceptable in international financial markets. Thus, the Fernandez government has seen the crisis as an opportunity to renegotiate the debt situation.

Clearly, adequate, quick and early action has been successful in most countries of East Asia. Two elements appear to be important for success: one, an 'all of government' approach, meaning involving all levels of government – the federal or central government as well as state and municipal governments, and the entire spectrum of the cabinet, with planning of measures involving the entire cabinet and not just the health authorities. Even in China, the lockdown was the exception, necessitated by early contagion after the initial viral outbreak. Once the national or central authorities learnt of this, they reversed the situation and acted decisively to stem the contagion in and around Wuhan, apparently successfully limiting its spread beyond.

There is one important exception that needs to be acknowledged, involving the rich island-state of Singapore, where there has been a resurgence of the virus, apparently because they ignored migrant workers' vulnerabilities. Singapore has a huge population of migrant workers with many living in crammed dormitory housing, and involved in many of the more 'dirty', 'dangerous' and 'depressing' jobs such as working in old-age homes. The resurgence of the epidemic after early success has been traced to the migrant workers, raising a lot of concern in other countries which have large migrant-worker populations. With the important exception of Singapore, adequate, early precautionary measures have been successful in East Asia.

Posing the Covid-19 dilemma as a choice between life and the economy is problematic. While big companies are generally much more politically influential in terms of bringing an end to 'stay in shelter' lockdowns and enabling employees to resume work, without adequate social protection measures, the fate of their dependants typically relies on their incomes as well. In an economy with strong linkages, many more livelihoods, typically of the vast majority in most developing countries, depends on resumption of paid employment, especially in the absence or limited availability of relief measures, often beyond the fiscal means of many countries. Nonetheless, the choice between lives and livelihoods remains a difficult one.

Thus, the design of lockdown measures becomes extremely important with coherent 'all of government' approaches necessary for 'whole of society' mobilization and cooperation. Transparency engenders community trust in the authorities. Lockdowns to restrict movements to reduce possible exposure to the virus need to be complemented by targeted testing and follow-up contact tracing, requiring community cooperation, not mass repression. If the authorities do not provide relief measures to compensate for loss of livelihoods, as in Kerala or Argentina, communities are less likely to cooperate, let alone actively support the authorities' measures, providing 'whole of society' cooperation with the authorities' 'all of government' efforts.

Covid-19 Recessions Different

The world economic contraction in the first half of 2020 was largely due to measures to contain or prevent Covid-19 contagion, restricting business operations and its many consequences, including reducing economic activity, output, incomes and spending. Covid-19 posed the cruel public policy dilemma of having to balance between livelihoods and averting infection, including the possibility of death. Therefore, lower worker and business incomes have reduced consumption and investment spending, and thus aggregate demand.

Covid-19 recessions have been quite varied and uneven, due to different circumstances and responses. Various aspects may bear some resemblance to earlier supply-side recessions, for example, those caused or worsened by post-war conversion of armaments industries, oil price shocks (in 1973, 1979, 2007, for example) and 'shock therapy'-induced 'transformational recessions' in 'post-communist' and other economies in the 1990s.

A general recession typically involves declines in many, if not most, industries, sectors and regions. Such output contraction typically implies underutilized production capacities, raising unemployment, albeit unevenly, during a general recession. A structural recession usually refers to falling output in one or a few related industries, sectors or regions, not sufficiently offset by other rises. Not all supply-side recessions necessarily involve structural transformation, especially if not deliberately induced or 'nudged' by government. A structural transformation – with 'unviable' activities declining as more 'competitive' alternatives grow – may not involve overall economic contraction if resource transfers, from declining activities to rising ones, are easy, rapid and low-cost.

Such resource transfers typically require 'repurposing' labour, as well as plant, equipment and other 'fixed capital' stock. Typically, unplanned or unmanaged structural transformations result in supply-side recessions as resources are withdrawn without being redeployed for alternative productive ends. Left to markets and corporate powers alone, such adjustments typically increase unemployment as industries become unprofitable – due to cost spikes, for example – and lay off workers. Growing unemployment lowers wages, although conventional wisdom insists that cheaper labour costs will induce new investments. Market resolution of such unexpected, massive disruptions is likely to be poorly coordinated, slow and painful, with high unemployment typically persisting for years thereafter. Alternatively, governments can guide, facilitate and accelerate desired changes with appropriate relief and industrial policy measures.

Slumps in travel, tourism, mass entertainment, public events, sit-down eateries, hotels, hospitality, catering, classrooms, personal services and other such activities have been due to physical distancing and other containment requirements and related precautionary behaviour. Such collapses will not be overcome with support, relief and stimulus measures as most such activities cannot fully resume soon, even in the medium term. Expansionary Keynesian fiscal and monetary policies to address collapses in aggregate demand have less relevance in addressing government-mandated restrictions intended to contain contagion and their many consequences, often unanticipated and unintended.

Of course, relief measures for those losing incomes can help mitigate the effects of the adverse supply and demand shocks involved. But much depends not only on direct, but also indirect, second- or even third-order effects, partly captured by Keynes's 'multiplier'. A necessary precondition for the multiplier to accelerate broader economic recovery is he prior existence of underutilized productive capacities and capabilities. Otherwise, increasing demand, enabled by easy liquidity, may simply raise prices when output and efficiency cannot be quickly increased profitably.

Many restructured economies, particularly those able to develop better or new productive capacities and capabilities, will emerge from the pandemic doing better than others. There are, and will be, greater need and demand for new as well as modified goods and services such as medical supplies, health facilities, care services, distance learning and web entertainment. Economies trying to adjust to the new post-contagion context – often termed the 'new normal' despite its likely dynamic and transformative nature – should optimally use industrial policy, or selective investment and technology promotion, to facilitate and expedite the desired restructuring by directing scarce resources from unviable, declining, 'sunset' industries with limited futures to more feasible, emerging, 'sunrise' activities with promising prospects. Enabling, incentivizing or even requiring needed resource reallocations can help overcome supply bottlenecks. China and other East Asian countries have already had some early successes in thus addressing their Covid-19 downturns.

All workplaces adversely affected by precautionary requirements will need to be safely reconfigured or repurposed accordingly. Structural unemployment problems, due to capabilities' shortages not coinciding with available labour skill supplies, can be better addressed by appropriate government–employer coordination to appropriately identify, raise and meet skill requirements.

Government policies, e.g., using official incentives, can thus encourage or induce adoption of desirable new practices, such as 'clean investments' for 'green' restructuring, for example, by using renewable energy and energy-saving technologies. Without such inducements, stimuli and support for desirable new investments, desired structural shifts may be much more difficult, painful and costly. Thus, the ongoing Covid-19 crisis should be seen as an opportunity to make much needed, if not long overdue, investments in desirable 'sunrise' industries, services and enterprises, including personnel retraining and capability enhancement as well as workplace repurposing.

Designing Relief, Recovery and Stimulus Measures

Following the initial shock from the Covid-19 pandemic, governments and central banks responded with massive injections of liquidity. Governments around the world reacted fast, with monetary and fiscal responses quickly accounting for significant shares of national output. With deficit financing actively discouraged by hegemonic neo-liberal financial pundits long in ascendance, bold fiscal measures were largely eschewed by much of the world. Many of the predominantly monetary measures pursued – especially in developing countries, particularly the so-called 'emerging markets' – largely failed to sustain consumption, let alone generate new job-creating investments.

Many measures were hastily conceived with recent financial crises and recessions in mind to contain the pandemic's economic contagion, typically injecting considerable liquidity, *inter alia* to prevent widespread bankruptcies, mass unemployment and protracted recession. Much of the money was directed to measures that have led to a Keynesian 'liquidity trap'. After failing to contain contagion through adequate precautionary measures, extended 'stay in shelter' lockdowns were deemed necessary, in turn precipitating recessions.

The long shadow of the financial follies of the last decade – enabled by 'unconventional monetary measures', especially in the North Atlantic economies, which retarded 'recovery' from the 2008–09 global financial crisis and the Great Recession which followed – seems likely to continue to hobble recovery, let alone contribute to progress. With improved understanding of the causes and likely extended duration of the slowdown, some policy-makers have reconsidered their earlier policy response measures. The unprecedented nature of the crisis has generated considerable uncertainty, discouraging household consumer spending and business investments as apprehensions encouraged holding cash.

Undoubtedly, much household and business liquidity, including additional resources made available by governments, was not spent due to uncertainty about the future and reduced spending options. Potentially available liquidity has not been fully utilized, as many interested and even needy borrowers were deemed uncreditworthy while those deemed creditworthy often bide their time before opportunistically making predatory acquisitions. Likely stimulus effects were further retarded by the limited multiplier effects of such liquidity measures. The early emphasis on liquidity provision appears to have enabled debt, inflation and financial speculation, keeping share markets buoyant while doing little to encourage the consumption and investment needed for recovery.

With firms preoccupied with economic uncertainty and continued economic vulnerabilities, investment and recovery have been delayed. In such a situation, government spending, investments and guarantees are needed to break vicious circles. Many countries have helped businesses by subsidizing wage and related costs on condition they retain employees. Meanwhile, income-contingent loans have been used to encourage consumer spending and desirable business investments – e.g., for renewable energy. Chinese municipal authorities have issued expenditure vouchers or coupons with expiry dates to buy certain goods and services to enhance consumption and thus aggregate demand in the short term.

Neo-liberal Economics Blocks Deficit Financing

As governments try to revive their economies after the debilitating lockdowns imposed following their failure to undertake adequate early precautionary containment measures to curb Covid-19 contagion, neo-liberal economists have been warning against needed deficit financing for relief and recovery. The range of deficit financing options has changed little since some were first legitimized by Roosevelt and Keynes in the 1930s, and used extensively to finance wartime government spending and post-war reconstruction and recovery.

First, debt financing has typically involved government borrowing. More recent understandings of sovereign debt stress the implications for most countries of borrowing either domestically or externally. For example, Japan's total government debt now greatly exceeds double its annual national income, but this is not considered problematic as most of the debt is domestically held by Japanese. Second, price controls, general or selective, may require subsidies. Price controls on extracted natural resources can also enable governments to capture resource rents to augment revenue. Third, widespread use of unconventional monetary measures since the 2008–09 Great Recession following the global financial crisis forced economists to reconsider earlier Friedmanite monetarist articles of faith about deficit financing by 'taxing' everyone via inflation. This has arguably even boosted 'modern monetary theory'.

Finally, an overvalued exchange rate has been favoured by elites who travel and purchase abroad, wanting strong currencies, which they portray as cause for national pride. After all, governments collect taxes in domestic currency but pay for international debt and imports with foreign exchange. However, a strong exchange rate only provides a temporary solution, worsening balance of payments difficulties in the longer term while also favouring consumers over producers and importers over exporters, besides encouraging consumption at the expense of savings. Increasing imports for consumption either deplete foreign exchange reserves or require external borrowing.

The ability of overvalued exchange rates to check inflation is doubtful as balance of payments deficits cannot be sustained indefinitely. Exchange rate-based currency board and stabilization arrangements in transition and developing economies are similarly problematic. Economies maintaining overvalued exchange rates have often experienced severe currency crises later. Quasi-nationalist development ideologies and weak elite opposition enabled many East Asian economies to use undervalued exchange rates to discourage imports and promote exports, with effective protection for import-substituting industries conditional on successful exports.

Neo-liberal commentators are once again warning against deficit financing. Instead of consistently counter-cyclical fiscal policies over the course of business cycles, they dogmatically insist on minimal annual budget shortfalls in the short term, and on balancing budgets by next year, regardless of the nature and duration of the recession. The stagnation of the last decade was due to the failure to reform adequately after the global financial crisis. Covid-19 recessions are undoubtedly different from recent financial crises, and will need bolder monetary, supply-side and industrial policy measures to catalyse and sustain economic relief, recovery and restructuring measures to address previous maladies and the post-lockdown malaise.

The crisis presents us with an opportunity to do better, to move forward. There is much to learn and do to progress, including abandoning the very modes of thinking which have led to the mess we are in. Exorcizing such ghosts of economic ideology from the past will be imperative.

Whither the 'New Normal'

The pandemic has exposed economic vulnerabilities building up for some time, especially since the 'counter-revolution' – against Keynesian and development economics in the 1980s – led to transnational corporation-led privatization, liberalization and globalization. As the world became more interdependent via trade, finance and communications, inequality and economic insecurity have waxed and waned unevenly, exacerbated by deregulation, reregulation, financialization and less public social provisioning, undermining public health and social protection.

Global economic prospects remain unpredictable, with uncertainties about the varied nature of pandemic recessions. Government responses have not only been diverse, but often poorly conceived due to the novel crisis and its ramifications. Impacts have varied with the contagion and policy responses, not helped by often confusing, if not misleading metrics. Such uncertainty is also reflected in the wide-ranging growth forecasts by major international organizations. The International Monetary Fund (IMF) has recognized the 'Great Lockdown' as due to 'self-imposed' contractions, leading to the 'worst recession since the Great Depression' (IMF 2020a). The Fund has supported government fiscal and monetary initiatives, declaring that it 'stands ready to mobilize its US$ 1 trillion lending capacity to help its membership' (IMF 2020b). The World Bank (2020) has also promised an additional US\$ 14 billion to help governments and businesses address the pandemic.

A March 2020 joint statement by G7 countries promised 'a strongly coordinated international approach', with no specific actions mentioned or forthcoming thereafter. Instead, countries have pursued their own divergent strategies, even banning exports of medical equipment. Meanwhile, the Trump Administration continued to prioritize 'America First' while undermining most multilateral institutions and even plurilateral arrangements, including those created by the US such as the G20. Already, G20 members have been dragged into US–China tensions, as the White House blames China for the pandemic and other American problems. Meanwhile Saudi Arabia, the G20 chair for 2020, is itself embroiled in its own political and economic quagmire, undermined by falling oil revenues, worsened by its oil price war with Russia.

Economic growth slowdowns, especially in manufacturing, services and trade, started prior to the Covid-19 outbreak. Initially, the pandemic's economic effects were expected to be short-term as factories and offices were closed, and strict 'stay in shelter' lockdowns were enforced to stop the contagion. The drop in economic output as the epidemic began and spread to industrial hubs has had international repercussions, with supply chains disrupted. Such supply disruptions have engendered and interacted with prolonged, wide-ranging demand shocks as Covid-19 crisis-induced policy responses and other uncertainties reduced consumption and invest- ment spending, slowing economic growth and undermining employment.

Almost 2.7 billion workers, around 81 per cent of the world's workforce, work and earn less due to the Covid-19 recession, with those in lower middle-income developing countries losing most. And almost 1.6 billion in the informal economy are in the hardest hit sectors or significantly impacted by lockdown measures. The longer the lockdowns persist, the greater the economic disruption and adverse impacts as the effects spread via trade and finance linkages to an ever-growing number of countries, firms and households.

Governments have adopted various monetary and fiscal measures to try to revive and sustain economic activity. Such measures include cash transfers to households, extending unemployment insurance or social security benefits, temporary deferral of tax payments, and increasing credit guarantees and loans to businesses. Early 'stimulus packages' assumed that the 'pandemic shock' would be short-lived and easily reversible. Even now, they largely ignore addressing the unsustainability, inequality, instability and other vulnerabilities of their economic, social and ecological systems.

Unconventional monetary policies have not addressed liquidity problems due to truncated business turnover. Increased liquidity provision has instead been captured by better 'credit risks', even fuelling inflation while doing little for the most vulnerable and needy, deepening pre-Covid-19 inequalities. Even before Covid-19, such policies were already creating stock-market bubbles and facilitating share-holder value extraction instead of financing investments in the real economy, thus contributing to growing inequality. Central banks have not been able to repair their balance sheets or draw back excess liquidity for fear of financial sector collapse, thus increasing fragility by injecting more liquidity, increasing speculation and fuelling inflation.

Without better planned coordination, relief measures for households and businesses were often wrongly portrayed as fiscal stimulus packages while output has been constrained by lockdown enforcement. Despite cuts in government expenditure, especially for public health and social protection, there was little political will to increase progressive taxation. Mounting government debt, already at historically high levels prior to the pandemic, has not helped. Instead, earlier tax cuts have increased public debt, while the failure to improve fiscal capacities after the 2008 global financial crisis has meant eschewing productivity-enhancing public investments, boosting revenue via progressive taxation, and strengthening universal health coverage and social protection.

Design and implementation of policies matter, crucially affecting likely effects. As countries prepare for recovery, governments must ask what 'recovery' can and should mean. To address the many problems, recent and accumulated, should not mean a return to 'business as usual'. Workplaces and social spaces – where people meet, socialize, shop, etc. – have to be redesigned and repurposed to meet precautionary public health requirements, such as physical distancing. The unsustainable, financialized and grossly unequal pre-Covid-19 economy needs to and can be fundamentally transformed. Covid-19 policy responses have rarely addressed deeper prior malaises, such as stagnant or falling productivity growth and declining labour remuneration. 'Industrial policy' policies to address global warming, resource exhaustion and other sustainability problems need to be considered and pursued.

This chapter draws heavily on various articles published by the Inter Press Service (IPS). Most of this work was undertaken in collaboration with others, including Anis Chowdhury, Vladimir Popov and Nazihah Muhd Noor. I am greatly indebted to, but do not implicate them in what I have included here. I am also thankful to Inesh Ramanathan for his help in revising this chapter for publication.

Notes

1 When a PHEIC (Public Health Emergency of International Concern) is declared, the WHO Director-General issues temporary recommendations under the 2005 IHR, including obligations for countries to provide sufficient public health rationale and justification to WHO about any additional measures beyond what WHO recommends. This is critical to ensure that the international response is evidence-based, measured and balanced, so that unnecessary interference with travel and trade is avoided. The WHO also recommended that the global community should provide support to low- and middle-income countries to respond to the threat, and to facilitate their access to diagnostics, potential vaccines and therapeutics.

2 'Report 9 – Impact of non-pharmaceutical interventions (NPIs) to reduce Covid-19 mortality and healthcare demand', 16 March 2020, https://www.imperial.ac.uk/mrc-global-infectious-disease-analysis/covid-19/report-9-impact-of-npis-on-covid-19/ , accessed 29 August 2020.

References

Chowdhury, Anis and Jomo Kwame Sundaram (2020), 'Kerala Covid-19 Response Model for Emulation', Inter Press Service, 9 April, https://www.ipsnews.net/2020/04/kerala-covid-19-response-model-emulation/, accessed 29 August 2020.

_____ (2020) 'Vietnam Winning New War Against Invisible Enemy', Inter Press Service, 14 April, https://www.ipsnews.net/2020/04/vietnam-winning-new-war-invisible-enemy/, accessed 29 August 2020.

_____ (2020) 'Covid-19: Brazil's Bolsonaro trumps Trump', Inter Press Service, 21 April, http://www.ipsnews.net/2020/04/covid-19-brazils-bolsonaro-trumps-trump/, accessed 29 August 2020.

_____ (2020) 'Argentina Responds Boldly to Coronavirus Crisis', Inter Press Service, 5 May, https://www.ipsnews.net/2020/05/argentina-responds-boldly-coronavirus-crisis/, accessed 29 August 2020.

_____ (2020) '"Passing the Buck" Becomes Reckless "Conspiracy Blame Game"', Inter Press Service, 12 May, http://www.ipsnews.net/2020/05/passing-buck-becomes-reckless-conspiracy-blame-game/, accessed 29 August 2020.

_____ (2020) 'Politics, Profits Undermine Public Interest in Covid-19 Vaccine Race', Inter Press Service, 26 May, http://www.ipsnews.net/2020/05/politics-profits-undermine-public-interest-covid-19-vaccine-race/, accessed 29 August 2020.

_____ (2020) 'Reviving the Economy, Creating the "New Normal"', Inter Press Service, 16 June, http://www.ipsnews.net/2020/06/reviving-economy-creating-new-normal/, accessed 29 August 2020.

Faiola, Anthony, Sudarsan Raghavan, Max Bearak and Terrence McCoy (2020), 'Public Health Experts: Coronavirus Could Overwhelm the Developing World', *The Washington Post*, 1 April, https://www.washingtonpost.com/world/the_americas/coronavirus-developing-world-brazil-egypt-india-kenya-venezuela/2020/03/31/d52fe238-6d4f-11ea-a156-0048b62cdb51_story.html, accessed 29 August 2020.

G7 (2020), 'G7 Leaders' Statement', 16 March, https://www.whitehouse.gov/briefings-statements/g7-leaders-statement/, accessed 29 August 2020.

Gage, Anna and Sebastian Bauhoff (2020), 'Health Systems in Low-Income Countries Will Struggle to Protect Health Workers from Covid-19', Center for Global Development, https://www.cgdev.org/blog/health-systems-low-income-countries-will-struggle-protect-health-workers-covid-19, accessed 29 August 2020.

Greenwood, Michael (2020), 'Quick and Affordable Saliva-Based Covid-19 Test Developed by Yale Scientists Receives FDA Emergency Use Authorization', *Yale News*,

15 August, available at https://news.yale.edu/2020/08/15/yales-rapid-covid 19-saliva-test-receives-fda-emergency-use-authorization, accessed 29 August 2020

International Monetary Fund (IMF) (2020a), 'World Economic Outlook: The Grea Lockdown', Washington, D.C.: IMF, April.

_____ (2020b), 'Policy Steps to Address the Corona Crisis', https://www.elibrary.imf.org doc/IMF007/28916-9781513536927/28916-9781513536927/Other_formats Source_PDF/28916-9781513537122.pdf?redirect=true, accessed 29 August 2020

Jomo Kwame Sundaram (2020), 'Covid-19 Straw Breaks Free Trade Camel's Back', Inte Press Service, 19 May, http://www.ipsnews.net/2020/05/covid-19-straw-breaks free-trade-camels-back/, accessed 29 August 2020.

_____ (2020), 'Economic Ghosts Block Post-Lockdown Recovery', Inter Press Service 9 June, http://www.ipsnews.net/2020/06/economic-ghosts-block-post-lockdown recovery/, accessed 29 August 2020.

Malley, Robert and Richard Malley (2020), 'When the Pandemic Hits the Most Vulnerable Developing Countries Are Hurtling Toward Coronavirus Catastrophe', *Foreign Affairs*, 31 March, https://www.foreignaffairs.com/articles/africa/2020-03-31 when-pandemic-hits-most-vulnerable, accessed 29 August 2020.

Nazihah Muhamad Noor and Jomo Kwame Sundaram (2020), 'East Asian Lessons for Controlling Covid-19', Inter Press Service, 26 March, https://www.ipsnews. net/2020/03/east-asian-lessons-controlling-covid-19/, accessed 29 August 2020.

Popov, Vladimir (2020), 'Why Some National Health Care Systems Do Better than Others', Inter Press Service, 13 May, http://www.ipsnews.net/2020/05/national-health-care-systems-better-others/, accessed 29 August 2020.

Popov, Vladimir and Jomo Kwame Sundaram (2020), 'Covid-19 Recessions: This Time It's Really Different', Inter Press Service, 4 June, http://www.ipsnews.net/2020/06/ covid-19-recessions-time-really-different/, accessed 29 August 2020.

Stiglitz, Joseph E. and Hamid Rashid (2020), 'Which Economic Stimulus Works?' Project Syndicate, 8 June, https://www.project-syndicate.org/commentary/stimulus-policies-must-benefit-real-economy-not-financial-speculation-by-joseph-e-stiglitz-and-hamid-rashid-2020-06, accessed 29 August 2020.

World Bank (2020), 'World Bank Group Increases Covid-19 Response to $14 Billion to Help Sustain Economies, Protect Jobs', Press Release, 17 March, https://www.worldbank.org/en/news/press-release/2020/03/17/world-bank-group-increases-covid-19-response-to-14-billion-to-help-sustain-economies-protect-jobs, accessed 29 August 2020.

World Health Organization (WHO) (2020), '2019-nCoV Outbreak is an Emergency of International Concern', 31 January, http://www.euro.who.int/en/health-topics/ health-emergencies/international-health-regulations/news/news/2020/2/2019-ncov-outbreak-is-an-emergency-of-international-concern, accessed 29 August 2020.

11

Thailand and Covid-19
What's Happened and What's Next

Pasuk Phongpaichit and Chris Baker

The first case of Covid-19 in Thailand was reported on 13 January 2020 – a female Chinese tourist from Wuhan. It was then widely predicted that Thailand would be the third worst hit by the virus, after China and Hong Kong, largely because of the large number of Chinese tourists – 11 million in 2019.[1] In the first few weeks, before controls were imposed, around a million Chinese may have passed through Thailand. But today, Thailand accounts for only 0.01 per cent of global deaths from the virus – less than 60 people over almost four months. In the United States, around that number are dying from the virus every hour.

In this chapter, we discuss why the impact has been relatively mild in Thailand, and what might be the social and economic impact from here onwards.

What's Happened: The Virus
There are two pieces of background information that are important here. First, Thailand has a relatively strong public health system. Its origins date back to the 1970s, when medical students were radicalized in the student movement.[2] Since then a strong commitment to *public* health has been institutionalized in the medical profession. In 2001, public health activists persuaded the government to launch a universal health care (UHC) system which gave virtually everyone near-free access to health care. There have been attempts to cancel, scale back or cripple the UHC, but activists have defended it brilliantly.

From the late 1970s, activist doctors also established a network of village health volunteers (O-So-Mo),[3] loosely modelled on China's bare-

---

Lecture delivered on 4 May 2020.

foot doctors,[4] to extend the reach of primary health care. This network now has about a million people (in a country of 70 million). According to the World Health Organization (WHO), this unique network played 'a crucial role' in tracking and tracing during the SARS (severe acute respiratory syndrome) epidemic in 2002–03 and bird flu epidemic in 2005–06. This public health system has been fundamental to the relative success of managing the virus (Treerutkuarkul 2008).

Second, Thailand has returned to military rule after coups in 2006 and 2014, becoming the only country in the world ruled by a government installed by coup. In 2019, an election was held to return to democratic parliamentary rule, but the electoral process was criticized for being non-transparent in multiple ways and ensuring that the military clique remained in power. As a result, some people have questioned the government's legitimacy and its competence.

Through January and February 2020, the spread of the virus was slow in Thailand. There were probably several reasons for this. First, though medics are reluctant to confirm this, the virus does not seem to like heat and dryness. Through February, Thailand was hot and dry. Second, as in much of Asia, social etiquette avoids touching. Third, much of Thailand had been covered with PM2.5 haze for several weeks, meaning that many people were already wearing masks, and the availability of masks was relatively good (there was a shortage only for a short time, maybe a week, as a result of panic buying and hoarding). Fourth, the network of health volunteers spread information about basic prevention techniques down to the grassroots level. Fifth, in treating serious cases of Covid-19, the doctors applied their experience from SARS, including using anti-retrovirals borrowed from HIV-AIDS treatment (an approach since proven to be effective). Sixth, there was probably an element of sheer luck. This virus is very fickle, hitting hard in some places but not in others. Thailand had no hot-spots in this early phase.

Against this background, there was a debate over policy. The medical lobby, which had experience with SARS and bird flu, wanted to impose an early lockdown, following the examples of China, Korea and Vietnam. But politicians opposed any measures that might injure the economy and, in particular, the huge tourist industry (international tourism accounts for about 12–15 per cent of GDP). As such, measures were relatively light – testing people arriving at airports, encouraging people to wash their hands often and so on.

From the beginning, the public health authorities adopted two critical policies. First, they did contact tracing on every infected case, using ooth public health officials and the health volunteer network. To give just one example, a Thai returned from Pakistan, passed through the airport tests without showing any symptoms, then died overnight on a train to southern Thailand, and was found to be positive.[5] Within a couple of days they had traced most of his contacts on the plane, through the airport and on the train, including people who stood near him on the railway platform, identified from security cameras. The health volunteer network made this tracing quick and efficient. Second, they adopted a policy of transparent public information, giving daily accounts of new infections, classified by the source of infection (from abroad, contact with a known case, etc.), and details of each death. The full information was available on websites set up by the Department of Disease Control.[6]

In early March 2020, two hot-spots appeared. The first was at a boxing stadium on 6 March. From this one event, around 150 people were infected. These included a good-looking young actor, whose equally attractive partner was soon also ill. Their media exposure, despite government attempts to smother them, greatly increased public awareness of the danger of the virus. A second hot-spot appeared in a nightlife area. At the same time, there was a growing number of new infections stemming from people crossing the borders, including Thais returning from abroad, visitors to border casinos and foreigners.

At this point the government reacted, in somewhat panicky fashion. Between 17–25 March, it closed down Bangkok nightlife; imposed a standard lockdown, closing all retail and service businesses except food; imposed a night-time curfew; shut down airports, first partially and then completely; and finally passed an emergency law giving government back the absolute powers it had lost in the 2019 election.

In general, people cooperated. Within days, supermarkets and convenience stores obliged people to wear masks, have their hands sanitized and be shot by a temperature gun before admission to the store.

The graph of daily new infections shown in Figure 11.1 comes from the Ministry of Public Health website, where data are updated daily. Thailand shows the same pattern as other places that adopted this policy, including Wuhan. After the lockdown, infections continued to rise for two to three weeks, then turned downwards. The steepness of the decline depended on the strictness of the lockdown (moderate in the Thai case – no full curfew, partial internal travel restrictions).

By the first week of May 2020, seven weeks after the lockdown, daily new infections had dwindled to single figures. Since then, the graph has been almost flat. The number of infections is certainly undercounted

Figure 11.1 *Daily new Covid-19 patients, February–May 2020*

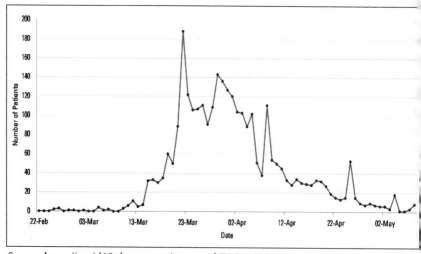

Source: https://covid19.th-stat.com/, accessed 7 May 2020.

because the testing regime has been passive (see below), but the methodology has been constant and so the shape of the graph is credible. There is no reason to believe the figures have been manipulated.

About two-thirds of all cases have been in Greater Bangkok. The other concentrations have been in the tourist resorts of Phuket and Pattaya, and in the far south (especially Yala) where people can cross a very porous border with Malaysia, and from where people have continued to go on pilgrimage. Outside these areas, the numbers of infections have been small. The public health volunteers played two key roles: they educated people about protecting themselves against the virus (wearing masks, washing hands, social distancing); and they helped to track-and-trace anyone known to have been in contact with the virus. Their role has been crucial.

The early Thai strategy focused on tracing the contacts of known infections. This strategy has one weakness in the case of this stealthy virus: people may be infected and be capable of passing on the infection to others while they themselves have minimal or no symptoms. How large the number of asymptomatic carriers may be is a matter of debate. In Iceland, where a 6 per cent sample of the whole population was tested, 43 per cent of those who tested positive had no symptoms (Harmon 2020). Other tests in other countries on smaller samples have found higher proportions of asymptomatic carriers. In early April, a lobby within the Thai public health community predicted that Thailand might have 200,000 or more asymptomatic carriers, and pressed for a more aggressive policy of testing (personal communication). The policy-makers argued that this method was unnecessary and expensive, and that test kits were hard to come by. But in Vietnam – a country comparable to Thailand in many ways – the authorities had adopted a policy of pro-active testing from late January, including developing domestic production of kits and smartphone contact apps, and claimed to have a record of zero deaths from the virus.

Around 12 April, the local public health authorities in Phuket began more proactive testing. By the end of the month, the central authority also changed policy and announced that it had begun 'active case finding', which meant identifying at-risk segments for conducting random tests, and also commissioned a local firm (Zenostic) to produce test kits. The target segments included people crossing the southern border, migrant labour (especially after the experience of Singapore, where, in early April, there was a surge of cases among migrant workers in Singapore, peaking at 1,400 a day[7]) and prisoners. From 1997, the public health authorities had developed a branch of the health volunteer network to cover the large (two to three million) migrant population, largely from Myanmar, and had used this network to ensure that migrants were educated about the dangers of the virus and cooperated in tracing.

By the beginning of June, Thailand had adopted a fortress strategy. Local transmissions had been controlled. Anyone entering the country was tested and then required to undergo a fourteen-day quarantine. Hotels were commandeered to accommodate them. From then until now (28 July 2020), there have been no cases of local transmission. On most days, a few cases are found among those in quarantine. Total infections are around 3,300, under 0.01 per cent of the global total, and total deaths around 60.

What's Next: The Impact

Even though the epidemic has been relatively mild compared to many other countries, the economic and social impact would be heavy and long-lasting, simply because the Thai economy is so exposed to the outside world. Exports were 67 per cent of GDP in 2018, and 40 million tourists visited in 2019.[8]

The Thai central bank predicted the economy would shrink −5.3 per cent in 2020, later raised to −8.1 per cent.[9] Both estimates are probably overoptimistic. The nearest guide to the possible impact is the Asian financial crisis of 1997–98, which began in Thailand and was severest here. The Thai economy shrank by 14 per cent over eighteen months; 2 million people in the formal economy were immediately made unemployed, and many more in the informal economy lost their livelihood; thousands of businesses went bankrupt; and 5 per cent of households dropped below the poverty line.

But four factors softened the impact in 1997–98. First, the tradi tional social safety net provided by family, community and village worked rather well. Millions of people left urban areas and returned to a rural origin. Most of them were first-generation migrants and still had good claims on the support of family and community. Second, because Thailand is a food-surplus community, almost no one faced starvation as a part of the severe distress. Third, government delivered relief, in the form of grant aid and micro-credit, directly to local communities, in order to avoid delay and leakage of working through the bureaucracy. Fourth, because the crisis was confined to Asia, the rest of the world pulled Thailand and other countries out of the crisis relatively quickly. When prices fell, exports increased, and people arrived to have a cheap holiday or buy up a bankrupt business at bargain prices.

This time will be very different. First, over the two decades since the Asian crisis, the urban population has greatly increased, maybe dou-bled. Many more of the workforce are more distanced from a rural origin – they were perhaps born in an urban area, and have less access to the traditional social safety net. Second, Thailand is entering the second year of an El Nino drought. Though the drought appears less severe than earlier predicted, people who have returned to a rural home and begun planting rice have been warned that there may not be enough water to bring the crop to harvest. Third, this government is centralized, bureaucratic and top–down-minded. It has no faith in its own people. It has no idea how to support the local economies to take the strain. And finally, the rest of the world will not help to pull Thailand out of the crisis, but in fact will make it worse. Mismanagement of the virus in the US, UK and elsewhere will ensure that the damage to the global economy is deeper and more long-lasting. Demand has plummeted. Global supply chains are breaking down. Shipping companies and airlines face bankruptcy. Tourists will not be returning soon.

The kind of lockdown implemented in Thailand on 26 March 2020 has had a very heavy impact on the economy, and especially on the urban informal sector – small shops and service businesses, vendors, casual and day labour. Something like 13–15 million people may have immediately lost their livelihood. There was also a heavy impact on farmers who pro-duce goods such as fruit for export. Exports were disrupted, and prices dropped steeply.

The two-fifths of total households at the bottom of the income pyramid have negative savings, meaning they have no savings or are already in debt. So, the loss of income meant immediate distress. Within days of the lockdown, long lines appeared at organizations offering aid, especially food. The government has probably not had any involvement in distributing food since the Second World War.

While Thailand has excelled in constructing a public health system, other forms of social security are very weak. In the early 2000s, the government made some beginnings, but subsequent military governments have favoured targeted, discretionary systems which depend on identifying those in need.

Soon after the lockdown, government offered monthly hand-outs of Baht 5000 (approximately US$ 170) for three months to households that could prove they had lost their employment or livelihood. On the day the scheme opened, 20 million people attempted to apply, crashing the application website. The government announced that only 9 million qualified for the hand-out (and at one point reduced the scheme to a single month, but had to renege), causing widespread anger. Many from the informal sector faced difficulty providing the required proof of loss of livelihood and handling the electronic application system. The government allowed those rejected to appeal. Other provisions in the package included a moratorium on debts to state institutions and support for SMEs (small and mid-size enterprises). Subsequently, the government added a hand-out to farmers. Around a million formal sector workers qualified for emergency unemployment benefit under the social security scheme, but over half were told to wait because the computer system failed. Eventually, 15 million people benefited from the Baht 5000 hand-out. But after three months, the scheme expired, with no extension or replacement.

From the beginning of May 2020, government began to ease the lockdown, first by allowing small shops and businesses to begin operation while laying down rules to ensure that social distancing was maintained. It launched a track-and-trace app (Thai Chana), requiring people to login at all formal shops and institutions. From early June, the lockdown was further relaxed, even allowing nightlife to reopen under some limitations. But strict controls on the border remained. The country had become a fortress. Inside the fortress, the virus is no longer a threat. But the walls have to be defended against chaos beyond. The local economy is stuttering back to life, but the external economy, on which Thailand so heavily relies, is still kept at arms' length.

There is no sign yet of a strategy to manage the longer-term slowdown stemming from the global crisis. China is likely to be the first major economy to revive, and this will have a positive effect on the Thai economy, though posing some political difficulties. The larger question is whether the remaking of the world economy by the Covid-19 crisis will render obsolete the strategy followed by the Thai economy for the past four decades (exports, foreign direct investment, tourism). If the major economies bring more manufacturing home, institutional investors concentrate more on their domestic markets and tourists venture less far afield, Thailand's old sources of growth will disappear.

Already before the Covid-19 crisis, there was debate on the soundness of the government's economic strategies of continuing to promote tourism and FDI (foreign direct investment) in high-tech industries, given that Thailand's growth rates had been lower than that of its ASEAN (Association of Southeast Asian Nations) neighbours for about a decade. Countries like Vietnam and Indonesia have become more attractive to foreign investors because of their younger labour force, larger markets and more stable politics. Critics also point to the impact of the open strategy on the environment, and the failure to resolve Thailand's inequalities in income and wealth. Dissident economists argue that Thailand needs policies which cultivate local sources of growth by reducing monopolies, reforming the tax system, shifting power away from the centre, improving social welfare programmes, enhancing the quality of education, and confronting global warming, which is already causing higher incidence of droughts and floods.

Some Conclusions

In Europe, the health services are being rightly cheered for their work during this crisis. In Thailand, they deserve the same applause but are not getting it, because their work is in the past or in the background, not in front of TV cameras. Two key factors account for the relative mildness of the outbreak in Thailand: first, the efforts of medical activists, extending over half a century, to create a *public health system* with universal coverage and with exceptional reach due to the network of health volunteers; and second, the qualified success of the medical lobby in negotiating with politicians over policy.

However, the economic and social impact is another matter. We are in uncharted territory. The disruption of the global economy is on a scale not seen since the Great Depression and Second World War. How societies will react is impossible to predict. There is strong possibility that the government in Thailand, as elsewhere, will seize this opportunity to strengthen authoritarian rule and minimize changes to the status quo. But big crises are also big opportunities to achieve major shifts in policy. By late 2020, the Thai government will have run out of money for outdoor relief. The fiscal space will have disappeared, and monetary policy will have little impact. The only way to maintain some economic momentum will be to mobilize the resources that are repressed by heavy centralization of power and the prevalence of monopolies in the economy. The current political leadership is unlikely to recognize this reality. But in the end, the Thai elite can probably be trusted to do what is necessary to save itself. And in this case, that may require radical change.

An earlier version of this paper is posted as 'Thailand and COVID-19: What's Happened and What's Next', *CSEAS Newsletter*, 78: TBC, available at https://covid-19chronicles. cseas.kyoto-u.ac.jp/post-025.html/.

Notes

1. Ministry of Tourism and Sports, https://www.mots.go.th/mots_en/more_news_new.php?cid=330, accessed 24 August 2020.
2. In 1976, when the authorities cracked down on the student movement in Bangkok, several medical students were among those who took refuge in the forest bases of the Communist Party of Thailand. From 1980, several of them returned under amnesty arrangements. They were instrumental in forming a Rural Doctors Club, which promoted a proposal for a volunteer network to deliver primary health care and basic health education at the grassroots. In 1978, Prime Minister General Kriangsak Chamanan embraced the policy of primary health care. In 1981, he met with some of the medical activists and adopted their plan for a volunteer network.
3. The Thai name for the network is Asa Samak Satharanasuk, universally known by the acronym O-So-Mo, sometimes written as Aor Sor Mor.
4. In China, a network of village-level workers to deliver primary health care was developed from the 1930s. They were more systematically organized after a speech by Mao Zedong in 1965. See Fang (2012).
5. 'Passenger with Covid-19 Dies on Train', *Bangkok Post*, 1 April 2020, and other reports on TV and online sources.
6. ddc.moph.go.th/viralpneumonia/eng/index.php; covid19.th-stat.com/en, accessed 31 May 2020.
7. https://www.voanews.com/covid-19-pandemic/how-singapore-flattened-covid-curve-among-migrants, accessed 24 August 2020.
8. Ministry of Tourism and Sports, https://www.mots.go.th/mots_en/more_news_new.php?cid=330, accessed 24 August 2020.
9. https://www.boi.go.th/index.php?page=economic_overview, accessed 24 August 2020.

References

Fang, X. (2010), *Barefoot Doctors and Western Medicine in China*, Rochester, New York: University of Rochester Press, 2012.

Harmon, Amy (2020), 'Why We Don't Know the True Death Rate for Covid-19', *New York Times*, 17 April, https://www.nytimes.com/2020/04/17/us/coronavirus-death-rate.html, accessed 18 April 2020.

Treerutkuarkul, Apiradee (2008), 'Thailand's Unsung Heroes', *Bulletin of the World Health Organization*, vol. 86, no. 1, January, pp. 1–8, https://www.who.int/bulletin/volumes/86/1/08-010108/en/, accessed 24 August 2020.

12

The Indian Economy Before and After the Pandemic

C.P. Chandrasekhar

Despite deploying diversionary rhetoric, the NDA (National Democratic Alliance) government has not been able to conceal two aspects of the Indian economic situation. The first is that the Indian economy is in a deep crisis, with the Covid-19 shock only intensifying a recession that had engulfed it even before the pandemic. The second is that while a crucial driver of the pre-pandemic recession was the extreme inequalities that characterize a class- and caste-ridden patriarchal society, the recession itself and the crisis precipitated by the effects of the pandemic and the government's response to it have hugely aggravated those inequalities in ways that will remain true for the long term.

The Economy Before the Pandemic

Revised estimates of GDP (gross domestic product) for 2019–20 released at the end of January 2020[1] made it clear that growth in the *pre-Covid lockdown year* 2019–20, as captured by a national income data series which in any case exaggerates the size and pace of expansion of the economy, was down to 4 per cent, the lowest since the new GDP series was launched. Since the centre's recognition of and response to the pandemic occurred in the last week of March 2020, this slowdown clearly pre-dates the Covid-induced crisis.

Pre-Covid-19 discussions on that growth slowdown attributed it to demand compression, reflected in sharply falling off-take of commodities ranging from capital goods to cars and biscuits. A long view must trace that demand compression to the failure of successive governments pursuing the capitalist path to address the extreme asset inequalities, and consequent

Lecture delivered on 29 April 2020.

income inequalities, that characterized Indian society. Moreover, after 1991, accelerated liberalization accentuated those inequalities by allowing further asset concentration (especially in the non-agricultural sector), withdrawing redistributive fiscal interventions, and engineering income redistribution in favour of the rich through regressive taxation policies and explicit and implicit transfers. Agriculture languished, not so much because of poor production performance, but because prices for farm produce remained depressed and the government's minimum support prices failed to provide a remunerative floor. Underemployment was high and most jobs were precarious. Agricultural and industrial wages recorded sluggish growth or even declines in real terms. And petty producers found it increasingly difficult to eke out a decent livelihood from their occupations. The adverse effect that this had on growth, by depressing mass-consumption demand and new investment in productive activities, was compounded by the effects of trade liberalization on domestic production and adherence to the neo-liberal tenet that proactive state spending financed with borrowing had to be reined in at all costs.

The long-term crisis these trends had triggered remained concealed however in the years after 2003, when large capital inflows from abroad, facilitated by financial liberalization, increased the volume of liquidity in the system. The increased liquidity triggered a credit boom, which financed not just consumption spending and housing investment, but large capital-intensive investments by large corporate groups, especially in the now deregulated infrastructure sector. It hardly needs emphasizing that growth of this kind led by private, debt-financed spending and riding on a credit bubble is not sustainable. That fact however was suppressed by the financial sector in general and the banking sector in particular, which concealed evidence of large volumes of non-performing assets resulting from debt defaults, using legitimate and illegitimate means. When that strategy was no more feasible, recognized defaults or non-performing assets spiked, forcing banks to provide for the losses, with resultant erosion of their balance sheet positions. This forced them to cut back on lending in order to forestall any further losses, resulting in a waning of the credit boom and of the growth process riding on that bubble. The fundamental weaknesses characterizing the Indian development path – failure to generate a mass market for consumption goods by redressing gross asset and income inequalities, and inability to finance much needed government expenditures by appropriating a part of the surpluses accruing to the private sector resulting in dependence on debt-financed spending – asserted themselves, and the system reverted to the long-term normal of low growth. To make matters worse, even as the recession overwhelmed the economy, the Modi government adopted the misguided and/or irrational policies of demonetization and a disruptive goods and services taxes (GST) regime intensifying the crisis.

The Fiscal Crisis

The unwillingness of the government to give up its fiscal conservatism in the wake of recession only deepened it. Provisional estimates from the Controller General of Accounts of actual revenues collected in financial year 2019–20, or the fiscal year that ended March 2020, point to an erosion of revenue receipts of crisis proportions. As compared with the original budget estimate of Rs 19.6 lakh crore, and a revised estimate (or late-in-year projection) of a lower Rs 18.5 lakh crore, actual revenue receipts are currently placed at just Rs 16.8 lakh crore. This implies that the actual figure is more than 14 per cent short of projections in the first budget of the second Modi government, and 9 per cent short of the projection (revised estimates) for financial year 2019–20 in the budget presented by Finance Minister Nirmala Sitharaman in February 2020. The revenue shortfall has meant that the centre's revenue receipts grew by just 2.9 per cent in 2019–20 as compared to the previous fiscal year, which implies that real revenues (adjusted for inflation) have in fact fallen. This deceleration in revenue growth occurred in a year of which only about a week fell in the lockdown period, so that the serious revenue shortfall was a pre-Covid phenomenon and cannot be blamed on the sudden stop induced by the pandemic.

Given the government's obsession with realizing unrealistic fiscal deficit targets, this compression of revenue growth has meant that the centre's dependence on exceptional transfers from the Reserve Bank of India (RBI) and on receipts from sale of public assets to meet even routine expenditures has increased significantly. When these 'exceptional' sources of receipts fall short of expectations, as happened in 2019–20, meeting even unambitious expenditure plans requires window-dressing of budgetary figures. On the ground, capital expenditures and welfare expenditures, including on health, would have fallen even relative to woefully inadequate budgetary allocations.

Underlying this fiscal mess is the failure to mobilize adequate resources through taxation at a time when the need is for substantial additional resource mobilization. A casualty of the business-friendly taxation stance of the NDA government has been a substantial loss of buoyancy with respect to direct tax generation, with tax revenues stagnating in nominal terms despite the low levels of the centre's direct tax to GDP ratio and rising income inequality in the country. Net direct tax collection, or gross direct taxes adjusted for tax refunds, rose marginally in nominal terms from Rs 13.17 lakh crore in 2018–19 to Rs 13.56 lakh crore in 2019–20. The factor dominantly responsible for this trend was the decision, in the midst of a demand recession, to seek to stimulate the economy with corporate tax concessions, announced in September 2019.

That September 'stimulus' took the form of a huge reduction in the corporate tax rate, from 30 per cent (or an effective rate of 34.61 per cent after surcharge and cess) to 22 per cent (or an effective rate of 25.17 per cent), for domestic companies that do not avail of tax incentives or exemptions. New domestic manufacturing companies incorporated on or after 1 October 2019 will pay corporation tax at the reduced rate of 15 per cent (which is an effective rate of 17.01 per cent), so long as they do not avail of incentives and exemptions. And the minimum alternative tax (MAT) applicable to companies that do avail of incentives and exemptions was reduced from 18.5 per cent to 15 per cent. This is a huge bonanza, which dominantly explains the contraction in direct tax revenues.

The second contributor to the compression in tax revenues is the limited buoyancy of indirect tax revenues garnered through the centre from goods and services tax (GST) imposts. In fact, in four out of twelve months of 2019–20, central revenues from GST were lower than the sum collected during corresponding months of the previous year. Overall, the centre's revenues from GST rose by 8 per cent in 2019–20, despite the lower-than-projected base level in 2018–19. To recall, the government had promised the states a 14 per cent annual increase in revenues from a base-level GST estimate, failing which they were to be compensated with collections from a special cess. This suggests that, at the minimum, the centre too would have expected a 14 per cent growth in GST revenues. The 8 per cent realized in 2019–20 was therefore way short of expected revenue growth. The GST regime was launched in July 2017. So the argument that teething troubles and initial glitches in implementation of a new 'game-changing' measure are responsible for shortfalls in GST receipts no longer apply. Clearly, the GST regime has proved a failure, even while it has substantially curtailed the limited space that was available for states to increase their 'own tax revenues', in pursuit of an unrealizable 'one nation, one tax' goal. That failure is now haunting the centre as well, besides severely damaging the fiscal position of the state governments.

The poor performance with respect to corporate tax revenue generation and generation of revenues from GST is a fall-out of the shift to a neo-liberal policy regime. A defining feature of such a regime is a lenient corporate tax structure, ostensibly aimed at incentivizing private investors and unleashing the 'animal spirits' they are presumed to possess. That also explains why, when a demand recession is dampening investment and curtailing growth, the government decides not to spend to revive demand but hand over money to the corporate sector with tax concessions, which firms will not divert to investment in depressed market conditions.

The GST too is a neo-liberal measure. The United States had a role to play in the spread of the value added tax (VAT) that inspires GST. The Shoup Mission to occupied Japan after the Second World War argued for its introduction.[2] Subsequently, USAID (United States Agency for International Development) promoted VAT and sought to popularize the system through financial and technical assistance to the developing countries. All through that period, the US government was unwilling to implement the system at home. Later, the World Bank and the International Monetary Fund (IMF) played a role in pushing the system. More than half the countries that introduced VAT in the twenty years starting 1991 did so on the basis of advice and assistance from the IMF's Fiscal Affairs Department. Thus, the spread of VAT does seem to have a lot to do with the transition to market fundamentalism and market-friendly polices starting in the 1980s.

Once these neo-liberal shifts on the taxation front began to adversely affect government revenues, within a neo-liberal fiscal framework of caps on fiscal deficits or spending financed with borrowing, a corollary was sluggish government spending and lower growth. That sets up a feedback loop, with low revenues which curtails government spending reducing growth, which then reduces revenues further, for any given level of fiscal buoyancy or responsiveness of revenue growth to income growth. Revenue growth shrinks both because neo-liberal fiscal reform reduces fiscal buoyancy *and* because growth itself begins to fall.

These trends have other external effects. Neo-liberal governments seek to address sluggish revenue growth with the short-sighted measure of selling profitable, revenue-earning public assets to obtain what are euphemistically termed 'non-debt creating capital receipts'. As the fiscal crisis intensifies, dependence on privatization receipts increases. The central government pursued that trajectory successfully in 2018–19, when, as compared with budgeted receipts of Rs 80,000 crore from privatization, the government actually managed to mobilize close to Rs 95,000 crore, hawking profitable assets and riding on a buoyant stock market. But as growth falters, so does investor enthusiasm for public equity or the firms themselves. In 2019–20, the government hiked budgeted receipts from privatization to Rs 1,05,000 crore. But as the economy slowed, it managed to mobilize only a little more than Rs 50,000 crore.

The picture is now clear. As the government gave up its role as development leader within a neo-liberal growth strategy, growth rode n a credit bubble. With that bubble going bust and precipitating non-performing assets in the banking system, the credit-led boom gave way to a slowdown. The neo-liberal fiscal response curtailed government revenues and expenditures further. Growth fell sharply, and so did revenues. In the event, the government was trapped in a fiscal crisis and the economy in a recession.

The Covid-19 Shock

It was an economy and government in these straits that were hit by the Covid-19 shock. Initially, it appeared that the coronavirus had put economic decision-makers and their advisors in a kind of no man's land. In the absence of either a cure or a preventive vaccine, the virus, which quickly moved across frontiers, overwhelmed underfunded and/or unprepared health systems. This made national isolation – through closures of borders and aggressive intra-border social distancing culminating in lockdowns – the widespread means of addressing the effects of the pandemic.

As expected, this meant a sudden stop in economic activity. Even without lockdowns, with trade and global value chains disrupted, production was adversely affected because of loss of market access or shortage of raw materials. With airports closed, flights banned and even domestic transportation restricted, the travel and tourism businesses were crippled. Social distancing and full-scale lockdowns then shut down production and closed a host of businesses. Masses of workers lost their jobs, especially given the rise in the share of casual and precarious employment in recent decades.

Unofficial estimates from the Centre for Monitoring Indian Economy (CMIE) placed the unemployment rate at close to 25 per cent in April and May, when the lockdown was most intense. Without jobs and already at the margins of subsistence, overexploited migrant workers at lower ends of the job market engaged on terms with no security of employment and no social security were reduced to dependence on crowded soup kitchens and community shelters.

The developments affected both supply and demand. With production chains broken, factories shut down and businesses forced to close, the supply of a range of goods and services, barring those considered essential, was suddenly blocked. This had its spin-off effects on upstream and downstream sectors. Even suppliers of essential goods, facing problems in transportation and distribution, curtailed production.

This supply shock soon translated into demand compression for energy and for most goods, especially an opaquely defined large set of 'non-essentials'. With incomes and earnings curtailed or wiped out, consump-

tion demand fell. The halt in production cut demand for intermediates
And with capacity idle and economic activity disrupted, investment froze
This was an unusual situation. In the past, exogenous supply-side shock
that reduced production and availability, such as the effects of adverse
weather conditions on monsoon-dependent agriculture, were limited to
a few sectors and a few regions in the country. This unevenness allowed
for quick action that transferred goods from surplus to deficit regions
Where national reserves could not address such shocks, trade came to the
rescue, with national supply enhanced through imports from abroad. In
this crisis, with the Covid-19 infection present worldwide, there was much
less flexibility. With social distancing as a global guideline and with stringent lockdowns in different cities, regions or countries restricting almost
half the world's population to their homes, production shortfalls were
globally widespread and amplified by their transmission through global
value chains. Moreover, trade was limited as transportation links were
cut off or weakened. This led to a synchronized reduction in production
and supply, except for essentials, which too were flying off the shelves in
many locations.

Implications for Policy

This situation was idiosyncratic from a policy point of view.
Normally, in capitalist economies, crises are driven predominantly either
by demand constraints or by supply constraints and shortfalls, with the
former being the norm. This calls for a counter-cyclical, expansionary
response from the state, which in the face of demand inadequacies does
not, like the private sector, hold back on investment spending, but expands
both consumption and investment spending to revive demand, reduce unu-
tilized capacity and kickstart private investment. But with both demand
and supply constrained under Covid-19, it was not clear that this was the
right option. Would an increase in spending not run up against blocked
production and supply, and worsen the situation with inflation?

However, the perspective behind that question was misplaced.
The lockdown was not a cure for the pandemic but a means of preventing it from galloping at a pace that would overwhelm health systems. So,
spending for the following reasons was imperative:

(i) to ramp up testing, tracing and isolation to contain the infection;
(ii) to substantially enhance and improve hospital facilities; and
(iii) to protect health workers and doctors.

Moreover, the lockdown itself results in a sudden stop in economic
activity, leading to large-scale unemployment and pushing informal sector

businesses and small and medium firms to bankruptcy. Hence it is imperative that the state protects all in need of basic necessities through direct provision of essential goods free of cost, as well as through money transfers to substitute for a part of the lost earnings. To support that effort and simultaneously sustain the viability of agriculture, large-scale procurement at reasonable prices is a must. It must also ensure that the huge informal sector and small business entities that do not have the reserves and the wherewithal to stay afloat and restart business as and when normalcy returns are provided the support needed to survive. This would involve not just credit but subsidies and transfers, so that, whenever the time comes, individuals and businesses would be in a position to return to managing their economic lives. Finally, expenditure would be needed to ring-fence essential economic activities so that they can continue to function and revive in the midst of the pandemic. Once all this is ensured, spending to boost demand and accelerate the recovery can be effective and is needed. In sum, the issue is not whether the government should step up spending, but by how much and in what areas.

The government's policy response cannot but entail a sharp increase in expenditure to cope with the medical fall-out and the 'sudden stop' in a wide range of economic activities imposed by the pandemic. That response had to come primarily from the centre, which has far greater fiscal flexibility than the state governments, whose revenue receipts are under strain for multiple reasons and are subject to stringent borrowing limits. Not surprisingly, many countries across the world opted for large stimulus packages, combined with monetary easing and a lowering of interest rates, to help households and businesses access liquidity and stay in place during the worst phase of the pandemic. But without the fiscal push, the lockdown can at most postpone the health emergency, and monetary measures can only help relatively stronger players.

That a fiscal push was not seen as the dominant component of the crisis response became clear when the Reserve Bank of India made its initial intervention with an off-cycle, emergency announcement of a monetary policy package. This package included a significant 75 basis-points reduction in the policy (repo) rate, a cash reserve ratio (CRR) reduction that freed liquidity and allowed banks to lend more, and permission to banks and non-bank financial companies to postpone payment of the next three equated monthly instalments (EMIs) on a host of loans including housing, auto and durable purchase loans.

This monetary policy push is related to the conservative fiscal stance. An important component of the economic policy perspective that advocates fiscal conservatism is a stress on the role of monetary policy in macroeconomic management. When inflation is moderate and the economy is in recession, or growth is slow, it is argued that central bank intervention injecting cheap liquidity at extremely low interest rates through measures like 'quantitative easing' is the way to drive recovery and growth. It is this perspective that has determined policy in the developed nations during recession years since the 2008 financial crisis, with limited or marginal impact. The real effect of this injection of cheap liquidity was an asset-price bubble in financial and real estate markets, which has been only partially corrected even after the coronavirus shock. Yet, the grip of finance has meant that there has been little deviation from these unconventional monetary policies for more than a decade.

A similar emphasis on monetary policy in the current situation in India, reflected in the RBI's Covid-19 response, also would not work. If production is stalled because of the effects of the crisis and demand is falling because many are being deprived of their wages and earnings, pumping money into the system is unlikely to serve any of the government's purposes. Banks are unlikely to lend to those without the means to service such debt. At most, some who need marginal support to prevent default on debt and producers who need some credit to last through the worst of the shock may be backed. But even they would get the promised support only if the banks take up the options offered by the RBI's policy initiatives. Burdened with non-performing assets (NPAs) and expecting more loan defaults due to the crisis, they may prefer to go slow on credit provision. Attempting to outsource part of the effort to address the crisis to the banks was unlikely to yield significant results, as proved to be the case.

In practice, the government chose a rather damaging and ineffective policy mix. A severe lockdown was imposed early, all of a sudden with just a few hours' notice. Business froze, workers lost their jobs, many could not survive more than a few days and could not avail of the only social security they had, which was to return to their families in the villages from where they had come, since transport links were shut down. Large numbers had no option other than to walk or cycle hundreds of miles in the middle of summer. The lockdown was combined with monetary measures aimed at increasing the flexibility of banks and non-bank financial companies to provide credit, which was unlikely to be effective since banks were already saddled with large volumes of non-performing assets.

Callous Fiscal Conservatism

On the fiscal front, after much delay, the finance minister unveiled a package on 26 March 2020. A close look made clear that the package was like a hastily put together and incomplete laundry list, woefully inadequate even as an initial response. To summarize, there were five broad components the package claimed to include. The first was a set of measures aimed at reaching essential food requirements to those who just cannot access or find it difficult to access these through the open market. The second was to quickly put money into the pockets of chosen sets among the poor, so that they can meet essential expenditures. The third was to facilitate economic activity of the self-employed, assuming they can undertake them in the near future, by giving them access to liquidity via credit channels. The fourth was to provide financial assistance to the state governments, which are the principal agencies working to contain the spread and mitigate the effects of the virus. And the fifth was to support the frontline medical workers, doctors, nurses and paramedics who are addressing the health impact of the virus at much personal cost.

As part of the first of these components, the government declared that it would provide, free of cost, the 800 million beneficiaries of the National Food Security Scheme, 5 kilograms of rice or wheat per person per month and 1 kilogram of pulses per household, for the next three months. (This was extended to another five months on 30 June 2020.) This was in addition to the 5 kilograms they were eligible to access on payment through the public distribution system (PDS). Beneficiaries of the Ujjwala scheme were also to be provided one free LPG cylinder per month for these three months.

The elements constituting the second component of the package included making an ex-gratia payment of Rs 1,000 per individual to poor senior citizens, widows and the disabled, and transferring an even smaller sum of Rs 500 each to 200 million accounts held by women under the Pradhan Mantri Jan Dhan Yojana (a national mission for financial inclusion). Besides, the government brought forward to 1 April, payment of the first instalment of three instalments of Rs 2,000 to be paid to 87 million farmers under the PM Kisan scheme. It also allowed organized sector workers who are covered under the Employees' Provident Fund (EPF) Scheme to avail of a non-refundable advance amounting to 75 per cent of their contribution or the equivalent of three months' wages, whichever is lower. In addition, the government promised to cover the contribution due to EPF from both employers and employees in companies with less than 100 workers for three months. Finally, it announced an increase in the daily wage to be paid for employment under the Mahatma Gandhi National Rural Employment Guarantee Scheme (MGNREGS) by Rs 20 – from Rs 182 to Rs 202.

Signalling the third component was a single announcement that the ceiling on loans without collateral, available in principle to self-help groups (SHGs), is to be raised from Rs 10 lakh to Rs 20 lakh. Elements of the fourth component were bald announcements that states can use funds from the Rs 31,000 crore available under the Building and Other Construction Workers' Welfare Fund to provide relief to workers in that sector who are badly affected, and from the District Mineral Fund for financing medical initiatives. And finally, in the fifth component, the government recognized the work being done and risks being taken by health workers, by providing them with medical insurance of Rs 50 lakh each.

Four features undermined the value of the package. First, the best of its components fell short of what was needed and what was potentially possible in the given circumstances. Second, some of the measures announced could not be implemented given lockdown conditions, and therefore did not deliver benefits during the period when they are needed most. Third, many elements of the package were not new initiatives but a mere extension or rescheduling of benefits available under schemes that were already in place. Finally, there was nothing in the announcement which indicated how exactly the government – using the potential benefit from the lockdown of delaying an expected explosion in infection and disease rates – was going to either protect frontline workers dealing with the crisis, or ramp up facilities to deal with those requiring to be tested and needing treatment. These features made the package a half-hearted response to an unprecedented health, economic and humanitarian crisis. It was almost as if the government felt that having imposed a lockdown, only marginal interventions were needed to address the crisis.

Perhaps realising the inadequacy of its first stimulus effort, the government announced a second package in May 2020, followed by two more. They were in character similar to the first in terms of their essential features, and involved an increasing reliance of off-budget measures with no real fiscal effort to back them.

The crisis resulting from the pandemic was severe because it affected both demand and supply in the economy. With the population locked down and economic activity near frozen, the flow of incomes to unorganized workers and even some formal sector employees, and of earnings of small and medium businesses and agricultural producers, had stopped. This meant that there were many – such as informal sector workers, especially poor migrant workers – who have little means to meet their essential requirements, and there were others who were having to hold back on consumption because their incomes had shrunk and savings eroded.

Simultaneously, as a result of the sudden stop in economic activity, stocks in some sectors were dwindling, were being held back in others because of hoarding, and in yet others, were not being transported and delivered in adequate quantities where needed. So, despite reduced demand, the prospect of shortages confronted even those who had the wherewithal to buy and consume.

This unusual crisis, the intensity of which is still to be gauged, required a huge outlay of physical and financial resources, the magnitude of which had to be decided without consideration of principles the government may adhere to in normal times. But undeclared considerations seemed to be holding the government back. A crucial component of the package announced was doubling the quota of rice or wheat available through the PDS to around 80 crore beneficiaries from 5 to 10 kilograms a month, and providing a kilo of free pulses to somewhere around 16 crore households. But restricting the access to foodgrain to only those holding the required cards not only deprived those, such as migrant workers, who are known to be excluded from the scheme, of the benefits of the measure, but also those who may not be eligible to be enrolled in the scheme when circumstances are normal but had been pushed into a dire situation by the impact the crisis had on their livelihood, and needed the support. Some way of including such sections, or universalizing access, must have been found. When a belated effort was made to reach out to those excluded, complaints were rife that the measure was barely implanted.

Moreover, given the crisis, there is no reason why the government could not have considered providing all 10 kilograms available to each beneficiary free of cost; for three months, that would have required around 25 million tonnes of grain. The government was then sitting on a huge amount of foodgrain stock, with some of it undoubtedly rotting, and was expecting to procure large quantities of rabi wheat because of a good crop. According to the prevailing buffer stock requirements, the Food Corporation of India (FCI) is required to have, as on 1 April 2020, a total of 16 million tonnes of rice and wheat as operational stock to service the PDS, and an additional 5 million tonnes as a strategic reserve, making for a total of 21 million tonnes. As of that month, stocks with the government stood at around 60 million tonnes.

So, even if the requirement for the three months had been distributed immediately, stocks would have been above buffer requirements. This physical resource could have been deployed not just to provide individuals and households with a reasonable quantity of free grain, but also to ensure supplies to a vastly expanded initiative to provide cooked meals to the homeless, the destitute, and migrant workers displaced from work and seeking to return home. But this opportunity seems to have been lost, even while images of return migrants – walking home and thronging locations in the hope of finding transportation – flooded the airwaves. The most favourable explanation for this failure would be that the government did not want to outlay the finances required to support the operation for fear of widening its fiscal deficit. And that would not be a reasonable justification in the midst of the unprecedented and still evolving crisis.

What is disconcerting is that even the niggardly push on the food front appeared positive when compared with what was available in the rest of the package. When a crisis of unprecedented proportions throws a large number out of work and leaves them without an income, the obvious solution is a direct income transfer that allows them to manage through the crisis and protect themselves as best as they can. In a city like Delhi, where even the official minimum wage for unskilled workers is close to Rs 15,000, a transfer to take account of an absence of incomes should aim to cover at least half that sum. The fact that the shortages that were resulting from the lockdown were pushing up prices suggests that it should be even more. So, Rs 7,500 per month per eligible adult was a reasonable floor to target, with the scheme being made applicable to individuals registered under different schemes of the government without a protected source of income. What we had instead was a one-time Rs 1,000 *ex gratia* payment for the most disadvantaged, and a one-time transfer of Rs 500 to poor women with Jan Dhan accounts. That, definitely, was little more than tokenism.

The increase in the ceiling on loans without collateral for SHGs was also a non-starter, to say the least. When all services and production units other than those engaged in essential services are closed, and when production is expected to contract even after the lockdown is lifted because of severely depressed demand conditions, expecting poor women organized in SHGs to borrow in order to launch or expand businesses is to stretch the imagination.

This suggests that the Rs 1.7 lakh crore figure as the size of the relief effort was an exaggeration. But that figure too, amounting to less than 1 per cent of GDP, was far from adequate. Even estimates favourable to the government place the actual fiscal effort in all stimulus packages together at around 1.5 per cent of GDP.[3] Meanwhile, the finance minister graciously allowed states to use resources that were already at their command through the Building and Other Construction Workers' Welfare Fund and the District Mineral Fund to provide relief and to finance testing, containment and treatment. The states probably did not need the permission, at least in the case of construction workers. The inclusion of these in the package appears to have been a means of sidestepping requests from the states, which largely drive the effort to contain the virus attack and mitigate its medical and economic fall-out, for more resource transfers.

Centralizing Power and Decentralizing Action

In fact, among the many damages wrought by the inapposite central government policy response to the Covid-19 pandemic in India is the one on the fragile framework of economic cooperation between the centre and the states. It is clear that the real task of mitigating the effects of the pandemic on the health and lives of citizens has fallen on the states. That is inevitable. As India prepares to lift the lockdown to stall the economic collapse it has caused and face the inevitable spike in the number of Covid-positive cases, 'the key to success . . . would be the preparedness of local governments in suppressing and managing outbreaks at the community level', as stated by David Nabarro, the World Health Organization's Special Envoy on Covid-19. Only state governments and decentralized governance structures can handle the task of managing the pandemic.

Yet, the centre has been presenting itself as leading the battle against the virus. Two moves have been central to that propaganda offensive. The first was the legal sanction it gave its self-assumed role of leader, by declaring the pandemic a disaster and invoking provisions of the Disaster Management Act. Armed with those powers, it promptly resorted to the issue of mandatory, but frequently revised, 'guidelines', followed by transporting central teams to monitor the performance of ostensibly recalcitrant state governments. There was to be no doubt as to who was calling the shots. The second move was to declare, with no preparation and warning, a stringent nation-wide lockdown, covering badly affected and unaffected parts alike, which had hugely adverse effects not merely on the economy but on the livelihoods and lives of the poorest sections, especially migrant workers.

Setting aside the debate on whether such actions were justified, the least that could be expected of an agency that wants to concentrate in its hands the emergency political powers that it claims are needed in the midst of this crisis, was that it also shoulder the collateral responsibilities. Principal among the latter was the responsibility to hugely hike expenditures from its own budget and to transfer substantial additional resources to the states faced with collapsing revenues at a time when their expenditures were rising sharply, since they are the ones called upon to address the Covid-induced crisis on the ground.

Most states have made requests for large transfers from the centre. Since it is the states that have to carry much of the burden of dealing with the crisis, the centre must give priority to mobilizing and transferring a large proportion of the additional resources needed by the states to them. This support is crucial because, as noted, even prior to the Covid-19 crisis, over 2019–20 as a whole, slowing growth and a failed GST regime had led to shortfalls in states' share in central taxes of more than Rs 1.25 lakh crore, and had reduced states' own tax collections by 1.6 per cent relative to the previous year. This meant that many states were approaching or even exceeding their fiscal deficit target limit of 3 per cent. With revenues collapsing starting April 2020, this tendency intensified. Yet, central fiscal support was near-completely absent, to the extent where state governments were being required to pick up food from the FCI at market prices. And the centre was not even willing to cover the rail fares of migrants departing from different states as they return home because they have no jobs, no incomes and no places to stay.

The state which has been the most successful in addressing the pandemic, among those prone to its spread because of international travel by students, workers and tourists, is Kerala. With a well-developed public health system and experience in dealing with the Nipah virus, it was also the one state that could appropriately plan to contain the pandemic. Kerala assessed that in the first instance it would need to spend an additional Rs 20,000 crore on containment and relief. Other states, much larger in size, had provided estimated expenditures that were much less, but would have to significantly step up their budgets as the war on the pandemic was waged.

These were huge sums that needed to be spent at a time when not only was support from the centre missing, but their own revenues had collapsed. Delhi obtained Rs 320 crore as revenues in April 2020 as against Rs 3,500 crore in the same month the previous year. The corresponding figures for Kerala were around Rs 150 crore and Rs 1,500 crore respectively. Moreover, the states were facing difficulty borrowing their way out of the crisis. To start with, there are strict limits set on their borrowing relative to their state domestic product. But more important, when they chose to frontload borrowing permitted over 2020–21, they found that there is not much enthusiasm for state government bonds in the market, pushing up interest rates for borrowing by Kerala, for example, to close to 9 per cent. With revenues collapsing, the centre not offering the required support and interest rates soaring, state governments that must respond to the pandemic are trapped in a fiscal crisis.

The easy way out is for the Reserve Bank of India to print money and buy into the bonds of state governments at relatively low rates of interest, or for the central government to borrow from the central bank and make transfers to the states, which is the better option. Even conservative economists who normally oppose such 'monetization' of government deficit-spending now agree that this is the only way to go. But neither the central bank nor the government that *de facto* controls its decision-making is willing to accept the obvious.

What is more, in the context of the pandemic-induced crisis, the centre decided to deprive states of their legitimate dues. As per the GST Act, for a period of five years after the transition to the GST regime, states had to be compensated for any shortfall in revenues relative to what they would have garnered under the old system. It had been agreed that the shortfall was to be computed relative to a trajectory where state revenues grew by at least 14 per cent every year, starting from a base value computed for 2015–16. It is clear with hindsight that even before the Covid-19 pandemic, when the centre's revenues were falling because of a combination of a recession and unwarranted corporate tax concessions, it had decided to revisit its commitment to compensate the states for shortfalls in GST revenues. Delays in transferring not just the compensation but also regular IGST (integrated goods and services tax) revenue shares were pointers to the new mood. Then the pandemic struck, affecting the revenues of both the centre and the states. Around five months later, in a move that governments in opposition-ruled states declared a betrayal, the centre announced that in financial year 2020–21, it would not fully compensate the states for the shortfall in revenues from GST. Claiming that the compensation commitment was applicable only to revenue shortfalls resulting from 'GST implementation', the centre held that it cannot be asked to compensate for any reduction in state GST revenues resulting from an 'Act of God' such as the Covid-19 pandemic. Despite strong objections from many states, the centre had its way, only agreeing to borrow and lend to the states back-to-back, to make up for the loss of GST revenues in excess of some arbitrarily estimated sum attributed to GST implementation. The states had to exhaust their borrowing limits and bear the interest burden to cover for the revenue loss.

In sum, Covid-19 has severely intensified a disproportionality that is built into the distribution of powers and responsibilities characteristic of the Indian federal arrangement. It has always been recognized that while the state governments were crucial players in the design and implementation of economic policy in India, there was considerable disproportionality between the capacity to mobilize resources at the central and state levels and the spending responsibilities that these tiers of government had to shoulder. The finance commissions were to decide on the proportion of resources raised by the centre that had to be transferred to the states to address this disproportionality. As has been repeatedly pointed out, in the process of centralization of power within India's quasi-federal framework, two among many tendencies have been operative. First, an effort by the centre to increasingly mobilize resources by means of imposts that do not require the resulting revenues to be included in the pool of revenues that must be shared with the states. Second, in violation of what the Constitution originally envisaged, efforts to frame the terms of reference of the finance commissions in ways that make them agencies that can impose fiscal austerity, defined as 'discipline', by limiting states' right to borrow and linking transfers to them to performance with respect to fiscal austerity targets.

That the centre is failing to fulfil its own direct responsibilities is clear from the fact that the set of Covid-19 packages it has announced is partly a revamp of already existing schemes, and partly a small increase in new expenditures. The combined total of these two sets of expenditures amounts to 1–1.5 percentage points of GDP, which is anywhere between one-fifth and one-tenth of what estimates suggest is actually needed. The centre has clearly shirked on its direct fiscal responsibility.

As a consequence of all this, as the case load spiked in India, the state governments collapsed into a fiscal and developmental crisis, and were grasping at straws like state levies on petroleum products and alcohol that are still outside the GST regime. But that was small recompense for the revenue losses they were running up, undermining their ability to continue the war against the virus and its fall-out.

The consequences of this centre-made crisis in the middle of a larger and near-unprecedented health-cum-economic emergency are likely to take both expected and unexpected forms. One is definitely a prolonged crisis, the impact of which would be disproportionately borne by the vulnerable majority. A second could be pressure on at least some state governments to contemplate exit from the GST regime that has deprived them not just of revenues but even of minimal fiscal flexibility in the middle of a great crisis. A third may be a strengthening of incipient tendencies for states to work around or even break from the federal compact established by the Constitution, which includes the increasingly fragile power and revenue-sharing relationship that no longer works.

Concluding Remarks
While capitalism, with its focus on private gain and its atomistic structure of decision-making, is fundamentally incapable of handling a Covid-type crisis which requires planned and coordinated action and allocation of resources, the Indian experience suggests that matters have been made worse by the limited scope and nature of the central government's response. The consequence has been not only that the health emergency has been poorly addressed with considerable delays, but also that the economic crisis triggered by the pandemic has been far more severe than need have been, with devastating effects on the poor. The pandemic

response has been inequalizing in multiple ways, hurting the poor the most in ways that accentuate extreme deprivation and worsening the economic position of states while subjecting them to increased control by the centre. That this is not merely the result of ineptness comes through from the fact that in the middle of the pandemic that calls for focused intervention, the government chose to massively hike duties on petroleum and products that are universal intermediates, paved the way for liberalization of the farm trade and allowed entry of big business into agricultural production, changed labour laws and environmental regulations in regressive directions, and accelerated the process of privatization. The intensity of the crisis is influenced by an overall tendency to engineer a redistribution of income and wealth in favour of the rich that the government's neo-liberal agenda entails. As of now, the crisis is still unfolding, and the full extent of the devastation it inflicts will be clear only much later.

Notes

1 National Statistical Office Press Note, https://mospi.gov.in/documents/213904//416359//PressNote_FRE%202019-20%20-%20Website 1611922195016.pdf//5efc1a5e-1e8f-29ec-4f34-d58ebd438ea3, accessed 29 April 2020.

2 Carl Sumner Shoup headed a seven-member team of economists mobilized by General McArthur after the Second World War to restructure the Japanese system of taxation.

3 In her speech presenting Budget 2021–22, the finance minister declared: 'Total financial impact of all Atma Nirbhar Bharat packages including measures taken by RBI was estimated to about Rs 27.1 lakh crores which amounts to more than 13% of GDP.' That, even if valid, included monetary measures. See https://www.indiabudget.gov.in/doc/Budget_Speech.pdf, accessed 5 February 2021, p. 2.

13

The Coronavirus and India's Economic Crisis

Continuity and Change

Surajit Mazumdar

The Government of India imposed a Covid-19-related nation-wide lockdown from 25 March 2020, initially for a period of three weeks. This lockdown was then extended three more times with the fourth phase being completed on 31 May 2020. The subsequent phase, termed as Unlock 1.0, was marked by a significant withdrawal of the restrictions in force except in some select zones identified as being particularly severely affected. This process of easing actually began with the third phase from 4 May and a big step forward in that direction came when the lockdown was extended for a fourth time by another two weeks after 17 May. The fourth phase also initiated a shift from a highly centralized structure prevailing till then to greater decentralization of decision-making, opening up the scope for greater regional variations in the level and nature of restrictions. It would be hard, however, to find in the series of decisions of the Government of India – to impose a lockdown, extend it and then to ease the applicable restrictions – any kind of a consistent underlying framework of decision-making where both public health considerations and the economic situation are given their due place. This is maintainable even after conceding the fact that the world's response to the Covid-19 threat has involved a bit of groping in the dark for everyone.

In addition to imparting a communal dimension to the response to the coronavirus crisis, the way the regime dealt with the crisis reflected yet again two features that have tended to mark its style of governance. The first is an exceptional ability to make whimsical and ill-thought-out decisions dictated by cold political calculation and the objective of managing perceptions rather than reality, and indeed, with potentially

Lecture delivered on 6 May 2020.

disastrous consequences for that reality. The second is an unshakeable and highly inflexible commitment to the mutually complementary agendas of privatization and fiscal conservatism that is blind to the prevailing conditions. Even before the impact of the coronavirus had been felt, these twin elements characterizing the government's behaviour had contributed to consistently aggravating an economic crisis in India. With the added threats of the impact of the Covid-19 pandemic coming into the picture, they almost certainly are pushing India in the direction of an economic catastrophe without any significant gain in averting a public health disaster.

From Lockdown to Getting the Economy Going: What Is Behind It?

When the nation-wide lockdown was announced on 24 March 2020, the number of confirmed coronavirus cases in India was still relatively low, around the 500 mark, and large parts of the country had not yet been touched by the virus. The official contention was that India had not entered the stage of community transmission of the virus and most of the infected people were either those who had carried the infection from abroad or their close contacts. That route of entry of the virus into India had already been almost entirely closed by the cessation of all incoming international flights along with the imposition of restrictions on public gatherings prior to the lockdown. Despite these measures, as extreme a shutdown of the entire country as was possible was suddenly chosen as the way to deal with the pandemic, and implemented without giving people any warning. As measured by the Stringency Index developed by the Blavatnik School of Government of Oxford University,[1] the Indian lockdown restrictions were the most severe in the world, the index value for India being at the maximum of 100 between 25 March and 14 April. Even in the second phase of the lockdown, this index value remained close to 100 and higher than that of almost all other countries, including those worst affected by the pandemic. In the beginning, therefore, it did not appear that the likely disruption of economic activity and people's lives that the lockdown would cause was given too much consideration in the shaping of the epidemic containment strategy. The eruption of what became a prolonged migrant workers' crisis was one visible consequence of this neglect, which also undermined the immediate objective of the lockdown.

The process of gradual withdrawal from lockdown restrictions, on the other hand, seemed to have a life of its own, independent of the situation with regard to the epidemic. The first steps towards such easing were taken when there was a sharp acceleration in the growth of confirmed Covid-19 cases in the country, in the first week of May. This acceleration was in complete contrast to the projections that had been put forward on 24 April by a member of the NITI Aayog (National Institution for Transforming India) who headed the government's high-level technical committee of public health experts, which is supposed to be guiding the Covid-19 prevention and control activities. According to those projections put out by V.K. Paul in a press conference, the number of daily new cases was to peak in early May and decline to near zero by the middle of the month.[2] The reality of acceleration, however, did not come in the way of easing restrictions, including the first limited steps to allow the return home of migrant workers stuck in different parts of the country and also of Indians abroad.

Even though the acceleration at the beginning of May had been followed by a slowing down of the rate of growth of cases to levels prevailing towards the end of April, the number of infected people continued to grow at a steady clip throughout May on the higher base it produced. The number of cases reported daily remained consistently on an upward trend and this continued till mid-September. Indeed, almost 1.56 lakh cases – 78.5 per cent of all confirmed cases reported till 31 May – were added to the tally in the month of May, as were 4,254 of the total 5,408 deaths. By mid-September, when the first peak in daily cases was reached, the total number of confirmed cases had multiplied many times further to cross 5 million, and over 83,000 Indians had died of Covid-19. Another almost 4.5 million cases and 55,000 deaths were reported in the two-and-a-half months after, till the end of November. In other words, almost 98 per cent of all Indians who had contracted the coronavirus infection did so after the unlock phases were initiated. At the state level, states in eastern and southern India, where the growth of the infection appeared to have been limited or contained earlier, the situation changed and the number of cases started rising, partly on account of movement of people from the more affected parts of the country or of cases imported from abroad. Even Kerala, initially the most successful among the major Indian states in controlling the epidemic, experienced a very sharp reversal of the decline in active cases as it had to deal with a big second wave resulting from transmission from outside the state and country.

Seen in a global comparative perspective, India's epidemic control strategy built around an unplanned, stringent lockdown hardly produced the greatest relative success in its chief objective of checking the spread of the virus (and this is even if we ignore the issue of lower testing numbers per capita). Notwithstanding the proud official claims repeatedly made about the effectiveness of India's Covid-19 containment strategy, made exclusively by comparing the numbers in India (confirmed cases and deaths) with those in some of the worst affected countries in the world, he truth is that the coronavirus pandemic exhibited a certain pattern in its worldwide spread in relation to which the Indian story was a standout one only in the sense of India being one of the worst affected by the pandemic.

As is clear from Table 13.1, the economically advanced countries of Western Europe and North America, with barely a tenth of the world's population, were initially hit much more by the coronavirus than the rest of the world. The pattern of spread of the pandemic till end May was also indicative of some relationship with per capita income levels of countries – with the poorer countries being less affected. In sharp contrast to the west's story was that of the region of origin of the epidemic, East Asia and Southeast Asia. What was seen in China's Hubei province, the first epicentre of the pandemic, was not repeated across this vast and heavily populated region, including in the rest of China.

While East and Southeast Asia have remained among those regions of the world where success in controlling the epidemic has been the highest if not complete, South Asia and Africa did eventually see a surge by May. Despite their relatively low per capita incidence of cases and deaths, they crossed the East Asian levels. Thus, the onset of the epidemic in these parts of the world was at a later point of time, and by the end of May, these parts were still behind many other parts, including the rest of Asia, in terms of where they were located on the epidemic curve. Subsequent events were to bear this out.

Thus, the Indian story of the coronavirus epidemic was broadly what geography, its economic status and, perhaps, demographic characteristics like age structure of the population would indicate it should have been when restrictions started getting eased. In per capita terms, the Indian situation was almost identical to that of the African continent, which has almost the same population size as India. The growth of the epidemic in India, however, was already faster than in Africa as a whole. During the lockdown India had also left behind thirty-six countries which initially had a larger number of cases than her – becoming in the process the country with the highest number of cases in Asia, with only Russia moving up to cross India. All of these, however, proved to be only early signs of what was to follow. The subsequent trajectory of the pandemic in India was one that made it, for months, one of the global epicentres. India became the country with the second largest number of cases, and third largest number of deaths, by some margins. It not only left Africa far behind, in per capita terms, its cases and deaths left behind almost the entire Asian continent other than West and Central Asia, including its South Asian neighbours. Despite the pandemic ebbing somewhat in India since mid-September while Europe and the USA saw new surges, by end-November,

Table 13.1 *India and the pattern of spread of the coronavirus pandemic til,* *31 May 2020*

Country/Region	Population	Total Covid-19 cases			Total Covid-19 deaths		
		4 May	17 May	31 May	4 May	17 May	31 May
World	100.0	100.0	100.0	100.0	100.0	100.0	100.0
US, Canada	4.8	34.9	33.4	30.8	29.1	30.6	30.4
Western Europe	5.5	33.8	28.5	23.2	54.6	49.1	43.8
Eastern Europe	4.2	6.7	8.6	9.1	1.9	2.3	2.7
Latin America and Carribean	8.4	7.3	10.8	16.2	5.6	9.2	13.7
West Asia	4.7	8.9	9.1	9.3	4.2	3.9	3.8
Central Asia	0.9	0.2	0.2	0.3	0.0	0.0	0.0
East and Southeast Asia	29.9	4.4	3.8	3.3	2.8	2.5	2.3
Excl. Hubei (approx.)	29.2	2.5	2.3	2.2	1.1	1.1	1.1
South Asia	23.9	2.2	3.5	5.2	0.9	1.4	2.1
India	17.8	1.3	2.0	3.0	0.6	1.0	1.4
Africa	17.3	1.3	1.8	2.4	0.7	0.9	1.1
Oceania	0.5	0.2	0.2	0.1	0.0	0.0	0.0
Low Income Economies	9.2	0.3	0.5	0.7	0.1	0.2	0.3
Low Middle Income	40.0	4.1	5.7	7.8	2.1	2.8	3.7

Country/Region	Population	Total Covid-19 cases/ million population			Total Covid-19 deaths/ million population		
		4 May	17 May	31 May	4 May	17 May	31 May
World	100.0	466	616	803	32.3	40.6	47.9
US, Canada	4.8	3445	4355	5230	198.8	262.6	307.9
Western Europe	5.5	2888	3225	3421	323.1	366.2	384.9
Eastern Europe	4.2	751	1273	1755	14.9	22.5	31.7
Latin America and Carribean	8.4	410	799	1562	21.8	45.0	78.9
West Asia	4.7	896	1209	1608	29.4	34.2	39.2
Central Asia	0.9	106	170	296	0.8	1.5	1.7
East and Southeast Asia	29.9	69	78	88	3.1	3.4	3.7
Excl. Hubei (approx.)	29.2	41	50	60	1.2	1.6	1.9
South Asia	23.9	45	90	177	1.3	2.4	4.2
India	17.8	34	69	138	1.0	2.0	4.0
Africa	17.3	35	65	111	1.3	2.1	3.2
Oceania	0.5	207	213	215	2.8	2.9	3.1
Low Income Economies	9.2	15	32	62	0.5	1.0	1.4
Low Middle Income	40.0	48	88	157	1.7	2.8	4.5

Note: Population shares are derived from the affected country population figures given in the same source (as on 31 May 2020).
Source: www.worldometers.info/coronavirus/ as at the end of 4, 17 and 31 May 2020, accessed 1 June 2020.

India's share in global cases and deaths were almost 15 per cent and over 9 per cent, respectively, way above the levels in May. The corresponding shares relative to Asia's totals were almost 57 per cent and over 47 per cent, respectively.

Thus, even though 68 days of lockdown had served to slow down the growth of cases in India, it was clear that it had not managed to suppress the epidemic or take it past its peak. Unlike in many other countries, therefore, the beginning of the retreat from the lockdown in India was initiated and continued even as the country remained a long distance away from turning the corner and starting the long journey downwards in terms of the number of daily active cases. It was not apparent, however, that any new and more sophisticated and effective epidemic containment strategy had replaced it – which perhaps explains the accompanying message that 'we have to learn to live with the virus'. This suggests that the authors of the Indian lockdown script chose to start withdrawing from it because it was proving to be unsustainable, precisely because despite its highly restrictive nature and already long duration, it had failed to fulfil the expectations of enabling a grip on the epidemic.

Even before the government announced the easing of lockdown restrictions in mid-May, it also put forward what it claimed was a big economic stimulus package, equivalent to 10 per cent of the country's GDP (gross domestic product), with the objective of achieving an 'Atmanirbhar Bharat' (self-reliant India). Several state governments also announced relaxations in labour laws, ostensibly to stimulate investment. Several elements of the economic package were such that the underlying assumption must have been that almost all the constraining effects of epidemic control measures on economic activity would disappear very soon. It seems therefore that the state of the economy had come to the fore, outweighing the concern with the epidemic and its spread that apparently dominated earlier decision-making. That perhaps the clock had indeed turned full circle was also indicated by the significant difference between the prime minister's addresses to the nation: the one announcing the first lockdown and the one which declared the coming of a Rs 20 lakh crore economic package. The clarion call had changed – what was supposed to be a war to vanquish a deadly virus had become one of 'converting a crisis into an economic opportunity'.

However, reviving a battered economy, let alone achieving economic resurgence, is different from implementing a lockdown. Coercion, fear and persuasion can all combine to ensure compliance with a lockdown, but the economy demands more specific, concrete actions from the government. Unfortunately, that was conspicuous by its absence in the 'stimulus' package and all subsequent measures that were announced. The package failed to acknowledge the reality of what the lockdown had done to an economy that was already in the throes of a crisis, and the effects of these on the people. A mutually reinforcing combination of a sinking economy, and a growing epidemic and larger public health crisis, as attention to other ailments and diseases get squeezed out due to diversion of limited capacity, may be recorded as the eventual outcome of the government's follies.

The Coronavirus Impact on the Indian Economy

International evidence tends to support the fact that the economic impact of the coronavirus has been relatively more uniform across countries, not reflecting the diversity seen in the incidence of the epidemic. In other words, successful containment of the epidemic has also been costly in economic terms. Thus, in the January–March quarter of 2020, if the European Union and the US experienced contractions in their GDP by 3.5 and 4.1 per cent respectively, so did China, Japan and Korea – by 6.8, 4.1 and 1.4 per cent, respectively.

India's January–March GDP (Q4 of 2019–20) data showed a considerable slowing down. However, this was no indication of the magnitude of the impact since the lockdown began only in the last week of March. Instead, it was a 23.9 per cent GDP contraction in the April–June quarter (Q1 of 2020–21), itself considered an underestimate, which eventually confirmed the devastating economic effects of the lockdown. Before these data came at the end of August 2020, there were several other indicators from official and private sources that pointed towards a catastrophe. While the negative growth picture moderated in the next quarter (July–September or Q2 of 2020–21) to –7.5 per cent, the picture of these two quarters are suffcient to confirm that India was not only among the worst affected by the pandemic, but its failed attempt to suppress the pandemic also produced one of the biggest economic contractions in the world. A comparison with the situation in other major economies over the same period, as shown in Table 13.2, bear this out.

The GDP data for India indicate that the contraction has been widespread, and it is only agriculture that appears to have posted positive growth in the first half of 2020–21. India's trade too was hit, and the fact that imports were hit more severely than exports (Table 13.3) was also an indication that India's growth performance was worse than in other countries constituting her export markets.

In the case of agriculture, too, studies have revealed how disruptive the lockdown provisions have been for operations, leading to decline in *mandi* arrivals of different crops, large-scale destruction of perishable

Table 13.2 *Growth in GDP compared to the same quarter of previous year, seasonally adjusted, selected countries*

Country/Country Group	April–June 2020	July–September 2020
Mexico	–18.7	–8.6
Turkey	–8.5	5.4
Korea	–2.8	–1.3
United Kingdom	–21.5	–9.6
United States	–9.0	–2.9
Euro area (19 countries)	–14.8	–4.4
European Union (27 countries)	–13.9	–4.3
G7	–11.9	–4.2
Brazil	–11.4	–
China (People's Republic of)	3.2	4.9
India	–23.5	–7.5

Source: OECD.stat., https://stats.oecd.org/index.aspx?queryid=350, accessed 16 December 2020.

Table 13.3 *Percentage change in India's merchandise trade (in US $) over the same period of previous year*

Item	April–October 2020–21/ April–October 2019–20 (H1+October)
Merchandise exports	–19.2
Non-oil and non-gems & jewellery X	–9.4
Merchandise imports	–36.3
Non-oil and non-gold imports	–30.1

Source: Government of India (2020a).

crops, fall in farm gate prices and reduced procurement – all implying significant loss of farm incomes (Rawal and Verma 2020; Rawal and Kumar 2020).

The employment situation, of course, was one of the most distressing dimensions of the massive production contraction. CMIE (Centre for Monitoring Indian Economy) data indicated, not surprisingly, large-scale job losses as an immediate effect of the lockdown – amounting to as much as 122 million by the beginning of May (Vyas 2020). While unemployment levels came down thereafter, it is unlikely that the earnings situation of workers has recovered or that they have the same kind of employment as earlier.

The Economic Crisis in a Longer-Term Perspective

The immediate and direct contractionary impact of the pandemic cannot, however, fully capture the damage that is being actually afflicted. This is because this impact is taking place on the back of an existing crisis, which also means greater longer-term damage is being done also to the economy's future prospects. As the full-year growth figures in Tables 13.2 and 13.3, and the three-year trend in Figure 13.2 already indicated, things were not well with the Indian economy even before Covid-19 appeared on the scene. An ongoing slowdown, expressed through the regular fall in quarterly GDP growth since the last quarter of 2017–18 (Figure 13.1), had been the centre of attention before anyone had heard of the novel coronavirus, and 'stimulus' and 'reform' packages and measures had also been announced in response to it.

However, the coronavirus pandemic should be seen as the third successive shock being inflicted on an already sluggish Indian economy – the November 2016 demonetization and the introduction of the new GST (goods and services tax) regime from July 2017 being the previous two. Even India's controversial new GDP series introduced in 2015 shows the effects of the earlier two shocks (Figure 13.2), despite it not being suited

Figure 13.1 *Growth of quarterly GDP over same quarter in previous year, Q4 2017–18 to Q4 2019–20* (percentages)

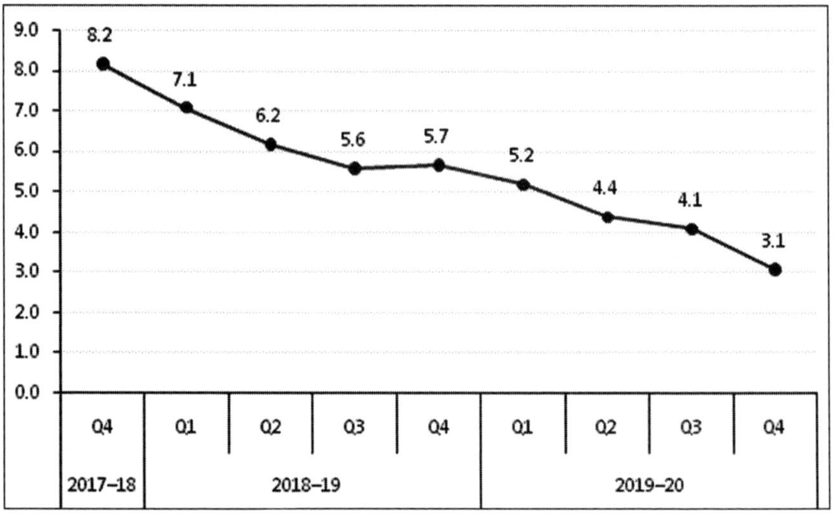

Source: Government of India (2020b).

Figure 13.2 *Growth rates of India's GDP (new series) at 2011–12 prices, 2016–17 to 2019–20*

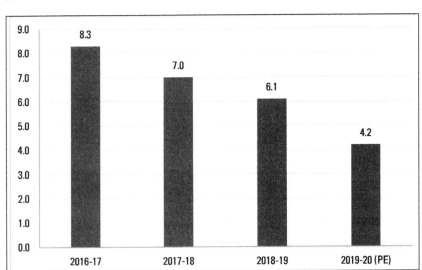

Source: Government of India (2020b, 2020c).

to capturing the exceptional adverse impact all of these had on the unorganized sector. It is clear, therefore, that the latest slowdown was only an aggravation of an existing trend. If we in addition take into account the widely believed possibility that even the growth of the period before was being overestimated by the revised GDP series, in one estimate by some 2.5 percentage points in the period up to 2016–17 (Subramanian 2019), the picture is starker. It would imply that India's GDP growth had already slowed down considerably from the beginning of the 2010s to around a 4.5 per cent per annum level, decelerated rapidly after 2016–17 as a result of two shocks being inflicted on it, and approached stagnation or contraction levels even before the coronavirus hit was experienced.

Even if we leave aside the controversy about the accuracy of GDP growth estimates, there are several other indicators which show that all has not been well with the Indian economy in the second decade of the twenty-first century. An extremely poor industrial growth performance, a sharp slowing down in growth of construction activities, stagnation in investment and a steady reversal of the previous decade's trend of a rising investment ratio, a similar reversal in the significance of India's external trade and a general weakening of expansionary impulses being transmitted from the world economy, and a sharp deceleration in the growth of commercial bank credit – these are among the symptoms of a decade-long weakening of the growth impulse.

As shown in Figure 13.3, the 2010s have been the worst manufacturing growth phase in four decades as measured by trends in the index of
industrial production. Indeed, it is reminiscent of the stagnation era that
started in the mid-1960s.

The construction sector in India had been booming since the
mid-1990s and grew even more rapidly in the first decade of this century.
Figure 13.4 shows a comparative picture of the growth of the sector since
2011–12 with periods of equivalent length in the first decade, using both
the older 2004–05 base year series as well as the official 2011–12 base
year back series. Either comparison shows that the sector's growth has
considerably slowed down in the decade ending 2020.

An extremely dramatic rise in the investment ratio of the Indian
economy led by private corporate investment was one of the standout
features of the five-year boom preceding the global crisis. However, that
has since given rise to a stagnationist trend in investment and a steady
decline in its ratio to GDP (Figure 13.5). The slowdown in construction
activities is a part of that, but there been also an almost complete stagnation in expenditure on machinery and equipment. This is also borne
out by the very sharply contrasting trends in both the production and
imports of capital goods in the two decades of the twenty-first century

Figure 13.3 *Simple averages of annual growth rates of manufacturing index of*
industrial production (IIP) since 1980

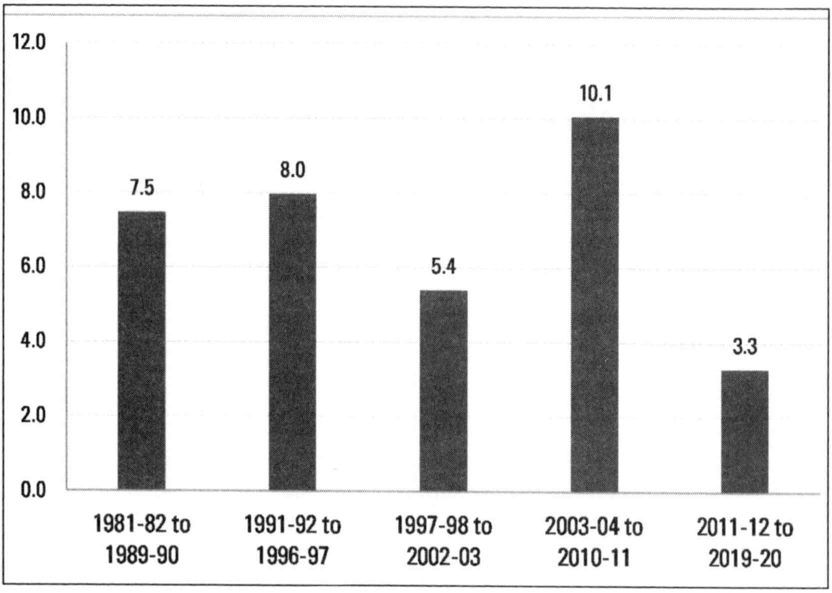

Source: Computed from data in RBI (2020).

Figure 13.4 *Index of construction GDP at constant prices* (alternative 9/8-year periods and GDP series) (respective year zero = 100)

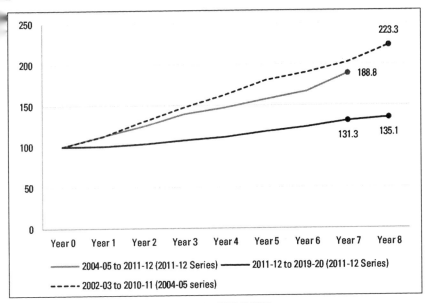

Source: Government of India (2011), (2013); RBI (2020).

Figure 13.5 *GFCF (gross fixed capital formation)/GDP current market prices (percentage), 2002–03 to 2019–20*

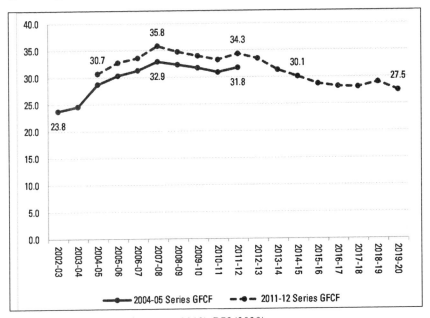

Source: Government of India (2011, 2013); RBI (2020).

Figure 13.6 *IIP for capital goods and quantum index of imports of machinery and transport equipment (2002–03 = 100), 2002–03 to 2019–20/2018–19*

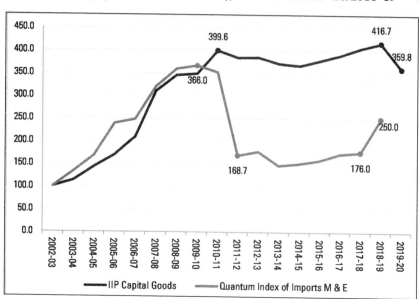

Source: RBI (2020).

(Figure 13.6). Even the temporary upturn in investment in 2018–19 proved to be very short-lived.

Like in the case of investment, a rapid growth of merchandise and services trade, both exports and imports, and significant capital inflows into India were part of the process by which India came to participate in the boom seen across 'emerging' economies before the global crisis. However, as is evident from Figure 13.7 and Table 13.4, this did not last into the current decade, where all the variables show almost complete stagnation.

It is in the background of all these signs of a severely demand-constrained economy that one must understand both the taming of inflation and the improvement in India's current account situation that has marked at least the second half of the 2010s decade. Attempts to address this demand problem by monetary easing towards the later part of the decade has proved ineffective and bank credit growth has remained tepid throughout, barely keeping pace with nominal GDP growth. This is in sharp contrast to the rapid expansion of the previous decade.

Underlying the persistent sluggish tendencies of the Indian economy is India's cheap labour economy and the wage and income stagnation of large sections of the population it entails – which has only been aggravated by the slowdown tendencies. The forced shift out of agriculture that

Figure 13.7 *Exports and imports of goods and services to GDP current market prices (percentage), 2002–03 to 2019–20*

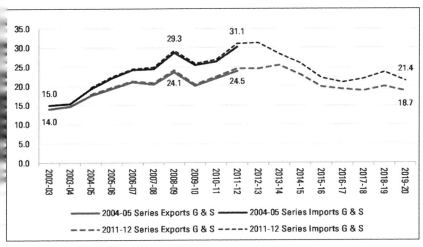

Source: Government of India (2011), (2013); RBI (2020).

Table 13.4 *Indices of US Dollar values of selected balance of payments items, 2002–03 to 2010–11 and 2011–12 to 2019–20* (first year = 100)

Year	Merchandise exports		Merchandise imports		Invisibles, net		Foreign investment	
	02–03 to 10–11	11–12 to 19–20	02–03 to 10–11	11–12 to 19–20	02–03 to 10–11	11–12 to 19–20	02–03 to 10–11	11–12 to 19–20
Year 0	100	100	100	100	100	100	100	100
Year 1	123.3	99	124.1	100.5	163.2	96.3	260.6	108.7
Year 2	158.5	102.9	184.5	93.3	183.3	103.3	254.3	71.1
Year 3	195.5	102.2	243.6	92.4	246.6	105.8	355.7	153.8
Year 4	239.7	86	295.8	79.4	306.5	96.7	494.5	81.9
Year 5	309	90.4	399.6	78.6	444.6	87.8	1030.8	99.2
Year 6	351.5	99.7	478.6	93.9	537.7	99.7	463.6	122.3
Year 7	339.3	108.9	466.4	103.6	469.8	110.2	1088.7	85.2
Year 8	476.4	103.5	594.9	95	465.3	118.7	1005.8	110.9

Source: RBI (2020).

Figure 13.8 *Commercial bank credit to GDP ratio, 2002–03 to 2019–20*

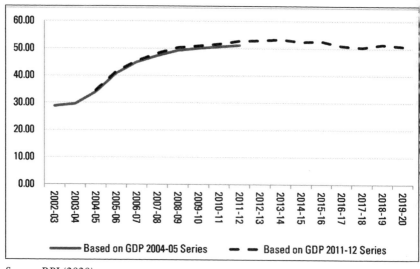

Source: RBI (2020).

was triggered from the mid-1990s by the agrarian crisis continued during the current decade with a further reduction in the proportion employed in that sector (Table 13.5). However, while the onset of the agrarian crisis had coincided with the start of the construction boom, making it the most important sector for absorbing those moving out of agriculture, in the 2010s, it happened in the background of a slowdown in construction. The persistence of a high level of self-employment (52 per cent of total employment), largely in own-account enterprises (OAEs), despite the reduction in cultivators is one expression of the problem of inadequate employment opportunities. However, with the non-agricultural unorganized sector, where much of the employment is also facing increasing difficulties, increasing unemployment and shrinking work participation (of both females as well as males) have come to characterize the Indian economy in the 2010s. If the unemployment rate emerging from the Periodic Labour Force Survey (PLFS) 2017–18 was at an all-time high, the same source also showed that the proportion of the Indian population that was in self-employment declined from 20.2 per cent in 2011–12 to 18.1 per cent in 2017–18, while those in wage employment declined from 18.6 per cent to 16.5 per cent (Rawal and Bansal 2019).

Limited income-earning opportunities in agriculture for the large mass of people with little or no land, and the entry of large numbers of them into labour reserves that non-agricultural activities could draw on, has for long meant a generalized tendency in India for earnings from

Table 13.5 *Employment structure in India (usual status basis)*

Sector	Share in workforce		
	2011–12	2017–18	2018–19
Agriculture	48.9	44.1	42.5
Industry	24.3	24.8	25.2
Manufacturing	12.6	12.1	12.1
Construction	10.6	11.7	12.1
Services	26.8	31.1	32.1
Share of informal enterprises in non-agricultural employment	72.4	68.4	68.4

Source: NSSO (2014); Government of India (2019, 2020d).

labour to remain depressed – even in highly productive activities, and even in periods of rapid expansion of investment and output. This is what had earlier facilitated high growth and accumulation in India being combined with sharp increases in inequality, which saw the top 10 per cent of the population raise its share in national income to over 55 per cent (Chancel and Piketty 2018) and the overlapping trend of dramatically rising share of corporate profits. Thus, while India's real per capita income increased by 2.41 times between 2000–01 and 2017–18, the average real wage in India's organized factory sector increased by less than 15 per cent over the same period.[3] That this was symptomatic of labour incomes in general is indicated by Table 13. 6, which shows the general levels of earning of Indian workers – both self-employed and waged – the bulk of whom make up the 90 per cent that has seen a steady slide in its share in national income over the last few decades.

The crisis of manufacturing and the sharp slowing down of construction activities seen in the present decade meant that growth in both output as well as employment terms became more concentrated on services. This reflected the inability of the beneficiaries of increasing inequality and expanding credit to sustain support from the demand side for any alternative growth pattern. This included the failure of the private corporate sector to sustain the investment boom of the previous decade – the drying up of opportunities in high capital-absorbing manufacturing, real estate and infrastructure had a cause as well as effect relationship with the demand situation. Cheap labour had also not proved adequate incentive for Indian and foreign firms to be able to convert India into a competitive location for production for the world market in much of manufacturing, and this became even less of a possibility in the post-global crisis world. The trade

Table 13.6 *The cheap labour economy: earnings by category*

PLFS April–June 2018/April–June 2019				
Item	Share in workforce (%)		Earning/Wage (in rupees)	
Gross monthly earnings of self-employed	52.2	52.1	12,304	10,648
Monthly wage/salary of regular workers	22.8	23.8	16,848	16,196
Average daily wage of casual workers	29.4	24.1	271	291
Annual Survey of Industries 2017–18				
Factory worker's average monthly wage (in rupees)			13,143	
Monthly per adult income 2018–19 (in rupees)*				
Bottom 50% of the population			4,944	
Middle 40% of the population			12,289	
Top 10% of the population			94,407	
Top 1% of the population			3,59,170	

Note: * Derived from Chancel and Piketty (2018).
Source: Government of India (2019, 2020d, 2020e); RBI (2020); Chancel and Piketty (2018).

balance remained in check because of the sluggish growth of import-using sectors rather than increases in exports.

Demonetization and hurried introduction of the GST regime served to inflict further body-blows on a floundering growth and accumulation process, particularly through their impact on the unorganized sector. The slowdown in the immediate period before the Covid-19 crisis struck thus reflected the process of the crisis spreading and becoming more generalized. The agrarian crisis became a larger livelihoods crisis that not only sustained through the boom of the first decade of the twenty-first century, but even helped in its generation by its effects on profits. As its demand and other effects assumed greater significance, however, it translated into a sustained crisis of accumulation and profit growth that became worse as the initially relatively more adverse effects on the unorganized sector in time also transmitted themselves to the organized sector.

Given this background to the impact of Covid-19 on India, the specific contractionary effects that the containment measures associated with the epidemic has produced, of course, aggravates every aspect of the crisis. However, it doesn't do so only temporarily, and there is little scope for the economy to return to even its previous situation, even after all the constraining factors specifically associated with Covid-19 containment cease to operate. That this 'normalcy' will fully return soon, not only in India but in the world economy, itself seems remote. Even when containment measures cease, reversal of some effects like the migration of labour back to villages is unlikely to be instantaneous, more so on account of the delay in their returning home and what they have had to experience in the process. Similarly, the still incomplete return of expatriate Indians to their employments abroad and the resultant flow of remittances to India may also not be restored quickly, if at all it will. Many service activities may face greater difficulty in returning to normal levels of activities in comparison to at least organized manufacturing because of the practices and regulations that will have to be adhered to as long as the Covid-19 threat continues. These will also tend to tilt the balance further against unorganized enterprises in several sectors. To add to all of this are the large-scale destruction of incomes and damage to the financial health of enterprises that the containment measures have caused – making it unlikely that there will be much pent-up demand to form the basis for any rebound in the economy unless it receives significant support from the state. Such support, however, is precisely what is missing in the so-called 'stimulus' package announced by the government, which neither responds to the immediate needs created by the massive economic contraction nor to the longer-term crisis of India's economy.

'Stimulus' as the Expression of an Unchanging Economic Policy Script

Trying to get India's economy going by trying to induce private investment, both domestic and foreign, even while completing the 'retreat' from the post-global crisis stimulus, has been the essence of the Government of India's policy for the entire decade of the 2010s. Started by the previous government, this has been continued with renewed vigour by the present one since it assumed office in 2014. The attempts to improve the 'ease of doing business', 'Make in India', 'Skill India', etc., were among several supply-side measures intended to kickstart the investment process. Once inflation rates came down, monetary easing, reduction of interest rates and pushing expansion of credit also became part of this effort despite the mountain of bad debts already existing on the books of banks and other institutions (sought to be cleared by basically writing off the bad debts). That year after year passed with neither exports nor investment showing any signs of revival made no difference, except the pursuit of the same strategy with greater doggedness. All this was accompanied by single-minded pursuit of the objective of bringing down the fiscal deficit, which had increased with the post-crisis stimulus. This effort relied primarily on expenditure compression as underlying economic realities and the lack of any effort to raise direct taxes meant that revenue growth remained poor except for the brief windfall gains from higher oil taxes when international prices fell after 2014. Figure 13.9 captures this story with reference to the central government's finances.

Even when the slowdown became too severe to be ignored, the prescription did not change. Attempts to talk the Indian economy out of a crisis by promising bold structural 'reforms' and a rosy future (the 5 trillion dollar economy) have particularly marked the tenure of Nirmala Sitharaman as finance minister. In content and in form, there is much similarity that can be found in the five-stage announcement of the Covid-19 'stimulus' package, the previous one announced in September 2019 in response to the slowdown, and the last two budget speeches of the finance minister.

The slowdown, however, led to a further aggravation of the fiscal crisis – a sharp drop in revenue growth in 2018–19 was followed by a contraction in 2019–20 (Table 13.7), as a result of which the central government's fiscal deficit shot up to 4.6 per cent of GDP. While the coronavirus impact on March revenues played some part in this, it was not the primary factor because revenue growth was non-existent even before that.

Figure 13.9 *Central revenues, expenditure and fiscal deficit as percentage of GDP at current market prices, 2011–12 to 2019–20*[4]

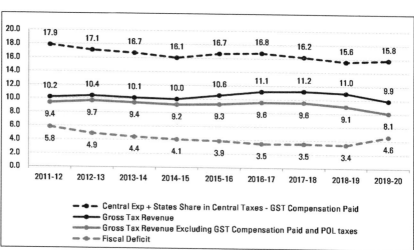

Source: Union Budget Documents (various years); RBI (2020); Controller General of Accounts Monthly Accounts (www.cga.nic.in, accessed 30 September 2020); Petroleum Planning and Analysis Cell (https://www.ppac.gov.in, accessed 10 October 2016 and 14 December 2020).

Table 13.7 *Growth compared to same period in previous year in nominal GDP and tax revenues* (percentage increase)

Nominal GDP 2018–19 (1st revised estimate)	11.0
Gross revenue from central taxes 2018–19	
Union Budget estimates (relative to actual)	18.4
Actuals	8.4
Nominal GDP 2019–20 (provisional estimate)	7.2
Gross revenue from central taxes 2019–20	
Budget estimates (relative to actual)	18.3
Actual collections (provisional)	(–)3.4
Revised estimates (from Budget 2020–21)	4.0

Source: Union Budget documents (various years); RBI (2020).

Part of this, in fact, can be attributed to the bizarre corporate tax cut that was included in the September 2019 'stimulus' package.

Given this long record of an unfolding economic reality and governmental obstinacy that has been in effective denial of it, the nature of the Covid-19 'stimulus' package is actually not surprising. With the revenue situation becoming graver, the central government's borrowing requirement in 2020–21 already has had to be increased substantially. In the absence of any new-found willingness to abandon 'fiscal prudence' and to consider, eventually if not immediately, a decisive shift in the direction of heavier taxation of the rich and the corporate sector, the government obviously cannot find any 'fiscal space' to step up spending. It is not surprising therefore that additional spending does not constitute any significant part of the stimulus measures. Almost everyone has seen through the hoax of the package having a size equivalent to 10 per cent of GDP and that the fiscal implications of it do not go beyond a tenth of that. However, past experience suggests that even the limited increase in expenditure may end up being 'financed' by cutting similar expenditures under other heads.

Evidence from the first half of the year (Table 13.8) shows this clear picture of continuity in the fiscal approach. In the background of the Covid-19 crisis, the Indian government once again resorted to the old method of generating revenues from increasing oil taxes. Despite the sharp increases in excise collections, however, revenue growth was still negative even in the second quarter of the year. However, the expenditure increases maintained in the first quarter did not carry over into the second even as the squeeze on the states' shares in central taxes increased. In other words,

Table 13.8 *Growth in central taxes and expenditure in the first two quarters of 2020–21 over same period of previous year*

Item	April–June 2020–21 (Q1)	July–September 2020–21 (Q2)
Gross tax revenues	–32.6	–13.1
Corporation tax	–23.3	–46.1
Income tax	–35.9	–10.1
GST total	–35.2	–1.3
Customs	–61	–23
Excise	–4.3	58.4
Assignment to states	–9.8	–22.6
Total expenditure of central government	13.1	–13.5

Source: www.cga.nic.in, accessed 28 November 2020.

the fiscal stance of the Indian government had already turned contractionary in nature.

In the absence of spending, obviously, the package is incapable of meaningfully compensating working people with already fragile household economies for the exceptional loss of income and employment. Indeed, the 'stimulus' package incorporated the earlier announced limited relief under the Pradhan Mantri Garib Kalyan Yojana (PMGKY) but added little to it. Some of the measures are little more than adjustments in the schedules of receipts and expenditures, with no net positive impact on the incomes of beneficiaries or expenditures of government. 'Relief' has been given to employers by legitimizing what in effect is a wage-cut (temporary reduction in the statutory provident fund contribution). Included in the package is also the 'enabling' of workers in running down their savings and future pensionary benefits in order to survive in the present. Thus, there is extraordinarily little which represents transfers from the government. Even the increased allocation to the Mahatma Gandhi Employment Guarantee Act (MNREGA) of Rs 40,000 crores is less significant than it seems as first sight, since the original allocation in the 2020–21 budget was almost Rs 10,000 crore less than what had been spent the previous year.

Another critical gap in the 'stimulus' package is the inadequate financial support to state governments, which will end up squeezing the aggregate level of public expenditure in the economy. States are already suffering from the combined effects of two consequences of the shortfall in revenues from central taxes in 2019–20. The first is that this also hit the states' share in central taxes, which came down from Rs 7,61,454 crore in 2018–19 to just Rs 6,50, 677 crore in 2019–20 – a drop of 14.6 per cent. The picture indicated in Table 13.8 is a reflection of this problem becoming worse in 2020–21. The second consequence has been the central government holding back the GST compensation payable to the states, which is likely to be repeated in 2020–21. Thus, instead of helping state governments overcome the hit their revenues are taking, the central government will end up aggravating their problem. Even the expansion of their borrowing possibilities has been made conditional on state governments accepting 'reform' measures.

The core of the attempt, if any, to attain the short-term objective of reviving economic activities from the immediate shutdown that can be found in the package is all about facilitating greater borrowing by individuals and enterprises that are already reeling under the impact of significant income and revenue losses. The longer-term focus accompanying it – facilitating greater privatization and concentration in the control of the nation's assets – is also the same tired old script the government has been plugging for years without any results. The current context, however, makes these look even more perverse than earlier.

When the ability to repay existing debt has taken a big dent, and even renewal of economic activity is likely to confront Covid-19-related abnormal and uncertain conditions for some time, how is increasing debt further a solution? Adding to the perversity is the fact that this 'solution' comes from a government that is reiterating the belief that it is the one economic actor that must keep its own borrowing under check, no matter what the circumstances. So, the rest of the economy has to be 'self-reliant' by increasing its debt, and not expect government spending to revive demand and income-earning prospects. Even those who might favour the 'reforms' announced, or hope to gain from them, recognize that these do not really constitute the immediate relief and stimulus that the economy and the desperate millions without work need – the disappointment at the government doing too little for once appears near-universal. Others would recognize the paradox of privatization being offered as a reform at a time when the pandemic has brought home the importance of the public sector the world over. Other peculiarities – like the promotion of 'self-reliance' through 74 per cent foreign direct investment (FDI) in defence production, of all things – have also not escaped attention. The renewed expression of commitment to privatization and the reluctance to expand public spending are linked. Together, they mean that the real roots of India's long-term economic crisis, and the immediate consequences of the specific Covid-19-related disruption, will both remain unaddressed.

Conclusion

India's economy was in a deep-seated crisis even before anyone had heard of the novel coronavirus. Economic policy-making had remained captive to the promotion of narrow interests, out of which emerged a universalization of what was an ever-present crisis for India's working people. Further, helping the economy on its path downhill were actions like demonetization and introduction of the goods and services tax (GST). The way in which the nation-wide lockdown was imposed resonated that same kind of 'decisiveness' without proper weighing of the economic costs and benefits, making the fall-out worse than might have been the case. As the Covid-19 crisis is aggravating every element of the existing crisis even while immediately producing acute distress, the almost formulaic policy response of the government reflects a continuing pattern. This apparently ostrich-like behaviour of the Indian government, seemingly in contrast to responses elsewhere in the world where governments appear to be assuming a larger role, is of course rooted in the class interests it represents. What the coronavirus crisis has revealed more sharply is the exceptional obstinacy as well as callousness that a secure but deeply authoritarian regime is capable of in the pursuit of these interests. That is what makes it incapable of 'deviating' even to the limited extent that the exceptional circumstances created by the Covid-19 crisis may have rendered possible, even been partially acceptable to powerful economic interests if not desired by them. As such, the only 'opportunity' that the Covid-19 crisis really offered – to pull India's economy out of the morass into which it is sinking – is being lost even as the situation with regard to the pandemic and its effects continues to add to uncertainty.

Notes

[1] https://www.bsg.ox.ac.uk/research/research-projects/coronavirus-government-response-tracker, accessed 1 June 2020

[2] V.K. Paul has sought to clarify his position and suggested that he had been misinterpreted. However, the fact is that a graph was presented which showed precisely what has been said here. See Koshy (2020).

[3] Based on data from the Annual Survey of Industries (ASI), http://mospi.nic.in/asi-summary-results/844, accessed on 1 June 2020, and Government of India (2011, 2013, 2020c).

[4] The data have been presented in a specific way to ensure that comparability across the entire period is not affected by (i) changes in the share of the centre and states in central taxes following the implementation of the Fourteenth Finance Commission recommendations; and (ii) the introduction of GST with a clause for compensation of states for revenue losses from the proceeds of a GST compensation cess levied by the centre.

References

Chancel, Lucas and Thomas Piketty (2018), 'Indian Income Inequality, 1922–2015: From British Raj to Billionaire Raj?', WID.world Working Paper Series, no. 2017/11, https://wid.world/document/chancelpiketty2017widworld/, accessed 1 June 2020.

Government of India (2011), 'National Accounts Statistics Back Series 1950–51 to 2004–05', Central Statistics Office, Ministry of Statistics and Programme Implementation.

——— (2013), 'National Accounts Statistics 2013', Central Statistics Office, Ministry of Statistics and Programme Implementation.

——— (2019), 'Periodic Labour Force Survey, Annual Report, 2017–18', National Statistical Office, Ministry of Statistics and Programme Implementation.

——— (2020a), 'INDIA'S FOREIGN TRADE: October 2020', press release, Ministry of Commerce and Industry, Department of Commerce, Economic Division, 13 November.

——— (2020b), Press Note on Provisional Estimates of Annual National Income 2019–20 and Quarterly Estimates of Gross Domestic Product for the Fourth Quarter of 2019–20, Ministry of Statistics and Programme Implementation, 29 May.

——— (2020c), 'National Accounts Statistics 2020', National Statistical Office, Ministry of Statistics and Programme Implementation.

——— (2020d), 'Periodic Labour Force Survey, Annual Report, 2018–19', National Statistical Office, Ministry of Statistics and Programme Implementation.

——— (2020e), 'Annual Survey of Industries 2017–18, Summary Results for Factory Sector', National Statistical Office, Ministry of Statistics and Programme Implementation.

Koshy, Jakob (2020), 'Coronavirus: "Zero Cases by May 16" Forecast Was Misinterpreted, Says NITI Aayog Member V.K. Paul', *The Hindu*, 22 May.

National Sample Survey Office (NSSO) (2014), 'Employment and Unemployment Situation in India, NSS 68th Round, July 2011–June 2012, NSS Report No. 554 (68/10/1)', Ministry of Statistics and Programme Implementation, Government of India.

Rawal, Vikas and Ankur Verma (2020), 'Agricultural Supply Chains during the Covid-19 Lockdown: A Study of Market Arrivals of Seven Key Food Commodities in India', https://www.networkideas.org/featured-articles/2020/05/Covid-19-lockdown-impact-on-agriculture/, accessed 1 June 2020.

Rawal, Vikas and Manish Kumar (2020), 'Covid-19 Lockdown: Impact on Agriculture', https://www.networkideas.org/featured-themes/2020/04/agricultural-supply-chains-during-the-Covid-19-lock-down-a-study-of-market-arrivals-of-seven-key-food-commodities-in-india/, accessed 1 June 2020.

Rawal, Vikas and Prachi Bansal (2019), 'The Surgical Strike on Employment: The Record of the First Modi Government', 4 June, https://www.networkideas.org/featured-articles/2019/06/surgical-strike-on-employment-the-record-of-the-first-modi-government/, accessed 1 June 2020.

Reserve Bank of India (RBI) (2020), *Handbook of Statistics on the Indian Economy*, https://www.rbi.org.in/Scripts/AnnualPublications.aspx?head=Handbook%20of%20Statistics%20on%20Indian%20Economy, accessed 27 October 2020.

Subramanian, Arvind (2019), 'Validating India's GDP Growth Estimates', CID Faculty Working Paper 357, Harvard University, July.

Vyas, Mahesh (2020), 'India Has a Jobs Bloodbath as Unemployment Rate Shoots up to 27.1%', *Business Standard*, 3 May.

14

Mexico: Confronting the Pandemic while Transforming the Political Landscape

Alicia Puyana Mutis and Lilia Garcia Manrique

Introduction: Understanding the Pandemic

The world is experiencing one of the biggest shocks in recent years. The coronavirus pandemic has impacted the lives of people in unimaginable ways. Economies have come to a halt with people staying inside their homes most of the time. In every way – biologically, economically, politically – the most menacing threat is the uncertainty of virus-related problems. We don't know how much it will cost, we don't know the best policy practices, and we don't know the behaviour of the virus in the long run.

Worldwide, the response to the current pandemic has been shaped by particular conditions existing in each country, reflecting, on one hand, a general lack of resources in the health system including proper supply of antivirals and vaccines, testing, and care capacities. On the other hand, it has been proved how difficult it is to reach a good balance between policies aiming to preserve life and caring for people's health, and those keeping the economy running and maintaining incomes. In any case, all countries face the need to solve economic crises induced not by the virus itself, but by the total lockdown imposed to control it (Ghosh 2020).

So far, it is not clear how the pandemic is going to evolve worldwide. Even the most sophisticated mathematical models on pandemics leave several unresolved questions. Parameters suitable for some regions (countries) may be unrealistic for some others. In terms of social impact, we can probably grasp the immediate effects in society but not the long-run effects. Once the shock impacts, there might be social, economic and even psychological hysteresis – a permanent, everlasting effect. In most of the scenarios, that means the shock is going to be pervasive over generations.

Lecture delivered on 9 May 2020.

The pandemic may remain an open wound unless governments implement sound public policies dealing with all these pressing issues, and effective vaccines are freely available for all persons.

The current configuration of an economic model based on orthodox economic theory – the appropriation of wild spaces, buzzing air traffic, chronically underfunded public health, marginalization of the elderly, structured ethnic and gender discrimination, and fragile supply chains – has made it easy for the proliferation of the virus. Present societies consider human beings, natural resources and the environment as commodities, available to be exploited and traded for profit. This perspective is more evident in a crisis like this one.

Now, there is larger acceptance of the many uncertainties surrounding the spread of the coronavirus. From a biological perspective, it has been suggested that the virus has a strong capability to mutate and evolve, making uncertain the recovery and immunity of those already infected. In particular, these features make it more challenging to get a successful and safe vaccine. In an economic sense, it is hard to say how hard it will hit each country and how it will impact their economic path, because we still don't know the full scale of the demographic and health shock. The extension and severity of this pandemic will depend on the characteristics of the society affected and the policy response of each country.

Compared with economic crises, during which there are extensive analysis disentangling the effects by sector (agriculture, extractive sectors, services, etc.), in a pandemic-triggered crisis the whole population is vulnerable, and because of that there should be a collective response. Another challenge is to identify the risk to sectors of society with the highest vulnerability, mainly because there are different kinds of vulnerabilities related to class, income, health, age, gender, ethnicity, medical predisposition, even blood type, that divide societies all over the world.

During the first seven months of this crisis, the only fact we knew is that the virus spreads very quickly, and once within an individual, it invades the respiratory system at a fast speed, leading very often to a fatal outcome. On the other hand, asymptomatic patients can also transmit the virus to others. Herd immunity is also considered to be one way of diminishing the effect of the pandemic. Nevertheless, this is a risky strategy since it signifies a high mortality rate and can leave important health complications in those infected. Finally, functional and affordable vaccines and treatments will take months, or more certainly years, to be developed.

For most of the developed countries, the pandemic has resulted in a crisis that they haven't managed to tackle correctly. Among the most deleterious cases are those of the United Kingdom and the United States of America, both with a high level of contagion and death rates. These countries had one common practice in particular: they pondered the economic outcome more than the social one. Besides, both have anaemic health systems that have been severely underfunded. Recently, Germany has been mentioned as the most successful developed country in administering the pandemic and its economic effects. The most successful cases are countries in the Asian region – China, Vietnam, Taiwan and South Korea among the most remarkable ones. These regions began a strict quarantine system before most other countries. Their citizens also demonstrated a strong commitment to policies following all governmental regulations. On the other hand, countries with lower population density, such as the Eastern European countries, Iceland and Norway, have also implemented successful practices.

In these times, it is essential to understand how the pandemic has inflicted harm and pain in most of the broad sectors of Latin American society and elsewhere, mostly because the enhancers of these shocks are endogenous and society-specific. Moreover, Latin America is affected by deep social, economic, gender and ethnic divisions, which would impair an already highly unequal distribution of costs and benefits during the pandemic and its economic effects. Latin American countries are still suffering from the profound impact of liberalization of the social security net. There was a drastic reduction in the provision of public goods and social services, particularly social security and public health, and education. Due to these neo-liberal reforms that tried to reduce costs and elevate efficiency, there was liberalization of the health system. This was guided by market-oriented principles and micro-economic practices (as just-in-time supply elements). The aim was to force the public health system to compete with private health providers. Most of the supply of medical resources relied on the supply chain which, for an increase in profitability, adopted dangerous strategies for reducing costs, such as practically eliminating stocks or closing rural hospitals and the number of intensive care units. Today, the Covid-19 pandemic has proven the high social, economic and political costs of liberalizing and privatizing public services. Chile is the clearest example in the case of Latin America.

In order to do a suitable assessment of the short- and long-term impact of the coronavirus, it is necessary to acknowledge the context of every country. For this purpose, we review some of the most important and pressing issues exacerbating the effect of the pandemic in Mexico and the suitability of the measures and policies taken to confront it, stressing some particular features that deserve special attention. First, the new political scenario that emerged from the unquestionable results of the last presidential elections; second, the centrality of social justice in the agenda of the new government, called La Cuarta Transformación (or the Fourth Renovation[1]); third, the lacklustre economic trajectory leading to multiple forms of inequality, such as ethnic or gender inequality,[2] alongside staggering corruption and violence. To solve these problems, the present administration adopted holistic government programmes accounting for sound responses to the pandemic. Since it aims to rescue the economy from long stagnation, reduce inequality and poverty, the president, Andres Manuel Lopez Obrador (AMLO) considers it a suitable response to the economic impact of the pandemic.

Mexico's Political Landscape

Since 1 July 2018, the political tsunami that erupted due to the results of the last presidential elections has impacted the economic and political arena in Mexico. The election was a landslide win for AMLO. His political party, the Movimiento de Regeneración Nacional (National Regeneration Movement – MORENA[3]), won the majority in the Senate and Deputy Chambers. Therefore, AMLO has a clear mandate to implement the political agenda he has been fighting for at least the last thirty years. Although political power is in his hands, he has faced the intensive opposition presented by the biggest investors in mining, the auto car and banking industries, and in a lesser degree, by the traditional political parties. He has been put on the spot in this regard, concerning most of the large infrastructure projects he presents as his main investment priorities. Criticism is also directed against the sustainability of social programmes in favour of the lowest income social groups while refusing to contract new public debt. A part of these attacks served the purpose of spreading fake news and putting in doubt policies with regard to containment of the pandemic. This misinformation represents a risk to the already vulnerable health system and a highly susceptive population. Nevertheless, the total approval rate of AMLO is 68 per cent with a 51 per cent approval of how the government has faced the pandemic (Lafuente and Beauregard 2020).

When the coronavirus crisis erupted, the economic and political situation in Mexico was complicated. The low-growth tendency aggravated the opposition from economiclly powerful groups and the traditional political elite became more belligerent. This lobby saw the pandemic as an opportunity to force AMLO to change his orientation. After AMLO's landslide electoral win in the 1 July elections, political opposition to him has been almost non-existent, or disoriented and divided by internal conflicts.

The more organized opposition has come from private sector interests or poorly articulated social and civil society groups that keep pushing for more market-oriented public policies.

The Lacklustre Mexican Economic Miracle: No Growth, Falling Labour Incomes

After almost forty years under structural reforms, liberalization programmes and NAFTA (North American Free Trade Agreement), there has been no real per capita economic growth. The average rate of growth in the period of neo-liberal economic reforms, 1982–2019, was 0.7 per cent, a massive decline compared to the growth registered during 1965–81 (Figure 14.1). During 1982–2019, Mexico recorded the lowest rate of growth since the beginning of the twentieth century, with serious effects on income, employment growth and productivity growth (Puyana and Romero 2015). The further fall in 2020 from the decline in 2019 will intensify poverty and inequality, a tendency that will continue despite the strong recovery estimates for 2021 (IMF 2020), and despite the efforts of President López Obrador to decrease both poverty and inequality.

A powerful catalyst of inequality is the sustained decline of labour income share in total national rent, a phenomenon registered all around the globe. The decline in Mexico, of 9.6 per cent, was one of the most severe in Latin America – a fall that implies a sustained transference from wages to capital profits and from lower to higher wages (see Table 14.1).

Figure 14.1 *Per capita GDP growth rates, 1960–August 2021, Mexico* (percentages)

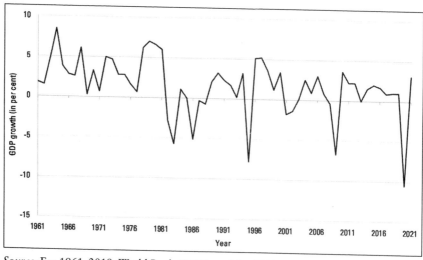

Source: For 1961–2019, World Bank (2020), and for 2020, IMF (2020).

Table 14.1 *Functional distribution of income in selected countries*

	Share of wages as percentage of GDP 1970–2017												Change in percentage 1970–2017
	1970	1980	1990	2000	2010	2011	2012	2013	2014	2015	2016	2017	1970–2017
Canada	53.2	53.3	53.4	50.1	50.4	49.9	50.7	50.7	50.2	51.5	51.3	50.7	–2.5
United States	58.1	56.8	55.9	57	53.3	53.3	53.3	53.0	53.2	53.6	53.7	53.5	–4.6
Brazil	34.2	34.7	45.4	45.4	41.6	42.2	42.8	43.2	43.5	44.6	44.7	s/n	10.5
Chile	42.7	38.1	33.8	39.8	36.1	37	38.7	38.4	38.3	38.3	s/n	s/n	–4.4
Colombia	39	41.6	37.4	32.8	32.7	31.4	32.2	32.7	33.1	33.5	33.6	33.9	–5.1
Mexico	35.7	36	29.5	29.7	27.6	27	27.1	27.9	27.4	27.3	26.6	26.1	–9.6

Source: For 1970–90, Comisión Económica para América Latina y el Caribe; for 2000–17, OECD (Organization for Economic and Development Cooperation) Statistics.[4]

This, in a context of deterioration of the labour market, a euphemism for the process of extracting an ever-increasing share of the value of work. The effect of liberalizing labour relations resulted in wiping out almost all labour protection norms and equating labour to civil legislation.

The 9.6 per cent fall of labour retributions implies a sustained transference from Mexican wages to capital profits, mainly to foreign private firms. Since the main or exclusive income, at least for 74 per cent of all households, is labour income, total inequality and poverty worsened. In effect, while only 5.1 per cent of the labour force are employers, 70 per cent are employees and wage-earners, 4.6 per cent do not receive any wage, and 20 per cent are self-employed mainly in the service sector and some in micro and mini enterprises. The sustained deterioration of the real minimum wage index, from 340 in 1976 to 30 in 2019 (see Figure 14.2), is worth mentioning.

Finally, it is important to recall the structure of employment by wages. More than 39 per cent of Mexican employees received a minimum wage (or US$ 5.6 a day). Nevertheless, today more people earn less than one minimum wage, as compared with what they did forty years ago. The wage distribution is negatively skewed (see Table 14.2). The mean average income is US$ 316 per month, and an income of US$ 600 per month is considered a middle-level income. In contrast, the wealthiest people have an income of US$ 33,000 per month. Most Mexicans earn less than US$ 600 a month, even though they have stable and formal jobs. With a diminished welfare state, even formal employees live from paycheck to paycheck and

Figure 14.2 *Real minimum wage index 1970–2019, Mexico*

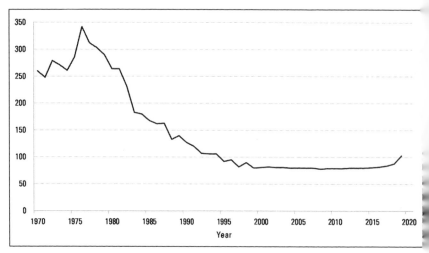

Source: Based on Puyana (2020).

Table 14.2 *Employment by minimum wages (MW) perceived as percentage of total number of workers, Mexico*

Year	At least one MW	More than 1 and at least 2 MW	More than 2 and at least 3 MW	More than 3 and at least 5 MW	More than 5 MW	No income
2017	15	27	20	13	5	6
2018	16	28	18	13	5	6
2019	19.86	31.57	18.06	8.93	3.61	6.0
2020*	22.64	35.74	15.56	6.71	2.77	5.3

Note: * Up to June 2020.
Source: INEGI (2020a).

have to work every day, whatever the conditions. In a post-coronavirus crisis scenario, it is very likely that those in the top income groups will dominate the poorer ones by means of their purchasing power, that is, in a 'vote with your feet' scheme. In the long run, there is a chance that this will increase economic and societal disparities.

The increased number of persons receiving up to one minimum wage and the deterioration of real minimum wage confirms the growing pauperization of the Mexican working class. Normally, the Mexican labour responds to economic crisis by reducing income and not by increasing unemployment as in Chile, Argentina or Colombia, for example. Even in

Figure 14.3 *Unemployment trends 2005–20, in percentages of total economically active population, Mexico*

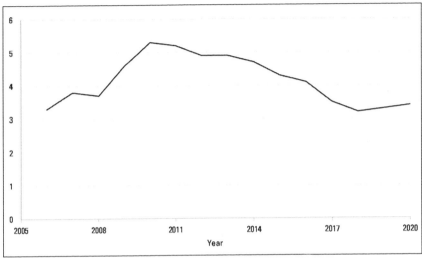

Source: INEGI (2020b).

the deepest crisis (1982, 1994, 2009, illustrated in Figure 14.1), unemployment reaches around 5 to 6 per cent of the economically active population and only for a few months (see Figure 14.3). With very low income, smaller savings capacity and non-existent unemployment insurance, unemployment has negative pervasive effects in those most vulnerable. Under such critical circumstances, few people can afford unemployment and have to move to the informal economy even at the cost of a drastic reduction of income. It is the real reason why unemployment stays almost at the same level as before the shock, as it had done in previous economic crises.

Another element distancing Mexico from other countries at similar level of development and from the United States and Canada, is the external index of its economy (the total trade of a country as per cent of its GDP). This shows how much of its product is imported and exported. With an external coefficient of 80 per cent of the GDP (42.5 per cent of imports and 38 per cent of exports), the Mexican economy is 2.6 times more open to competition in domestic and external markets than the American one.

Two major effects of this situation are worth mentioning: first, the high GDP propensity to import close to 5 per cent, meaning that a 1 per cent GDP increase would generate a 5 per cent increase in imports. Second, the disparate integration of the Mexican and the USA economies forces us to take a careful look at how asymmetrically Mexico's economy depends on the US. While about 3.3 per cent of the GDP in the US is linked to trade with Mexico, in staggering contrast, 50 per cent of the Mexican GDP depends on trade with the US – a dependency 16.7 times higher than the other way round (Puyana 2020). All these characteristics of the Mexican economy have been attributed to the liberalization and privatization processes instrumented since the mid-eighties last century, which were reinforced by the NAFTA and its substitute, the Mexican–USA–Canada Agreement, which entered in force during July 2020.

Mexico: A Highly Unequal Society

After almost forty years of lackluster economic performance and increasing concentration of wealth and income, there is no wonder why even with the unconditional transfer programmes instrumented since the mid-1980s, wealth concentration are still ruling out in the country. In 2018, according to official figures, around 45 per cent of the Mexican population lived in poverty and 17 per cent in extreme poverty. All in all, 29 per cent cannot afford to cover their basic needs like health, education and proper nutrition, and 37 per cent don't have enough income to afford a basic nutrition basket. Additionally, 56 out of 100 workers are in the informal sector (CONEVAL [National Council for the Evaluation of Social Development Policy] 2019).

As elsewhere in Latin America, in Mexico, the transition to the liberal economic model implied a worsening of inequality and poverty. Curtailing human rights, reduced access to social services and public goods, and intensive curtailment of labour protection were accepted as the way to 'put prices right', which in effect were mainly tools to reduce the power of labour force and to extract increasing share of the value it creates.

In Mexico, the value of the Gini income-concentration index revolved around 55 per cent, one of the highest in the region (Puyana 2019: 50–74). The distribution of income by deciles reveals some features of how the Mexican inequality looks like. In 2017, the income of the lowest decile (2.2 per cent) was slightly larger than one in the majority of the Latin America countries, while the share of the 10th decile (34.8 per cent) was somehow lower than Brazil, Chile and Colombia. At the same time, the Palma ratio which contrasts the income captured by the 5th and 9th deciles of distribution against the 10th receives a lower proportion (51.8 per cent). This ratio indicates that the Mexican middle class is relatively less affluent and does not capture a larger share of the pie as in Argentina, Peru or Ecuador, and some developed countries (ibid.) (see Table 14.3).

Information on wealth concentration is not abundant but those existent studies are relevant to understand inequality in Mexico. Some suggest that, in 2014, 63 per cent of total wealth was concentrated in the

Table 14.3 *Income distribution for some Latin American countries, deciles, 2017*

	Income share by			Ratio for Latin American countries		Ratio (Palma) for each country			
	Decile 1 (A)	Decile 10 (B)	Deciles 5 to 9 (C)	(B/A)	Palma (B/C)	Argentina	Germany	United States	Denmark
Argentina	1.9	29.4	55.1	15.47	0.53	1.00	1.25	0.94	1.32
Brazil	1.0	41.9	45.9	41.90	0.91	1.71	2.14	1.61	2.26
Chile	1.9	37.9	48.9	19.95	0.78	1.45	1.82	1.37	1.92
Colombia	1.4	39.0	48.2	27.86	0.81	1.52	1.90	1.43	2.01
Costa Rica	1.6	37.0	50.2	23.13	0.74	1.38	1.73	1.30	1.83
Ecuador	1.6	33.8	51.9	21.13	0.65	1.22	1.53	1.15	1.61
Mexico	2.2	34.8	51.2	15.82	0.68	1.27	1.60	1.20	1.68
Peru	1.7	32.3	52.8	19.00	0.61	1.15	1.44	1.08	1.52
Spain	1.9	26.2	56.8	13.79	0.46	0.86	1.08	0.82	1.14
United States	1.7	30.6	54.1	18.00	0.57	1.06	1.33	1.00	1.40
Germany	3.1	24.8	58.2	8.00	0.43	0.80	1.00	0.75	1.06
Denmark	3.7	23.8	59.0	6.43	0.40	0.76	0.95	0.71	1.00

Source: Puyana (2019)

Figure 14.4 *Labour poverty index (Índice de la tendencia laboral de la pobreza [ITLP]), Mexico*

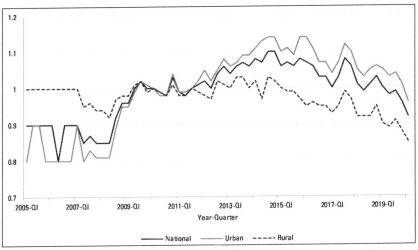

Source: CONEVAL (2020).

richest 10 per cent of the Mexican population, and the top 1 per cent of the very rich accounted for more than the 37 per cent (CEPAL 2010). This in part is explained by the high unequal concentration of financial assets where 80 per cent is owned by the richest 10 per cent.

Many researchers link the liberalization of the Mexican economy since the middle of the 1980s to an induced and sustained increase of the labour poverty index. The index went from 0.8 in 2005 up to 1.1 in 2014–15. Besides, rural labour poverty increased proportionally more that the national and urban average, perpetuating this everlasting divide (see Figure 14.4).

The Government Economic Programme

Since assuming the presidency on 1 December 2018, AMLO has fostered a regime change known as the *Fourth Renovation*. The president presented it as a *moral economics* (López Obrador 2020), the political economy road map to guide the government actions by an ethical compass. To restart economic growth, his first step is to mend the delicate social fabric destroyed by neo-liberalism, by reducing inequality and poverty via an array of income distributive programmes favouring the lowest income segments of the society. Second is fighting corruption and reducing the luxury of high government bureaucracy.[5] Third is procuring security and fighting impunity by acting on its social and economic causes. This package translated into drastic reducing and reordering of public expenditure[6] to finance his social programmes and infrastructure projects,[7] while promising not to increase taxes or to impose new levies, not to contract new public debt in real terms, and to freeze petrol, gas, electricity and water tariffs. These actions would recuperate real wages and invigorate the demand of low-income social groups. Since campaigning, he insisted on eliminating corruption, tax evasion and fraud, public sector extra-high salaries. Also for fighting drug organizations, he proposed expropriating bank accounts and properties of drug cartels and non-fully justified increases in wealth of top government officials. With these resources, the government will have enough solvency to finance its social programmes while maintaining fiscal discipline, that is low taxation and fiscal deficit. Nevertheless, some figures might prove him right, or at least nearly so. While refusing to increase taxes, the government eliminated all tax reductions, exceptions and devolutions, which amounted to 3 per cent of the GDP and initiated a tax recovery initiative, to induce big companies to pay several years' owed taxes. Fifteen large corporations owed overdue taxes for around 5 trillion pesos, i.e. 1.5 per cent of the 2019 tax income. Three of them have already paid 3 trillion pesos.[8] In Mexico, large corporations only pay 2 per cent tax of their income, while workers pay between 30 to 35 per cent of their labour income. One of the most startling examples is the automobile industry. Due to the generous incentives given forty years ago, they receive tax returns equivalent to 150 per cent of the levies paid. This is beyond important, since in Mexico the total amount of tax recovery is less than 16 per cent of the GDP.

Another driver of the recovery plan includes a very severe austerity plan. In AMLO's words, it is not acceptable for a poor country with a society divided by deep inequality to pay for an imperial, inadequate, expensive government. Particularly, public servants like politicians at the top level have lived (still there are some of them) in extravagant exhibitionist luxury. This fearsome determination against corruption has created an uneasy atmosphere for the wealthiest in the country.

Amongst others, the following are some of the more relevant social programmes:

i) universal pension for older people where 10 million persons are entitled to receive a 2,500 pesos monthly transfer;

ii) scholarships of 800 pesos per month burse for 13 million low-income students attending public education system, from pre-school to middle school;

iii) 20,000 pesos in non-guarantee loans (*a la palabra*) for micro- and mini-industrial and commerce enterprises;

iv) Stipendium for youngsters between nineteen and twenty-nine years out of work and study: one million persons a year would be enrolled receiving US$ 175 (3,800 pesos) a month for a year;

v) Young People Sowing Future: a programme for rural young people to work in small peasant agriculture;

vi) Production for well-being: For 2.8 million small and medium-size peasants, that is the 85 per cent of all agricultural producers, giving preference to 657 thousand small producers of indigenous origin;

vii) Programme to support 0.42 and 0.17 million small coffee and sugarcane producers, respectively;

viii) Guarantee Price Programme for 2 million small producers of corn, beans, wheat for bread, rice and milk, that will increase their income by 30 per cent a year;

ix) Welfare Universities Benito Juárez: Thirty-one universities started activities in March 2019 with 100 schools. Priority was given to high-density population areas with high degree of social backwardness, marginalization and violence, such as Oaxaca (eleven schools), Mexico City (ten schools), Veracruz (eight schools),

Chiapas and Guanajuato (six schools). Some 32 thousand open positions for students would receive a monthly scholarship of US$ 102.0 (2,400 pesos).[9]

An important element of AMLO's political agenda was to solve the effects on the provision of social services which were systematically and severely underfunded, the health system in particular (Gobierno de México 2020a). That is why, during the first fifteen months of his government, he visited 200 hospitals asking and interviewing doctors, nurses, paramedics, administration employees as well as the public about the state of the service. He found that at least 200 unfinished and abandoned hospitals, clinics and health units (their construction was suspended for financial and technical reasons, and their infrastructure severely damaged by earthquakes and hurricanes), 0.2 million workers did not have formal contracts and the system was understaffed (at least, by 0.2 million specialized personnel). Nevertheless, the amount of resources that this administration is considering for the health system is not enough to pay for accumulated deficits or to improve both the coverage and the quality of the service.

The Mexican health system is concentrated in mainly seven subsystems:[10] IMSS (Mexican Institute of Social Security, covering all private-sector formal workers), ISSSTE (Social Security Institute of the Public Sector Workers), PEMEX (Social Security of the PEMEX the State Oil Company), SEDENA (Social Security for the Arm Forces), SEMAR (Insurance service for navy services), SP (Popular Security) and IMSS Bienestar (IMSS Welfare). From these seven options just SP and IMSS Bienestar are available for people without formal employment or affiliation to any of the above mentioned systems. Besides these government-funded options, people may opt to pay for a private social and medical insurance, an option extremely expensive and inaccessible to the bulk of the population. All in all, the resources allocated to these public services represents 2.5 per cent of GDP (see Gobierno de Mexico 2020a for more detail). This is half of what may be suitable to cover health needs of all Mexicans. According to demographic and epidemiologic analysis, just to cover thirteen medical interventions like maternity care, infectious diseases, chronic diseases, preventive care and health promoting services, etc., Mexico should invest at least 5 per cent of GDP in health services. So Mexico still has a long way to go.

Since 2010, the public funding for IMSS increased from 44.4 per cent of the total health budget to 48.6 per cent in 2020. This was in sharp difference from the contraction of finances for other institutions as the Seguro Popular and Seguro para el Bienestar. Nevertheless, increases in public expenditure, even those for IMSS with a high share of budget, are small in per capita terms. In any case, there was a real reduction of total health public expenditure, from 2.8 per cent of the GDP in 2010 to 2.5 per cent in 2020. This year's Forecasted National Budget for Expenses (PPEF) had a 19 per cent reduction in share for illness prevention, 6 per cent in share for diabetes and obesity, and 7.8 per cent in HIV programmes (Méndez Méndez 2019). Once again, this shows the discrepancy between Mexican society's demography and effective public policies. Some caution is needed to understand the proper significance of such a decline. Dr López Gatell (the Deputy Health Minister) commented that under the outsourcing system, private laboratories perform 70 per cent of the laboratory analysis the public systems require annually (Gatell 2020). Also, the majority of all the acquisition of the medicines was outsourced to private firms, and additionally, important shares of the budget were directed to non-essential administrative activities. By eliminating this intermediation, savings gave space for increases in basic public health expenditure and disease prevention. Worldwide, Mexico presents some of the highest rates of diabetics, obesity, high tension and respiratory problems (Gatell 2020; Gobierno de México 2020a).

Nevertheless, for a per capita increase in heath expenditure per capita, demographic changes – morbidity, general growth and the ageing of the population – have to be considered. Expenditure has to grow at a higher rate than population in order to improve the system and to have the capacity needed to confront actual and future epidemics. Population dynamics are neglected when designing the strategies and resources to the health system. For example, life expectancy increased from 71.4 years in 1990 to 76.5 in 2020 and the proportion of people older than 65 years from 5 per cent to 9 per cent in the same period. But the number of years lost due to incapacity or early mortality increased, indicating perhaps a direct relation between age and morbidity rates. Mortality rates for people over 65 years increased from 2.5 to 4 per cent. This increase is due to more persistent transmissible diseases like chronic diseases that are more expensive in treatment and last longer. At the same time, in 2019, a severe scarcity of medical personal specialized in attending elder people was confirmed (Méndez Méndez 2019)

In 2010, the gap in resources between social security systems for those in the formal sector (IMSS, ISSTE, PEMEX, Sedena and Semar) and those without security service (SP and IMSS Bienestar) was wider. Now this gap is smaller, but this is an effect of a reduction of funding to both services. Disparities between health services are also remarkable – IMSS Bienestar has ten times lesser resources than someone with access to Pemex,

Figure 14.5 *Affiliation by decile in social security systems, 2018*

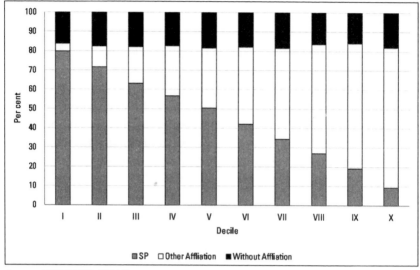

Source: CONEVAL (2019).

and four times lesser than those in IMSS (Méndez Méndez 2019). Besides, people in the lower income distribution are those who rely the most on the SP which has the most remarkable cut in budget (see Figure 14.5).

In 2020, the present administration modified the supply chain of medicines, transferring from subcontracted private companies to public sector entities the acquisition supply, storage, logistic and transportation activities. This change was mainly to eliminate corruption and cronyism in these processes. Still, with a chronically underfunded health system there are raising doubts of the capability of the public sector to successfully achieve these goals (Vega and Ureste 2019). These processes are highly specialized and need a lot of special equipment and resources, characteristics that the public sector lacks. AMLO promised to deliver to everyone in need – all the required medicines, as well as social programmes fostering prevention and better health, especially for vulnerable sectors such as the indigenous population. Although this is necessary, it is a demanding task given the existing limited resources still affecting the public sector.

As part of the proposals of the current government levering resources in the population, it has created the Health Institute for Welfare (INSABI [Instituto de Salud para el Bienestar]). This programme is open for everyone, even for those outside the formal security system. It is a sound and egalitarian programme, since the government has fully financed its development. The way to guarantee its sustainability is to consider and take proper account of the Mexican demographic dynamics, the population growth, and the changes in the demographic structure by age and the morbidity of the older population.

How the Coronavirus Affected Mexican Society and the Official Response

Within the uncertainty of the coronavirus trends, the public has to rely on measurement, diagnosis and policy implementation. For this, the government has to reassure that it is handling the crisis on behalf of the entire community, not of some few. Good and in time information and accurate accounting of the most relevant indicators is vital to produce the best strategies to control the epidemic. The fatality rate being one of the most critical indicators. It measures the total deaths divided by confirmed cases, the latter dependent on the number of tests. Total deaths are determined mainly by the demography of the country, the prevalence of existent illness, how far people live from hospitals and how well-equipped the hospitals are. After some pandemics that Mexico has experienced in the last twenty-five years – for example, the one caused by the influenza virus A H1N1 in June 2009 – epidemiological models predicting the spread of the virus were ready to be implemented for this new one as well as the record of the measures taken by the respective authorities. Since the beginning of January 2020, there was an urge for a policy response and time to prepare it until March when the first death was registered and the government suspended all activities at schools and universities, taking out of circulation around one-third of the total population. In contrast, some developed countries had a slower response and unprepared policies.

The coronavirus crisis has impacted more the poorest segments of population – that in major proportion are also those systematically discriminated, like indigenous and African-descendent communities. In Mexico, the health system has been underfunded since at least the 1980s. Regardless of this, there are people with access to three health insurance schemes, financed by public funds, depending on their type of work contract. On the other hand, people are labouring in the informal sector, with no access to health and social security protection; this creates higher inequality in an already unequal society. Nevertheless, the Mexican health system is one of the latest safety nets of a welfare state established around 1945, now severely diminished. After the Second World War and up to 1982 when the debt crisis erupted, Mexico had a progressive public education and health policies. The effort to consolidate and extend them was curtailed by the structural reforms and the neo-liberal model which privatized these sectors and introduced a free-market criteria. Besides, there have been numerous scams within the public health system – for example, non-working chemotherapies and, very recently, a non-existing and overpriced medical protective equipment.

Mexico registered the first confirmed case of Covid-19 on 28 February 2020; by 21 May (84 days later) there was a total of 56,000 confirmed cases, that is 382 total cases per million. By 11 June, there was a drastic increase in cases (see Table 14.4); though compared with other countries like USA (6,300), UK (4,294), Spain (6,198) and Italy (3,905), Mexico was doing better (1,003), but not as well as India (216). These numbers also have to do with the total number of tests carried out per population, and in this regard, Mexico has a lower rate of test per million people – a total of 2,866 – whereas the US (69,423), UK (91,957) and India (3,780) have done better. The most recent figures seem to reveal Mexico has a lower incidence rates than other countries at different rates of development and disparate political and ideological orientations (see Table 14.4).

The Mexican curve of confirmed cases suggests the country has higher rates than India, but lower than Chile, Peru and Brazil. Nevertheless, it is important to mention that Mexico only conducts tests for cases that received medical attention in hospitals. Figure 14.6 represents confirmed cases given the rate of testing. More testing could provide a different rank-

Table 14.4 *Relative rates of coronavirus incidence: cases, deaths and tests per million until 18 August 2020, Mexico*

	Total cases per million population	Tests per million population	Death per million population
UK	4,294	91,957	608
Spain	6,198	95,507	580
USA	6,300	69,423	350
Ecuador	2,521	7,271	211
Brazil	3,706	6,422	190
Peru	6,339	38,117	179
Chile	8,065	40,877	139
Mexico	1,003	2,866	119
Iran	2,146	13,978	102
Russia	3,443	95,080	45
Colombia	859	8,750	28
India	216	3,780	6

Source: WorldoMeter: Coronavirus pandemic.[11]

Figure 14.6 *Daily confirmed Covid-19 cases from first registered contagion until 18 August 2020*

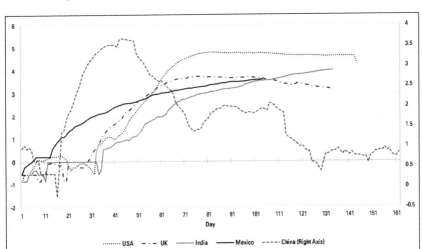

Source: Elaboration based on data from Our World in Data, 2020.[12]

ing. Assuming a higher testing rate, the number of cases will be higher, but the trend of the curve will be the same.

Given the low capacity of the Mexican health system, the health minister implemented the sentinel surveillance, the method proposed and used by the World Health Organization (WHO). This survey calculates an expansion factor to get an approximation of the real infected population. Nevertheless, this expansion factor is hard to calculate, varies between countries and has been criticized for its sampling process. The population that is fully sampled are the most severe cases, mainly or first treated in hospitals (less severe cases would be never counted or would be so with some delay). Those that report mild symptoms are only sampled by a 10 per cent rate. For Mexico, the mean of the expansion factor is 8.3 according to the Health Secretary, Mexico (Gobierno de Mexico 2020b).

So far, the distribution of cases across the thirty-two states shows a high concentration in the most populated areas with the highest population density – 42 per cent of all confirmed coronavirus cases are concentrated in Mexico City (CDMX) and Mexico State. Less populated areas – namely Colima, Baja California Sur, Campeche, Nayarit, Tlaxcala, Aguascalientes, Zacatecas, Quintana Roo, Durango – show lower contagion rates, or rather they are in an early stage of the pandemic (see Figure 14.7). Ninety-one per cent of the cases are concentrated in twenty states. The high rates registered in Tabasco and Veracruz, states with relative low population density, lower income and high concentration of indigenous and African-

Figure 14.7 *Concentration of coronavirus cases: accumulated, active and deaths, in percentages in Mexican states, 18 August 2020*

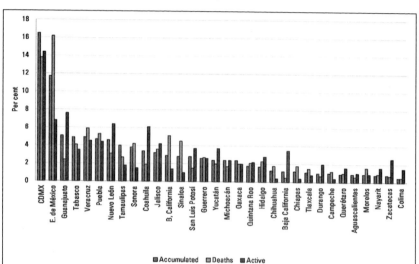

Source: Own elaboration based on data from Gobierno de México (2000c).

Figure 14.8 *Mexico: active cases per 100,000 inhabitants, 18 August 2020*

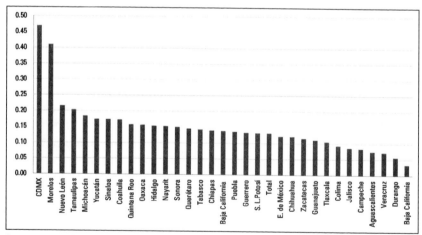

Source: Own elaboration based on data from Gobierno de México (2000c).

descendent communities, seem to confirm this discrimination by ethnicity and income in Mexico as well.

This tendency is confirmed by the incidence rate across the population, illustrated in figures 15.8 and 15.9 depicting the active cases (Figure 14.8) and the deaths (Figure 14.9) by million persons in the thirty-two

Figure 14.9 *Deaths by coronavirus per 100,000 inhabitants, Mexico, 18 August 2020*

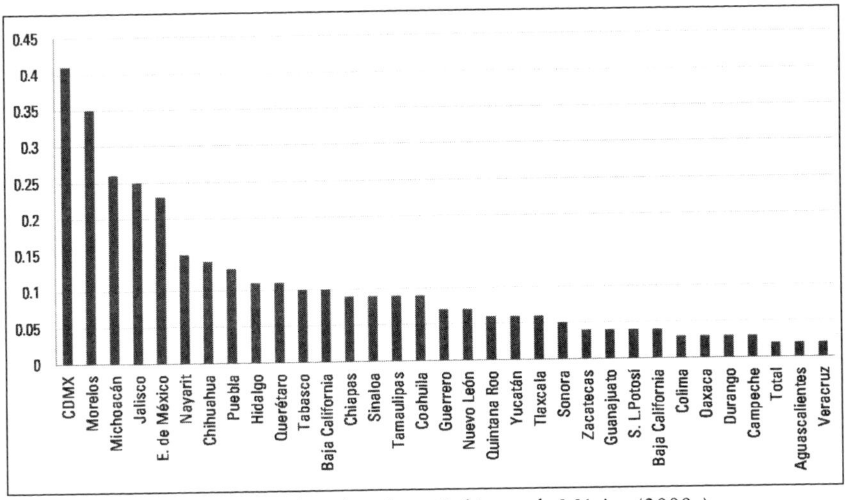

Source: Own elaboration based on data from Gobierno de México (2000c)

federal states. While Mexico City is the one with more active cases and deaths, an interesting reordering is evident, attributable to the different weight of their respective populations. Nuevo Leon, a rich state with lesser population than Mexico State has lower proportion of cases, while five of the states where the bulk of indigenous and African-descendent population is concentrated (Puebla, Tabasco, Chiapas and Yucatan) are above the national average.

Figure 14.10 illustrates the fatality rates, that is the quotient of active cases to deaths. This time Mexico City is not leading the table, an indication of having better medical infrastructure and relative mayor availability of intensive care units and mechanical respiratory equipment. It is surprising that a high fatality rate is in Nuevo Leon, the second richest state, after Mexico City. Some of the poorest states, with important indigenous communities seem to be doing far better than Nuevo Leon.

Municipalities of the Mexico City, the most densely populated state of the republic, presents great divergences in health infrastructure (see Table 14.5). While Iztapalapa has good infrastructure, with a rate of 1 clinic per 197 habitants, Milpa Alta has only 1 clinic per 2,400 habitants. Again, those with the highest ratio of clinics and doctors are the ones with the highest rate of infection. Most probably, this may reflect different population density and testing capacity. The systemic problem in the public health system is better illustrated in Table 14.5.

WHEN GOVERNMENTS FAIL

Figure 14.10 *Fatality rate by states, 18 August 2020*

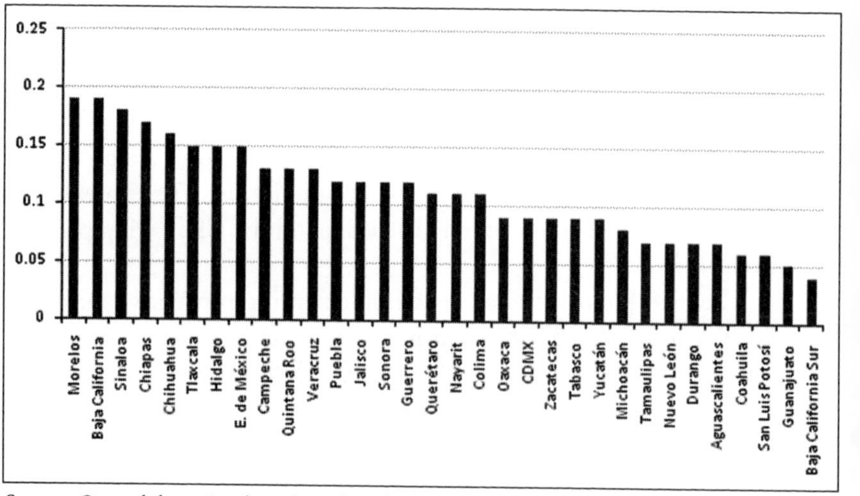

Source: Own elaboration based on data from Gobierno de México (2000c)

Table 14.5 *Capacity of health system per inhabitant by municipalities in Mexico City, 2018*

	Clinics	Doctors	Nurses	Beds	Confirmed cases	Per cent by population
Iztapalapa	197	68	43	137	3247	17.8
Gustavo A Madero	115	33	18	56	1954	16.8
Tlalpan	508	266	128	335	1232	18.2
ÁlvaroObregón	1634	392	218	620	1006	13.4
Coyoacán	839	323	230	672	964	15.8
Cuauhtémoc	354	145	75	237	920	17.3
Iztacalco	1568	477	290	850	931	23.9
Miguel Hidalgo	521	185	102	229	702	19.3
Xochimilco	2649	1325	832	4673	902	21.7
Venustiano Carranza	1167	447	332	1311	836	19.6
Azcapotzalco	648	176	76	226	748	18.7
Benito Juárez	674	173	105	336	605	14.5
Tláhuac	2165	925	444	1197	761	21.0
Milpa Alta	1379	734	434	2759	397	28.8
Magdalena Contreras	1244	934	987	9380	365	15.0
Cuajimalpa	2400	1569	1311		273	13.7

Source: Own elaboration based on information from CONEVAL (2019).

Has Mexico Already Stopped the Contagion?

On 14 March 2020, i.e. sixteen days after the first confirmed case of Covid-19 in Mexico, the educational ministry announced the suspension of activities in elementary and secondary schools effective from 20 March. By then, universities and some firms had already moved to home-office schemes and virtual lectures. These measures isolated forty million persons, one-third of the Mexican population. These preventive measures were taken sooner than in the USA and the UK, saving perhaps thousands of lives.

The health ministry has been implementing preventive measures with easily comprehensible instructions. As first action, a daily conference at 7 pm was established, where the deputy health minister Hugo Lopez Gatell presented, in a clear way, the daily number of confirmed cases, deaths, and answers any question concerning the pandemic in Mexico. He has an extensive experience in dealing with epidemiological crisis – he was the one in charge during the H1N1-virus (swine flu) pandemic in 2009. Another initiative which has become very popular is a friendly cartoon called 'Susana Distancia', a play on words to mean 'keeping the distance', which promotes the 1.5 meters of preventive distance between people. So far, the pandemic has spread all over the country and at different speed, in the intensity as depicted in figures 14.7 to 14.10.

Criticism has been directed from the outset of the pandemic towards the team of specialists dealing with the pandemic (physicians, epidemiologists, mathematicians and so on) as well as to some government health policies. Critics concentrated on the speed and intensity of the spread of the pandemics, the ways of registering active cases and deaths, and the question as to why the government is not testing as the Chinese do. The government has established an information system that practically puts all the data of the pandemic in real time allowing the public to follow the trajectory of the epidemic.[13]

So far, it is feasible to suggest that the way Mexico has approached the pandemic is correct given its national complexity. Nevertheless, there are some doubts about the ending of the quarantine measures. For some, it is too early, since the country is still showing an increasing trend in the curve. The opening is gradual, not uniform for the whole country depending on the traffic light signal established by the team of experts, that is, a scale of how high the risk of infection is given the number of cases in the country.[14]

As far as the response to the economic effects of the pandemic is concerned, AMLO suggests that the policies and programmes put in motion are adequate and only needs to be intensified and speeded up. He vehemently opposed contracting debt or increasing debt in real terms, contrasting with policies of other countries. He observes that, given the disparity in capital accumulation that is driving the significant proportion of inequality in Mexico, those who possess most of the capital will be getting most of these fiscal budget funds. On the other hand, small and medium enterprises and entrepreneurs, which provide 52 per cent of the GDP and employ around 72 per cent of the working population, will be negatively affected by the austerity and the lockdown policy if they do not receive financial support. The only available relief response is a credit of US$ 400 (10 thousand pesos) available, intially until May and later extended by a few months more. Still, most of these enterprises have been struggling since mid-March.

One of the central responses to the economic problems due to the coronavirus crisis is the unconditional, direct transfer[15] programmes. Even before the crisis, the total amount of resources directed to these programmes was about 3 per cent of GDP, and for this year, 2020, there was an increase of 2.8 per cent. During the first ten months of the new government, there have been at least 20 million people receiving some economic transfer and by the end of 2020, 80 per cent of poor households would receive financial support. Moreover, programmes like pensions for senior people (above 65 years of age), Benito Juarez scholarship for young students, scholarships for university students, and financial transfers for people with disabilities and social security for elderly people, are now guaranteed by the Constitution, making it hard for future administrations to overlook or erase these social programmes.

Although these unconditional transfers may prove to be the right policies, it is true that there is still a long way to go. Nevertheless, it is necessary to consider as well the severe inequality, poverty and less than mediocre economic growth Mexico experienced during the last four decades before the new government was inaugurated and the pandemic erupted in Mexico in March 2020. According to Oxfam Mexico (Oxfam 2020), during 2020 only, 40 per cent of people living in poverty have received some kind of economic help. The ones that received the biggest share of these social programmes are children, teenagers and senior people; the most significant gap is for people between twenty and 59 years of age (ibid.). The main beneficiary of the unconditional-transfer programmes are the poorest segments of society, and some sections of informal workers, leaving out around 56 per cent of them. All in all, to reduce inequality and poverty, and controlling the effects of coronavirus, a more robust and extended net of social benefits, job-creating programmes should have to be put in place as soon as possible. For that, fiscal expenditure has to be extended far beyond savings from corruption and republican austerity, and tresspassing the limits of the neo-liberal fiscal discipline by increasing direct taxes and fiscal expenditure as to have a really progressive fiscal system. As CEPAL has noticed, countries that contracted debt to manage the pandemic have not had better economic situation than Mexico and others that have not done that.

Conclusion

The coronavirus has highlighted the lethal effects of the Mexican embedded inequality. Even with timely response from the government, the idea of a quarantine, like those measures in the developed world, are not feasible. A high share of labour informality and a chronically underfunded health system are the main drivers of this pressing situation. With a health system, the main goal of which is market oriented, the manoeuvrability to respond to the pandemic was very small. The increase in contagion is highly correlated with a higher testing rate in Mexico in the last days; still, it is one of the lowest when compared with other countries.

The government fighting against inequality represents a struggle against years of inappropriate policies. Still, some measures championed by this government are not the most suitable ones. Guided by austerity, there are budget reductions in areas such as prevention of chronic diseases and obesity. Besides, the direct transfer programme is insufficient and leaves the majority of those working in the informal sector (people between twenty and 65 years of age) without an effective direct transfer programme. With these omissions once again, those in most need are uncovered and unprotected.

The disruption caused by the Covid-19 crisis in Mexico is just a crisis that once again demonstrates the fragility and vulnerability of a country with uneven distributed costs and resources. Although it is potentially transmittable to everyone, those with a lot of resources would easily overcome the problem or would be more resilient to this shock. It is necessary to implement policies that do account for all the heterogeneity of the Mexican society, mainly with regard to inequality. Even if the main idea of fighting for corruption and keeping balance of the national budget is reasonable, it should also take into account the social cost of stopping, all of a sudden, resource flow to certain areas. Otherwise, this could result in a costly miscalculation of the present administration.

Notes

[1] The other three renewing acts being: the Independency, the Benito Juarez Liberal revolution in the nineteenth century and the Mexican Revolution in early twentieth century.

[2] Almost 25 per cent of the Mexican population are identified as indigenous and 2 per cent as African descendants. These sections of the population are particularly vulnerable. While, in 2015, around 10.3 per cent and 7 per cent of the indigenous and African-descendents respectively, did not have any education; for the rest of the population it was only 5 per cent. Besides, there are larger disparities regarding access to social security and health services (Puyana 2020).

[3] Morena is the colloquial, affectionate popular name given to the Virgen de Guadalupe referring perhaps to the belief that the Virgen de Guadalupe helps specially the poor Mexicans. México is a religious society where Catholicism has been the main doctrine.

[4] https://stats.oecd.org/index.aspx?queryid=60702, accessed 18 April 2020.

[5] The first step towards this was reduction of the presidential salary by more than a 50 per cent and requiring no civil servant to earn more than the president. In some not so few cases, this resulted in cutting wages by more than two-thirds. Protests immediately erupted claiming violations of constitutional rights.

[6] For example, the much criticized cancellation of the new international airport in Mexico City.

[7] The new oil refinery, the Maya Railway, the 100 universities, amongst others.

[8] They did pay after threatening to go to litigations. In 2019, the tax authority collected 35 trillion owed taxes and expects in 2020 to collect around 70 trillion. If so, effective taxes could increase to 18 per cent of the GDP. For detailed comments on this topic, see González (2020).

[9] For full detail of the programme, see Gobierno de México (2020a).

[10] Instituto Mexicano del Seguro Social (IMSS), Instituto de Seguridad y Servicios Sociales de los Trabajadores del Estado (ISSSTE), Petróleos Mexicanos (PEMEX), Secretaría de Defensa Nacional (SEDENA), Secretaría de Marina (SEMAR), Seguro Popular (SP).

[11] https://www.worldometers.info/coronavirus/, accessed 20 June 2020.

[12] https://ourworldindata.org/coronavirus, accessed 16 August 2020.

[13] https://covid19.cdmx.gob.mx/nuevanormalidad, accessed 21 june 2020.

[14] The traffic light can be consulted at https://coronavirus.gob.mx/semaforo/; and for Mexico City at https://covid19.cdmx.gob.mx/nuevanormalidad.

[15] The resources are transfered to a savings or bank account of the beneficiaries. All the intermediaries were eliminated, reducing the costs of the programme.

References

CEPAL (2010), 'La hora de la igualdad. Brechas por cerrar, caminos por abrir', Santiago de Chile: CEPAL, https://repositorio.cepal.org/bitstream/handle/11362/13309/S2010986_es.pdf, accessed 25 June 2020

CONEVAL (2019), 'Estudio Diagnóstico del Derecho a la Salud 2018', Ciudad de México, https://www.coneval.org.mx/Evaluacion/IEPSM/Documents/Derechos_Sociales/Diag_derecho_Salud_2018.pdf., accessed 25 June 2020.

_____ (2020), 'Evaluacion de la Política Social', https://www.coneval.org.mx/Evaluacion/IEPSM/Paginas/Consideraciones2020.aspx, accessed 25 July 2020.

Gobierno de México (2020a) 'Plan Nacional de Desarrollo 2019–2020', https://lopezobrador.org.mx/wp-content/uploads/2019/05/PLAN-NACIONAL-DE-DESARROLLO-2019-2024.pdf., accessed 27 May 2020.

_____ (2020b), 'Conferencia de de Prensa. Informe Diario Sobre Coronavirus COVID-19 en México', https://www.gob.mx/presidencia/articulos/version-estenografica-con-ferencia-de-prensa-informe-diario-sobre-coronavirus-covid-19-en-mexico-240164?idiom=es, accessed 25 of August 2020.

_____ (2020c) 'Secretaría de Salud', https://covid19.sinave.gob.mx/Log.aspx, accessed 13 August 2020.

González, A.R. (2020), 'Interview with Raquel Buenrostro Director of the Servicio de Administración Tributaria SAT', in *La Jornada*, 3 June 2020, https://www.jornada.com.mx/2020/06/03/economia/019n1eco, accessed 4 June 2020.

Gatell, López (2020), 'Conferencia Informativa', 5 June 2020, https://www.youtube.com/watch?v=9QCAf3C-GBo, accessed 20 June 2020.

Ghosh, Jayati (2020), 'The Pandemic and the Global Economy', *Dissent*, 20 April 2020, https://www.dissentmagazine.org/online_articles/the-pandemic-and-the-global-economy, accessed 24 June 2020.

INEGI (2020a), 'Encuesta Ingreso y Gasto de los Hogares 2020', https://www.inegi.org.mx/rnm/index.php/catalog/310/datafile/F34/V2020, accessed 12 June 2020.

_____ (2020b), 'Encuesta Nacional de Ocupación y Empleo, 2020', https://www.inegi.org.mx/programas/enoe/15ymas/, accessed 30 July 2020.

IMF (2020), 'World Economic Outlook', June, https://www.imf.org/en/Publications/WEO/Issues/2020/06/24/WEOUpdateJune2020, accessed 17 August 2020.

Lafuente, J. and L.P. Beauregard (2020), 'El 68% Aprueba el Mandato de López Obrador, Pese a Rechazar su Gestión de la Inseguridad y los Feminicidios, in El País', 1 July, https://elpais.com/mexico/2020-07-01/el-68-aprueba-el-mandato-de-lopez-obrador-pese-a-rechazar-su-gestion-de-la-inseguridad-y-los-feminicidios.html., accessed 25 August 2020.

López Obrador, A.M. (2020), *Hacia una Economía Moral*, México City: Planeta, 2020.

Méndez Méndez, J. S. (2019), 'La contracción del Gasto Per Cápita en Salud: 2010–2020', CIEP, ciep.mx/tQyr, accessed 2 June 2020.

Oxfam (2020), 'La Política Social en Tiempos de la 4T: Nota Metodológica', Oxfam, México, https://www.oxfammexico.org/sites/default/files/Nota%20Metodológica%20Oxfam%20México%20COVID%2019.pdf., accessed 15 June 2020.

Puyana, A. (2020), 'Del Tratado de Libre Comercio de América del Norte al Acuerdo México-Estados Unidos-Canadá. ¿Nuevo Capítulo de la a Integración México-Estados Unidos?', *El Trimestre Económico*, 2020, vol. 87, no. 347, pp. 635–68.

_____ (2019), 'Inequality, Work, Poverty and Economic Policies: A Link to Explain the Latin American Protracted Malady' *Efil Juornal of Economic Research*, vol. 2, no.5, ISSN: 2619-9580, http://www.efiljournal.com/efil-journal-25-2019/, accessed 15 June 2020.

Puyana, A. and J. Romero (2015), *México: de La Crisis de La Deuda Al Estancamiento Económico*, El Colegio de México, CDMX.

Vega, A. and M. Ureste (2019), '¿Cómo Planea el Gobierno Distribuir Medicamentos? Estos Son los Costos y los Riesgos', Animal Político, 14 June 2019, https://www.animalpolitico.com/2019/06/gobierno-distribucion-medicamentos-costos-riesgos/, accessed 10 June 2020.

World Bank (2020), World Development Indicators, https://databank.worldbank.org/source/world-development-indicators, accessed 17 August 2020.

PART THREE

Food and Agriculture in a Time of Disease

15

The Bengal Famine
and Its Lessons for the Present

Utsa Patnaik

Today, my brief is to speak about the massive famine in Bengal in 1943–44 that claimed 3 million civilian lives, and its lessons for the situation we are in today. No doubt the organizers had in mind my paper published in 2018 on the 75th anniversary of the famine, created by the wartime policies of the British government with respect to India (Patnaik 2018). Analysing the reasons for that, the famine does throw up important lessons for present times when a global pandemic is stalking the world.

The first lesson has to do with the danger of the exercise of arbitrary and absolute power by any government with tunnel vision, pursuing a single objective with no concern for the maintenance of livelihoods, or for the very high cost the poor in particular have to pay in the course of its achieving that objective. The second lesson is that even though policies at the macroeconomic level profoundly affect our lives and in fact become a matter of life and death for the poor majority, governments get away with following bad and inhuman policies because not even the trained economists whose job it is to understand, take the trouble to understand how adverse their impact can be on the people. This ties up with the third lesson, that intellectuals have to change their slothful ways. Progressive intellectuals were not active then in critiquing these policies that killed millions, and they continue to be unacceptably complicit to this day with the theories and policies of ruling establishments which adversely impact ordinary people, until a crisis makes them wake up suddenly, but usually they wake up far too late.

First, let us discuss why the 1943–44 famine in Bengal took place. After the Japanese attack on Pearl Harbour in December 1941, the USA

Lecture delivered on 5 May 2020.

entered the war against Japan. Singapore had already fallen to Japanese forces which were advancing northwards through Burma. Allied forces poured into Bengal province in India to counter the Japanese advance. A massive war boom started as air strips and barracks were quickly built and factories came up for producing munitions, uniforms, bandages, chemicals and so on, while civilian consumption goods production was drastically reduced. Under an agreement signed between the colonial Indian govern-ment and the British government, the cost of financing the hugely increased war spending by the Allies was put on the Indian Budget, which had to meet these costs in rupees without any upper limit on spending and with only a promise that India would be repaid once the war ended, whenever that might be. The British government deposited, against this rupee war spending by India for the Allies, equivalent sums denominated in sterling (called recoverable sterling expenditure) in the account of the Reserve Bank of India in London. These sterling deposits were treated as reserves, and rupee notes could be printed up to two-and-a-half times their value.

But the sterling deposits were mere notional paper entries for they were frozen, not a single penny could be drawn, so they were of no actual economic value to Indians. The rupee sums for financing the war constituted, in reality, a forced loan of enormous and unlimited extent that Britain was taking from Indians without their knowledge or consent, that too with no guarantee of actual repayment as promised once the war ended. To treat the equivalent entries of sterling with the RBI as 'reserves' was invidious since reserves are meant to be actually there to be used in case of dire need, for example for food imports, whereas these so-called 'reserves' did not exist in reality since not a penny could be drawn. The deposits were an accounting measure designed to extract massive resources from the Indian people through a deliberate policy of inflation.

Taking a forced loan from India in the form of what he called 'profit inflation' was the brainchild of John Maynard Keynes, who in 1940 was made an economic advisor to the British government and given special charge of Indian monetary matters. Keynes was considered to be an expert on India's monetary and financial matters owing to his thirty-four years of close engagement with Indian affairs. The first job Keynes had ever held, for two years starting 1906, was at the India Office in London, and his first book published in 1913 when he was thirty years old, based on this experience, was titled *Indian Currency and Finance*. He gave lecture courses to students on Indian money and finance for several years after joining the faculty of Cambridge University, and he was a member of a number of official commissions set up on Indian finances from 1913 to 1926 – the Chamberlain, Babington-Smith and Hilton Young Commissions, and for a while the Indian Fiscal Commission. He worked closely with the Secretary of State for India in the British government, Edwin Montagu (later known for the Montagu–Chelmsford reforms).

The deliberate nature of rapid inflation imposed on India is very clear from Keynes's own exposition of his theory of 'profit inflation' that he considered to be a practical necessity for extracting wartime resource (see quotes below). For him it was equally applicable everywhere including Britain. But in practice it was applied to India alone, and not to Britain owing to strong working-class opposition there to his ideas.

Demand management is a two-edged economic weapon. When there is unemployment of labour and resources as in a depression, public expenditure using deficit financing in moderation will increase mass demand by a multiple, inducing expansion of output and employment. Because during the Depression Keynes had advocated, against prevailing views, for the first time such public expenditure to reduce unemployment and raise consumption, the working class in Europe had reason to be grateful to him. (The German trade unions had advocated slightly earlier, the same policy for countering depression.)

But equally, when required by the state, mass consumption demand can be compressed drastically either through increased taxation, or using the policy of rapid inflation that Keynes systematically espoused to finance war. Both in his *Treatise on Money – the Applied Theory of Money* (1930) and *How to Pay for the War* (1940), Keynes explicated his idea of deliberately promoting inflation to lower mass consumption in order to raise forced savings. He said that 'the rich were too few'; and in view of the unusual demands of war finance it was absolutely essential to reduce the consumption of the ordinary population of workers, to ensure 'forced transferences of purchasing power' from them to capitalists, who should then be taxed. Keynes was very considerate when it came to the rich in Britain, for although they were few, they concentrated most of the nation's assets in their hands, a matter he ignored. What he called 'virtuous finance' would be to deliberately promote an inflation which he called a 'profit inflation', which would reduce the real consumption of the people thus releasing the forced savings required for war investment. This is precisely what was done in India: although the policy of deliberate inflation that he advocated was in general terms and applicable to Britain as well, strong trade union resistance in Britain prevented it from actually being put into effect there.

Keynes wrote in the *Treatise on Money – the Applied Theory of Money* (1930) where he discussed the First World War:

The war inevitably involved in all countries an immense diversion of resources to forms of production which, since they did not add to the volume of liquid consumption goods purchasable and consumable by income earners, had just the same effect as an increase in investment in fixed capital would have in ordinary times. The investment thus required was – especially after the initial period – on such a scale that it exceeded the maximum possible amount of voluntary saving which one could expect, even allowing for the cessation of most other kinds of investment including the replacement of wastage. *Thus forced transferences of purchasing power in some shape or form were a necessary condition of investment in the material of war on the desired scale.* The means of effecting this transference with the minimum of social friction and disturbance was the question for solution. (Keynes [1930] 1979, pp. 152–53; emphasis added)

He then went on to discuss the three different methods through which such 'forced transferences of purchasing power' could be achieved: first, by reducing money wages while keeping prices steady; second, by letting prices rise more than money wages so as to reduce real wages; and third, by taxing earnings. Taking up the third course, he thought that 'the rich were too few' and therefore 'the taxation would have had to be aimed directly at the relatively poor, since it was above all their consumption, in view of its aggregate magnitude, which had somehow or other to be reduced' (ibid., p. 153). But the additional taxation of wage-earners would have to be substantial, it would meet trade union resistance and would be difficult for the government to implement.

'It was a choice, therefore, between the remaining alternatives – between lowering money wages and letting prices rise . . . it would be natural – and sensible – to prefer the latter' (ibid., pp. 153, 154). Keynes argued that it would be as difficult to enforce the required 25 per cent money-wage cut, as to impose heavier taxes. *'I conclude therefore that to allow prices to rise by permitting a profit inflation, is in time of war, both inevitable and wise'* (ibid., p. 155; emphasis added).

Keynes went on to say that while a profit inflation would raise profits by lowering wages, it was essential that after adopting such a policy towards capitalists that 'pours the booty into their laps', the state should tax the capitalists and not permit them to lend at interest to the state:

It is expedient to use entrepreneurs as collecting agents. But let them be agents and not principals. Having adopted for quite good reasons a policy which pours the booty into their laps, let us be sure that they hand it over as taxes and that they are not able to obtain a claim over the future income of the community by being allowed to 'lend' to the State what has thus accrued to them. *To let prices rise relatively to earnings and then tax entrepreneurs to the utmost is the right procedure for 'virtuous' war finance.* For high taxation of profits and of incomes above the exemption limit is not a substitute for profit inflation but an adjunct of it. (Ibid., p. 155; emphasis added)

Thus Keynes thought that while workers would not accept direct measures like money-wage cuts or increased taxes, they would accept rise in prices even though their money wages were not rising as fast, reducing their real consumption to the same extent as the two other measures. Irving Fisher was later to term this a belief that workers suffered from 'money illusion'. Keynes was mistaken in his belief, for trade union leaders were not so obtuse as he thought. In articles published in newspapers and journals in Britain during 1939 and 1940, Keynes repeatedly advocated inflation as a method of raising resources, and this met with stiff resistance from workers' unions, whose leaders like Aneurin Bevin categorically responded that deliberate inflation was unacceptable. The working class was prepared voluntarily to contribute resources for fighting fascism, but it would not agree to a policy of deliberate inflation that tricked them into lowering their consumption. They were right to resist, for rapid inflation is the most regressive possible method of raising resources since it hits to the hardest extent the poorest among workers. In Britain Keynes was forced by this strong trade union opposition to give up his initial ideas. It is strange that Keynes was also against rationing of necessities even in wartime, but fortunately for Britons, his views in this respect too were not accepted. In *How to Pay for the War* (1940) Keynes did mention inflation again briefly, but to ensure unity he opted for a system of graded extra taxes on income, exempting the poorest completely. To implement this new policy he made a quick estimate of British national income in 1941 and its distribution, arriving at a per capita annual income of £131 – this was thirty times the per capita annual income of Indians.

Taxes were greatly raised in India too, but the main reliance was on profit inflation, with the state acting directly as the principal agent of increased spending. As foreign forces massed in Bengal, spending by the colonial government for the Allies saw an explosive 6.7-fold rise of the central budget in the three years from 1940 to 1943, and only a quarter was met through doubling tax revenues, while three-quarters of this huge spending was met by simply printing notes. From under Rs 100 crore in 1939–40 the central government outlays rose to Rs 670 crore by 1943–44. This was an unprecedented degree of spending – an inflationary policy of such a magnitude was not seen anywhere else in the world. For the detailed data on public spending reproduced from the Reserve Bank of India reports, see Patnaik (2018).

There was no prior information leave alone debate in India: rapid profit inflation and hence severe reduction of real purchasing power, was arbitrarily thrust on an unsuspecting population whose per capita income was one-thirtieth of that of the average Briton. Keynes showed an unwavering commitment to serving his country, to the point of ruthless disregard for the cost to colonized peoples, and no one was in a better position than he was to know the impact of compressing demand so drastically. The political class in India was caught completely unawares and unlike in Britain, there appeared to be no intellectual understanding and hence no opposition was articulated at the analytical level to profit inflation, at least not to our knowledge, nor was there any later demand for reparations for the immense and avoidable loss of lives through starvation.

To get a sense of what this order of spending means, we can take some present-day figures for India. During fiscal 2019–20 the central government outlay (not counting devolution to the states) was about Rs 15 lakh crore or 8 per cent of that year's GDP of about Rs 190 lakh crore. (One lakh crore is a thousand billion, namely 10 raised to the power 12.) Let us imagine what would happen if within two years from now, by fiscal 2022–23, the central government budget spending in rupees rose from 15 lakh crore to 100 lakh crore, with revenues doubling to 30 lakh crore and the deficit of 70 lakh crore being met by printing notes. In short, the total budget spending by the central government in two years' time would then amount to just over half of the present total GDP of about 198 lakh crore (estimated for 2020–21 taking into account the economic effects of the current pandemic). That is what happened in India between 1941 and 1943: the explosion of spending meant that the 1943–44 total outlays accounted for half of British India's entire pre-war GDP; the annual monetized deficit alone in every war year from 1941 to 1946 was three times the normal budget. Nowhere in the world were more irresponsible monetary policies followed than in India, and nowhere did food prices rise as rapidly in so short a time.

From the demonetization debacle of 2016 we know that even today India lacks the technical capacity to print notes quickly, and this was the case to an even greater extent at that time. The frenetic rise in money supply took place with the new notes being printed in London, and flown over to India. We know that in a poor country there would be very strong multiplier effects of public spending on demand for necessities, since the poor cannot afford to save, and consume all their income. Indians had to meet not only the cost of housing, transporting and provisioning the Allied forces but also meet the booming wage-goods cost of the many lakhs of workers newly employed in war construction and in other war-related enterprises. But grain output could not possibly rise so fast; indeed rice output had been declining for three decades in Bengal owing to area diversion to commercial crops, so the adjustment to such suddenly increased demand was bound to be through rise in prices rather than rise in output.

While the wholesale price index rose 300 per cent in India as a whole, in Calcutta, between January 1942 and February–April 1943, the price of rice per maund (a maund equalled 82.13 pounds or 37.23 kilogram) quadrupled from Rs 6 to Rs 24, and by October 1943 it had nearly doubled again to Rs 40. Price rose even more in small towns to between Rs 50 to Rs 100 (Palme-Dutt [1997, p. 263] quoting Bhowani Sen). In terms of annas per lb. (pound) of rice, the price rise was from 1.2 to 4.7 and further to 7.8 at the dates mentioned. The per capita annual income in India was Rs 64 in 1940, or Rs 5.33 per month. Assuming iron rations, that 1 lb. of rice daily or 30 lb. per month was the only food item that one person consumed (and that she spent nothing on any other item like fuel, clothing and so on), in January 1942 this cost 35 annas, amounting to two-fifths of average monthly income. But by February–April 1943 the monthly rice cost for one person dependent on open market purchase, at 140.4 annas or Rs 8.78, *exceeded* by two-thirds her total monthly income of Rs 5.33.

The government, keen on maintaining war-related production, had quickly put rationing in place by procuring foodgrains and other necessities mainly from the hinterland of Bengal, focusing on making food, cloth and fuel available to what it deemed to be essential workers – those in war-related industries, transport and construction, and the middle classes. The urban population of greater Calcutta suffered consumption decline but most had access to rationed food. The entire burden of financing the outlays was effectively passed on to the unprotected rural population. In the villages those dependent on purchasing food did not know what hit them. As the price of rice quadrupled in eighteen months, rose nearly 8-fold within twenty-one months and then local stocks physically disappeared, they first faced shortage, then hunger, then famishment and finally death. The classes earliest and worst affected, naturally were those entirely or mainly dependent on the market for purchasing foodgrains and other necessities. They were the rural wage-paid labourers, the poor peasants with a little land but mainly dependent on wages, artisans, fisherfolk and service providers. Small and middle peasants who had parted with their rice output at unprecedentedly high prices were left without food as prices rose even higher. The situation was tailor-made for speculators who by holding on to stocks contributed to further price escalation.

The reduction of their consumption to extract forced savings for financing Allied spending was so savage and compressed into such a short time that 3 million of the poorest civilians died of starvation. The famine mortality during 1943–44 amounted to 5 per cent of the total population of undivided Bengal, and these deaths by starvation over two years comprised *more than six times* the below half a million total estimated mortality in Britain of armed forces and civilians combined, over the entire period of the war.

If we look at the age structure of the Indian population, 37 per cent were children aged 14 years or less. Assuming the same proportion of the young in Bengal's population as in India, even if we further assume that parents fed their children first so that the famine mortality of children was lower, making up say 30 per cent of the total and not 37 per cent, at least 9 lakh (0.9 million) children starved to death during 1943–44, twice the total war mortality in Britain.

In my 2018 paper I had termed the Bengal famine a genocide by economic means, for the rapid inflation was deliberately brought about by government policy, and there were other humane alternatives available for raising finance. In rounded terms, £1200 million was the total amount of war finance raised by reducing Indian consumption on account of recoverable spending for the Allies (not counting the additional £400 million monetized deficit on India's own account). The annual value over 1941 to 1946 of the total recoverable expenditures that killed so many was £200 million, which was a relatively small sum for the Allies. In Britain additional annual taxation of only £4.5 per head or 3.4 per cent of average income, during the six years, would have met the outlays. If the USA had chipped in the additional annual taxes needed would have been only £1 per head annually.

But of course, ordinary working people in colonies were hardly regarded as human beings by imperialists and were considered to be dispensable; Keynes and his friends habitually referred to ordinary Indians as 'blacks' and Winston Churchill, with whom he worked closely, had famously said that the Hindus were a 'foul race' and were 'protected by their mere pullulation from the doom that is their due' (quoted in Murray 2009, p. 20). They were too hardened to be affected by the carnage in Bengal; in a letter to a friend, the editor of the *New Statesman* and *Nation*, Keynes blamed the recent Indianization of the civil service and hence its alleged inefficiency, for the famine! Imperialists never took moral responsibility for their own actions. At Bretton Woods in 1944 the

Indian delegation including its British finance member pressed the British delegation headed by Keynes to release at least a small part of the frozen sterling deposits immediately against dollars for badly needed food imports from USA. Its request was torpedoed by Keynes, who said that sterling debt was a bilateral matter between Britain and India – even though India had financed Allied forces, not British forces alone. By 1946 the per head grain availability had dropped to 137 kilogram in India compared to 157 kilogram in 1937, and the drop was of course much steeper in Bengal.

Lessons from the Real Cause of the Famine for the Present

The first and immediate lesson relates to the danger of arbitrary decisions taken by the state in pursuit of a single over-riding objective, showing complete tunnel vision with no consideration of the actual cost to the majority of the population. In the process the original objective is itself lost. If the Japanese Army had reached India the country's armed forces would have fought it, and civilian mortality would have been certainly much less than 3 million lives sacrificed through arbitrary Keynesian profit inflation to keep the expensive Allied troops operational. As Covid-19 started spreading abroad in early 2020, the Prime Minister in India, at 8 p.m. on 24 March, announced a complete all-India lockdown from the next day, which meant that all productive activity and the bulk of services had to shut down, and all transport except medical and essential transport came to an end. There was no preparation for this arbitrary and drastic step whatsoever and no prior knowledge was conveyed even to the Chief Ministers of the constituent states of the Indian Union as their subsequent bitter complaints have made clear. The November 2016 demonetization had been similarly announced arbitrarily at night and had left workers and businesses deprived overnight of wages and working capital for many weeks, forcing enterprises to shut down. Workers rendered unemployed, especially inter-state migrant workers, had headed to their distant villages and were able to do so at that time because at least transport was available. Although they had no guarantee of work, in their villages they could expect some support from their extended family and social networks. It is estimated that there are at least 100 million inter-state, namely long-distance migrant *workers* in India, and since a substantial proportion have families with them the migrant *population* involved is at least 300 million. With the agrarian crisis of recent years, the actual numbers today are likely to be higher than the data sources indicate.

With the 24 March shutdown the suddenly unemployed workers, deprived overnight of incomes, could not even travel to their home states and villages since no transport existed. Casual labourers were soon evicted from the crowded urban shanties in which they lived since they could not pay rent, and they expected to run out of food as well within a few days. As the lockdown was extended after every two to three weeks repeatedly and their meagre resources were exhausted, they saw no alternative but to defy the lockdown and walk to their villages located many hundreds of kilometres away. Not only fellow Indians but the world has seen harrowing scenes of their long march on empty stomachs, running the gauntlet of stick-wielding police, with many deaths on the way through hunger and through road accidents. This disgraceful state of affairs could have been avoided through some prior planning and preparation whereas in practice the individual state authorities and charitable organizations were left to cope with a chaotic situation, with the central government belatedly organizing special trains to transport workers several weeks after they lost their jobs. The individual states are financially stressed by the central government's failure to deliver in time the promised compensation for loss of tax revenues after the introduction of the Goods and Services Tax (GST) in 2017, which had concentrated tax collection with the central government. The GST replacing state-level sales taxes was a measure undermining the federal revenue imperatives of a vast and diverse country, to which the state governments should never have agreed in the first place.

The forced migrant labour exodus has been a major factor in the continuing spread of the pandemic. The apparently laudable aim of containing the pandemic through the lockdown was itself subverted by its arbitrary, sudden and unplanned nature which completely ignored the very existence of the millions dependent on daily wages who were made to lose their means of subsistence overnight, even as relatively trivial measures were announced by the government to please the middle class (such as moratorium on fines for late credit card payments).

Just as tunnel vision combined with imperial arrogance led to ignoring the impact on the poorest Indians in the 1943–44 drive to finance war spending, after 75 years in an independent India with representative democratic governance, the labouring poor have been ignored in the drive to contain the pandemic, resulting during those weeks in almost as many people becoming victims of hunger and accidents, perhaps, as of the virus. Of course, the scale of distress is much less, not comparable at all to the colonial famine, and not comparable either to the great influenza pandemic a century ago in 1918–19, which had killed 13 million to 15 million Indians with an indifferent colonial state looking on. But even a single unnecessary death is unacceptable in an independent India where the very people who are suffering the most have elected to power those who implement the policies that affect their lives.

A great deal of the criminal neglect we see is related to the class–caste structure in the country and the deeply elitist and casteist ideology of the minority who run governments and head institutions, for most of whom the labouring poor are usually invisible even though the economy would cease to function without their labour. While their recent crisis has been projected as a humanitarian one, which indeed it is, few have recognized that it represents a violation of the fundamental rights as citizens of the country as enshrined in the Constitution of India. The 2016 demonetization had also represented a violation of the fundamental right to life. Every other country in the world affected by the pandemic has taken immediate measures to reach compensating incomes by the government to those losing their means of livelihood through the lockdown, but in India even after four months millions continue to be without their earlier means of sustenance. Economic disenfranchisement has made a mockery of their political enfranchisement and of the hopes with which many had voted the incumbent government to power.

The second and related lesson to be drawn from the earlier famine for today's circumstances is that macroeconomic policies followed by the state have a profound impact on the lives of ordinary people, but appear to be little understood and hence are inadequately contested. When state policies are welfare-reducing for the majority, it is the duty of educated citizens who belong to the well-to-do hence relatively unaffected minority, to point out the adverse effects, and they need not be economists alone. But while there was an explosion of art, song and literature on the Bengal famine, no *analytical* critique of the real reason for the famine, namely deliberate inflation imposed on the people, or explicit opposition to this economic policy was seen at that time whether from public intellectuals or from patriotic political leaders, even though many of the latter were intellectually very able persons. There was a great contrast in this respect with Britain which saw stiff working-class opposition preventing the same policy from being implemented.

The best detailed account of the macroeconomic policies followed then (without mentioning the famine at all) remains P.S. Lokanathan's *India's Post-War Reconstruction* (1946), followed many years later by Amartya K. Sen (1981) in *Poverty and Famines*. In the chapter dealing with the Bengal famine, Sen had rightly concluded that '[t]he 1943 famine can indeed be described as a "boom famine" related to powerful inflationary pressures initiated by public expenditure expansion' (p. 75) and had traced the 'failure of exchange entitlements' to such inflationary pressures .

In the early 1940s, Keynes's brightest Indian students at Cambridge most certainly must have understood why in Bengal, the poorest civilians were starving to death, but they found it expedient to maintain silence rather than criticize persons as influential and powerful as Keynes and Churchill. The Indian student Keynes most favoured obtained on his recommendation the post of an executive director of the newly set up International Monetary Fund. Silence is equivalent to complicity, and unfortunately such complicity is seen to this day on the part of far too many intellectuals, particularly those connected in the past or at present with the government, who have ignored the poverty-raising impact of official neo-liberal policies on the bulk of our population; while some continue to make false claims of poverty decline.

In the absence of the direct colonial control that prevailed earlier, so much of the neo-imperialist drive of Northern countries today relies on ideology, on peddling incorrect or outdated theories in new guise, to pressurize decision-makers in the global South to follow policies which harm their own populations to the benefit of the North. Intellectual critiques of these policies are therefore now important as never before. For more than a quarter century since the early 1990s, policies reducing mass welfare have been followed in India by successive governments pliantly bowing to the intense pressure exercised by international finance capital. This has been done regardless of the political complexion of the governments, though the intensity of welfare-reducing policies and their adverse impact has grown over time. But we have not seen the expected degree of incisive analysis or consistent protest by progressive mainstream intellectuals participating in official policy-making bodies, who appear to have been either completely, or substantially hegemonized by the dogmas of finance capital.

This set of policies usually labelled as 'neo-liberal' is strongly reminiscent of colonial policies albeit in a modern setting, and its two main pillars have been reintroduction of free trade and periodic compression of public spending. Both policies reversed four decades of the Nehruvian strategy of protecting small producers from the vortex of global prices and following expansionary fiscal policies to generate development. The Nehruvian strategy had been mercilessly pilloried by the foreign and expatriate Indian ideologues of finance capital who wanted to see India opened up again to meet the demands of advanced capitalist countries. But it had a sound logic, and we see before our eyes the result of abandoning that logic in the adverse trends of employment decline and severe decline in food security over the last three decades of neo-liberalism.

The first neo-liberal policy of reintroducing free trade, by removing protection to small producers including farmers and exposing them to global price volatility as in colonial times, has undermined their livelihoods and induced through un-repayable debt, over 3,20,000 farmer suicides since 1997 to date. The second neo-liberal policy of periodic fiscal contraction has affected income growth and employment in the material productive sectors very adversely. Further, technological change in manufacturing, which becomes mandatory in a trade-liberalized economy for firms to remain globally competitive, means that positive growth of manufacturing investment and output is now marked by negative growth of employment. The latest employment figures show an unprecedented rise of open unemployment to 6 per cent of the workforce.

During the four decades of state-directed or *dirigiste* measures of protecting the economy and increasing public development spending, the food security of the population had improved with the per capita foodgrain availability climbing slowly to 177 kilogram average by the three years centred on 1991, a substantial gain compared to the average of 145 kilogram during the three years centred on 1952. But with the inception of neo-liberal policies which affected both output and demand, this trend was reversed. Grain output per head started falling with area and resource diversion to export crops, and grain availability again fell to 162 kilogram by 2007, as fiscal compression led to demand compression. Public stocks far in excess of buffer needs have been periodically building up, because the decline in effective demand of the population hence increase in hunger, was faster than the decline in per capita output. A contributory factor was misguided targeting of the food subsidy and wrong poverty estimates, resulting in the exclusion of millions of the actually poor from below-poverty-line ration cards, hence exclusion from affordable foodgrain rations from the public distribution system. Of late output per capita has been rising, but demand compression induced by the 2016 demonetization followed by the current pandemic, means that unsold grain stocks are at a historic high of 89 million tons (counting unmilled rice) and availability is bound to have declined even further.

A most grotesque argument is that fall in per capita grain consumption in India is the outcome of diversification of diets as incomes rise and so is nothing to worry about. Those putting forward this argument are ignorant of three decades of discussion using detailed data provided by national governments to the United Nations Food and Agriculture Organization (FAO), that has shown conclusively that as a population gets richer and goes for more diversified diets with more animal products, its per capita demand for grain *rises* quite steeply. This is because while direct consumption of grain may fall, use of grain as feed rises fast for producing animal products – milk and poultry products in particular, even in countries where vegetarianism is prevalent. The FAO database shows that by 2011, annual per capita consumption of grain (for food + feed) was in kilogram, 152 + 9 = *161* in India, compared to 148 + 27 = *175* for the Least Developed Countries, 151 + 40 = *191* average for Africa, 152 + 122 = *274* for China, 125 + 331 = *456* for the European Union and 106 + 396 = *502* for the United States. India is at the bottom of the global charts, even lower than the Least Developed Countries.

Poverty Has Risen Not Declined, and the Current Pandemic Is Producing Further Impoverishment

Let us end with a brief discussion of an intellectual scam of global proportions that has been in operation for at least three decades, namely the spurious claims of poverty reduction, a claim made both by national governments in developing countries and by the World Bank. In reality, far from reducing, poverty has been increasing in most countries during the three decades of market-oriented reforms, which made privatized health care, utilities and education so expensive – even as unemployment rose and incomes were compressed – that the mass of the people have been not only deprived of adequate access to these services but have been forced to cut back on food intake. The nutritional intake data from the National Sample Survey (NSS) show that per capita energy intake measured in kilocalories per day has declined and so has per capita protein intake in grams per day. The decline started earlier in rural areas while in urban areas it started somewhat later. The same surveys give every five years (when large samples are canvassed) the consumer expenditure and nutritional intake of private persons in households ranked by levels of spending on all goods and services, from the poorest to the richest. We find from the 2011–12 sample survey, that the thirty-day monthly spending needed to access rural/urban nutrition norms of 2200/2100 kilocalories per day, namely the poverty lines using the official definition of norms, were Rs 1,300 in rural India and Rs 2,250 in urban India and the percentage of rural/urban persons below these levels was as high as 67/68 per cent compared to 59/57 per cent in 1993–94, which marks a significant rise in poverty. The required spending per capita, namely the daily poverty lines for rural and urban India were thus Rs 43.3 and Rs 75 respectively.

But the revised official monthly poverty lines presented by the government for 2011 in rural/urban areas were only a fraction of this, Rs 816 in rural and Rs 1,000 for urban areas, namely in daily terms Rs 27.2 and Rs 33.3 respectively, which when applied naturally gave grossly underestimated poverty percentages of 26 and 14 in rural and urban areas respectively with 22 per cent as the national average. The national poverty line of Rs 29 would not have bought even two (1-litre) bottles of drinking water. What it measured was destitution, not poverty. After the initial year of correct poverty estimation, 1973–74, the official poverty lines only allowed the consumer lower and lower nutritional intake over time, diverging downwards more and more from the nutrition norm, a matter on which both the government and intellectuals following the same method have maintained a deafening silence, thereby misleading the public.

The reason for such large underestimation of poverty lines and hence of poverty percentages lay in an undeclared, silent *abandoning of the nutrition norm* by the national governments, not only in India but in China and all other countries too, when calculating poverty lines. These governments applied the nutrition norm only once, in an initial year termed the base year (1973 in India and 1985 in China) to consumer expenditure and nutrition data, to obtain the correct spending level satisfying the norm, but after that never again applied the nutrition norm to ascertain poverty, but simply used consumer price indices to bring forward to later years, the base year rural and urban poverty lines (see Patnaik 2013). This unstated change in the definition of the poverty line is logically incorrect and represents *a fallacy of equivocation*, where the same term, 'poverty line', is used in two completely different senses: one directly using nutrition norms, the other simply price-indexing the original, by now decades-old poverty line.

Since, unlike many other countries India has a very sound database giving us every five years the consumer expenditure and nutritional intake data from the NSS, this author was able to carry out the estimation of correct poverty lines which were by 2011 at least double even the revised official ones. Abandoning its own definition of poverty line has meant *cumulative* underestimation by the government over a long four decades, so that by year 2011 the official poverty lines were a fraction of true poverty lines. The latest consumer expenditure survey for 2017–18 has been removed from the public domain, so bad are the findings, so we can give examples only from the earlier survey.

In rural Punjab in 2011–12, the official poverty line was Rs 1,054 per month or Rs 31.1 per day and only 7.7 per cent were declared to be poor. But from the basic data we find that this poverty line permitted a person only 1,500 calories daily energy intake, far below the required norm of 2,200 calories for working health. The actual poverty line meeting the norm was Rs 48.3 per day, and 31 per cent was in poverty, over four times the official claim. In rural Gujarat which has a large tribal population, the official claim was that 21.5 per cent of persons were poor using its poverty line, but at this official poverty line, we find that only 1,080 calories per day could be accessed, which is a starvation level. Accessing the norm level of nutrition required a level of spending which could not be afforded by 90 per cent of the state's rural population. Similarly striking was the case of rural Puducherry in 2009 where the official estimate declared poverty to have virtually disappeared with only 0.2 per cent falling below the official poverty line of Rs 21 per day, not mentioning of course that at this spending level only 1,150 calories daily could be accessed. The true poverty line was over double this, and 56 per cent of persons were poor. In every such case of inadequate calorie intake at official poverty lines, the protein intake too was below minimum required levels.

In China, as in India, the same procedure of merely indexing the 1985 base year line was followed and by mid-2011 the official rural poverty line was a paltry 3.5 yuan daily, which would have purchased just over 1 litre of bottled water. However China in December 2011 raised its annual poverty line to 2,300 yuan or 6.3 yuan per day, which price-indexed to year 2017, comes to 2,952 yuan or 8.1 yuan per day. This sum allowed the purchase of 2.05 litres of bottled water, no doubt marginally better than the less than 2 litres of bottled water commanded by the poverty lines in other countries, but still far too low in absolute terms to meet minimal food and other expenses. While China has done better than other developing countries, its claim of drastic poverty reduction to below 1.7 per cent of its population by 2017 is misleading for just as in India, its price-indexed poverty line is far too low to permit anything but a hungry and miserable level of living no longer satisfying any reasonable nutrition norm leave alone adequately meeting non-food expenses. The true poverty line is likely to be at least three times the official one. The current pandemic and global slowdown will affect the poor in China severely no less than in India and so it is very important for its government to recognize that in reality, poverty is much higher than it currently claims.

The World Bank's international poverty line is derived from the national poverty lines of thirteen countries, all increasingly underestimated over time, and so its claim of decline in absolute poverty is completely spurious just as national claims of decline are spurious. Poverty decline cannot be claimed when the nutrition standard against which poverty is measured is itself allowed to decline, and decline drastically, with a deafening silence being maintained on the matter of the declining standard.

The World Bank obtained its latest US$ 1.90 international poverty line by taking an average of the rural poverty lines of thirteen poorest countries mainly located in sub-Saharan Africa, and in these countries, just as in India and China, poverty lines had been increasingly underestimated to provide by now only starvation levels of living. It then multiplied these local currency poverty lines by its purchasing power parity (PPP) numbers to arrive at the dollar value. For example if India had been one of the thirteen countries, then, since in 2011 the market rate of exchange, namely Rs

45.45 for one dollar, was estimated to buy 3.2 times the same basket of goods in India that 1 dollar could buy in the US, the local currency rural poverty line of Rs 27 would be multiplied by 3.2 and the result, Rs 86.4 would amount to US$ 1.9. Of course, the World Bank's US$ 1.9 so defined, as we have seen, would have bought less than 2 litres of bottled drinking water whether in the US or in India. Those who are found to survive still at or below this miserable level of spending are not the poor, but home-less beggars and the destitute. There is a real and deep racism embedded in the World Bank's assumption that in developing countries US$ 2 a day can be at all thought of as a poverty level of consumption, while the USA's annual 'poverty threshold' for a young family of four with two children is US$ 6,550 per capita or US$ 18 per capita per day, nine times higher.

Economics was not an independent subject until quite recently: Adam Smith and Karl Marx studied history and philosophy and were therefore well versed in logic (not only formal, mathematical logic but also applied logic). Economists and econometricians working with data today the world over, seem to be universally innocent of the most elementary logical principles, that have been known for a thousand years. If they had the slightest idea of these principles, at least those academics who are honest would not have adopted one definition of poverty line directly linked to nutritional norms, and then when estimating applied an altogether differ-ent definition delinked from any norm, while suppressing the fact that the different definition meant lower and lower nutritional intake over time. To attribute ignorance to the estimators however is to be extremely kind, for in reality for many, a degree of opportunism, of taking the line of least resistance by going with the dominant flow, also plays its part. National governments and the World Bank are likely to continue with their illogical estimation procedures no matter how fraudulent and absurd the results, because it is so convenient for them to be able to mendaciously claim poverty reduction, when the market-oriented neo-liberal policies they have advocated and inflicted on country after country, have in reality not just increased relative poverty, but increased absolute poverty substantially.

It is all the more important for honest academics to refuse to go along with these fraudulent estimation procedures leading to spurious claims of poverty reduction, and to make realistic estimates of the actual cost of living. They face a powerful global establishment, but then, arriving at what is true has been always a struggle for academics, which cannot be shirked because what is at stake is the welfare of millions of people who are being badly short-changed by being told they are not poor, when in reality they cannot afford food, medical treatment or education for their children. The extent and depth of the current increase in hunger and deprivation owing to the pandemic will not be understood and no effective counter-measures will be taken, as long as illusions are retained on past decline in poverty, when in fact it has been on the rise for a quarter century.

In India a very big mistake was to abandon the universal public distribution system in 1997 and go for targeting the food subsidy which immediately excluded millions of the actually poor from accessing affordable foodgrains, since they were not classified as eligible for 'below poverty line' ration cards that alone provide rations at significantly less than market prices. Recent surveys have shown that while 81 per cent of rural households and 67 per cent of urban households had ration cards, the holders of 'below poverty line' cards among them were only 26.5 per cent of rural and 10.5 per cent of urban households.

Even before the 2020 pandemic, the November 2016 demonetization had plunged the country into recession, and the NSS 2017–18 consumption expenditure data (quickly removed from the public domain by the government) showed for the first time, absolute decline in the household per capita real spending on all goods and services compared to 2011, across all spending classes of persons. (Per capita real food expenditure had been declining for many years before that.) The current lockdown beginning in the second quarter of 2020 has worsened greatly an already bad situation with respect to employment, incomes and access to food and health care. It is well known that public spending in India on health has been among the lowest in the world, and declined further under neo-liberal reforms to hardly 1 per cent of GDP. Even in normal times over 1,200 people on average die every day from tuberculosis (TB) and more than 500 persons die from malaria, although neither should be fatal as effective treatment is available, but they die mainly because they are too poor to afford the treatment especially for TB which requires many months of medication.

The economic measures urgently required today have been repeatedly put forward by competent scholars, but to what extent even the steps announced by the government so far will actually be implemented remains to be seen. There is unlikely to be any real official departure from the income-deflating tenets of neo-liberalism, but without such a jettisoning of the neo-liberal package no pulling back from recession and subsequent expansion is possible. First, those who have lost their jobs are facing starvation so the immediate priority is to put cash in their hands to spend, using the district-level administration in combination with local government bodies to distribute cash to all applicants, sufficient to meet their food costs for at least three months. The Mahatma Gandhi National Rural Employment Guarantee scheme has to be expanded and funded without limit as it is a demand-driven scheme. Second, in the medium run there has to be a large real expansion of public spending to support small-scale producers focusing in particular on labour-intensive, employment-generating areas of production including agriculture, small industries and local infrastructure. Third, immediate free distribution of excess food stocks should be followed up by removing the targeted system completely in favour of a universal public distribution system, and foodgrain exports should be curtailed until the country reaches reasonable levels of domestic consumption. Fourth, a supplementary budget is required to increase the allocation to public health to 5 per cent of GDP namely to about Rs 10 lakh crore. Fifth, minimum support prices for farmers need to be made effective at the state level through actual procurement, and to address price volatility, there needs to be public procurement of cash crops by restoring the procurement function of Commodity Boards, a function which had been abolished in the mid-1990s. Piecemeal measures of cash transfers to bank accounts undertaken so far, which reach only a small fraction of those actually in distress, will not do the job either of relieving distress or of stimulating revival.

References
Government of India (GoI) (2013), *Press Note on Poverty Estimates*, July.
Keynes, J.M. (1913), *Indian Currency and Finance*, London: Macmillan.
_____ ([1930] 1971), *A Treatise on Money – the Applied Theory of Money*, in *The Collected Writings of John Maynard Keynes*, vol. VI, Macmillan and Cambridge University Press, for the Royal Economic Society.
_____ (1940), *How to Pay for the War*, Melbourne: Macmillan.
Lokanathan, P.S. (1946), *India's Post-War Reconstruction and Its International Aspects*, Delhi: Indian Council for World Affairs.
Murray, A. (2009), *The Imperial Controversy: Challenging the Empire Apologists*, Croydon, UK: Manifesto Press.
Palme-Dutt, R. ([1940] 1997), *India Today*, London: Gollancz; Indian reprint, 1997, Calcutta: Manisha Granthalaya.
Patnaik, U. (2013), 'Poverty Trends in India 2004–5 to 2009–10: Updating Poverty Estimates and Comparing Official Figures', *Economic and Political Weekly*, vol. 48, no. 40, 5 October.
Patnaik, U. (2018) 'Profit Inflation, Keynes and the Holocaust in Bengal 1943–44', *Economic and Political Weekly*, vol. 53, no. 42, 20 October, pp. 33–43.
Sen, A.K. (1981), *Poverty and Famine: An Essay on Entitlement and Deprivation*, Delhi: Oxford University Press.

16

Impact of the Covid-19 Pandemic on Indian Agriculture

Abhijit Sen and Vikas Rawal

Covid-19 Infections in India and the Lockdown

India's response to deal with the Covid-19 pandemic reflects an utter lack of planning and preparation. The central government announced a nation-wide lockdown when the country had just about 500 known cases of Covid-19 infections and these were mostly concentrated in a few states. The lockdown was imposed indiscriminately across the entire country including not just large cities where Covid cases were concentrated, but also smaller cities, towns and villages. In April and May 2020, the Indian strategy to contain the spread of Covid-19 infections was largely based on coercion and policing to force people to stay indoors even in areas where infections had not been reported, and with complete disregard to constraints that people from poorer sections of the population, with precarious access to livelihoods, under considerable threat of food insecurity and lacking decent housing conditions, were going to face by staying indoors for a prolonged period.

The lockdown continued for about ten weeks. It was withdrawn when the cases were still rising and the peak was still far away. While the nation-wide lockdown did not achieve much in terms of containing the spread of infection, it created a serious crisis of livelihoods. It also forced an unprecedented level of movement of migrant workers as the fear of grave food insecurity and economic distress forced them to flee to their native villages. With inter-state travel rising further after the lockdown was lifted at the end of May, the spread of Covid-19 cases not only saw a steep rise but also spread across the entire country. As seen in Figure 16.1, the share of top five states in the total number of active cases, a measure

---

Lecture delivered on 2 May 2020.

Figure 16.1 *Number of active cases (in thousands) and share of top five states (in per cent) in total number of active cases, India*

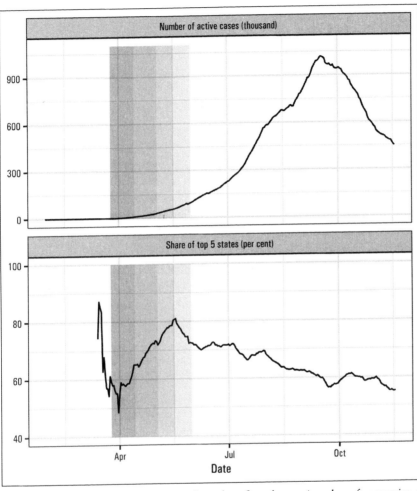

Notes: Active cases are estimated as number of confirmed cases (number of recoveries + number of deaths).
Shaded areas show the four phases of the lockdown.
Source: Based on data from https://covid19india.org, accessed 19 November 2020.

of concentration of Covid-19 infections, fell steeply once the government started relaxing lockdown restrictions and inter-state travel picked up. Over the next few months, Covid-19 reached every nook and corner of the country (Figure 16.2).

It is questionable whether an indiscriminate nation-wide lockdown was the best response when the country had just about 500 known cases of infection, when these cases were limited to a few large cities and when

Figure 16.2 *Geographical spread of active Covid-19 cases, 19 November 2020*

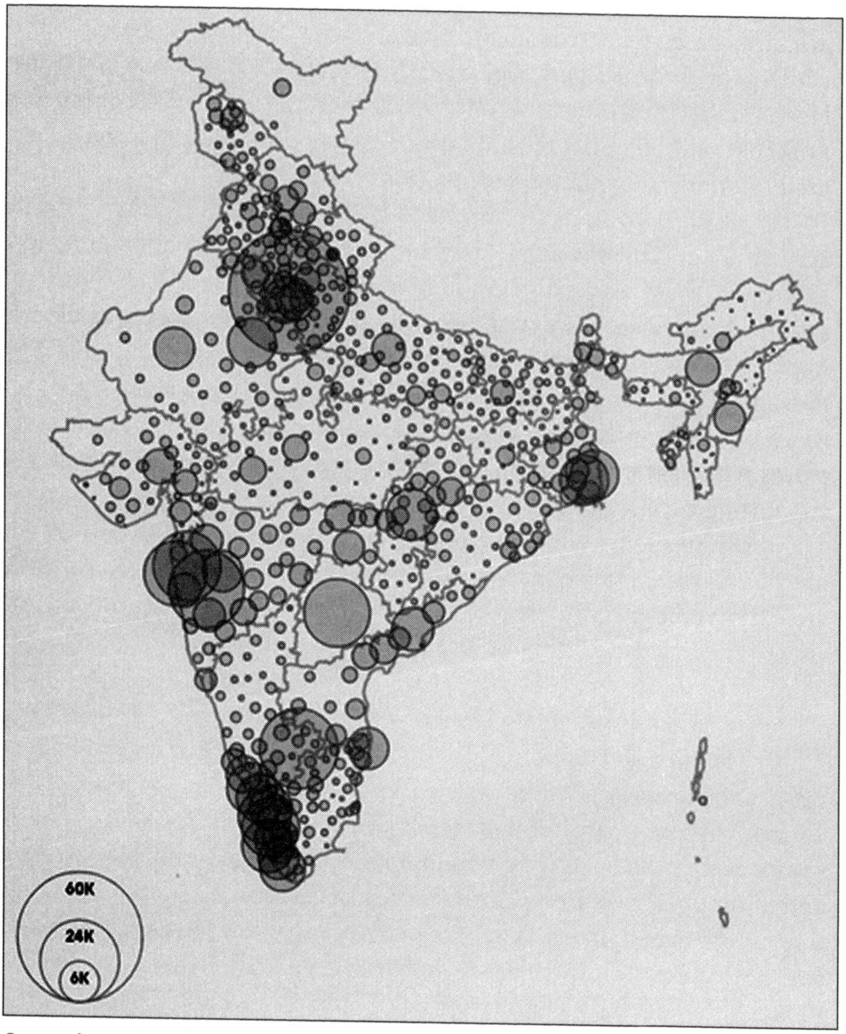

Source: https://covid19india.org, accessed on 19 November 2020.

contact tracing was relatively easy. Imposition of this lockdown without any planning or preparation for tackling the pandemic dealt a massive blow to India's economy and caused enormous hardships to working people of the country. The informal rural economy was hit the hardest. The central government's refusal to acknowledge the economic crisis and its mismanagement in handling the situation aggravated the suffering of the people and deepened the crisis further. The Central Statistical Organization has estimated that India's GDP contracted by 23.9 per cent in April–July and by 7.5 per cent in August–November over the year 2020.[1] These quick estimates are widely believed to be an underestimation as they are primarily based on data from the formal sector. The informal economy, of which agriculture is a part, was severely affected because of the lockdown. However, not much macroeconomic data on the informal economy are available yet and whatever data are available do not seem to have been used to inform the quarterly estimation.

Policies to mitigate the spread of Covid-19 infection impacted agriculture in different ways. First, because of the sudden and unplanned lockdown, there was a disruption in agricultural market operations and supply chains were disrupted. Second, in an economy that was already facing a slowdown, the lockdown resulted in massive contraction of demand. Third, loss of incomes of farmers adversely impacted their ability to invest. Fourth, the lockdown caused a shortage of labour in some places while agriculture in many other places had to bear the burden of supporting excess labour.

While some of these effects were short-lived and the stress was alleviated once restrictions were withdrawn, in some other respects the effects have been more prolonged, and have continued to influence the situation despite the lifting of lockdown restrictions.

Disruption of Supply Chains

Sudden imposition of the lockdown caused a disruption in the entire agricultural marketing system. No preparations were made to ensure continuation of agricultural marketing or to ensure safety of food supply chains before the lockdown was announced. The government exempted agricultural markets from lockdown restrictions on 27 March 2020, five days after the first round of restrictions was imposed. However, even after this exemption was provided, in the absence of complementary measures to facilitate safe and unhindered functioning of transport facilities across the entire supply chain that connects farmers to consumers, to ensure availability of labour and to ensure safety of those involved in transportation and marketing, these administrative decisions remained completely ineffective for several weeks.

Data on market arrivals from the Agmarknet database show that there was a significant fall in arrivals of most crops that are usually harvested in March–April (Figure 16.3). A significant number of agricultural markets shut down when the lockdown was first announced. The number of *regulated* markets reporting arrivals of wheat in the Agmarknet database fell from 746 in the week ending 22 March to just 235 in the week ending 29 March. Similar falls were seen for other commodities that are

Figure 16.3 *Weekly arrivals of different commodities in markets*

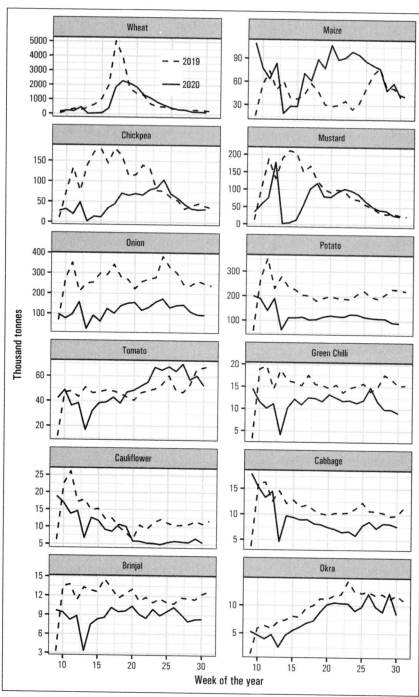

Source: Based on data from the agmarknet.gov.in database.

harvested during this period including chickpea, rapeseed and mustard, and vegetables like potato, onion, tomato and cauliflower.[2]

Data on weekly arrivals presented in Figure 16.3 show that the arrivals of most crops in the weeks immediately after the lockdown was announced were significantly lower than the arrivals in corresponding weeks in the previous year. It is likely that during these weeks, a lot of the produce, particularly of perishable commodities, was sold to local traders, agents, village-level retailers or directly to consumers at low prices. As a result, the total arrivals in regulated markets registered in the Agmarknet system remained considerably lower in 2020 than in previous years, even several months after the lockdown was first imposed.

Public Procurement and Foodgrain Stocks

Public procurement is limited mostly to rice and wheat. However, for these two crops, procurement by the government has become exceedingly important in recent years. The lockdown was imposed when wheat was about to be harvested in the major wheat-growing states. The imposition of lockdown and closure of market operations resulted in a delay of about two weeks in procurement. Although it started late, and disruptions due to Covid restrictions and spread of infection kept taking place throughout the wheat procurement season, a substantial proportion of the wheat crop was procured by the government. As in past years, procurement was limited to a few states, with Madhya Pradesh, Punjab and Haryana topping the list in terms of highest procurement. Only a small proportion of the crop was procured in other wheat-producing states.

Few other crops cultivated in the rabi season are procured by the government. Until 19 June 2020, 1.8 million tonnes of chickpea, 0.5 million tonnes of pigeonpea (*tur/arhar*) and 0.76 million tonnes of mustard oilseed crop were procured by the government through the National Agricultural Cooperative Marketing Federation of India (NAFED).

Over the last three years, the Food Corporation of India (FCI) has been sitting on massive excess stocks of foodgrain (Figure 16.4). Stocks held by the FCI include grain required to meet the operational requirements of government programmes such as the public distribution system (PDS) as well as grain held as a strategic reserve to meet exigencies or shortfalls in production (and procurement). The stocking norms of the government specify the quantity of grain that the FCI should hold at different points of time in a year. However, over the last three years, the FCI has steadily accumulated more and more grain, and public stocks have grown to be hugely in excess of the stocking norms. As shown in Figure 16.4, the amount of surplus stocks held by the FCI steadily increased after October

2018 and by 1 May 2020, before the procurement season for rabi 2020 started, the government had 878 lakh tonnes of grain (including unmilled paddy), which was 668 lakh tonnes in excess of the stocking norms.

Why is the FCI holding such a large surplus of grain? The volume of public stocks of foodgrain has increased so much because, with increasing cost of production, public procurement has become more and more important for the profitability of agriculture, resulting in a significant increase in public procurement even if limited to just wheat and rice, and only in a few states. On the other hand, the government has been unwilling to correspondingly expand the scale of subsidized public distribution of food so as to avoid an increase in the fiscal burden due to food subsidies.

When the government takes grain from the FCI, it reimburses FCI at the economic cost of the grain, which includes cost of procurement as well as storage and handling costs. In the past, even when governments did not lift all surplus food stocks that the FCI held, they covered most of the FCI's costs. However, under the NDA (National Democratic Allliance) government, this has changed. In the last few years, less than 60 per cent of the FCI's food subsidy expenditure has been covered by the government. While finance ministers window-dressed their own budgets and showed low fiscal deficit, the FCI was made to show losses in its books and to cover these through borrowings (mainly out-of-balance-sheet borrowings from the National Small Savings Fund of Government of India). This window-dressing has resulted in burdening the FCI, an organization of strategic importance (as has become clear in the present crisis), with a debt of over Rs 3.79 trillion (as of 30 September 2020).[3]

Over this period, instead of lifting the surplus grain that was being procured and using it to expand public distribution, the government forced the FCI to sell surplus grain through the Open Market Sales Scheme (OMSS), often at a loss (that is, at a price less than the economic cost to FCI). The OMSS was created in the mid-1990s for the government to be able to intervene to moderate sharp rises in the prices of foodgrain in the open market. Since the early 2000s, OMSS has been used to sell surplus grain to traders and exporters and to state governments for state-level welfare schemes. However, the record of sales shows that in most years, other than to state governments, very little grain has been sold through the OMSS even at prices that were below the economic cost of grain to FCI. This is because the existence of large surplus stocks on the one hand raises the economic cost of grain for FCI, and on the other, puts downward pressure on open market prices. In 2019–20, FCI had managed to sell only about 14.5 lakh tonnes of wheat through OMSS until December 2019. Given the large amount of stocks and the urgency to clear the godowns for rabi procurement, the government directed FCI to reduce the OMSS price of grains. Having reduced the price, the FCI was able to sell an additional 21.8 lakh tonnes of wheat between January and March 2020, taking the total sale of wheat in 2019–20 to 36.3 lakh tonnes. Of this, about 23 per cent was sold to state governments for use in state-level schemes. The total OMSS sale of rice during 2019–20 was 16 lakh tonnes, of which 98 per cent was to state governments and about 10 per cent was after imposition of the lockdown in March.

On 26 March 2020 the Finance Minister announced that under the Pradhan Mantri Garib Kalyan Anna Yojana (PMGKAY), '80 crore individuals, i.e. roughly two-thirds of India's population' 'would be provided double of their current entitlement over next three months' and that 'this additionally would be free of cost'.[4]

Four points need to be noted about food distribution by the government during the period of the Covid pandemic. First, the amount distributed was barely enough to match the additional quantity of grain procured during the rabi 2020 season. As a result, the overall stocks did not fall significantly. So the opportunity provided by the pandemic to get rid of massive excess stocks of grain and use these to ensure that everyone had access to food was missed (Figure 16.4).

Secondly, while the government distributes about 4.3 million tonnes of grain every month under the NFSA (National Food Security Act), 2013, the distribution of grain through PMGKAY has been signifi-

Figure 16.4 *Public stocks of foodgrain, India, 1973–2020*

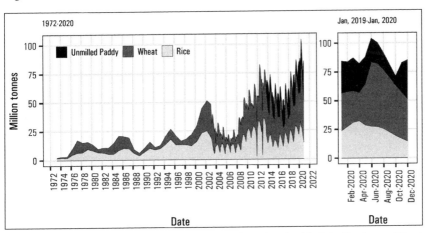

Source: Data from the websites of the Department of Food and Public Distribution and Food Corporation of India. Annual data before 2005 as archived at https://indianstatistics.org.

Figure 16.5 *Subsidized distribution of grain through the NFSA and the PMGKAY, March–September 2020*

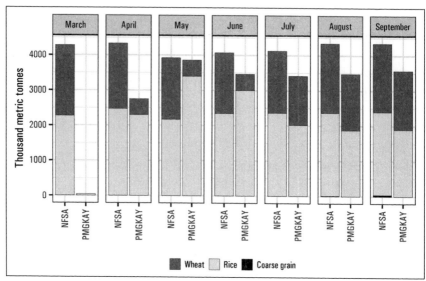

Source: Based on data from https://annavitran.nic.in, accessed 1 November 2020.

cantly lower (Figure 16.5). In other words, the government was not able to double the amount of subsidized grain distributed.

Thirdly, the government did not take any serious steps to expand the coverage of public distribution of food. As a result, subsidized foodgrains remained out of reach for many households that became vulnerable to food insecurity due to loss of livelihoods following the lockdown.

Fourthly, school meal programmes and distribution of food through other nutrition programmes stopped in most states after the lockdown was first announced. Only a few states created alternative systems of delivery of food commodities to the homes of students, babies and mothers in lieu of the cooked food they used to get in schools and day-care centres. The offtake of grain from FCI for these programmes between April and July in 2020 was about 16 per cent less than that in the same months the previous year.

Fifthly, wages in public works programmes such as MGNREGS (Mahatma Gandhi National Rural Employment Guarantee Scheme) could have been paid partially in grain, and this could have been used to expand employment creation. Such possibilities of expanding the reach of existing social protection programmes using available resources were not exploited.

Disruption of supply chains and the fall in demand (due to the lockdown and the economic crisis) influenced prices across the entire supply chain. The combined effect of these factors has been varied across commodities – in particular, between prices of essential and non-essential commodities, and between commodities having different degrees of perishability – between producer, wholesale and consumer prices, and in different phases of the lockdown and opening up. In the case of rice and wheat, prices were also significantly influenced by the accumulation of public stocks and public distribution. Imports contribute significantly to domestic supply of commodities such as edible oils, pulses and onion. As discussed in the next section, disruption in imports for a few months resulted in a short-term depletion of domestic stocks and supply for some of these commodities. On the other hand, with considerable surplus and low prices, India exported substantial quantities of rice and sugar after a brief disruption caused by the lockdown.

The first few weeks after the announcement of the lockdown saw a decline in producer prices of most commodities as the disruption of the agricultural marketing system and the tardy progress of public procurement forced the farmers to sell their produce at low prices. Even in the case of wheat, the only crop for which a significant amount of produce was bought by the government, delays in public procurement and lack of procurement in large parts of wheat-growing areas meant that in many states, farmers were forced to sell produce at prices below the MSP (minimum support price). The situation was much worse in the case of chickpea and mustard, major rabi crops for which very little government procurement happens. For these crops, prices were considerably below MSP in all the *mandi*s. The price of mustard during the period of the lockdown varied between Rs 3,700 and Rs 4,000 per quintal, while the MSP was Rs 4,425 per quintal. In most *mandi*s the price of chickpea varied between Rs 3,500 and Rs 4,000 per quintal, while the MSP was supposed to be Rs 4,875 per quintal. Potato prices plateaued during the first few weeks after the announcement of the lockdown. Onion prices saw a sharp decline in all the major *mandi*s. While onion was selling at about Rs 2,000 per quintal before the lockdown, by the end of the third phase of the lockdown, the price of onion ranged between Rs 500 and Rs 1,000 per quintal in different *mandi*s. Tomato prices have also been extremely volatile. In the Kolar and Mulabagilu markets in Karnataka, where the volume of market arrivals increased sharply because the produce could not be transported to Andhra Pradesh or Tamil Nadu, tomatoes sold for as little as Rs 200 per quintal on some days during the lockdown. In Junnar (Narayangaon) in Maharashtra, the modal price of tomato on 8 May was just Rs 150 per quintal.

In the case of rice and wheat, increased release of grain from public stocks after May worked to depress open market prices, and the producer

Figure 16.6 *Mandi prices of selected commodities, 2018–19*

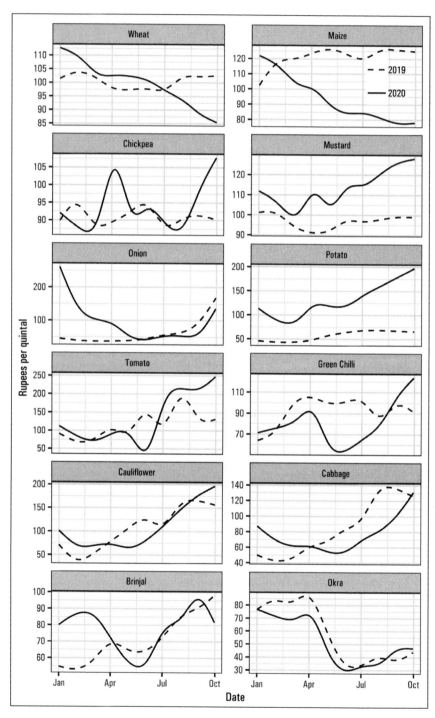

as well as retail prices of these remained low. In particular, *mandi* prices of wheat fell steeply after July, when public procurement ended. In the case of many perishable crops – for example, potato, onion and tomato, the three most important of these crops – prices increased steeply after the lockdown was withdrawn. This is peculiar and suggests that supply chain disruptions was only one of the causes of price rise. It seems more likely that for some of these crops, the produce was acquired at low prices by traders directly from farmers, stored and released in wholesale markets when the prices increased. Since these crops are perishable and require storage in regulated conditions, only traders who have access to such storage capacity could have held the produce.

Trade

Rice, shrimp, bovine meat, sugar and chilli are the most important agricultural commodities exported by India. Although exports of all these commodities fell sharply in April after the lockdown was announced, there was quick recovery thereafter (Figure 16.7).

Exports of rice are particularly interesting. Rice exports showed a sharp rise after an initial fall due to the Covid lockdown. The increase in rice exports was primarily on account of non-basmati rice, which is mainly exported to Southeast Asian countries. With large public stocks of wheat and rice, and increased distribution of grain through the PMGKAY, domestic prices of rice have been low. Because of this, Indian exporters have sold rice at prices below the price of rice of other major rice exporters such as Vietnam and Thailand (Figure 16.9). Total rice exports in August 2020 were at the highest level of rice export in any month in the last ten years.

The disruption lasted longer for imports than for exports. Edible oils, pulses and cashew (in shell, for processing and re-export as kernels) are the most important commodities imported by India. After a disruption in imports for about four months, imports of edible oils and pulses increased sharply in August (Figure 16.8). This jump in imports may have been partly to replenish depleted stocks.

The Situation in Respect of Employment

Over the last two decades, there has been a great increase in the proportion of rural workers who migrate or commute to towns and cities to work in non-agricultural activities such as construction labour, loading/unloading in *mandi*s, shop assistants, mechanics, hawkers, as well as salaried workers. Some of these workers travel to destination states that are several thousand kilometres away. Most of them, including those who have salaried jobs in private establishments, are employed through informal

Figure 16.7 *Exports of major agricultural commodities*

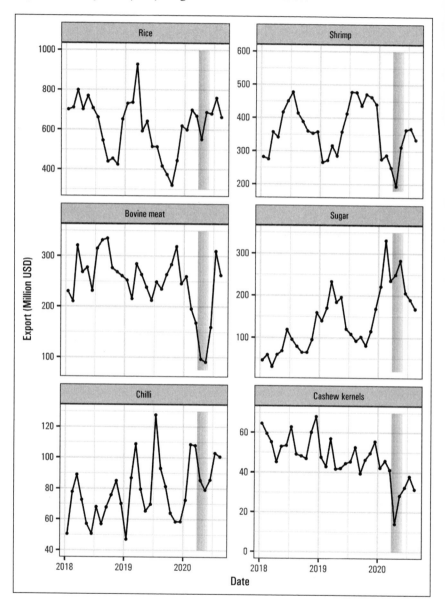

contracts. With the announcement of the lockdown, a large number of informal workers who were also migrants were out of work either temporarily or permanently. In any case, a large number were without any earnings during this period. As a consequence, and given the relatively higher cost of living in urban centres, migrant workers have been trying to return to their villages.

Figure 16.8 *Imports of major agricultural commodities, August 2020*

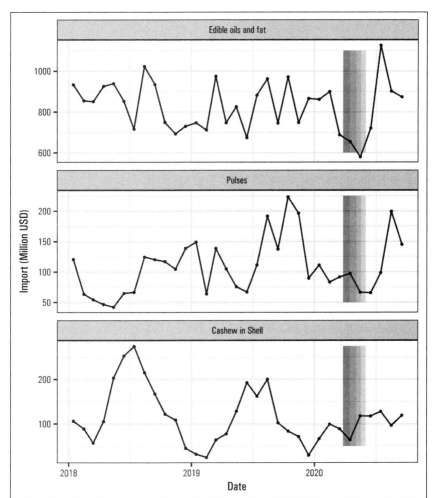

It is clear that the government had made no plans for ensuring that migrant workers engaged in informal activities were provided means of subsistence when the lockdown was announced. In addition, the government created obstacles to their returning to their native villages as employers wanted this reserve army of labour to remain on stand-by, without food or salary, so that they could be made to work once the lockdown was lifted.

Despite these obstacles, a large number of migrant workers managed to return to their native villages, at great risk and enduring immense hardships, often walking hundreds of kilometres, some on bicycles and others using whatever means of travel was possible, such as hidden in container trucks, tankers and so on. In this process, they faced grave dangers

Figure 16.9 *Quantity of exports and unit export price of rice, by month*

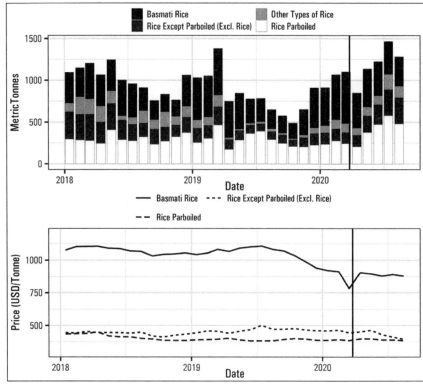

Source: Based on data from the Department of Commerce, Ministry of Commerce and Industry, Government of India.

and many lost their lives on the way. In many cases, these migrant workers were subjected to police atrocities on the way to their villages and made to spend weeks in isolation upon arrival before they were allowed to be with their families.

With many migrant workers back in the villages and local workers unable to commute to the towns, everyone was dependent on employment availability within the village. Village studies in the *India's Villages during the Covid-19 Pandemic* series showed that employment availability within villages was meagre during the lockdown (Rawal, Kumar and Pais 2020). Wages in villages are much lower than what workers earned in non-agricultural employment in towns and cities, and are likely to have been depressed further because of the huge excess supply of workers in the villages because of the lockdown.

Although the lockdown made it impossible to do face-to-face surveys, several telephonic surveys were conducted, particularly among migrant workers stranded in the cities, to collect information on their situation. Given that these telephonic surveys had to be designed suddenly in the wake of the lockdown, their coverage was limited, and the methods of sample selection and surveying left much to be desired. In particular, most of the surveys covered mainly urban workers – or rural workers stranded in urban areas – and did not provide much information about the situation in rural areas. Nevertheless, in the context of lack of any official data, even these surveys were useful in illustrating the conditions of employment and loss of livelihoods, and deserve to be summarized.

The Centre for Monitoring Indian Economy (CMIE), which has been conducting regular surveys on employment, moved its surveys to the telephonic mode in view of the lockdown. CMIE surveys undersample informal sector workers and do not capture women's employment very well. Since these sections are likely to be worst affected by the lockdown, CMIE data are likely to underestimate the fall in levels of employment due to the lockdown and overestimate the extent of recovery after the lockdown was withdrawn. The estimates of levels of work participation rates seem to be biased downward for women because the CMIE surveys do not capture women's employment very well, and biased upward for men because the survey selected disproportionately high numbers of households primarily dependent on salaried employment and businesses. There are also problems of comparability between face-to-face surveys done before the lockdown and telephonic surveys done during the lockdown. Despite this, the CMIE surveys showed a massive increase in unemployment, from 8.7 per cent in March 2020 to 23 per cent in April 2020 (Vyas 2020). As shown in Figure 16.10, there was a significant drop in work participation rates among men and women of working age in both rural and urban areas. The drop in work participation rate was particularly high among the youth.

The misery of informal workers was widely covered in the media. Bereft of employment and incomes, they struggled to access food and pay rents for typically small living quarters. A survey of stranded informal workers in the National Capital Region (NCR) by the Centre of Indian Trade Unions and the Communist Party of India (Marxist) which covered about 8,870 migrant workers found that 58 per cent of them worked on casual contracts and 13 per cent of them were self-employed. About 56 per cent of the survey respondents had earnings less than Rs 10,000 per month.

Surveys conducted by SWAN (Stranded Workers Action Network) covered 10,929 workers and showed that only 4 per cent of the informal workers had received full wages during the period of the lockdown and 78 per cent of them had not received any wages at all. Many workers who had received payments from their employers during the period of the

Figure 16.10 *Work participation rates for men and women aged 15–59 years, rural and urban population, India*

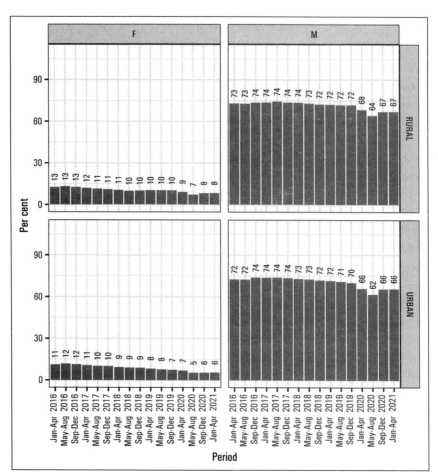

Source: Estimates based on the CMIE Consumer Pyramids Survey data.

lockdown had been told that these were advances that would be adjusted against wage payments when they returned to work. Over 97 per cent of the self-employed workers in the sample had had no income for over a month (SWAN 2020).

A telephonic survey conducted by the Centre for Sustainable Employment, Azim Premji University (APU), in collaboration with ten NGOs covered 4,000 workers from twelve states. This survey is the only one in which the sample included a substantial proportion (60 per cent) of rural workers and data were provided separately for the same. The survey found that 80 per cent of surveyed workers in urban areas and 57 per cent in rural areas had lost their jobs. In rural areas, 66 per cent of casual workers, 62 per cent of regular salaried workers and 47 per cent of self-employed workers had been rendered unemployed during the lockdown. On average, weekly earnings of rural casual workers fell by 50 per cent, while earnings of rural workers self-employed in non-agricultural occupations fell by 92 per cent during the period of the lockdown. About 42 per cent of rural salaried workers received reduced or no salary during the period of the lockdown. Of all the farmers covered in the survey, 37 per cent reported having sold their produce at a reduced price because of the lockdown, 37 per cent reported inability to harvest their crop and 15 per cent reported inability to sell the produce (APU 2020).

The rural employment guarantee programme (MGNREGS) could have been leveraged to generate employment in rural areas. However, in the initial weeks of the nation-wide lockdown, even MGNREGS works, which typically require an assembly of workers at a worksite, were not allowed. MGNREGS works were exempted from lockdown restrictions only by the end of April (Manish Kumar 2020). When worksites for MGNREGS employment were opened, there was a surge in demand for employment under the scheme (Figure 16.11), and very soon most states exhausted the financial resources that were allocated for the scheme. Between 31 March and 19 November 2020, about 18 million new rural households applied for enrolment in MGNREGS. As of 19 November, about 9 million households that had applied for enrolment were awaiting their job cards which entitled them to seek employment under the scheme. As shown in Figure 16.11, provision of employment through MGNREGS started to slow down after June as financial resources started to dry up.

Figure 16.11 *Person-days of employment generation in the Mahatma Gandhi National Rural Employment Guarantee Scheme, by month, 2011–20*

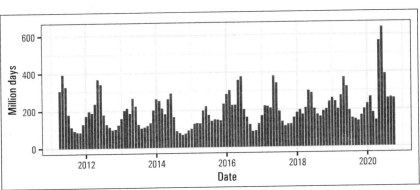

Source: Based on the MIS data of MGNREGS, http://mnregaweb4.nic.in/netnrega/ MISreport4.aspx, 10 December 2020.

By the middle of November, total spending on MGNREGS and pending dues for the work had exceeded the total amount of resources (Rs 791 billion) that were allocated to the scheme for the entire financial year. It was not clear how the rural employment guarantee programme would be run in the remaining four months of the year unless additional resources were allocated by the central government for the programme.

Lack of availability of employment in rural areas forced many workers to start migrating again shortly after the lockdown restrictions were removed. With the onset of the monsoon, the demand for migrant labour for paddy transplanting picked up in states such as Punjab and Haryana. As urban enterprises started to resume activities, the network of labour contractors was used to mobilize migrant workers again. While the government dilly-dallied to operate trains to take migrant workers back to the states of their origin when the Covid-19 crisis was in its early stages, the government was prompt in facilitating their return to the cities when the infections had increased manifold.

The New Farm Laws

The government has used the opportunity provided by the pandemic and the restrictions on political assembly to bring about major changes in the legislative framework under which agricultural marketing and supply chains function. While some of these changes were on the agenda of the central government for quite some time, introducing these through national laws was not considered feasible because of anticipation of resistance from farmers. With the Covid-19 restrictions considerably weakening the possibility of political resistance, introducing these changes through national laws became a feasible strategy.

On 3 June 2020, the Government of India approved three ordinances. These ordinances were converted into Acts after they were passed in the monsoon session of Parliament, in September 2020, amidst considerable opposition and without a clear majority of members supporting the bills in the upper house. Once presidential assent was given on 27 September 2020, the Farmers' (Empowerment and Protection) Agreement on Price Assurance and Farm Services Act (FAFSA), the Farmers' Produce Trade and Commerce (Promotion and Facilitation) Act (FPTCA), and the Essential Commodities (Amendment) Act (ECAA) came into force.

Of the three new Acts, FAFSA provides a national framework for contract farming in which farmers enter into contracts with buyers for a period ranging between one season and five years for supply of agricultural produce of specified quality, grade and standards at a mutually agreed prices. The second Act, FPTCA, is directly aimed at deregulation of the agricultural marketing system. The thrust of the Act is to remove trade barriers and restrictions that resulted in fragmentation of agricultural markets, and to remove various taxes and cesses that were imposed on agricultural trade. As per the FPTCA, any area or location outside the physical boundaries of the market yards run by marketing committees or notified under the state APMC Acts can be considered a 'trade area', and agricultural trade occurring in such trade areas is exempted from regulation under the state APMC Act. The FPTCA removes, in one go, all restrictions on intra-state or inter-state trade of agricultural produce. Besides direct engagement with farmers, the Act allows private traders to set up private market yards or electronic trading platforms to facilitate trade and commerce of scheduled agricultural produce (agricultural produce which is notified under state APMC Acts). Under the Act, price fixation is entirely left to mutual consent between the buyer and the seller, and no role is left for the state to mediate for ensuring that a fair and remunerative price is paid to the farmers. The Act bars the state governments of APMC markets from imposing any levies, cesses or taxes on trade under FPTCA.

The Essential Commodities Act, 1955 (ECA) was enacted to ensure a smooth supply of essential commodities. Among various provisions, it allowed the government powers to impose restrictions on the stocking of essential commodities. Historically, the effectiveness of these regulations in curbing the volatility of retail prices has been questionable. In addition, unpredictability of government intervention to use ECA to put limits on stockholdings of specific commodities created uncertainties which disincentivized private investment in storage infrastructure. This is an important factor behind technological backwardness in the area of private storage of food commodities in India, diseconomies associated with small-scale operations, and high post-harvest losses. With the enactment of the Essential Commodities (Amendment) Act, 2020, the government has considerably weakened the provisions for imposing limits on stockholdings by various operations in the food supply chain. The new legislation allows for government regulation only in extraordinary circumstances such as war, famine, natural calamities or extraordinary rise in prices. Further, stock limits are not applied if the stocks are less than the installed capacity of an agro-processing company or export demand for exporters.

These three Acts drastically change the legislative framework under which agricultural marketing takes place in India. The thrust of these changes is to reduce the scope of control and regulation of domestic agricultural trade by the government. The case for liberalization of agricultural marketing rests mainly on two arguments: first, that liberalization would result in increased competition, which in turn will result in better price realization for farmers; second, that liberalization will result in an increase in investment from the private sector in agricultural marketing. Are these the likely implications of these legislative changes?

The prices that farmers get are determined by overall supply and demand conditions and, within the overall limits determined by the conditions of demand and supply, by the extent of concentration of market power in the supply chains, and the position of individual farmers in the system of agrarian class relations.

At the macro-level, deregulation of input prices over the last three decades has resulted in a steady increase in the cost of production, which has put upward pressure on the MSP. On the other hand, increasing integration with the world market, large build-up of public stocks of grain and an economic slowdown have exerted downward pressure on prices in the open market. Consequently, in recent years, open market prices have been considerably lower than the MSP for a number of key crops. Given this, government procurement has become critical for ensuring returns from rice and wheat cultivation. On the other hand, low price realization has become a widespread problem for crops and regions that are not covered by public procurement.

Unless these structural issues are addressed, it is unlikely that the changes brought about by these laws can ensure that farmers get remunerative prices for their produce. On the other hand, a greater penetration of large agribusiness companies, through contract farming arrangements or by way of direct purchase of produce outside the system of regulated markets, would only give greater monopsonistic powers to these large buyers and may work against the interests of the farmers.

It is also highly likely that public investment in marketing infrastructure would fall in the coming years because of the poor resource position of the central government, the even more dire situation of state government finances, and the likely fall in the revenues of the market committees of existing regulated markets. It is also likely, given the deep economic crisis in the country and fall in public investment, that private investment in the agricultural supply chain will remain subdued in the near future.

In other words, we do not expect that these new Acts will result in increased investment in agriculture and agricultural marketing, or make agriculture more remunerative. They are, almost certainly, likely to pave the way for greater penetration of agribusiness in agriculture.

Making agriculture remunerative for farmers is a key challenge. This requires an overarching review of the policy changes that have been introduced in the areas of input pricing, trade liberalization and pricing of agricultural produce as part of the liberalization programme. These changes have been the main cause of the deep agrarian crisis that rural India finds itself in today. Addressing this crisis requires a major course correction in policies for the agricultural sector.

Some Concluding Reflections

The impact of the Covid-19 pandemic needs to be seen in the context of three aspects of the agrarian economy of India.

First, over the last decade or so, India has seen an absolute decline in the number of people working in agriculture. Even among rural households, there has been a significant tendency of diversification out of agriculture, and an increased dependence on non-farm employment. This diversification into non-agricultural occupations has been associated with a great increase in rural–urban migration, a lot of it being short-term and circular. The increase in migration has been associated with a great expansion of densely populated slums in the cities with poor civic amenities. This has had implications for disease transmission and vulnerability of people in the context of the pandemic. This change in pattern of employment also has implications for agriculture. For at least some part of the last fifteen years or so, rural wages saw a considerable rise. Rural–urban migration also meant that, in some parts of the country, agricultural production had to take place with fewer workers and, at least at some points of time in the agricultural calendar, there could be short-term labour shortages.

Second, there is strong evidence of increasing frequency of extreme weather events due to climate change. Various models have tried to quantify the impact of climate change on yields. The impacts are regionally varied and varied across crops, but it is clear that there is an even greater need to ensure that the increase in crop yields per unit of land and water is sustained in the coming decades (Jayaraman and Murari 2014). Given the range of estimates of the impact of climate change on yields, an annual increase of about 1 per cent in crop yields would be required to counter the adverse impact of climate change on crop yields. This is feasible, but enabling conditions for this, in particular technological change for improving efficiency of resource use, need to be created.

Third, greater globalization over the last three decades has meant an increasing reliance of countries on world trade for the food supply. There is a distinct possibility that this will change in the post-Covid world. In this context, India has its own historical specificities. Despite an overall move towards neo-liberalism, the large size of India has meant that imports have never been the mainstay of food supply in India. Apart from oilseeds, for which India has considerable dependence on imports, domestic production remains critical for national food security. Reliance on domestic production for food supply is likely to become even more critical in the coming years as other countries try to secure their food supply in the wake of the experience during the Covid-19 pandemic. Agricultural policies in the future will have to take this into account. The need for planning will become particularly significant as relative prices in the economy start to vary significantly from the rest of the world.

The immediate impact of the unplanned nation-wide lockdown was in terms of a severe disruption of food supply chains and a widespread loss of incomes particularly for workers employed in the informal economy including agriculture. The wisdom behind imposing a nation-wide lockdown at a few hours' notice and without having prepared for expanding the social protection system to meet the needs of the vulnerable population is seriously questionable. Although India has large public stocks of foodgrain, the potential of using these to ensure that everyone has access to foodgrain and to create employment through large-scale food-for-work programmes has not been utilized. The increase in social protection has been meagre and nowhere near what is required to mitigate the adverse impacts of the lockdown. The Covid-19 pandemic is at its worst as we write this. Many states are bracing for the second and third waves of the infections and local-level lockdowns are being proposed once again. Unfortunately, with no comprehensive strategy to combat the economic crisis or the pandemic, the agrarian crisis is set to deepen.

This paper builds on the work done by scholars at the Society for Social and Economic Research (SSER), New Delhi. We are thankful, in particular, to Jesim Pais, Manish Kumar and Ankur Verma who have been part of the effort to study the impact of Covid-19 on the rural economy.

Notes

[1] See the paper by Surajit Mazumdar, 'The Coronavirus and India's Economic Crisis: Continuity and Change', in the present volume for further details.

[2] See Rawal and Verma (2020) for a more detailed discussion of the disruption of agricultural markets in the first phase of the lockdown.

[3] https://fci.gov.in/finances.php?view=107, accessed 1 November 2020.

[4] https://pib.gov.in/PressReleaseIframePage.aspx?PRID=1608345, accessed 10 December 2020.

References

APU (2020), 'Covid-19 Livelihoods Survey: Early Findings from Phone Surveys', Centre for Sustainable Employment, Azim Premji University, https://cse.azimpremjiuniversity.edu.in/wp-content/uploads/2020/05/APU_Covid19_Survey_Webinar.pdf, accessed 10 December 2020.

Jayaraman, T. and Kamal Murari (2014), 'Climate Change and Agriculture: Current and Future Trends, and Implications for India', *Review of Agrarian Studies*, vol. 4, no. 1, February–June, pp. 2–49, http://www.ras.org.in/index.php?Article=climate_

change_and_agriculture_83&q=jayaraman&keys=jayaraman, accessed 10 December 2020.

Kumar, Manish (2020), *Choking the Lifeline of the Rural Economy: MGNREGS during the Covid-19 Lockdown*, SSER Monograph 20/2, New Delhi: Society for Social and Economic Research (SSER), http://archive.indianstatistics.org/sserwp/sserwp2002.pdf, accessed 10 December 2020.

Rawal, Vikas, Manish Kumar and Jesim Pais, eds (2020), *India's Villages during the Covid-19 Pandemic* series, New Delhi: Society for Social and Economic Research (SSER), https://coronapolicyimpact.org/2020/04/07/indias-villages-during-the-covid-19-pandemic/, accessed 10 December 2020.

Rawal, Vikas and Ankur Verma (2020), *Agricultural Supply Chains during the Covid-19 Lockdown: A Study of Market Arrivals of Seven Key Food Commodities*, SSER Monograph 20/1, New Delhi: Society for Social and Economic Research (SSER), http://archive.indianstatistics.org/sserwp/sserwp2001.pdf, accessed 10 December 2020.

SWAN (2020), '32 Days and Counting: Covid-19 Lockdown, Migrant Workers, and the Inadequacy of Welfare Measures in India', Stranded Workers Action Network (SWAN), https://bit.ly/2XIOT2a, accessed 10 December 2020.

Vyas, Mahesh (2020), 'Unemployment rate over 23%', Centre for Monitoring Indian Economy (CMIE), https://bit.ly/2XasvzW, accessed 10 December 2020.

17

Covid-19: An Opportunity for Breaking with the Global Food Supply Chain

Walden Bello

Food has been very much front and centre in the Covid-19 story.

First of all, hunger is following closely on the heels of the pandemic, especially in the global South. The United Nations World Food Programme says that the pandemic will double the number of people experiencing acute food insecurity, from 130 million in 2019 to 265 million in 2020. This figure is likely to be a gross underestimate, says Vijay Prashad of the Tricontinental Research Centre, who claims that over 2.5 billion people might eventually be rendered hungry by the pandemic (UN World Food Programme 2020).

Indeed, one can say that unlike in East Asia, Europe and the United States, in South Asia the food calamity preceded the actual invasion by the virus, with relatively few infections registered in India, Pakistan and Bangladesh as of mid-March 2020 but with millions already displaced by lockdowns and other draconian measures taken by the region's governments.

In India, as the renowned journalist and founder of the People's Archive of Rural India (PARI) P. Sainath put it, 'We gave a nation of 1.3 billion human beings four hours to shut down their lives. . . . One of our legendary civil servants had said, "A small infantry brigade being pushed into a major action is given more than four hours' notice"' (quoted in Parth 2020). With little money for food and rent, migrant workers were forced to trek hundreds of kilometres home, and scores were beaten up by police seeking to quarantine them as they crossed state lines. Estimated at some 9 to 139 million, these internal migrants, largely invisible in normal times, suddenly became visible as they tried to reach their home states, deprived

Lecture delivered on 15 March 2020.

of public transportation owing to the sudden national lockdown. With people dying along the way, a constant refrain in this vast human wave were the desperate words – If coronavirus doesn't kill us, hunger will!

The second point I would like to underline, and will devote the rest of this presentation to, is that the pandemic has shown that the global supply chain – the dominant agribusiness model – is fragile and threatened with breakdown, with incalculable consequences, and it is time to do away with it.

The Fragility of the Global Food Supply Chain

This fragility of the global food supply chain was impressed upon us a couple of weeks ago by a joint declaration of the World Trade Organization (WTO), World Health Organization (WHO) and Food and Agriculture Organization (FAO). The three institutions warned: 'When acting to protect the health and well-being of their citizens, countries should ensure that any trade-related measures do not disrupt the food supply chain.'[1] One particular case appeared to have triggered the agencies' concern: the blockade of food exports in Rosario, Argentina. According to an FAO report:

> Rosario in central Argentina is the country's major grain export hub, as well as a major soybean area. Argentina is the world's largest exporter of soymeal livestock feed. Recently, dozens of municipal governments near Rosario have blocked grains trucks from entering and exiting their towns to slow the spread of the virus. Many are defying the federal government's order to unblock their roads, citing health concerns. Soybeans are therefore not being transported to crushing plants, affecting the country's export of soybean meal for livestock. Similarly, in Brazil, another key exporter of staple commodities, there are reports of logistical hurdles putting the food supply chains at risk. Internationally, if a major port like Santos in Brazil or Rosario in Argentina shuts down, it would spell disaster for global trade. (Cullen 2020)

The Rosario blockade was carried out by local governments and civil society groups that wanted to protect themselves from what they saw as a global supply chain that had allowed the virus to hitchhike to their communities. But the FAO was not sympathetic to their concerns. What was critical, said Qu Dong Yu, head of the FAO, was for the international community to avoid disruptions of corporate-controlled global food supply chains.

The event that informed the response of the FAO and other international agencies to the Rosario blockade was the food price crisis of 2007–08, when export restrictions imposed by food-exporting countries, worried about domestic supplies, contributed to food shortages and skyrocketing prices of food in food-importing countries, resulting in 75 million people joining the ranks of the hungry and driving an estimated 125 million people in developing countries into extreme poverty.

Now, the FAO and the WTO are certainly right to be worried that disruptions of global and regional supply chains could contribute to the spread of hunger. But what is really disturbing is the absence of any awareness that global and regional supply chains are themselves the problem when it comes to ensuring global food security. The 2007–08 food price crisis should have taught these agencies this sobering lesson, but there is the same uncritical endorsement of the corporate food supply chain.

The 2007–08 crisis was triggered by a number of developments, including financial speculation in commodities as well as the transfer of land to cultivating biofuels. However, these short-term triggers would have not led to a global crisis had not a number of structural conditions been created, chief among them the globalization of capitalist industrial agriculture through the creation of a process of production, the dynamics of which was 'the suppression of particularities of time and place in both agriculture and diets', as Harriet Friedman put it. 'More rapidly and deeply than before, transnational agrifood capitals disconnect production from consumption and relink them through buying and selling. They have created an integrated productive sector of the world economy, and peoples of the Third World have been incorporated or marginalized – often both simultaneously – as consumers and producers' (Harriet Friedman, quoted in Baviera and Bello 2012).

The 2007–08 food crisis and the 2008–09 global financial crisis should have shown the multilateral agencies the fragility of global supply chains – in the food system in the case of the first, and in the industrial system in the case of the second – when the financial crisis led to a global recession that halted production in many factories in China. The two crises should have triggered serious interrogation of the resiliency of the global supply chain.

Instead, in the case of agriculture, the global supply chain stretched farther and farther, and local and regional food systems withered even more. The FAO estimates that global agricultural trade more than tripled in value to around US$ 1.6 trillion from 2000 to 2016. More and more local and regional food systems that provide most of domestic production and consumption of food have retreated, so that today, as one study reveals, modern food supply chains, dominated by large processing firms and supermarkets, capital-intensive with relatively low labour intensity of operations, constitutes roughly 30 per cent to 50 per cent of the food systems in China, Latin America and Southeast Asia, and 20 per cent of the food systems in Africa and South Asia (Reardon, Bellemare and Zilberman 2020).

The bulk of the evidence is that the gains from 'high-standards' agricultural trade promoted by value chains that impose strict quality controls on local producers are captured by foreign investors, large food companies and developing country elites. Vertical integration and consolidation at the buyer end of export chains are strengthening the bargaining power of large agro-industrial firms and food multinationals, displacing decision-making authority from the farmers to these downstream companies, and expanding the capacity of these companies to extract rents from the chain to the disadvantage of contracted smallholder suppliers in the chains.

The smallholder, in short, is being squeezed out at almost every level, from production to finance to meeting sanitary and phytosanitary standards, all of which benefit corporate agriculture, with its big buyers, big suppliers and big middle men. One well-known liberal research institute sums up the smallholders' plight thus:

> Increasingly globalized and liberalized agri-food markets are dominated by supermarkets, distributors, processors, and agroexporters that are introducing and expanding food safety and quality standards that many smallholders are unable to meet. These developments are further shifting the competitive advantage away from smallholder farmers toward large-scale producers. (Fan *et al.* 2013)

Increasingly, foreign investors are pushing out smallholders even from land ownership. Many land acquisitions, notably in Africa, are really land grabs, says one important report, since 'The competition for investment, the weak capacity of States, and the complex implications of titling and clarification of property rights are all factors that have impeded the establishment of robust regulatory frameworks to protect local communities from land grabs.'

We said earlier that the FAO and other multilateral agencies continue to endorse the global supply chain despite the many problems associated with it. This goes against the impression of many in the NGO (non-governmental organization) community and the government that the FAO and other multilateral agencies have become more sympathetic to the needs of small farmers. This image is erroneous. To take just one example, in Myanmar, which is considered the last frontier of development in Southeast Asia, the FAO teamed up with the Asian Development Bank and the Livelihood and Food Security Trust Fund to draw up an agricultural development plan that, in their own words, focuses on ensuring that

> farmers and agro-enterprises are integrated into effective value chains and are competitive in regional and global markets. This is achieved by facilitating the process of transforming the agricultural sector from a situation where a substantial proportion of farming is carried out primarily for subsistence or for local markets into a sector in which most farming is carried out for profitable commercialization and is connected to the local, national, and international markets.[2]

The FAO continues to promote a business model that would subordinate smallholders to corporate industrial agriculture.

Why Food Self-Sufficiency Makes Sense

The very real drawbacks of integrating local agricultural systems into the global supply chain and eroding food self-sufficiency are commonsensical, but, trapped by neo-liberal ideology, the FAO and other multilateral institutions have simply brushed them aside. Agricultural analyst Jennifer Clapp (2017) has provided several critical reasons why moving towards greater food self-sufficiency makes very good sense. Let me just cite four:

(1) When a large proportion of a country's population is at risk of hunger in instances of sudden food shortages due to the vagaries of world markets, as happened in 2007–08, it is vital to carefully consider ways to improve domestic food production.

(2) Countries with volatile export earnings can assure their unimpeded access to food by reducing reliance on global food markets via greater domestic food production.

(3) In fact the majority of the world's countries, Clapp notes, do have the resource capacity to be food self-sufficient. But of those countries that have the resource capacity to be food self-sufficient, a number are net food importers. Many sub-Saharan African countries, for example, were net agricultural exporters in the 1960s–70s, but became net importers of food after the 1980s. Some of those countries that have become reliant on imported food since the 1980s still have the capacity to produce sufficient foodstuffs domestically, including Guinea, Mali, Sudan and the Democratic Republic of the Congo.

(4) Countries facing the threat of trade disruptions as a result of war, political tensions or other emergencies may also benefit from

greater levels of food self-sufficiency. Most countries consider the ability to ensure food supplies in times of crisis to be a national security issue, and depending on the risk that imports will be cut off due to conflict or political tensions or emergencies, countries may want to invest in their domestic agricultural capacity. This imperative is especially relevant now, during the Covid-19 pandemic. But it is one that not many countries can effectively address immediately, because they have lost the capacity to be self-sufficient owing to neo-liberal prescriptions and corporate power.

The Covid-19 Crisis and the Opportunity for Food Sovereignty

The Covid-19 pandemic is a crisis that can translate into an opportunity to move food production away from the fragile, corporate-controlled globalized food supply chain based on narrow considerations, such as the reduction of unit cost, to more sustainable, smallholder-based localized systems. While, in the short term, global supply chains must be kept running to ensure people do not starve, the strategic goal must be to replace them, and some measures can already be taken even as the pandemic is at its height. For instance, in many cities under lockdown, produce from the countryside is available even as the global supply chain stops functioning – but the produce rots and peasants lose money because lockdowns prevent food from entering the city. Or peasants and fishers cannot do productive work even if they observe precautions such as the two-metre social distance rule because of emergency directives that are not appropriate to the local situation. If, under appropriate emergency rules, the combined force of peasants and fishers can be unleashed, in a safe and cautious manner, much of the current problem of the supply chain for cities can be significantly reduced. In addition, it can help prevent/mitigate any possible future food supply shortages, where poor peasants and the landless rural poor are themselves among the first to suffer and to starve.

These are measures for the short term. When talking about strategic transformation, there are solid reasons for reversing the trend towards the globalization of food production and moving towards more food self-sufficiency. However, the rationale goes beyond just ensuring food self-sufficiency to achieve food security, to fostering values and practices that enhance community, social solidarity and democracy.

This paradigm shift was the 'road not taken' after the food price crisis of 2007–08 as the transnational agrifood interests and their ideologues asserted their power to preserve and expand the system. There were, however, representatives of the peasantry and civil society groups who met in Nyeleni, Mali shortly before the crisis broke out, to articulate a different vision and different path from the agribusiness road, one that has become popularly known as 'food sovereignty'. The resulting Nyeleni Declaration proclaimed that the aim of food sovereignty was 'a world where . . . all peoples, nations and states are able to determine their own food producing systems and policies that provide every one of us with good quality, adequate, affordable, healthy and culturally appropriate food'.[3]

Led by peasants and smallholders who still produce some 70 per cent of the world's food, this movement proposes an alternative food system, the cornerstone principles of which include the following:

(1) Local food production must be delinked from corporate-dominated global supply chains, and each country should strive for food self-sufficiency. That means the country's farmers should produce most of the food consumed domestically. This is not, it should be stressed, the corporate concept of 'food security' which says that a country can also meet a great part of its food needs through imports.

(2) The people should have the right to determine their patterns of food production and consumption, taking into consideration 'rural and productive diversity', and not allow these to be subordinated to unregulated international trade.

(3) Localization of food production is good for the climate, since the carbon emissions of localized production on a global scale are much less than that of agriculture based on global supply chains.

(4) Traditional peasant and indigenous agricultural technologies contain a great deal of wisdom and represent the evolution of a largely benign balance between the human community and the biosphere. Thus, the evolution of agrotechnology to meet social needs must take traditional practices as a starting point rather than regarding them as obsolete.

(5) A technology supportive of food sovereignty is agroecology, which is marked by recycling nutrients and energy on the farm rather than introducing external inputs and diversifying plant species and genetic resources over time and space.[4]

To be sure, there are many questions related to the economics, politics and technology of food sovereignty that remain unanswered, or to which its proponents give varying and sometimes contradictory answers. But a new paradigm is not born perfect. What gives it its momentum are the irreversible crisis of the old paradigm and the conviction of a critical mass of people that it is the only way of surmounting the problems of the old system and opening up new possibilities for the fulfilment of values that people hold dear. As with any new form of organizing social relationships, the unanswered questions can only be answered – and the ambiguities and contradictions can only be ironed out – through practice, since practice has always been the mother of possibilities.

It has been said that one should never let a good crisis go to waste. The silver lining of the Covid-19 crisis is the opportunity it spells for food sovereignty.

Notes

1 World Trade Organization, World Health Organization and Food and Agricultural Organization, Joint statement, 31 March 2020, reproduced in *The Maritime Executive*, 31 March 2020, https://www.maritime-executive. com/article/wto-who-and-fao-call-for-action-on-food-trade, 30 October 2020.

2 *Agricultural Development Strategy and Investment Plan* (ADS), Draft 4, Government of Myanmar, Asian Development Bank, Food and Agricultural Organization, and Livelihood and Food Security Trust Fund, Nay Pyi Taw, 4 September 2017, p. 74.

3 'Nyéléni Declaration on Food Sovereignty 27 February 2007, Nyéléni Village, Sélingué, Mali', *The Journal of Peasant Studies*, vol. 36, no. 9, 2009, https://www.tandfonline.com/doi/full/10.1080/03066150903143079?src=recsys, accessed 13 April 2020.

4 These points have been summed up from various sources: Alonso-Fradejas *et al.* (2015), Borras Jr *et al.* (2015), Edelman (2014), La Via Campesina (2000), cited in Desmarais (2007) and Lodi (2015).

References

Alonso-Fradejas, Alberto, Saturnino Borras Jr., Todd Holmes, Eric Holt Gimenez and Martha Jane Robbins (2015), 'Food Sovereignty: Convergence and Contradictions, Conditions and Challenges', *Third World Quarterly*, vol. 36, no. 3, https://www.tandfonline.com/doi/full/10.1080/01436597.2015.1023567?src=recsys, accessed 12 April 2020.

Baviera, Mara and Walden Bello (2012), 'Food Wars', *Monthly Review*, vol. 64, no. 3, July–August, https://monthlyreview.org/author/marabaviera/, accessed 13 April 2020.

Borras Jr, Saturnino, Jennifer Franco and Sofia Monsalve Suarez (2015), 'Land and Food Sovereignty', *Third World Quarterly*, vol. 36, no. 3, https://www.tandfonline.com/doi/full/10.1080/01436597.2015.1029225?src=recsys, accessed 12 April 2020

Clapp, Jennifer (2017), 'Viewpoint: Food Self Sufficiency: Making Sense of It, and When It Makes Sense', *Food Policy*, vol. 66, January, https://www.academia.edu/30775341/Food_self-sufficiency_Making_sense_ of_it_and_when_it_makes_sense, accessed 12 April 2020.

Cullen, Maximo Torero (2020), 'Covid-19 and the Risk to Food Supply Chains: How to Respond', http://www.fao.org/russian-federation/news/detail-events/en/c/1268744/, 29 March.

Desmarais, Annette (2007), *La Via Campesina: Globalization and the Power of Peasants*, London: Pluto Press.

Edelman, Marc, Tony Weis, Amita Baviskar, Saturnino Borras Jr., Eric Holt-Gimenez, Deniz Kandiyoti and Wendy Wolford (2014), 'Introduction: Critical Perspectives on Food Sovereignty', *Journal of Peasant Studies*, vol. 41, no. 6, https://www.tandfonline.com/doi/full/10.1080/03066150.2014.963568?src=recsys, accessed 13 April 2020.

Fan, Shenggen, Joanna Brzeska, Michiel Keyzer and Alex Halsema (2013), *From Subsistence to Profit: Transforming Smallholder Farms,* Washington, D.C.: IFPRI, p. 7.

Lodi, A. Haroon Akram (2015), 'Accelerating Towards Food Sovereignty', *Third World Quarterly,* vol. 36, no. 3, https://www.tandfonline.com/doi/ full/10.1080/01436 597.2015.1002989?src=recsys, accessed 12 April 2020.

Parth, M.N. (2020), 'Urban India Didn't Care about Migrant Workers till 26 March, Only Cares Now Because It's Lost Their Services', *Firstpost,* 13 May, https://www. firstpost.com/india/urban-india-didnt-care-about-migrant-workers-till-26-march-only-cares-now-because-its-lost-their-services-p-sainath-8361821.html, accessed 30 October 2020.

Reardon, Thomas, Marc Bellemare and David Zilberman (2020), 'How Covid-19 May Disrupt Food Supply Chains in Developing Countries', International Food Policy Research Institute (IFPRI), 2 April, https://www.ifpri.org/blog/how-covid-19-may-disrupt-food-supply-chains-developing-countries, accessed 7 April 2020.

UN World Food Programme (2020), 'Covid-19 Will Double Number of People Facing Food Crises Unless Swift Action is Taken', 21 April, https://www.wfp.org/news/ covid-19-will-double-number-people-facing-food-crises-unless-swift-action-taken, accessed 30 October 2020.

La Via Campesina (2000), 'Food Sovereignty and International Trade', position paper approved at the Third International Conference of La Via Campesina, Bangalore, India, 3–6 October 2000.

Contributors

Martín Abeles is Director, United Nations Economic Commission for Latin America and the Caribbean (ECLAC), Buenos Aires. His main areas of expertise are macroeconomics, international finance and development economics. He has been a research fellow at various academic institutions and held different positions at the Ministry of Economy in Argentina. He is currently Director, Master's Programme in Development Economics at the National University of San Martín (UNSAM) in Argentina.

Chris Baker is a historian. His early work is on the political history of south India. He has worked extensively on Thailand's political economy, history and literature. In 2017, he (with Pasuk Phongpaichit) won the Fukuoka Grand Prize which 'honors individuals or groups that have made outstanding achievements in preservation and creation of the unique and diverse cultures of Asia'.

Walden Bello is a well-known activist, academic and writer from the Philippines. He is currently International Adjunct Professor of Sociology at the State University of New York at Binghamton, and co-chairperson of the Bangkok-based research and advocacy institute Focus on the Global South. He received the Right Livelihood Award (also known as the Alternative Nobel Prize) in Stockholm in 2003 for his work showing the negative impact of corporate-driven globalization.

C.P. Chandrasekhar is former Professor of Economics at Jawaharlal Nehru University, New Delhi. His areas of interest include the macroeconomics of development and the role of finance and industry in developing countries. He is a regular columnist for *Frontline, Business Line* and *Economic and Political Weekly*. Among his recent publications are *Demonetisation Decoded: A Critique of India's Currency Experiment* (co-authored with Jayati Ghosh and Prabhat Patnaik, 2020) and *Karl Marx's 'Capital' and the Present: Four Essays* (2017).

Martín Cherkasky is an economist at the United Nations Economic Commission for Latin America and the Caribbean (ECLAC), Buenos Aires. He studied economics at the University of Buenos Aires (UBA) and the National University of San Martín (UNSAM). His research focuses on macroeconomics, international finance and economic growth.

Giovanni Andrea Cornia taught development at the University of Florence from 2000 to 2017, where he was made Honorary Professor of Economics in 2017. From 1995 to 2000, he was Director, United Nations University World Institute for Development Economics Research (UNU-WIDER), Helsinki. He also worked as lead economist at the United Nations Children's Fund (UNICEF) headquarters in New York and the Innocenti Research Centre (IRC) in Florence. His work has focused on inequality, macroeconomics, poverty, mortality and child well-being.

Jayati Ghosh taught economics at Jawaharlal Nehru University, New Delhi for nearly thirty-five years, and is now Professor of Economics, University of Massachusetts, Amherst, USA. She has authored and edited (alone and in collaboration) twenty books and published more than 200 scholarly articles, in addition to writing frequently in the popular media. She has been Executive Secretary, International Development Economics Associates (IDEAs) and serves on a number of international commissions.

Jan Kregel is Director of Research at the Levy Economics Institute, USA. He has served as Rapporteur of the President of the United Nations General Assembly's Commission on Reform of the International Financial System, directed the Policy Analysis and Development Branch of the United Nations Financing for Development Office, and was Deputy Secretary of the United Nations Committee of Experts on International Cooperation in Tax Matters. In 2011, Kregel was elected to the Accademia Nazionale dei Lincei. He is a life fellow of the Royal Economic Society (UK) and an elected member of the Società Italiana degli Economisti.

Sashi Kumar is a journalist, filmmaker and media entrepreneur. He founded the Media Development Foundation, which runs the Asian College of Journalism, the Asianet TV channel and statewide cable TV network in Kerala, and Asiaville, a digital infotainment and education venture. He was a producer and presenter on Doordarshan, West Asia correspondent of *The Hindu* and chief producer of PTI-TV. He scripted and directed *Kaya Taran*, a movie based on the 1984 anti-Sikh riots and has acted in a few feature films. His columns 'Unmediated' in *Frontline* form part of a book by the same title, published in 2014.

Matías Torchinsky Landau is a consultant at the United Nations Economic Commission for Latin America and the Caribbean (ECLAC), Buenos Aires. His research focuses on economic growth, international trade and input–output analysis.

Lilia García Manrique is a PhD scholar in economics at the University of Sussex. Previously, she has worked as a research assistant at the Latin American Faculty of Social Science (FLACSO).

Surajit Mazumdar is Professor of Economics at the Centre for Economic Studies and Planning, Jawaharlal Nehru University, New Delhi. He was also on the faculty of Ambedkar University Delhi (AUD), Institute for Studies in Industrial Development (ISID), New Delhi and Hindu College, University of Delhi. The focus of his research is on the Indian corporate sector, industrialization and the impact of globalization on the economy in India.

José Antonio Ocampo is Professor of Professional Practice in International and Public Affairs at the School of International and Public Affairs, Columbia University. He is Chair of the Committee for Development Policy of the United Nations Economic and Social Council (ECOSOC) as well as of the Independent Commission for the Reform of International Corporate Taxation. He has occupied numerous positions at the United Nations and in Colombia, including UN Under-Secretary-General, Economic and Social Affairs; Executive Secretary, ECLAC; Minister of Finance, Minister of Agriculture, and Director of the National Planning Office of Colombia; and member of the board of directors of Banco de la República.

Prabhat Patnaik has taught at the University of Cambridge, UK and at Jawaharlal Nehru University, New Delhi, where he held the Sukhamoy Chakravarty Chair at the time of his retirement and is currently Professor Emeritus. His books include *Accumulation and Stability under Capitalism* (1997), *The Value of Money* (2009), *Re-envisioning Socialism* (2011)and *A Theory of Imperialism* (co-authored with Utsa Patnaik, 2016). His most recent book, *Capital and Imperialism: Theory, History, and the Present* (co-authored with Utsa Patnaik, 2021), is winner of the Paul A. Baran–Paul M. Sweezy Memorial Award. He is the Editor of the journal *Social Scientist*.

Utsa Patnaik is Professor Emeritus, Centre for Economic Studies and Planning, Jawaharlal Nehru University, New Delhi. Her main research interests are the processes of transition from peasant-predominant societies to industrial society; colonialism and imperialism; and food security and poverty. Her books include *Peasant Class Differentiation* (1987), *The Long Transition* (1999), *The Republic of Hunger* (2007), *A Theory of Imperialism* (co-authored with Prabhat Patnaik, 2016) and *Capital and Imperialism: Theory, History, and the Present* (co-authored with Prabhat Patnaik, 2021).

Pasuk Phongpaichit is Professor of Economics, Chulalongkorn University, Bangkok. She has written widely on Thailand's political economy, history and literature. In 2017, she (with Chris Baker) won the Fukuoka Grand Prize.

Alicia Puyana is full-time Professor of Economics at FLACSO-MEXICO, and is a member of IDEAs, Oxford Development and other academic boards. She has been a visiting fellow at St Antony's College, Oxford and London School of Economics. Puyana is the author and editor of books and articles on economic growth, economic regional integration, oil economics and extractivism, growth and inequality, ethnic and gender discrimination in Latin America, and ethics in economics.

Vikas Rawal is Professor of Economics at Jawaharlal Nehru University, New Delhi. His research has mainly focused on agrarian issues, food security and employment. He has conducted field-based research in many states of India. He has also worked on global issues related to agriculture and food. His recent book (co-edited with Dorian K. Navarro), *The Global Economy of Pulses*, was published in 2019 by the Food and Agriculture Organization of the United Nations (FAO).

Erik S. Reinert is Professor at the Tallinn University of Technology and Honorary Professor at University College London. Reinert holds an MBA from Harvard University and a PhD in economics from Cornell University. Much of his work is dedicated to teaching and researching the theory and history of uneven development. His book, *How Rich Countries got Rich and Why Poor Countries Stay Poor* (2007), has been translated into around twenty-five languages.

Abhijit Sen retired as Professor of Economics at the Centre for Economic Studies and Planning, Jawaharlal Nehru University, New Delhi. He was a member of the Planning Commission for two terms and chaired the Commission for Agricultural Costs and Prices apart from many other high-level committees of the Government of India. His work encompasses macroeconomics, planning and development, and agricultural economics. He is currently President of the Indian Society of Agricultural Economics.

Jomo Kwame Sundaram is Senior Advisor at the Khazanah Research Institute, Fellow of the Academy of Science, Malaysia, and Emeritus Professor at the University of Malaya. He is Founder-Chair, IDEAs, and was Assistant Secretary-General for Economic Development in the United Nations system from 2005 to 2015. He received the 2007 Leontief Prize for Advancing the Frontiers of Economic Thought.

A. Erinç Yeldan is Professor of Economics and Dean at Kadir Has University, Turkey. He is one of the executive directors of IDEAs, and serves as a member-elect of the International Resource Panel of the United Nations Environment Programme (UNEP). He is also a member-elect of the Science Academy (Bilim Akademisi) in Turkey. Yeldan's recent work focuses on development macroeconomics, vulnerability and fragmentation of labour markets, deindustrialization, the economics of climate change, and on empirical, dynamic general equilibrium models.